DICTATING REALITY

MARTIN MOORE AND THOMAS COLLEY

DICTATING REALITY

The Global Battle to Control the News

Columbia University Press / *New York*

Columbia University Press
Publishers Since 1893
New York   Chichester, West Sussex

Copyright © 2025 Columbia University Press
All rights reserved

Library of Congress Cataloging-in-Publication Data
Names: Moore, Martin, 1970– author | Colley, Thomas author
Title: Dictating reality : the global battle to control news /
Martin Moore and Thomas Colley.
Description: New York : Columbia University Press, 2025. |
Includes bibliographical references and index.
Identifiers: LCCN 2025010385| ISBN 9780231212908 hardback |
ISBN9780231212915 trade paperback | ISBN 9780231559621 ebook
Subjects: LCSH: Government and the press | Press and politics |
Information warfare | Mass media andpropaganda
Classification: LCC PN4751 .M66 2025 | DDC 070.44/932 23/eng/20250—dc20

Cover design: Noah Arlow
Cover image: Shutterstock

GPSR Authorized Representative: Easy Access System Europe,
Mustamäe tee 50, 10621 Tallinn, Estonia, gpsr.requests@easproject.com

To my children (MM)

To my parents (TC)

CONTENTS

ABBREVIATIONS

AFL	America First Legal, United States
AMLO	Andrés Manuel López Obrador, President of Mexico
ASPI	Australian Strategic Policy Institute
BBC	British Broadcasting Corporation
BJP	Bharatiya Janata Party, India
CCP	Chinese Communist Party
CGTN	China Global Television Network
CIA	Central Intelligence Agency, United States
CNN	Cable News Network
CPMI	Joint Congressional Inquiry Committee (on Fake News), Brazil
CRI	China Radio International
EBU	European Broadcasting Union
IFCN	International Fact-Checking Network
ISD	Institute for Strategic Dialogue
KESMA	Central European Press and Media Foundation, Hungary

MBL	Movimento Brasil Libre—The Free Brazil Movement
MORENA	National Regeneration Movement, Mexico
MTI	Magyar Távirati Iroda (Hungarian News Agency)
MTVA	Media Service Support and Asset Management Fund, Hungary
NATO	North Atlantic Treaty Organization
NCO	National Communications Office, Hungary
NDTV	New Delhi Television (India)
NGO	Nongovernmental Organization
NMHH	National Media and Infocommunications Authority, Hungary
OANN	One America News Network
Ofcom	Office of Communications, UK
OSINT	open-source intelligence
PAN	National Action Party, Mexico
PLA	People's Liberation Army, China
PRI	Institutional Revolutionary Party, Mexico
PSB	Public Service Broadcasting
PSM	Public Service Media
PT	The Worker's Party, Brazil
RT	Russia Today
TASS	Information Agency of Russia
TRP	television rating point
UGC	user-generated content
UPM	unit production manager
VGTRK	All-Russia State Television and Radio Broadcasting Company
VPN	virtual private network

DICTATING REALITY

1

NEWS AS REALITY

"When you think of it," he continued, "the first half of the twentieth century was just that: a titanic confrontation between artists. Stalin, Hitler, Churchill. After them came the bureaucrats because the world needed a rest. But today the artists are back. Look around you. Wherever you look there is nothing but avant-garde artists who, instead of depicting reality, are busy creating it. Their style is the only thing that has changed. Today, instead of the artists of yesteryear, we have reality-show personalities. But the principle is the same."

—GIULIANO DA EMPOLI, *THE WIZARD OF THE KREMLIN*

A short drive from Riga, in rural Latvia, there is an old Soviet secret bunker that was built to house Communist Party elites in the event of a nuclear attack. Tucked between forested hills to absorb blast tremors, the bunker sits nine meters below ground, hidden underneath a drab, rectangular concrete rehabilitation center that was once a holiday retreat for senior party members. Its presence is suggested only by the strange green cubic air vents that jut out suspiciously throughout the grounds. Having been shrouded in secrecy for decades, it is now open to members of the public, who can see it as it was when the Soviet Empire collapsed. Visitors step through the double blast doors into a maze of corridors painted in a dull green-gray, with individual rooms on either side furnished with little more than a plain wooden bed and a rotary-dial telephone. An operations room is covered in maps depicting likely nuclear strike locations, with evacuation routes and blast radius estimates crudely hand-drawn with highlighters. A golden bust of Lenin dominates the wood-paneled conference room, as if he were still monitoring attendees for ideological purity. At one end of the bunker in the old communications room a banner on the wall in Russian reads: "БЕЗ СВЯЗИ НЕТ УПРАВЛЕНИЯ. БЕЗ УПРАВЛЕНИЯ НЕТ ПОБЕДЫ!" This roughly translates as: "Without communication there is no control. Without control there is no victory."

Soviet leaders were always acutely conscious of the importance of media and communication for sustaining their power. This is why, in Soviet Russia, the press was considered an instrument of the party. Its purpose was to inform the people about what the party was doing on their behalf and to educate the people about why the party was right.[1] If this meant misrepresenting reality to suit the party's needs, so be it. In November 1983, for example, nine months after the Soviet leader Yuri Andropov had suffered total kidney failure and three months after he had entered the Central Clinical Hospital in Moscow, where he would soon die, he was pictured looking fit and healthy in the USSR's official newspaper, *Pravda* (which translates as "Truth").[2] Almost three years later, it took ten days before the party newspaper reported on the nuclear disaster at Chornobyl, which the Soviet authorities had initially covered up. Even then the information was sparse, and *Pravda* accused the West of politically motivated reporting on the catastrophe and "enjoying somebody else's misfortunes."[3] The purpose of the Soviet press was not to tell people what was actually happening; it was to serve the interests of the leader, the party, and the government.

This world of state-controlled news and parallel political realities appeared to end in 1989. That was the year the Berlin Wall fell and the

Soviet Empire began to crumble. It was also the year that Tim Berners-Lee, working among particle physicists in a Geneva suburb, invented the World Wide Web, making it possible for anyone to access information from anywhere and to self-publish virtually anything. Together, the opening up of the Soviet Empire and the democratizing potential of the internet made it seem as though states had lost the ability to control news and information. Indeed, the whole idea of state-produced news—like claiming that Andropov was fit and healthy—channeled through a clutch of compliant news outlets suddenly seemed fantastically anachronistic. In this new, unconstrained digital environment, governments would simply have to accept that they could not limit what was published or stem the free flow of news and information. As John Perry Barlow famously wrote in 1996: "Governments of the Industrial World, you weary giants of flesh and steel, I come from Cyberspace, the new home of Mind. On behalf of the future, I ask you of the past to leave us alone. You are not welcome among us. You have no sovereignty where we gather."[4] Yet, though the era of total information control may have been over, the battles for narrative supremacy had only just begun.

"By the grace of God," President George H. W. Bush said in his 1992 State of the Union Speech, "America won the Cold War." History is written by the victors, and in the immediate aftermath of the Cold War the one remaining superpower wrote a story of American triumph. "Communism died this year," Bush said, and our country is "the undisputed leader of the age."[5] This story was amplified across the globe, not yet via the nascent web but by cable TV news and notably by the one contemporary international TV news channel—the Atlanta-based CNN. Originally launched in 1980 by Ted Turner, the outlet expanded globally in 1985, and by 1991 viewers in almost any high-end international hotel room could watch as Boris Yeltsin stood up to Communist hardliners in Moscow. The channel, although independent of the US government, presented a US-centric perspective on the world. Nowhere was this more apparent than during the 1990–91 Gulf War. Operation Desert Storm—as the US-led coalition operation was named—was so carefully choreographed for TV audiences that it prompted the postmodern French philosopher Jean Baudrillard to question whether a war had even taken place (as opposed to "a programmed and melodramatic version . . . of the drama of war").[6] Indeed, CNN—and its emerging US and European TV news competitors—was considered so influential that in 1993 the US secretary of state Madeleine Albright suggested that simply by choosing to focus attention on a particular region cable TV news could prompt international intervention or withdrawal. This came to be known as "the CNN effect."[7]

Many countries bristled at the dominance of this US perspective. For them, these TV news channels were portraying reality in a way that promoted the United States and its leadership of a unipolar order. In response, they launched their own international news channels, although unlike in the United States, many of these were financed or heavily subsidized by national governments. The Qatari government bankrolled Al Jazeera in 1998. Saudi Arabia followed by launching Al Arabiya in 2003. Two years later, following the Color Revolutions in Ukraine, Georgia, and other former Soviet states, Russia launched Russia Today (subsequently rebranded as RT). A year after that France started broadcasting France24, justifying the channel with full-page advertisements claiming it would give people "All the news you're not supposed to know."[8] In 2007 Iran began PressTV, and in 2009 China announced its "Going Out" project to extend its global media presence and to "Tell China's Story Well" to international audiences.[9]

These news channels would become central to the countries' efforts to promote their perspectives and contrast them with those of American broadcasters. But as more and more of the global public shifted online and then onto social media, linear TV news channels would not be enough for government messages to dominate, either at home or abroad. The media and communications environment was becoming increasingly chaotic— characterized by fragmented audiences, individualized news feeds, and information abundance, not scarcity. People were now not just passively consuming news but selecting it, reacting to it, sharing it, and debating it. If governments, parties, and political leaders wanted their stories to dominate, they could not simply instruct news editors, as some had done in a world of print media and broadcast TV. Or if they did, their stories were unlikely to command attention or respect. They would have to figure out new ways of shaping reality in their favor.

Initially it seemed as though the structure of the internet and this cluttered new digital information environment would make it difficult if not impossible for governments and political leaders to get their preferred stories to dominate. The internet was structurally decentralized, highly distributed, and networked rather than hierarchical. Yet at the same time, it provided opportunities previously inaccessible to parties and politicians to reach the public directly, to bypass legacy media outlets, and to act like a publisher. Moreover, as time went on and internet services became recentralized around a handful of transnational tech platforms such as Google and Meta (owner of Facebook, WhatsApp, and Instagram), it became easier for governments and parties to take advantage of these global services to spread content, amplify their voices, and mobilize followers. Simultaneously, many news publishers found their distinctiveness diminished, their content replicated, their revenues depleted, and their audiences atomized. This made them vulnerable to what the scholar Alina Mungiu-Pippidi refers to as "media capture"—being taken over and controlled "either directly by governments or by vested interests networked with politics."[10]

NEWS AS A GROUNDING FOR REALITY

If governments were to win narrative supremacy, news would be essential. Why? Because news is the primary means by which people understand reality beyond their immediate experience, and it shapes how their political attitudes evolve. As the founding theorist of modern journalism, Walter Lippmann, wrote in 1920, "A sound public opinion cannot exist without access to the news." Those who produce the news ascribe to themselves the responsibility of giving the public a realistic picture of *the world outside*. As such the newspaper is, as Lippmann wrote, "the bible of democracy."[11] This is why news occupies a privileged position within democratic society, legally and constitutionally. To be recognized as a legitimate news provider is to be recognized as an institution that seeks to present verified, truthful information about what is really happening in the world. Yet news is also constructed. "Unable to report everything that happened . . . [journalists] must select some actors and activities from the many millions they could choose."[12] They then shape these actors and activities into stories—or "cook them into story forms" as the historian of journalism Michael Schudson called it—that help people interpret the world and figure out where they stand within it.[13] In the process of choosing what to cover, journalists omit alternative actors and events. Because of that, a news story can be entirely factually accurate but still present a highly selective version of reality. If governments, parties, and political leaders are able to direct the news, they can ensure not only that their preferred stories dominate public discourse but also that they can "narrow the range of what kind of truths can be told" to those that present the government in a positive light.[14]

Controlling the news is therefore a key way for political leaders and parties to gain "discourse power" or "narrative dominance."[15] The more dominant their preferred stories are, the more easily they can shape the terms of political debate and generate support for their policies.[16] A party in government can then, for example, more easily convince its people that it is fighting a just, defensive war rather than a war of annihilation and use this to gain public support. A country can convince the international community that it is a benign and tolerant partner and generate more favorable terms of trade. The more dominant political actors' narratives become, the more they can marginalize competing narratives, to the point that no other version of reality makes sense to their followers.[17] Like the former Bolsheviks who were carefully airbrushed from photographs during Stalin's purges, other interpretations of reality are not just discredited—they cease to exist. The result is that people can come to perceive entirely different realities, in which war is peace, a fair election is fraudulent, and dictatorship is democracy.

EXPERIMENTS WITH NEW METHODS OF STATE NEWS CONTROL

It is this power to shape how citizens perceive reality that is motivating governments to experiment with different strategies to control and influence the news worldwide. This book details how seven different governments have done this, as they fight for domestic power and international influence. Rather than focusing on either autocracies or democracies we cover both, examining the seven countries on a spectrum, from leading autocracies such as China to liberal democracies such as the UK. We examine the strategies and methods of leaders and their governments from across the world, including Vladimir Putin's Russia, Narendra Modi's India, and Andrés Manuel López Obrador's (AMLO) Mexico. We identify key figures who have led government efforts to direct news narratives—from the meticulous media management of Antal Rogán in Viktor Orbán's Hungary to the social media machinations of Carlos Bolsonaro in Jair Bolsonaro's Brazil. Each of these governments has sought to mold the news to achieve narrative dominance, with more autocratic states relying on direct control and more democratic states relying on co-optation and indirect influence. Analyzing this spectrum of states together, we provide original evidence of how methods of influencing the news traditionally associated with authoritarian states are being adopted by democratic governments. Although no single chapter is devoted to the United States, like Banquo's ghost it haunts the book throughout. Many of the techniques to influence the news documented throughout this book have been integral to Donald Trump's media strategy prior to and since his re-election in 2024.

These battles for narrative supremacy are taking place at a time when many governments are approaching the news as an instrument of "political warfare," "cognitive warfare," or "information warfare": something they see as being "weaponized" by their adversaries for strategic gain.[18] This is troubling because presenting reality accurately is often a secondary concern when approaching news as an instrument of warfare. Instead, the priority is to ensure that one's preferred stories are told, believed, and acted upon more widely than those of one's competitors. As we shall see, when one's priority is narrative dominance and when news is approached as a national security issue, the importance of factual truth and democratic debate can be lost along the way.

Of our seven cases, the Russian government's approach has evolved the most in the digital era, from its oversight of an open and chaotic information environment at the end of the twentieth century to its institution of an ever-more controlled one in the first decades of the twenty-first. The reinstitution of government control began shortly after Putin took power. His administration first defenestrated Russia's nascent media moguls (sometimes literally), such as Boris Berezovsky. Next, it enhanced and expanded state media—launching international news services (RT, Vesti/Russia-24, and Sputnik) and restructuring domestic ones. From there it moved onto Russia's tech platforms—gaining control of VKontakte and Yandex.[19] But Russia's military operations have accelerated its use of news as an instrument of political warfare—from Georgia in 2008, through its occupation of Crimea and fighting in Ukraine's Donbas region from 2014, to the full-scale invasion of Ukraine in February 2022. After this point, as chapter 2 shows, the process of disinforming the public became industrialized. Like Newton's Third Law of Motion, every claim made by the Ukraine government elicited an equal and opposite counterclaim by Russia's state-controlled news media: Russia was an oppressor: Russia was a liberator. Russia bombed a Ukrainian hospital: Ukraine bombed its own hospital. The Russian military has killed Ukrainian civilians: the Ukrainian civilians are not dead, they are crisis actors. Since the invasion, the parallel realities spun within Russia's domestic news networks have become constant and all-encompassing. And remarkably, as the Russia experts we interviewed explain, many citizens accept them.[20] Russia, as the veteran journalist Luke Harding puts it, is creating its own "sovereign reality."[21]

The Putin government's strategy has been to frame Russia as the underdog, the victim of a decadent and rapacious West that is determined to destroy Russia. In contrast, the Chinese state has adopted the characteristics of an alternative hegemon, positioning itself as the rising global superpower. Unlike the Soviet Communist Party, the Chinese Communist Party (CCP) never relinquished domestic information control after the Cold War. To them, the increase in freedom of expression brought about by Gorbachev's policy of glasnost was a primary cause of the Soviet Union's collapse, and they had no intention of replicating it.[22] This meant they were cautious about the early internet and instituted methods of censorship and control from its inception. Yet as globalization took hold, the CCP became self-conscious about the discrepancy between China's growing geopolitical power and its muted international voice, and so they decided to go out into the world. Rather than adopting the digital guerrilla tactics of Russia, however, they took a more economic and infrastructural approach: investing in foreign media, installing pipes and satellite dishes, and subsidizing Chinese communications companies. Like Russia, they poured funds into state international news services (notably the news agency Xinhua and China's leading international news channel, CGTN), but instead of using these to sow chaos, they would use them to cultivate an impression of measured neutrality, similar to that of the BBC (without the corresponding independence). These outlets would report news, but news that is unrelentingly positive toward China and that presents the West as dysfunctional, unequal, and undemocratic. Eventually, as chapter 3 shows, the CCP aims to create a "New World Media Order" and increase its "international discourse power" to the point where it becomes recognized not as an authoritarian state but as a world-leading democracy.[23]

In Hungary, Viktor Orbán's Fidesz party borrowed elements of the Russian and Chinese governments' methods of news control but disguised them beneath a veneer of democratic legitimacy. This is why, for liberal democracies, the Orbán model is both instructive and alarming. Orbán was able to achieve monopolistic control of news in Hungary while maintaining the semblance of a free press. From 2010, he and Fidesz slowly but surely captured the main pillars of the country's media ecosystem. They neutered the media and communications regulator, purged the public service broadcaster, annexed almost all commercial news media, and colonized social media. In each case they were scrupulously careful to maintain the impression that their actions were lawful (even if it meant changing the law first) and could be defended as "democratic" (if illiberal). Chapter 4 details how they did this through the stories of five people who were integral to the process: András Koltay, the head of Hungary's media and communications regulator; Balász Bende, a lead presenter on Hungary's public service news; Lőrinc Mészáros, Viktor Orbán's childhood friend and "cashier"; István Kovács, the founder of the influencer promotion company Megafon; and Antal Rogán, the stage manager of Fidesz's communications strategy. After

Orbán won a convincing fourth election victory in 2022, he could be justifiably smug about his party's direct and indirect control of Hungary's entire news ecosystem. He had created, in effect, a counterfeit public sphere.

To corral the news media in India, Narendra Modi and the Bharatiya Janata Party (BJP) employed some of the tactics of Orbán and Fidesz while introducing others of their own. Like Fidesz, the BJP used two key levers of government influence—money and access—to draw news outlets into a complicit and dependent relationship. This meant targeting government advertising revenue at supportive news channels and denying it to critical ones. It meant giving interviews and information to docile news owners and biddable news anchors and freezing critical ones out. In India's case, the result has been a plethora of news channels that give the impression of diversity, but most of them try to outdo one another in their support for the BJP government. These outlets have sacrificed their independence, choosing instead to become what the journalist and presenter Ravish Kumar calls the "Godi Media"—or "lapdog media." Chapter 5 explores how India's news media became so homogeneous and so homogeneously pro-BJP through the story of the man who exemplifies the country's news journey, Arnab Goswami. At the same time, it shows how Modi's BJP consolidates this top-down management of the news with legions of social media warriors, who take the government's narrative battles directly into people's instant messaging feeds.

A similar social media strategy was adopted by Brazil's former president, Jair Bolsonaro. As a political outsider who was considered a clown by Brazil's major news outlets, co-opting mainstream media was not an option for Bolsonaro. He was fortunate, however, in that he pursued his political career in a country that had fully embraced social media and instant messaging. He, his sons, and their associates took full advantage of this, building an army of keyboard warriors, a portfolio of online influencers, and an alternative news ecology disseminated via Facebook, YouTube, and Instagram. Bolsonaro's Brazil provides a fascinating illustration of how a political leader and then a government can put theories of networked power into practice.[24] As chapter 6 sets out, those working with Jair Bolsonaro, most importantly his son Carlos, developed a complex, multifarious, coordinated digital news ecosystem through which they could disseminate hyperpartisan political narratives, assail Bolsonaro critics, and delegitimize Brazil's democratic institutions.

As president, Bolsonaro liked to express himself in religious terms, but it was another political leader from the Americas—this time from the left—who sought to make his own word gospel. As chapter 7 reveals, no head of government has exploited digital media's direct access to the public more than Andrés Manuel López Obrador (AMLO), Mexico's president from 2018 to 2024. During his six years in office, AMLO would live stream to the Mexican people on television and YouTube almost every day, normally for two to three hours. AMLO did not just try to compete with the news; he sought to replace the news. Why tune into a news program to find out what your government is doing if you can hear it from the president each morning at seven A.M.? Journalists were invited to attend these *mañaneras* and could ask questions, but they were there more as a congregation than as a Fourth Estate. AMLO consciously intended that these daily press conferences—sermons would often be a better description—were seen as a depiction of what his government was actually doing (as opposed to what the media said it was doing). Journalists and news outlets who chose to question his truth or criticize what his administration was doing would find themselves chastised, condemned, and excommunicated. But AMLO is just one of several leaders who have sought to establish themselves as the voice of truth in their societies by undermining established news outlets and setting up direct channels of communication with the masses. A similar logic underpins the media strategy of Donald Trump, who systematically attacks the "fake news media" while positioning himself as the primary source of truth for American citizens via his social media service, Truth Social.

The efforts of these governments and their leaders to control the news have not gone unchallenged. Indeed, as they have pursued their aims, we have seen a new type of truth-seeker emerge whose very reason for being is to test the truthfulness of political claims and the credibility of political narratives. Yet these fledgling fact-checking organizations and open-source intelligence (OSINT) collectives are fragile and vulnerable to attack from the governments and parties they are investigating. Chapter

8 documents how attempts to make these new methods of truth-seeking more sustainable—as the BBC has tried to do in the UK with BBC Verify—are being hampered by the very governments one would expect to be championing them. Unless this new breed of truth-seeker is nurtured and cultivated, the methods of news capture explored in this book will spread and multiply.

Based on our careful analysis of these seven very different countries, we identify more than a dozen techniques governments are now using to control and influence the news. Some of these are *harder* and more *structural*—such as building media and communications infrastructure or taking ownership of existing media channels. Others are *softer*, although similarly damaging, such as denying political access to news outlets or refusing to conform to democratic news norms (such as refusing to hold press conferences). One set of methods targets news producers and includes the many ways in which governments now denigrate and delegitimize "mainstream media" to sow distrust among the public. Another set of methods is designed to enhance government control over news distribution, whether through operating or regulating digital platforms or artificially inflating the popularity of government messages on social media. Rather than separating the approaches of authoritarian and democratic states, as previous media scholars have done, we show that the methods used by autocracies, illiberal democracies, and liberal democracies overlap as each tries to take advantage of the transformation of the communications environment to ensure that their versions of reality dominate.

WHY IS GOVERNMENT CONTROL
OVER NEWS A PROBLEM?

Are these efforts to manage and direct the news necessarily bad? Sometimes governments may justifiably feel misrepresented by mainstream media and simply want their messages communicated more fairly. Some news outlets can frame stories in a highly selective and partisan manner. Equally, even if governments go beyond persuasion and try to direct news and public opinion, this is a far from uncommon practice. Not only is it symptomatic of authoritarian regimes; it can be seen in contemporary democracies, where political leaders use their power over news media to propel them to office and sustain them in government. Silvio Berlusconi, for example, used his media empire flagrantly to help him win elections in Italy in the 1990s and 2000s and to prevent scandals from engulfing him as prime minister. Moreover, since there is now a general consensus that the digital information environment is disordered and chaotic, one could legitimately argue that greater state intervention is necessary and overdue to prevent our digital spaces from being overwhelmed by disinformation and malign actors.

However, news capture by governments is a significant problem, and it will have serious consequences if not addressed. Governments are not reliable truth-tellers because their priorities are skewed by the need to gain or retain power. Many of the narratives they push through the news media are misleading, polarizing, and destructive. Jair Bolsonaro used his networked news ecosystem to tell millions of Brazilian citizens that COVID-19 was not harmful (it went on to cause the deaths of seven hundred thousand Brazilians), that his administration was defending the Amazon rainforest from predatory international organizations (when it was engaged in mass deforestation and the decimation of Indigenous populations), and that the 2022 election process was fraudulent (helping to spark the January 8, 2023, Brasilia riots). In India, during COVID-19, government ministers and pro-government news channels promoted the false belief that Muslims were to blame for spreading the virus, calling it "CoronaJihad," leading to anti-Muslim violence and boycotts.[25] In Mexico, AMLO's critics charged that his incessant rhetorical attacks on journalists led to the upsurge in physical assaults and killings of journalists during his administration.[26]

THE PRIMACY OF NARRATIVE REALITY

News capture is also a problem because these governments are trying to control news so that it supports their own "strategic narratives"—the main stories driving their political strategies. Whether the reported news is true or false matters much less to them than whether it backs up these narratives. In a different field of study, the educational psychologist Jerome Bruner referred to this way of thinking as "narrative reality" to distinguish it from reality informed by empirical evidence or by rational deduction.[27] Narrative realities conform to different strictures and standards from scientific or logical realities. Unlike argument, which is based on logical deduction from a series of premises, narratives convey reality by setting out a plot that explains how events play out over time. The story is populated by characters who play certain roles (friends, allies, enemies) and takes place in a setting (such as "the Caliphate," "the international system"). A persuasive narrative ties the events together into a coherent whole, which conveys a central point ("vote for me," "support the war"). Strong political narratives are like carefully woven tapestries whose individual elements might be eclectic, even jarringly different, but that tell a compelling story when threaded together. Each of the elements of the narrative may or may not be true, but that is not how the narrative is judged. As Bruner writes, "Narrative 'truth' is judged by its verisimilitude rather than its verifiability."[28] It is more important, in other words, that audiences find the story believable rather than whether it is factually accurate: that it *feels* right rather than whether it *is* right. When politics becomes dominated by narrative reality, politicians and parties compete to win narrative supremacy using whichever stories they think will best achieve their political objectives, regardless of their veracity.

Political storytelling is not in itself a problem. Indeed, all politicians are storytellers; it is central to what makes them politicians. In *Dreams from My Father*, Barack Obama told a story of hope that emerged from his search for his father and his journey to discover his own identity that helped him ride a wave of enthusiasm to victory in 2008.[29] Donald Trump nurtured a personal story of business acumen via *The Art of the Deal* and *The Apprentice*, which he has used to boost the idea that he can achieve international deals that others cannot.[30] However, political narratives become democratically dangerous when narrative reality is given precedence over rational logic and factual accuracy; when a single narrative is given primacy to the exclusion of others; and when leaders position themselves at the center of this narrative as the ultimate source of truth. Rather than democracy, this type of political system is more synonymous with theocracy: societies in which the narrative is set out in a holy text, where politics and religion are fused, and where the state is run by a divinely appointed autocratic leader. Such societies reject evidence-based research and logical reasoning when it contradicts or undermines the holy scripture or the authority of the theocratic state. This can have harmful consequences. We saw this, for example, in European states' approach to medicine until after the Reformation. Before then, dissection was illegal because the church stipulated that a human body had to be buried whole or the soul could not go to heaven. Medical "knowledge," such as it was, was derived from classical texts like those by Hippocrates and Galen (because they did not jeopardize the church's official narrative). It was not until people challenged the Catholic Church, and doctors began to treat patients on the basis of observation and research, that illness could be properly treated and medicine made effective. In this way, making narrative reality paramount impeded scientific understanding and technological development. We see a similar tendency to prioritize narrative reality over empirical reality in how governments are approaching the news today.

Prioritizing narrative reality over empirical reality can also fuel polarization and foment conflict. Many successful contemporary political narratives, communicated via memes, posts, and reels, are not painted in muted shades of gray but in loud primary colors ("Brazil above everything, God above everyone!"). Political opponents are not complex, rounded individuals but pantomime villains ("Sleepy Joe!"; "Crooked Hillary!"; "Crazy Kamala!"). Critics and supporters of other political parties are not principled or well-meaning, they are enemies with malign intent. Whoever the villains and the enemies in the narrative are, what matters to the storyteller is that they are wicked and scary enough to cohere and mobilize their own supporters. Such a deliberately dualist and bellicose representation of politics reflects the ideas of the German philosopher (and Nazi party member) Carl Schmitt, whose work has enjoyed a renaissance after having been disregarded for decades following the Second World War.[31] Just as morality is defined by good and evil, and aesthetics by beauty and ugliness,

Schmitt argues that politics is defined by the distinction between friend and enemy.[32] The enemy is "existentially something different and alien, so that in the extreme case, conflict with him is possible."[33]

This demonization of enemies is found throughout our case studies. In Xi Jinping's China, for example, state news focuses on and disparages the United States. In Russia, RT reviles and scorns the "collective West." On news channels in Modi's India, the Muslim minority is blamed for allegedly victimizing the Hindu majority. In Viktor Orbán's Hungary, news outlets vilify George Soros, the EU, and the "Jewish International". In Mexico, AMLO singles out the *mafia de poder* (the mafia of power). In the United States or the UK, depending on who you ask, it might be "woke elites," illegal immigrants, or "the Deep State." Whoever the villains of the story are, what matters to the storyteller is the creation of an enemy to serve a purpose in the narrative; news is simply an effective vehicle by which to do this. As we explain in the concluding chapter, it is therefore critical that news does not succumb to the politics of narrative reality. Nor should the news defer to the leader and the party as the only source of authoritative truth.

WHAT IS "REALITY"?

This raises a broader question of what we mean when we talk about "reality" in this book. Without the space for a philosophical treatise, we would summarize our approach as pragmatic and parsimonious. People perceive things differently and interpret the world in different ways. However, we follow Aristotle and his materialist successors in believing there is a material world that can be observed and documented. Through such observation and documentation we can develop knowledge, and the accumulation of that knowledge can help us better understand and interact with the world and one another. All of this knowledge can and should be tested, and part of this conceptualization of reality recognizes that existing knowledge can be proved wrong, or falsified, as the philosopher Karl

Popper wrote in the 1930s: "In so far as a scientific statement speaks about reality, it must be falsifiable: and in so far as it is not falsifiable, it does not speak about reality."[34] Following this, we therefore think that efforts to better understand the world through research, observation, and verification are desirable, as both the functioning of democracy and social cohesion require a shared understanding of reality so that citizens can relate to one another, make well-informed decisions, and jointly decide who should govern them.

In this book we show how political actors are taking advantage of the vast changes in our media and communications environment to push their versions of reality and position themselves as arbiters of truth. By doing so, some of them have deliberately created false, distorted, and conspiratorial realities by "knowing but ignoring correct information" and "believing and using incorrect information."[35] By saying this we are not taking a politically partisan position (in the sense of left versus right). As the case studies in this book show, government attempts to create such distorted, parallel realities can come from conservatives, reactionaries, socialists, or progressives, and from across a range of political systems. We do, however, adopt an empiricist position—in the sense that we do not believe that the creation and dissemination of these parallel realities is justified by some distant, "bigger" truth. Nor do we adopt the postmodern position that truth or reality is entirely dependent on one's personal perspective: that *my* truth is equivalent to *the* truth. We adhere to the idea of truth as being about things that are knowable, public, and verifiable. Truth should therefore be considered, as the philosopher Charles Sanders Pierce wrote, as "that of which any person would come to be convinced if he carried his inquiry, his sincere search for immovable belief, far enough."[36] We also recognize the emergence of other important players—large technology platforms—in the digital communications environment, and we do not underestimate their power and influence. However, this book focuses on the role of governments—and how their powers are utilized by leaders and political parties as they attempt to shape the news in their favor.

The book is based on years of original exploratory research, encompassing extensive analysis of news output across television, radio, news websites, and social media, as well as dozens of interviews with journalists, academics, and political actors. Because the techniques governments use to control and influence the news vary greatly, we have necessarily used a range of methods and sources. In Brazil we have been able to use evidence gathered by government inquiries and court cases (such as the Fake News Inquiry and the Inquiry Into Anti-Democratic Acts). For Mexico and India, we had access to the full online archives of AMLO's press conferences and Narendra Modi's broadcasts. In the UK we were able to speak to people within BBC Verify and observe the team at work in New Broadcasting House. For other countries, such as Russia and China, we had more limited access to people or materials and relied more on media analysis and interviews with journalists and subject matter experts, coupled with social media research.

Ultimately, this research is motivated by concern that government efforts to gain control over the news pose a growing threat to democracy, knowledge, and shared understanding. If this continues, we risk a world in which the public sphere—the space in which citizens communicate and deliberate as they form and express their opinions and beliefs—becomes increasingly authoritarian.[37] A world in which citizens place their trust in charismatic leaders who they hope will save the nation, in the process granting them the power to dictate reality as they see fit. A world in which independent sources of news and information wither and societies retreat into tribes. A world in which countries prioritize sovereign reality over objective reality, and international dialogue becomes increasingly conflicted. The global battle to control the news has begun. The direction it now takes will, we believe, shape not just our political future but the way we perceive reality.

2

WAR IS PEACE

Putin's Russia

Violence finds its only refuge in falsehood, falsehood its only support in violence. Any man who has once acclaimed violence as his method must inexorably choose falsehood as his principle.

—ALEXANDER SOLZHENITSYN, 1970 NOBEL LECTURE

On March 16, 2022, the Mariupol theater was destroyed. With its white walls and conspicuous red roof and surrounded by green tree-lined parkland, the theater stood apart from Mariupol's gray skyline: a symbol of the southeastern Ukrainian port's artistry and culture. That day it housed more than one thousand civilians seeking protection from the airstrikes and shelling that accompanied Russia's advance on the city. Civilians had daubed the word "children" in Russian in massive white letters on the pavement at the building's front and rear, hoping to save it from aerial attack. It made no difference. Two giant explosions rocked the building. The building's back half was flattened. The theater's white columned façade remained standing, jutting out like an enormous grave-stone for the hundreds of innocents buried beneath it. Estimates varied that between three hundred and eight hundred civilians were killed, mostly women and children.[1]

International media outlets instantly blamed the Russian military, which had systematically targeted civilian buildings from the outset of the war. Dozens witnessed the attack. However, with years of experience of Russia's use of disinformation across its wars in Georgia, Syria, and Ukraine, investigative journalists knew they needed proof. The Associated Press combined witness testimony and satellite footage with detailed 3D mapping of the building before and after the explosion. Amnesty International hired a physicist to model the explosion's impact and likely source. The conclusion was unanimous: the Mariupol theater was destroyed by two 500kg bombs dropped in close succession by Russian aircraft. The attack was just one of thousands of attacks on civilians attributed to Russia during the war.[2]

To read Russian news about the incident was to enter a parallel universe, however. According to Russia's news agency, TASS, the attack was not conducted by Russia. The building had been blown up by the Ukrainian army's Azov battalion—a militia that had been folded into the Ukrainian army and had previously included documented neo-Nazi elements.[3] Azov were the ideal culprits for Russian propagandists, who had argued since Russia first invaded Ukraine in 2014 that the Ukrainian regime was fascist and that Russia was really invading Ukraine to protect ethnic Russians from "genocide." According to Russian state media, the battalion had taken their own civilians hostage and were using the theater as a military base: a common argument often (mis)used in war to argue that a building is a legitimate military target even if it contains civilians.

Russia had initially used the same argument when it destroyed the Maternity Hospital Number 3 in Mariupol just one week before, one of forty-three verified attacks on medical facilities in the first month of Russia's offensive.[4] But then Russia changed tack. Russia's Defense Ministry circulated social media images claiming that a pregnant woman being helped out of the ruined hospital was a "crisis actor" and that the incident was staged by the Ukrainians as a "provocation."[5] As Maria Zakharova, the spokesperson of the Russian Foreign Ministry, stated with a remarkably straight face: "It is well known to everyone that the Russian armed forces do not bomb cities."[6]

* * *

Parallel realities are inherent in war. The protagonists, whether they are democracies or dictatorships, almost always claim they are acting defensively because defending against aggression provides just cause to go to war in international law. Both sides claim to be fighting for peace. To preserve morale and undermine their opponents, both sides typically downplay their casualties and overestimate those of their opponents. Enemy atrocities are usually embellished; one's own are typically played down or denied.

Discerning the truth from news coverage of war is especially challenging. War is often accompanied by calls to restrict information for national security reasons. Armies censor information from the front. The "fog of war" makes it harder to know what is real. Even with the vast amount of war coverage available on screens today, it is difficult to know what is really happening. Journalists are treated like spies or "foreign agents" when they seek the truth about events on the ground. News media are pressured to produce patriotic coverage in the national interest regardless of how closely this represents reality. The only reality that participants will likely agree on is how brutal the experience of war is. But even that is often hidden by regime propagandists desperate to maintain recruitment for their cause.

Truth may be the first casualty of war, as the old adage goes, but Russia's war against Ukraine has taken the subversion of truth in war to a new level. The full-scale invasion, which began in February 2022, is in many ways an imperial war of aggression to annex Ukrainian territories in order to realize Russian president Vladimir Putin's nineteenth-century vision of a renewed *Russkiy Mir* (Russian World). But according to Russia's president, his elite supporters, and Russia's state media, Russia is not imperialist and it has not attacked civilians. It has fought to protect them from a genocidal fascist Kyiv regime and their NATO puppet masters who want to destroy Russia.

In a remarkable act of Orwellian doublespeak, the Russian foreign minister Sergei Lavrov stated that the goal of Russia's February 2022 "special military operation" (so named because calling it a war was banned) was to "stop any war that could take place on Ukrainian territory or that could start from there."[7] War, apparently, was peace.

From the outset, Russia has promoted its parallel reality about Ukraine to maintain domestic support (or at least acceptance) for the war and to reduce international opposition. It has done so across all available media, old and new: from billboards to bots, from talk shows to Telegram. Its disinformation has been systematic: every bullet, bomb, missile, and drone has been ammunition not just for industrial warfare but for industrial disinformation warfare. Mountains of evidence have documented Russia's targeting of civilians, abductions of Ukrainian children, and the rape, mutilation, and execution of Ukrainian civilians and prisoners of war.[8] But for Russia these incidents have not been a risk to its war effort but an opportunity. Each allegation can be used to produce a counteraccusation claiming that Ukraine has been attacking its own civilians. This deeply cynical strategy has reinforced Russia's alternative reality in which it is Ukraine's liberator and the real villains are the Ukrainian government and its NATO backers.

This chapter documents Russia's news war against Ukraine and how it has evolved in the two years since February 2022, using analysis from Russian domestic and international media and interviews with Russian and Ukrainian journalists, academics, and international experts. It shows how the full-scale invasion of February 2022 was in part a consequence of the parallel reality that Russian domestic state media had been promoting ever since Russia first annexed Crimea in 2014. At that time, Russia was building a reputation for a sophisticated and subversive approach to international news, with outlets like RT and Sputnik inviting foreign audiences to question whether their governments and established media outlets were presenting reality accurately. But as the war dragged on and Russia's expectations of quick victory evaporated, its domestic news took a dark turn, relying on increasingly fascist and genocidal rhetoric and Soviet-era censorship and repression.

MARGARITA SIMONYAN AND THE EVOLUTION OF RUSSIAN NEWS

To explain how Russia constructed its alternative reality about Ukraine, few stories are more telling than that of Margarita Simonyan. Simonyan first developed international notoriety as the editor in chief of RT, Russia's leading international news outlet, which was set up in 2005. Her evolution into one of the key "Faces of Kremlin Propaganda," as the US State Department describes her, parallels the evolution of Putin's regime itself.

Simonyan's rapid rise to become a leading Putin propagandist is a rags-to-riches story. Born in the southern Russian city of Krasnodar in 1980, she had a poor upbringing and described being brought up in a rat-infested family home by her Armenian parents. She was eleven when the Soviet Union collapsed. Academically capable, as a teenager she lived through Russia's politically and economically chaotic "wild 1990s," although she also spent almost a year in the American town of Bristol, New Hampshire, on a future leaders program. "Maggie," as her host family affectionately referred to her, then returned to Russia to become a journalist.[9]

Simonyan's first war as a journalist was Putin's first as leader—the Second Chechen War from 1999. At twenty-one she got a job as a regional television journalist for the state-run All-Russia State Television and Radio Broadcasting Company (VGTRK). She quickly achieved national prominence with her coverage of the 2004 Beslan school siege, in which more than thirty Chechen separatists took 1,100 hostages on the first day of term at School Number One in Beslan, North Ossetia, demanding Chechnya's independence. The separatists killed several hostages during the three-day siege. In response, the Russian military stormed the school using a staggering array of heavy weaponry, including rocket-propelled flamethrowers, grenade launchers, and T-72 tanks. More than 330 people were killed during the siege, mostly children. Although the separatists were responsible for killing many of these, the Russian military faced accusations that most deaths were because of their heavy-handed response.[10]

Simonyan, meanwhile, was accused of aiding the government by providing misleading coverage—claiming that the terrorists had made no demands when they had actually promised to release hostages if Russian soldiers left Chechnya. She also underreported the number of hostages (claiming there were only 354 rather than more than 1,100) to make the situation look less embarrassing for Putin.[11] Shortly after that Simonyan was promoted and sent to Moscow to join the Kremlin press pool. A year later, at just twenty-five, Simonyan was made editor in chief of Russia's new international news outlet, Russia Today (later rebranded as RT to obscure its Russian origins).

Simonyan's RT initially aimed to provide quality journalism to match established outlets such as the BBC and CNN while conveying Russia's perspective on international affairs. But with little international interest in good news stories about Russia, Simonyan's outlet changed tack after Russia's war against Georgia in 2008. It mainly stopped talking about Russia— "there is little coverage of Russia today on Russia Today" the *Guardian* foreign correspondent Luke Harding told us.[12] Instead, RT evolved into a tool of Russian information warfare, with the apparent aim of subverting Western governments and undermining their established media outlets. As Simonyan later boasted about Russia's invasion of Georgia in 2008, "the Defence Ministry was fighting with Georgia, but we were conducting the information war . . . against the whole Western world."[13]

Simonyan's RT did this by developing a subversive antiestablishment form of journalism that gained large followings with sympathetic international audiences. Captured by the outlet's slogan "Question More," RT sought to undermine trust in established Western media outlets by offering viewers "alternative" perspectives. Preferring not to make direct accusations or publish blatant falsehoods itself, it provided a platform for anti-Western, antiestablishment politicians, and conspiracy theorists from the far right and far left of Western politics. Most of these sought to undermine their own government's and established media's accounts of events. This enabled RT to claim it was innocently airing alternative perspectives that are usually silenced by "mainstream media." In reality RT's coverage served Russia's aim of undermining the credibility of Western governments and Western media outlets. RT would relentlessly cover stories highlighting division and dysfunction in liberal democracies:

"anything that causes chaos."[14] According to one report, more than 90 percent of RT and Sputnik's articles on UK domestic politics were about political dysfunction.[15]

RT tried to highlight dysfunction across many liberal societies, but the United States was its main target. Simonyan's RT portrayed America as a domineering and decadent power that was wrongfully imposing liberal values of sexual tolerance, secularism, the extension of LGBTQ rights and gender fluidity against the interests of ordinary people worldwide. This complemented the Putin regime's attempt to portray Russia as the defender of traditional conservative values, the church, and the family.

RT's antiestablishment and antiliberal ideas closely reflected those of numerous right-wing populists that gained traction across Western countries following the 2008 financial crisis. RT and Sputnik backed them and any other cause that promised instability. Russia's outlets promoted Scottish independence and the UK's "Brexit" vote to leave the European Union, and they were named by the United States as key actors in the Kremlin's attempts to influence the 2016 US presential election in favor of Donald Trump.[16] Simonyan herself was mentioned twenty-seven times in a preliminary US government report into Russia's interference in 2016.[17]

In the 2020 US election, RT adopted what we call the "partisan parasite" propaganda model: they made their coverage largely indistinguishable from American domestic, right-wing outlets such as Fox News and One America News Network (OANN). They hosted op-eds about why voters should vote for Trump, amplified his unfounded conspiracy theories about voter fraud, and framed the Democrat Joe Biden as corrupt and unelectable.[18] Meanwhile, RT repeatedly referred to the accusations of its electoral interference as "Russiagate" and continued to deny involvement. A mocking admission eventually came on Russian domestic TV in November 2022 after the US mid-term elections that year, when Russian TV pundits crowed about "Happy US Election Interference Day." They celebrated President Joe Biden's losses in the elections, but lamented that the Republicans ("our guys," led by "Comrade Donald") had underperformed.[19] Yevgeny Prigozhin, then leader of the Wagner mercenary group who had been linked to the Internet Research Agency troll farm in

St. Petersburg, admitted that "We have interfered (in US elections), we are interfering and we will continue to interfere."[20]

As well as adapting its news to undermine liberal societies, RT tailored its content to social media. Staffed by young international journalists well-versed in social media vernacular, RT's Twitter and Facebook accounts provided snarky, edgy banter on political events. Through humor and satire RT lambasted liberal media outlets whenever they appeared to offer partial accounts of events, and they ridiculed celebrities who gave what RT considered to be excessively politically correct opinions on gender and race. Their content was intended to be entertaining and engaging. As our research on the 2020 US election showed, RT gained almost eighty times more Facebook comments than China's CGTN, whose content rarely deviated from the Chinese Communist Party's (CCP) official line.[21] Unlike the dull propaganda of the Soviet era, seemingly meant to bore people into submission, outlets like RT successfully combined news, propaganda, and entertainment, at one point becoming the most watched news channel on YouTube.[22] All the while RT claimed to be innocently offering an alternative perspective: a news outlet asking challenging questions rather than a Kremlin mouthpiece.

RT's state propaganda function has been clearest when Russia has faced criticism for its international behavior. Then RT joins Russia's more outspoken state news agency, Sputnik, in reproducing disinformation overtly. When Russia-backed separatists shot down Malaysian Airlines flight MH-17 on the border with Ukraine in 2014, even posing for photographs amid the wreckage, RT blamed Ukraine, claiming it was an attempt to shoot down Putin's private jet.[23] RT was sanctioned by the UK broadcast regulator, Ofcom, in 2015 for alleging that a chemical weapons attack in Syria by Russia's ally, the Assad government, was staged by the BBC.[24] Sputnik accused Barack Obama and Hillary Clinton of creating the Islamic State (Daesh) and blamed the West for spreading COVID-19 to interfere with China's internal affairs.[25]

Through this and other output RT and Sputnik contributed to what came to be known as Russia's "firehose of falsehood" approach to propaganda. Rather than promoting a single alternative narrative and spinning events to fit the story, as is common in Western political communication, Russian media aimed to produce high volumes of news across multiple channels as rapidly as possible without any commitment to consistency or to objective reality.[26] Following Russian agents' poisoning of the former spy Sergei Skripal in Salisbury, UK, in 2018, researchers identified 138 different narratives spread by RT and Sputnik about the attacks, many of which were contradictory.[27] The purpose, as Simonyan put it, was to convince audiences that "There is no objectivity—only approximations of the truth by as many different voices as possible."[28] If RT could convince people of this, it could get audiences to see all stories and perspectives—including Russia's—as equivalent. Alternatively, audiences might become so overwhelmed by multiple narratives that they would be unable to distinguish between truth and fiction and give up trying. This approach, described by Luke Harding as a form of "weaponized relativism,"[29] is very different from the more traditional authoritarian approach to news employed by China (see chapter 3), which usually prefers tight control of a single pro-government message that is relayed repetitively on all possible media channels.

RT and Sputnik were eventually banned from many liberal democracies after Russia escalated its war against Ukraine to a full-scale invasion in February 2022. Simonyan was sanctioned by the United States, Canada, the EU, and the UK shortly after that and again in September 2024 after the United States published a report claiming that RT was functioning as a branch of Russian intelligence and that it once more attempted to influence the 2024 US election. Simonyan had achieved international notoriety—claiming that she had been described by the CNN journalist Christine Amanpour as an "expert" "international troll."[30] But she had also gained domestic influence. She had been promoted to editor in chief of Russia's state news agency, Rossiya Segodnya, become editor in chief of TV Novosti, and was ranked by Forbes in 2017 as the second most influential woman in Russia and the fifty-second most influential woman in the world. Tellingly, this was thirteen places higher than Hillary Clinton, who had been bumped from second on the list after losing the 2016 election to Trump, a result Simonyan's RT had done its best to promote.[31]

SIMONYAN AS DOMESTIC AGITATOR

Simonyan's tenure at RT drew international attention to Russia's use of news to subvert other societies, but fewer international observers paid attention to how Russia was creating a parallel reality *within* Russia regarding the war in Ukraine. This inattention is partly why so many described Russia as "invading Ukraine" in February 2022 when that was actually the ninth year of an invasion that began in 2014.

In the domestic parallel reality Russia constructed about the war in 2022 and 2023, Simonyan played a different role. She was most prominent as a talk show pundit on Russian state television, conveying the Kremlin's core messages about Ukraine. Alongside her punditry, she was highly active on Telegram, threatening the West with nuclear annihilation in one message and posting her favorite recipes in the next. But her international profile changed after February 2022. Simonyan had gained international recognition for being at the vanguard of a novel but subversive approach to digital news, but after February 2022 she gained increasing notoriety for advocating greater repression and censorship in Russia and for contributing to Russian state television's increasingly genocidal rhetoric toward Ukrainians and its aggressive threats toward other countries. Her evolution reflected the evolution of methods Russia used to promote its narratives about Ukraine as the war progressed.

RUSSIA'S DOMESTIC PARALLEL REALITY

Margarita Simonyan is a central figure in Russia's domestic industrial disinformation ecosystem, but she is just one part of a system that encompasses cutting-edge and traditional news formats. Based on our analysis of Russian news across multiple platforms and interviews with experts who have lived, worked, and conducted research in Russia and Ukraine, there were five key ways Russia promoted and sustained its alternative reality regarding its war in Ukraine in 2022 and 2023:

1. **Inconsistent tactics, consistent strategy:** telling multiple, conflicting stories about a given event but making sure they reflected Russia's overall strategic narrative.
2. **Talk show spectacle:** using stage-managed talk shows on Russian state television to disseminate Kremlin narratives.
3. **False flag industry:** systematically attacking civilians and committing war crimes to fabricate evidence that Ukraine was committing war crimes.
4. **Beyond censorship:** using neo-Soviet methods of control, censorship, and repression.
5. **Meta-fakes:** exploiting social media to spread fake content, fake websites, and fake fact checks about the war.

INCONSISTENT TACTICS, CONSISTENT STRATEGY

Just as it had done over the previous decade, Russian domestic news about the war in 2022 and 2023 often told audiences multiple contradictory stories, making it more difficult for them to discern truth from fiction. But beyond creating confusion and undermining the idea of objective reality, the regime had a more fundamental goal: it wanted Russians to believe that the war was defensive, not offensive; that Russia was liberating people rather than colonizing them; and that Russia was protecting citizens rather than attacking them. Russia had come to be known internationally for news that propagated fifty shades of gray, but in its domestic news what mattered more was to convince Russians that black was white.

So while Russia communicated a wide range of "tactical narratives" to explain specific events during its full-scale invasion, its "strategic narratives" about the war's overall purpose were relatively consistent, having become more so since 2014. Russia claimed Ukraine's government was fascist and that Ukrainian "nationalists" were committing genocide against "good Ukrainians" (those who speak Russian and therefore are Russian, according to Putin). Ukraine's "fascist" government was backed by NATO and the "collective West," which was driven by Russophobia and wanted to destroy Russia. In response, Russia was fighting a patriotic defensive war against fascism, just as the Soviet Union had done against Nazi Germany in World War II. Russia was also fighting to defend itself, and civilization more broadly, from the decadent excesses of Western liberalism.[32]

These stories characterized Russia as good and Ukraine as evil. Russia was saving people, not targeting them. As Simonyan herself claimed, "Nobody is fighting against Ukrainians! We're liberating Ukraine!" "No one is bombing peaceful Ukrainian cities!"[33] Russia had "never waged any wars of conquest. Russia waged defensive wars. Russia enlarged its territories either by defending itself or saving people."[34] In contrast, not only does the West wage wars to destroy other governments, its promotion of sexual freedoms and gender fluidity will cause the "destruction of mankind" because "no one will give birth anymore."[35]

As long as audiences accepted Russia's strategic narratives about the war's overall purpose, it mattered less to the regime whether citizens believed a specific story. During the siege of Mariupol, Russian news claimed that in addition to the Ukrainian army itself its forces were variously fighting neo-Nazis, NATO, British special forces, "LGBT brigades," Satanists, terrorists, nationalists, and mercenaries.[36] These images of the enemy may have been inconsistent and illogical, but it did not matter. They were used flexibly to demonize an enemy that supposedly hated Russia, and against which it needed to defend people.[37]

A common claim Russia made shortly after its February 2022 campaign began was that the United States funded dozens of biolabs across Ukraine to create lethal pathogens to use against Russia. The United States had already explained that it had provided some funding to Ukraine's limited number of biological labs, but these were for preventative public health purposes, not military ones.[38] Russian military officials went further than this—accusing the United States of training migratory birds to carry infectious diseases from Ukraine into Russia. Apart from the general ridiculousness of the idea none acknowledged the obvious contradiction: how could such birds target Russians and not Ukrainians given that Russia had long claimed that Ukrainians and Russians were the same people?[39] But as the Russia expert Jade McGlynn explained to us, what mattered to Putin's regime was not whether citizens believed a specific tactical narrative but that they believed the overall strategic narratives the state was using to justify the war. A Russian citizen may have thought "I don't really believe in biolabs, but I do believe the broader message that the United States interferes in Russia's near abroad." If they believed the regime's larger truth that "the West was using Ukraine to target and destroy Russia," they would be more likely to support—or at least accept—Russia's war.[40]

Russia could use these strategic narratives to draw support because the state had been telling similar stories about Ukraine and the West for years. The idea that Russia was fighting against fascism dates back to the Great Patriotic War (the name for the Soviet Union's war against Nazi Germany in World War II). Russia used the same argument to justify its war against Georgia in 2008. As the ethnographer Paul Goode told us, the Great Patriotic War narrative is "the one story most Russians agree about, so it is a useful way to unify the population."[41] The idea that NATO was a threat to Russia and was driven by rampant Russophobia was used by the Soviet Union while denying the Chornobyl nuclear disaster of 1986. Soviet authorities waited two days before telling citizens about the disaster, and three days before evacuating the area, and tried to hide the scale of the fallout in the coming weeks. Meanwhile, the outlet Moscovskie Novosti printed an article titled "A Poisonous Cloud of Anti-Sovietism," which blamed the international reaction to Chornobyl on "a pre-meditated and well-orchestrated campaign . . . to soil the political atmosphere in the East-West relationship and . . . to cover up criminal acts of militarism by the USA and NATO."[42] Repeating these narratives gave the impression that the war in Ukraine was not a radical break from the past but a continuation of a history in which Russia repeatedly saves itself, and civilization more broadly, from dark forces who seek to destroy it.[43]

The irony of having promoted these strategic narratives was that the regime itself appeared to believe them when it embarked on its "special military operation." According to intelligence sources, Putin sincerely believed that Ukraine's population was pro-Russian and would greet Russian soldiers as liberators and that the West was too decadent and disunited to resist.[44] In this respect, Russia's parallel reality about Ukraine was not just a justification for its full-scale invasion in February 2022. It was arguably a contributing cause because it was the basis of Putin's assumption that the operation would bring swift victory at minimal cost.

TALK SHOW SPECTACLE

Throughout 2022 and 2023, five nights per week, millions of Russians sat down to watch Evening with Vladimir Solovyev, one of many pro-Kremlin news shows on Russian state television. Solovyev, a former radio DJ turned state TV presenter, stood in the center of the studio, usually dressed in a slimming black buttoned suit. He was flanked by a semicircular panel of state-selected pundits, politicians, generals, and media elites to discuss the progress of the war. Solovyev usually began with a monologue that set the tone for the ensuing discussion. After Russian military setbacks he came across as solemn and grumpy. Sometimes he was sarcastic, particularly about NATO and Ukraine's capabilities. At other times he ranted angrily, calling for nuclear strikes on Western democracies one minute and for poorly performing Russian commanders to be shot the next. Having delivered his opening monologue, Solovyev turned to the pundits surrounding him. Margarita Simonyan was usually to his left and was the first speaker he turned to. Each presenter offered a slightly different perspective, giving the impression of genuine debate. The combination of stories, arguments, and tirades they put forward were a bellwether for what the Kremlin wanted to say about the war at a given moment. When Solovyev was not fronting his TV show, he was presenting his phone-in radio show, Full Contact, in which he responded to calls from Russian citizens and railed about the war. He was so well known for spreading the Kremlin's agreed narratives that his critics nicknamed him "Putin's voice."[45]

Solovyev's journey to becoming a leading face of Russian state propaganda was more meandering than Margarita Simonyan's. Highly educated, he achieved advanced degrees in economics and briefly worked as an

academic in the United States, but when higher education proved insufficiently lucrative, he reportedly worked as a bricklayer, cleaner, gardener,
delivery driver, karate instructor, and even a fire extinguisher salesman.[46]
He only moved into presenting in his mid-thirties. He quickly built a reputation as a dynamic radio host, graduating to presenting television news
in the early 2000s. At that time he openly defended journalistic independence. "The phrase 'the journalist does what the boss says' does not apply
to us," he stated in one television interview. "The journalist is always independent."[47] In 2008 he was filmed saying that any leader who started a war
with Ukraine would be a "criminal"—sentiments that would have landed
him in jail had he voiced them after February 2022.[48] But over the years
he changed his tune, morphing from an advocate of journalistic independence into a regime propagandist. By the time of Russia's annexation of
Crimea in 2014, Solovyev was a leading face on Russian state news and a
full-throttled Putin mouthpiece, so much so that Putin awarded him the
Order of Service to the Fatherland, alongside three hundred journalists,
for his pugnacious pro-Russia coverage.[49] The one-time fire extinguisher
salesman had become a firebrand.

If Solovyev was not to one's taste, similar shows were hosted on other
state TV channels, such as *Your Own Truth*, presented by Babayan Roman,
60 Minutes, presented by Olga Skabeyeva, or *Vesti Nedeli* (News of the week),
hosted by Dmitry Kiselyov. These talk shows and their celebrity anchors
dominated evening television. Even before February 2022, Solovyev broke
the Guinness World Record for the most live TV coverage by one host in
a week after he fronted five consecutive five-hour shows.[50] But after February 2022, Russia canceled many soaps and light entertainment shows, free-
ing up more of the state TV schedule for war news. As the Russian-born
journalist Arkady Ostrovsky writes, "Berlusconi once said 'What is not on
TV doesn't exist.' Putin took this one stage further: things that did not exist
could be turned into reality by harnessing the power of television."[51]

Television news may not be as dominant as it once was in Russia, but in
2022 and 2023 it was still a key driver of the domestic news agenda. Between
2013 and 2018, 90 percent of Russians got their news from television, and
it was their most trusted news source.[52] By February 2022, viewership had

dropped to two-thirds of Russians, and 40 percent used Telegram for news too.[53] But even if television viewership was reducing, it remained the main news medium for most Russians. Clips from Russian state television often went viral on social media, and the same pundits had millions of followers on the main platforms.

Russia's news talk shows operated similarly to other aspects of Russia's news ecosystem. When Russia was accused of attacks on civilians, pundits denied them and offered alternative explanations. One might claim that Ukraine was attacking its own people; another might accuse the West of conducting false flag operations to discredit Russia. The narratives talk shows used were often inconsistent, but as the Ukraine-based journalist James Rushton told us, "they don't care." "They'll say their army can defeat NATO in 72 hours, but then they say they are losing because they are fighting the whole of NATO. You'll hear these things in one hour of TV."[54]

The shows claimed to offer genuine debate, but this was illusory. "It's a pseudo talk show," Luke Harding explains. "It's faux debate. It's all very carefully constructed. No one says anything by chance."[55] The talk shows were reportedly briefed by the Kremlin about which topics to cover and which to avoid, which views should be endorsed and which should be criticized.[56] Until February 2022, few in the West knew about Russia's news talk shows and their persistent demonization of Ukraine since 2014. But after February 2022, Western journalists paid closer attention, translating clips of pundits' most outrageous claims to show curious followers how Russia's portrayal of the war inverted reality.

Julia Davis is one of the best-known investigative journalists documenting Russia's war news on state television. A part-Russian part-Ukrainian US citizen, since 2014 she recorded the most egregious examples of Russian disinformation and dehumanization on her website, russialies.com, and on her YouTube channel, Russian Media Monitor. Scouring Russian state news for hours every day, she is committed to holding to account the Putin regime for its actions in Ukraine and the regime propagandists who promote them. As she told us, previously Russia had "very carefully separated their propaganda toward the West from their domestic propaganda" so that they could present a more moderate image to international audiences. "The face they present to the world is completely different when they think no one outside Russia is watching."[57]

Davis's archive provides a chilling record of how Russian talk shows used increasingly dehumanizing and genocidal rhetoric toward Ukraine after February 2022. It documents hundreds of videos in which Russian pundits described Ukrainians as "animals," "insects," "pigs," and "cockroaches." "When a doctor is deworming a cat," Solovyev explained in one clip, "for the doctor, it's a special operation, for the worms, it's a war, and for the cat, it's a cleansing." "Exactly," Simonyan responded, laughing.[58]

The talk shows' dehumanization of Ukraine escalated with every Russian military setback. Russia had expected to take Kyiv in three days and decapitate President Zelensky's government. But a month later Russia had lost the "Battle for Kyiv." Six months later, in September 2022, Ukraine won back a huge swathe of eastern territory surrounding Kharkiv and liberated the southern city of Kherson in November. Russia then took more than six months to capture the eastern town of Bakhmut; its grinding, First World War–like offensive advancing a few meters per day at the cost of tens of thousands of casualties.

With Ukraine resisting strongly, pundits' frustration grew and their rhetoric intensified. Russian propagandists, and Putin himself, had long argued that there is no such thing as the Ukrainian nation and that Ukrainians are really Russians experiencing a "disorder of the mind."[59] State television took this argument further. Davis cited Pavel Gubarev, leader of the Donbas People's Militia, explaining that Ukrainians were really "Russian people, possessed by the devil" and the purpose of Russia's war was to "convince them" that they were not Ukrainian. He then added, "But if you don't want us to change your minds, then we will kill you. We will kill as many of you as we have to. We will kill 1 million or 5 million, we can exterminate all of you."[60] In another clip, a state Duma (parliament) member, Alexei Zhuravlyov, estimated that 5 percent of Ukrainians (approximately two million people) would need to be killed for "Denazification" to succeed. In an interview with RT's former head of Russian language programming, Anton Krasovsky, the musician Akim Apachev estimated that "10 percent of passionate Ukrainians would need to be [killed] . . . and the rest will become Russians again. That's it."[61]

This genocidal rhetoric was especially concerning because it could be found across Russia's information environment. It was evident in Putin's speeches, state media pundits' commentary, and as Ian Garner showed in his research on the "Z Generation," in ordinary Russians' social media conversations.[62] The rhetoric was also reflected in the Russian military's behavior toward Ukrainian civilians. Official reports, including from the UN Commission of Inquiry on Ukraine, documented Russia's unlawful confinement, torture, rape, and killing of civilians, the castration of Ukrainian prisoners of war, the deliberate destruction of civilian infrastructure, and the forced deportations of at least 16,211 Ukrainian children.[63] Russia's talk shows provided daily justification for these atrocities, based on the false reality that "coercion to fraternal relations by force" was the only way to convince Ukrainians they were Russians all along.[64]

The rhetoric on Russia's talk shows may have been a crude manifestation of "twenty-first century fascism," as Luke Harding suggests, but it reflected a sophisticated understanding of how information spreads in the digital age.[65] Solovyev and his fellow presenters made apocalyptic threats against other countries in the knowledge that these would be clipped, translated, and repackaged by Russia watchers on social media. They knew that these would probably go viral on Western social media platforms, whereupon they would be picked up by leading Western news outlets. Russia's channels would then pick up on this coverage and repackage it to claim that their threats were succeeding and that their enemies were running scared.

Alternatively, Russian talk shows would take news stories about problems in other countries and frame them as being caused by those countries' support for Ukraine. When Britain experienced fruit and vegetable shortages in the winter of 2022, the host of *60 Minutes*, Olga Skabeyeva (nicknamed the "Iron Doll of Putin TV"), claimed that "some restaurants in once-Great Britain will be serving squirrels" because it continued to spend so much supplying weapons to Ukraine.[66]

Russian state television also drew as often as possible from "useful idiots" abroad, a term Lenin used to describe foreigners who, knowingly or unknowingly, relayed Kremlin propaganda. Russian state news often featured clips of former Fox News anchor Tucker Carlson, who regularly praised Putin and repeated many of Russia's favorite pieces of disinformation verbatim, including that the United States was funding bioweapons research in Ukraine and that Ukraine was experiencing seven casualties for every Russian casualty.[67] In Russia's news laundromat, nothing was wasted: every news item, tweet, video, or comment was a potential resource for a cycle of disinformation that continually reinforced Russia's strategic narratives about the war.

FALSE FLAG INDUSTRY

In the sixteenth century, when pirates wanted to board a ship, a common ruse was to hoist a flag of a nation the ship was allied to. Believing the pirate ship to be an ally, the target would allow the pirate ship to come closer. The pirates' "false flag" would make it easier to board the target ship, take it over, and plunder it.

Since then the term "false flag" has come to be used for any political or military action taken with the intent to blame an opponent. Countries wishing to invade others use false flags to claim they were attacked first so they can claim that their war is defensive and therefore legal in international law. Nazi Germany, for instance, infamously sent seven SS soldiers dressed as Poles to take over the Gleiwitz TV tower in German territory, to make it seem that Poland was invading Germany and not the other way around. At some point, most major countries have been accused of conducting false flags to justify war. But never before has a state used false flag claims at the industrial scale Russia has against Ukraine.

Russia had two main rationales for its industrial use of false flags since invading Ukraine in 2014: to deflect responsibility for attacks on civilians it had already conducted, or to claim that its future actions had been provoked. When Russia annexed Crimea, Putin argued that the "little green men" who occupied Crimea were really local self-defense militias who needed Russian help because Ukraine's fascist government was attacking civilians. In fact they were Russian special forces, and Ukraine's government was neither fascist nor attacking its own people.

Similarly, Russia fabricated false flags to justify its February 2022 offensive. Six days beforehand, on February 18, Russian state television posted grainy footage of a nighttime skirmish portraying Ukrainian "saboteurs" trying to destroy a chlorine plant in separatist-held eastern Ukraine. Despite the mission's clandestine nature, the soldiers had recorded their actions on their headcams, which pro-Russian separatists conveniently recovered. Further analysis revealed that the incident was staged: the sound overlay originated from a Finnish military exercise in 2010, and the video's metadata showed it was filmed on February 8, ten days previously.[68]

As Russia's offensive proceeded, a grim pattern emerged: Russia would attack civilians, and when accused it would mirror these accusations and blame Ukraine. As it advanced on Mariupol, Russia announced it would create "humanitarian corridors" out of the city. Yet these only went back to Russia, aiding Russia's "filtration" campaign, documented by the UN, to force Ukrainians into Russian territory.[69] More cynically still, Russian promptly mined and shelled the routes, then blamed Ukraine for doing so.[70] When evidence emerged in April 2022 that Russian forces had tortured and executed dozens of civilians at Bucha, north of Kyiv, Russian news first blamed Ukrainian forces for attacking "collaborators," then blamed Ukraine for shelling civilians, then claimed that the crimes were staged by the British in a psychological operation.[71]

Sometimes Russia's false flag claims came from official channels. In May 2022, the Russian Ministry of Defense claimed that UK intelligence operatives were "putting civilian bodies in basements in the Sumy region" to manufacture evidence of a "Russian massacre."[72] Other claims spread from social media. The pro-Russian social media channel, Operation Z, claimed to its eight hundred thousand followers in May 2022 that Ukrainian doctors had been told to help transport bodies of women and children to a building in the city where a simulated Russian air raid would be held to create footage discrediting Russia.[73]

Together these claims generated a bizarre portrayal of contemporary warfare. In wars of attrition, the main logistical challenge is to deliver soldiers, munitions, and materiel to sustain operations at the front. But in Russia's alternative reality, there was a second logistical challenge taking place behind the scenes: a struggle to transport corpses and media teams to bombed out buildings just in time to concoct evidence that falsely implicated Russia in attacking civilians.

The problem Russia had was that there was no credible evidence that the Zelensky government was fascist or that it deliberately attacked its own civilians. Consequently, Russia had two choices. It either needed to fabricate evidence of attacks, which were usually easily discredited, or its military could attack civilians themselves and claim that Ukraine was the perpetrator. The latter approach was more convenient because there were other reasons Russia attacked Ukrainian civilians too. It attacked them to terrorize them into submission. It attacked them to compel them to flee, ethnically cleansing them from territory Russia could then repopulate with Russian nationals. It attacked civilians to punish them for resisting, as if this would somehow shake them out of false consciousness and make them realize that they were Russian all along.[74]

However, attacking civilians to generate false flag propaganda also further incentivized brutality against them. The more violent the atrocity, the stronger footage Russia could generate of what it said were Ukrainian atrocities. Russia therefore had little incentive to discourage its soldiers from committing war crimes because it would lose its steady flow of episodes it could blame on Ukrainians. This was a dark and diabolical approach to war. The worst *genocidaires* of the twentieth century mainly tried to hide their crimes. They did not encourage them to create news coverage they could then use to accuse their opponents of genocide.

BEYOND CENSORSHIP

Two months after Russia's "special military operation" began Russian pundits were getting frustrated. Russia's offensives had stalled, and Russia had seen numerous protests against the war. Something had to change. As ever, Russia turned to its television pundits to seed messages about what might happen next. Putin turned to his faithful messenger, Margarita Simonyan. Before February 2022, whenever democracies moved to restrict RT and Sputnik's broadcasting or advertising rights, Simonyan would deftly argue that RT was being denied freedom of speech by states that constantly lecture Russia about why freedom of speech is crucial in a democracy.[75] But by April 2022, Simonyan had reversed her position. Freedom of speech was unimportant after all. Censorship was what was needed:

> We had two periods in our history with limited or no censorship. From 1905 to 1917. We remember how that ended. And during *perestroika* and the following 1990s. We remember how that ended. It ended with the country's collapse. No big nation can exist without control of information. Those who made us add to our constitution, that censorship is prohibited, they understood that well, those who taught us for decades, that "No, no, no, society must be free. A developed economy cannot exist without a developed political system or a free political system." All of that is total BS [bullshit]. Just look at China. Do you like China's economy? I like it. Do they have any freedom in the political life of their country, in the informational life of their country? No, they don't and they never had it. Maybe that's not bad. Maybe that's a good thing. . . . We need to change our info-politics. This is the turning point, to look at everything that is happening in our country in a different way, starting with the phrase in our constitution that "censorship is prohibited."[76]

One year later, the war was going no better. With Russia having lost over half of the territory it had gained since February 2022, it now faced a Ukrainian counteroffensive and growing elite criticism about the war.[77] Simonyan's husband, the film producer Tigran Keosayan, went even further on an appearance on Evening with Vladimir Solovyev. "We need *more* than censorship," he argued earnestly. "Authorities have to dare to take drastic measures" to create a system with "zero tolerance for an opinion that contradicts the policies of the government."[78] "Question More" may have been RT's slogan when it wanted international audiences to doubt their governments, but inside Russia the Simonyan family called for a system in which audiences question nothing.

In an influential recent book, the political scientists Sergei Guriev and Daniel Treisman described Putin as a "spin dictator": one of a new breed of "information autocrats" who rule based on subtly manipulating public opinion to maintain genuine popularity, unlike traditional "fear dictators" who rule by overt repression.[79] From February 2022, however, Putin more closely resembled an old-school tyrant, relying on ever-stricter information control, censorship, and repression to maintain his parallel reality about Ukraine.

In truth, Putin's efforts to take control of Russia's media and information systems had been increasing ever since he came to power. As the political scientist Timothy Frye documents, this began with television in the 2000s, newspapers in the 2010s, and the internet thereafter.[80] Putin adopted an approach that leaders such as Viktor Orbán in Hungary would later follow (see chapter 4): avoid taking over outlets directly if possible, and instead ensure their takeover by proxies, such as pro-government businessmen. In 2001, the leading independent television outlet, NTV, was taken over by the state energy company Gazprom, and was repurposed to parrot the Kremlin's official line. In 2003, the government shut down the fourth major terrestrial TV channel, TVS, having already taken control of the other three.[81] Newspaper takeovers followed: *Kommersant* in 2011, *Gazeta.Ru* in 2013, *Lenta.Ru* and *Grani.Ru* in 2014.

Increased control over the internet followed. The Kremlin took control of VKontakte, a popular Facebook imitator, and Yandex, a successful alternative to Google search, placing them in the hands of pro-regime oligarchs. It banned Virtual Private Networks (VPNs) in 2017 (although many Russians still use them) and demanded that IT companies give the government their encryption keys so the state could monitor online conversations.[82] Leaks from Roskomnadzor, Russia's internet regulator, detailed over 1.2 million URLs banned in Russia by 2022.[83] Before the full-scale invasion of Ukraine, Russia was 150th in Reporters Without Borders' 2021 Press Freedom Index.[84]

Putin continued to allow some independent media in the margins but constantly tried to restrict their funding and harass their journalists. At least thirty-eight journalists were killed in Russia between 2000 and 2020, including six from the outlet Novaya Gazeta alone. Still, before the

February 2022 offensive, independent outlets could just about operate in Russia as long as they self-censored on politically sensitive topics, avoided direct criticism of Putin and his friends, and accepted the latent threat of punishment and violence.[85]

After February 2022 things got much worse. The Kremlin passed new media laws making it illegal to describe the Ukraine conflict as a "war" or an "invasion"; it was a "special military operation." Putin deployed a tactic increasingly used by autocrats and illiberal democrats worldwide, by criminalizing inconvenient truths as "fake news." People could get fifteen years in jail for circulating "fake information" about the war, and five for criticizing the military.[86] In response, protesters held up blank placards in Moscow's Red Square: an inspired critique of censorship that was later used by Chinese protesters against their country's ongoing COVID-19 restrictions in November 2022.[87] An estimated 16,380 Russians had been arrested under the new legislation by the summer of 2022.[88]

On March 1, 2022, Roskomnadzor blocked the broadcasting of two of Russia's last independent outlets, Ekho Moskvy (Echo of Moscow) radio and TV Rain.[89] Most independent outlets quickly shut down their Russian operations and fled the country. Ekho Moskvy later resumed coverage from Berlin, Meduza and TV Rain from Latvia, and the Moscow Times from Amsterdam. Russia tried to block these from domestic audiences, declaring them "undesirable organizations" and "foreign agents."[90] Russia also banned the BBC, alleging that it was part of an "information war unleashed by the West."[91]

Russia's neo-Soviet methods of news control, censorship, and repression were shown most strongly in occupied Ukraine. In the invasion's first week, Russia conducted airstrikes on TV stations and radio masts in Kyiv, Korosten, Lyschansk, and Kharkiv.[92] On March 4 Russia installed new equipment to the telecommunications masts in newly occupied Kherson and Melitopol that blocked Ukrainian broadcasts and only broadcast Russian channels. Russia shut down the Ukrainian internet in Kherson region on May 30. Many of Russia's efforts were unsophisticated. In May 2022, images emerged from occupied Mariupol of TV vans blaring out Russian state news shows explaining how Russia was saving Ukraine, including in front of the bombed Mariupol theater, where hundreds of civilians had just been killed.[93] Other methods were ruthlessly bureaucratic. Ukrainian citizens who reported to the authorities in Russian-controlled territory recall being given a Russian passport in one hand and a Russian SIM card in the other.[94] Without the SIM card they could not easily get online, and they later discovered that without the passport they could not open a bank account, receive health care, or get welfare payments. Meanwhile, their children were learning from new Russian history books that Russia's invasion was a legitimate act of self-defense against a Ukrainian neo-Nazi state.[95] Like much of the fighting, these were twentieth century methods of authoritarian control in a twenty-first century war.

META-FAKES

On April 8, 2022, a Russian missile struck the train station in the city of Kramatorsk in the Donetsk region of eastern Ukraine. For weeks the station had been an evacuation hub for Ukrainian civilians fleeing the Russian advance. On that cloudy spring morning, more than a thousand evacuees queued patiently to catch a train to the relative safety of western Ukraine. The evacuation was well known, having been featured on local news and on the city authorities' social media feeds. This did not deter the attackers. At 10:28 the missile struck, shattering glass, splintering limbs. The effect was catastrophic. The single strike killed at least fifty-eight Ukrainian civilians and injured over one hundred. Early investigations confirmed that the weapon used was a Tochka-U ballistic missile containing cluster munitions, whose motor unit had landed 50 meters southwest of the station entrance. It had "payback for the children" painted in Russian on it, an oft-used slogan in Russia's post-2014 disinformation campaign accusing "fascist" Ukraine of attacking children as part of its "genocide" in the Donbas.[96]

Several days later a video went viral on Twitter, purportedly by the BBC, claiming that Ukraine, not Russia, was really responsible. Mimicking the font, style, and branding of the BBC's social media videos, it claimed that the missile's serial number was consistent with those used by the Ukrainian army and that Russia no longer used that missile. Ukraine must therefore have fired it. However, the video was fake, as was the BBC branding. A swift investigation revealed that it emerged on a Telegram account run by Readovka, a pro-Kremlin news outlet with over one million followers.[97] It had also gone viral on the popular Chinese platform Sina Weibo, accumulating 119,000 views.[98] Russian state television channel Rossiya 24 published the video, looking for another opportunity to promote the Kremlin's claim that only Ukraine attacks civilians. Meanwhile investigative journalists discovered that pro-Kremlin journalists had posted shortly after the attacks that the strikes had hit soldiers, before quickly deleting the posts when the real victims had been revealed.[99] Open-source intelligence analysts rapidly accumulated dozens of images and videos showing Russia deploying Tochka-U missiles. A report by Human Rights Watch detailed overwhelming evidence that Russia was responsible.[100] But, as always, Russia blamed Ukraine.

These examples capture how Russia combined the opportunistic use of social media with more traditional news outlets to invert reality about the war. Tempting as it is to think of social media as separate from "traditional" or "mainstream" media, there is no clear distinction between the two. Russia used them together as part of a hybrid news ecosystem to maintain domestic backing for its war against Ukraine.

From February 2022 Russia tried to control its citizens' use of social media, but unlike China (see chapter 3) it lacked the resources to do this effectively. Before February 2022 approximately three-quarters of Russia's 145 million people used YouTube, 71 million used Facebook, and 65 million used Instagram.[101] Shortly after the February 2022 offensive began, Russia banned Twitter, and Meta's platforms Facebook and Instagram. It declared Meta's apps "extremist organizations" and accused them—ironically—of creating an "alternative reality" about the war.[102] Two years later, in April 2024, Russia convicted Meta's communication director Andy Stone of "inciting terrorism" and sentenced him in absentia to six years in a penal colony.[103]

Crucially, Russia left two international platforms open to Russian citizens at the time of writing: YouTube and Telegram. Russia repeatedly failed to coerce YouTube into taking down content that criticized Russia's war but did not block it.[104] Partly this was because YouTube had a global reach, enabling pro-Putin news outlets and bloggers to reach international audiences with their output. Another reason was that the ban could have backfired. Refuse access to YouTube to three-quarters of the Russian population and millions more might have invested in VPNs to bypass the restrictions, giving them access to other Western platforms too.

Even more important was Telegram, which quickly became the key social media battleground of the war. Russia banned Telegram in 2018 but reinstated it in 2020, having failed to stop citizens from using it. In January 2023, 40 percent of Russians consumed news on the app.[105] It became the main source of war news for Ukrainians too—they could receive up-to-date information on air strike locations, missing persons, and regular communication from the highly active account of President Zelensky himself.

On Telegram the Kremlin used the same social media techniques to promote its alternative reality as it had done for the previous decade. The state's leading media celebrities had huge Telegram followings, and they used their accounts to broadcast official narratives and amplify disinformation that supported them. In the first three months of the February 2022 operation, according to Jade McGlynn, pro-Russian Telegram users commonly referred to Ukraine as "country-404"—a reference to the "404 error" one gets online when a webpage does not appear to exist.[106] They persistently portrayed Ukrainians as Nazis and criticized the West for moral decay and Russophobia. As Russia's military failures mounted, they called on patriotic Russians to support their country no matter what and railed against "traitors" who opposed the war. The ubiquity of smartphones and cameras on the battlefield provided pro-military channels with an endless supply of combat footage with which to manufacture "war porn," portraying the successes and invincibility of the Russian military.[107] Still, the government was unable to stem criticism from various "milbloggers," who provided relatively accurate and often scathing updates on Russia's progress in the war.

Russia's inability to control platforms such as Telegram forced it to operate in a more chaotic, unpredictable communication environment than its closely controlled state news. But one advantage was that social media content provided almost limitless material with which to create disinformation. When Russia fabricated content from scratch, its efforts were often crude and easily debunked. However, rarely was it necessary to fabricate content on social media. Anyone with decent IT skills could lift footage from social media, overlay alternative text and sound, and create the false impression of genuine news. This will get even easier in the future as generative AI improves. Russian information operatives will not even need to spend time searching for the right image—AI can create it.

A week before Rossiya 24 had aired the fake BBC news video claiming Ukraine had attacked the evacuees at Kramatorsk railway station, it published social media images claiming to show Ukrainian soldiers handling mannequins in an effort to stage the Bucha massacres. This footage had been lifted from a TikTok video from the Russian actor Philippe Fedorchuk, in which he explained that a production team was "preparing a mannequin for a movie stunt" at a film set in St. Petersburg.[108] All someone had to do was appropriate the content and repackage it with new text and graphics to create the Kremlin's preferred impression. Russia could then amplify this content artificially through bot networks and inauthentic accounts. None of these techniques was especially new. Social media companies and fact-checking organizations such as EUvsDisinfo had been monitoring Russia's use of them for over a decade.[109]

Russia's propagandists did not care when fact-checkers revealed their fabrications, Julia Davis explains. When they're caught "they just shrug their shoulders and just say that 'everything is propaganda.' And that's why they will keep doing it."[110] Instead, Russia imitated the fact-checkers. One of the most popular pro-regime Telegram channels early on was War on Fakes, set up a day before Russia's February 2022 offensive by the pro-Kremlin journalist Timofey Vasiliev.[111] Imitating independent fact-checkers, War on Fakes claimed to be an "objective," "unbiased" site that debunks fake news because it sees "signs of an information war launched against Russia." In fact, it tried to discredit accurate news reporting about Russia's actions by labeling factual content as fake. War on Fakes told its audience that Ukraine attacked its own people at the Kramatorsk railway station, that the Bucha massacres were staged, and that Russian missiles strikes on Ukrainian apartment buildings and hospitals were really by Ukrainian missile defense forces. Boasting 750,000 followers, War on Fakes posted content in Russian, Arabic, Chinese, English, French, German, and Spanish. As with the other weapons in the Kremlin's news arsenal, it worked symbiotically with official channels, although it is unclear how directly it was linked to the Kremlin. The Ministry of Foreign Affairs, RT, and Margarita Simonyan herself, all posted War on Fakes content.[112] In this way, Russia hijacked methods designed to counter its disinformation to reinforce its own version of reality.

HOW SUCCESSFUL WAS RUSSIA IN PROPAGATING ITS PARALLEL REALITY?

On a sunny morning in Kyiv in the spring of 2023, the journalist James Rushton spoke to us via Zoom, recalling his experiences of living and working across Ukraine during the war:

> I remember coming back from Odesa in a sleeping car with a Russian who had moved to Ukraine in 2005 to 2006. He was a doctor. He phoned his mother at St. Petersburg and asked why Russia is doing this [to Ukraine]. He sees himself as Ukrainian now. She said "because you are all Nazis." It's so common. Almost everyone has had to cut off contact with family members, because the reality is they live in Russia; they sit and stew in Russian propaganda. It may seem ridiculous to us, but not if you're exposed to it for years, twenty-four hours a day. So many Ukrainian families say the same. Their Russian relatives are saying "why don't you let the Russian army do what they need to do? You have been brainwashed." It's an inversion of reality. The Russian relatives are the brainwashed ones.[113]

Anecdotes like these suggest that Russia had great success getting people to believe its narratives about Ukraine in 2022 and 2023. A Ukrainian blogger, Volodymyr Zolkin, concurred, having interviewed dozens of parents of captured Russian prisoners of war in early 2022: "Often a Russian mother does not ask her son about his health, but immediately tells us the propaganda she was told on Russian television. They have a TV instead of a brain."[114] But is it that simple? Was Russian state news that effective in shaping public opinion? Talk to Russia experts and the picture is more complicated.

The first complication is that it is hard to assess what Russians truly believe due to the unreliability of opinion polls, especially since February 2022.[115] But past research has shown that Russian citizens tend to be critical media consumers who are accustomed to state news being government propaganda.[116] This should mean they were not easily convinced by how the war was being portrayed on state news.

Despite this, having surveyed or interviewed hundreds of Russian citizens, Joanna Szostek identified a "paradox of disbelief," whereby Russian citizens claimed to be skeptical about official information but then repeated it anyway. Recalling her interviews with well-educated Russian students, she says that "I'd ask them about Russian state TV and nine times out of ten they'd say they know it's propaganda, that it's state controlled. They were quite dismissive of it. But then they all repeated messages from Russian TV," for example, that "the West is working to destroy Russia, and that Russia needs to defend against it."[117] This suggests that there was public belief in Russia's strategic narratives about the war even though citizens could recognize government propaganda.

Another tempting argument for why Russian citizens accepted their government's narratives about the war is because they lacked access to other news sources. However, as previously explained, because Telegram and YouTube were open to Russians and many used VPNs, Russians could initially access alternative news about the war relatively easily. Most simply chose not to do so. "The issue is not a lack of exposure to different points of view," Szostek continues. "Rather it is that they generally accept the worldview that is offered by the Russian state. It is appealing to them."[118] As the Russia watcher Francis Scarr observes, one should not think about the tens of millions of Russian citizens who consume state media as lacking agency. The regime has effectively channeled prejudices that go back to the 1990s, when many Russians felt humiliated as the West won the Cold War while political and economic order in Russia collapsed. Many Russians, Scarr concludes, have been told "exactly what they want to hear."[119]

Asking whether Russians believe their government's parallel reality about the war may even be the wrong question. "It is not about true and false," Joanna Szostek argues, "it is about us and them. It doesn't matter what's true. What matters is if you're on Russia's side, defending 'our guys'. It is the projection of a set of values in which loyalty is superior to honesty."[120] "They turn it into a sports game," the journalist Julia Davis explains. "You have to root for your own team. It doesn't matter if your team is doping, cheating. You are not a patriot if you are not supporting your team. So even if they are lying, and get caught in a lie, they say 'isn't it better to support our side rather than their side?'"[121]

The Russian government offered its citizens a more appealing version of reality than one in which their country was engaging in a criminal war of aggression in Ukraine. The political actor who spreads disinformation is inviting their audience to join them in a "collective fantasy" in which "both the target and the creator are complicit" in their deception.[122] Putin's propagandists invited Russia's citizens to join them in a fantasy world in which Russia's war in Ukraine was just, it was a force for good in the world, and its enemies were the real villains. Research shows that Russians liked these ideas, even those who had doubts about the war.[123] The alternative would be to admit the folly of Russia's war against Ukraine and risk arrest and imprisonment in the process. The path of least resistance was to accept the fantasy, however reluctantly.

Russia's ultimate aim, as Luke Harding told us, has been to create a "sovereign reality": a world in which citizens loyally accept the state's version of events regardless of its veracity.[124] National truth rather than factual truth. Russia has been at the cutting edge of state efforts to distort reality in the digital age, including co-opting media outlets and giving them to friendly oligarchs, hobbling independent news outlets, attacking critical journalists, and amplifying state messages with fake websites, troll farms, and bot armies while undermining Russian outlets' international competitors. And as we will show, where Russia has gone other governments have followed, as they have tried to warp reality to serve their interests.

But in 2022 and 2023 Russia's faltering war against Ukraine has also shown that the more Russia's sovereign reality has differed from material reality, the more repression has been needed to sustain it. With every military setback, Russian state rhetoric has become more vengeful and genocidal, and the regime has been forced to rely on methods of control and censorship from a bygone era. To refuse to live in Russia's alternative reality has been framed as an act of betrayal or treason. As Margarita Simonyan tweeted about the antiwar protests across Russian cities sparked by the February 2022 offensive: "If you are ashamed of being Russian now, don't worry. You are not Russian."[125]

* * *

On August 23, 2023, citizens near the northwestern Russian town of Kuzhenkino filmed a small passenger plane falling vertically from the sky before crashing violently into a field. According to TASS, Russia's state news agency, there were ten passengers, all of whom died in the crash. Among them was Yevgeny Prigozhin ("Putin's chef"), leader of Russia's infamous Wagner mercenary group, which had been fighting in Ukraine in addition to intervening in a range of conflicts across the Middle East and Africa.[126]

Two months before, to the day, Prigozhin had ordered his units to march on Moscow in a mutiny against the Putin regime. Astonishingly, he admitted on Telegram that the Russian government had lied to its citizens about the war for years and that Ukraine was not attacking citizens as the government claimed.[127] He complained that the Russian army had failed to support Wagner and that the army had recently attacked his forces. As Wagner troops drove north into Russia, it skirmished with the Russian military, shooting down several helicopters and planes and killing several pilots. Wagner forces occupied the southern town of Rostov-on-Don. Images of cheering crowds spread across Telegram. A second force sped toward the capital. Panic ensued in Moscow. Western news outlets reported feverishly that the Putin regime might be under threat.

As Prigozhin's forces advanced on the capital, narratives on Russian state news became inconsistent because pundits were unsure what the official line was. Anchors begged audiences to take information only from "official channels," and news shows tried to censor information about how much progress Wagner forces were making toward Moscow. Yet footage of this from citizens' smartphones was proliferating rapidly across Telegram, piercing Putin's parallel reality faster than Russia's tightly controlled state media could respond.[128] This included farcical images of construction vehicles digging up the highway to Moscow to slow down Prigozhin's forces. Having developed a reputation for mastering how to communicate in the digital age, the Putin regime's desire for information control suddenly made it look distinctly analogue.

Yet the coup ended as abruptly as it began. Prigozhin, having apparently received assurances from Putin that military failures in Ukraine would be addressed, fled to exile in Belarus. Later that evening state propagandists on Vladimir Solovyev's show were still struggling to work out what the official narrative was. Margarita Simonyan had apparently been boating on the Volga River before returning, in her words, to an "armed mutiny in Mother Russia." She had not even had time to mute her phone, which pinged with notifications during the broadcast. She was incredulous that despite Putin having given a TV speech accusing the mutineers of "high treason," Prigozhin appeared to be escaping without prosecution. Issuing a rare criticism of her "boss," she said it was a "mockery of legal norms." In a remarkable statement by an elected politician, perhaps anywhere other than wartime Russia, the State Duma minister Andrey Gurulyov said that "a bullet to the forehead is the sole salvation for Prigozhin." "The only way out," he continued, was for the mutineers "to kill themselves before a bullet finds them."[129] Two months later Prigozhin was dead in the plane crash. And while Putin denied involvement, to his critics this looked like the state assassination that had already been trailed on state news.

In the weeks following the mutiny, Putin acted as many autocrats do after facing a direct threat to their position: more repression, more censorship. Suddenly, the "milbloggers" who had been allowed to criticize the war faced arrest for "inciting extremist activity."[130] A rumor spread on Twitter suggesting that Vladimir Solovyev might be indicted because some of his televised rants had criticized the conduct of the war.[131]

A few days later Russian talk shows tried to invert reality once more. Apparently "There was no armed mutiny."[132] There was no division among the Russian armed forces. It was just another Western plot to destabilize Russia. The Russian military and Russian society were united behind their leader.

War is peace. Freedom is slavery. Ignorance is strength.[133]

3

SELLING "DEMOCRACY"

Xi's China

Why should a government which is doing what it believes to be right allow itself to be criticised? It would not allow opposition by lethal weapons, and ideas are much more fatal than guns.

—LENIN

I n December 2021, then-US president Joe Biden convened the Summit for Democracy. As his first year as president drew to a close, Biden painted a picture of a world facing a titanic contest between democracy and authoritarianism. In this existential struggle, Biden framed China as the greatest threat to democracy: the world's most powerful autocratic state. A state apparently bent on reshaping the international order in its interests.

More than one hundred countries were invited to the Summit, conducted virtually due to the COVID-19 pandemic. To explain the Summit's purpose, the United States invited Nathan Law, the exiled democratic politician from Hong Kong. With his youthful looks and clad in a black

T-shirt, Law looked more like a well-groomed student than a prominent politician. However, Law had been Hong Kong's youngest ever elected official—voted into parliament at just twenty-three years of age. He had been a key figure in the Umbrella Movement of 2014, in which tens of thousands of Hong Kong residents met under umbrellas of all colors and sizes to protest the Chinese Communist Party's (CCP) attempts to eliminate free and fair elections in the territory. He won election to Hong Kong's legislature in 2016, but he was then disqualified from his seat along with five other pro-democracy lawmakers. In 2017 he was arrested at a protest against a celebration of China's renewed rule of Hong Kong in 1997. Dragged away by two policemen, he was jailed for six months. Later released, he was also prominent during Hong Kong's pro-democracy protests from 2019, in which some protesters reportedly carried farewell letters to their families out of fear they would be beaten to death.[1] With fellow protesters imprisoned, he fled into exile in the UK following the institution of the 2020 National Security Law—a draconian edict in which any criticism of the state could be labeled a threat to national security.[2] In advocating for Hong Kong to retain democratic freedoms that China had promised to preserve when it took over Hong Kong from the British, Law was deemed a subversive, secessionist traitor.[3] Now he was a fugitive from the Chinese state.

Law's prerecorded speech to the Summit was short—just three minutes long. In that time he described how quickly Hong Kong had declined from the "freest city in Asia" to "an authoritarian police state" thanks to the unchecked power of the Chinese Communist Party. He then criticized China's repression of ethnic minorities in Xinjiang and Tibet. According to Law, "for too long the world has embraced the rise of China without developing mechanisms to hold it accountable."[4]

The responses in China's media were predictable for a state with a long-standing reputation for being hypersensitive to criticism.[5] The state news outlet, the *Global Times*, described Law as a "despicable sinner and soulless pawn." Hong Kong's Secretary for Security, Chris Tang Ping-Keung, described him as a "coward and traitor" with "evil intentions," which was shown by his "repeated political lies" and "slander" toward the Chinese government.[6] The state-run Xinhua news agency described Law as a "pawn of the West" who should be "crucified on the pillar of historical shame for betraying the country and the Chinese people."[7]

But another aspect of China's response to the Summit for Democracy was more striking. Immediately before, during, and after the conference, the Chinese government and state media assertively promoted an alternative reality: China was not the authoritarian state that Law claimed it was. In fact, it was a "Whole Process People's Democracy." Shortly after the Summit the CCP released a White Paper provocatively titled "China: Democracy That Works" (implying other forms of democracy do not). According to the paper, what makes China a democracy is that the Chinese Communist Party truly serves the people, unlike elites in Washington who serve themselves or commercial interests.[8] China's democracy involves public participation at all times, the *China Daily* claimed, rather than temporarily engaging citizens with empty promises during election periods.[9] According to China's leading international broadcaster, CGTN (China Global Television Network), Chinese democracy was not only more effective and genuinely democratic than American democracy—it was *the* most effective democracy.[10]

In this chapter we show how the Chinese Communist Party sells its parallel reality that China is the world's leading democracy. We draw partly from our prior research on the content and style of Chinese state news, especially CGTN.[11] We combine this with secondary analysis of China's attempts to buy influence and ownership of news platforms abroad, and its use of social media to promote the country and to limit criticisms of its human rights record. China's approach to international news is heavily based on control, and is an extension of its restrictive approach to domestic news. Unlike Russia, whose international news often prioritizes subverting democracies over promoting Russia, China's news is relentlessly self-promotional and seeks to "Tell China's Story Well" to international audiences. And as you will see, it is adopting an increasingly diverse set of methods to promote its "democratic" credentials.

CHINA AS A DEMOCRACY?

China is hardly the first dictatorship that has claimed to be democratic. Communist China under Mao Ze Dong was modeled on Leninist ideas of democratic dictatorship, in which elected functionaries rule on behalf of the people but without political opposition. From the "German *Democratic* Republic" (East Germany) to the "*Democratic* Republic of North Korea," dictatorships worldwide crave the legitimacy of being perceived to be democratic, however illusory such claims are. Neither is China's claim new domestically—its propaganda has long declared that its citizens enjoy "democratic" rights and freedoms. The veteran journalist Karl Strittmatter recalls walking around Chinese cities festooned with banners telling citizens that they "live in a free, democratic country governed by the rule of law."[12] The difference in recent years is the CCP's increasingly confident assertion that liberal democracy is not "real" and that China is the true democracy the world should emulate.

How could China credibly claim this? The Economist Intelligence Unit's Democracy Index categorizes China as an authoritarian state, sitting 148th out of 167 countries.[13] It does not have free elections, universal suffrage, or a multiparty system. Chinese citizens can participate in local elections, but these are mainly rubber-stamping exercises to elect preselected CCP officials. Independent candidates are "often kept off the ballot or out of office through intimidation, harassment, fraud, and in some cases detention."[14] China's constitution claims its people "enjoy freedom of speech [and] of the press," but neither of these exist in reality.[15] Freedom House placed China as the third least free country in the world for media freedom in 2021 and as "the world's largest prison for journalists."[16] There are no free trade unions, no independent judiciary, and no real equality before the law. Ethnic minorities face systematic repression.[17] The state does not practice religious tolerance and routinely uses torture, airing forced confessions on state media to deter further dissent.[18]

The idea that these behaviors constitute democracy seems absurd. However, China's attempts to promote its democratic credentials should not be dismissed so readily for several reasons. First, China's "discourse power"—its use of media channels to promote a positive image and influence international politics[19]—has increased markedly in recent years, thanks largely to its impressive economic growth and the scale of its international investments through policies such as the Belt and Road Initiative. Meanwhile, several of the world's leading liberal democracies have experienced political crises in which their legitimacy and performance have been questioned. As China points out whenever it can, its main rival, the United States, looks increasingly dysfunctional and divided domestically and less influential internationally. Thus, when the CCP claims its governance is more responsive to its citizens than the United States is (and therefore in its terms more "democratic"), China speaks more loudly than it used to.

Second, China's investments in controlling how news is produced and distributed worldwide have given it more influence over international news than ever before. China is investing far more than any other country in trying to control the international news agenda: through state media, social media, physical infrastructure, and smartphone technology. This has given it more tools with which to bombard audiences with unremittingly positive news about China and its "democracy" and more ways to silence stories that reveal China's repressive, authoritarian nature.

Third, contesting the meaning of democracy may be more strategically astute than it first appears. A prominent explanation for how liberal democracies "won" the Cold War is that citizens came to believe that liberal democracy would bring them a better life than socialist authoritarianism. Global polls continue to show that strong majorities in almost every country favor democracy as a political system, even though there has been a decline in faith in the *performance* of democracy in numerous countries.[20] Rather than cede this rhetorical ground, as the Soviet Union appeared to do, why not fight for it? Why not attempt to appropriate the meaning of democracy to serve one's own political purposes? Alternatively, if that is unrealistic, why not try to relativize the concept of democracy, claiming that what counts as democracy is a matter of perspective? That would mean that any government could claim it is "democratic,", and simply argue that different democracies have distinct features. American democracy has "American characteristics" and China's democracy has "Chinese characteristics." If people accept this, China can negate one of the key rhetorical weapons the West uses against it: that China's government is undemocratic and thus less legitimate. That is the rhetorical terrain on which China is now fighting, and it is deploying an unparalleled arsenal of media techniques to do so.

DOMESTIC ORIGINS: THE CCP'S CONTROL OVER NEWS

China's approach to promoting the parallel reality in which it is a world-leading democracy is partly an extension of the CCP's domestic approach to information control. Although, contrary to the CCP's claims, its approach more closely resembles totalitarianism than democracy.

Nathan Law knows this better than most. Meeting us at a coffee shop in North London on a busy street just south of Arsenal Football Club, Law's experiences testify to the CCP's authoritarian approach to news, to information, and to its critics. Casually dressed in a quilted khaki-green jacket, and with a copy of the *Financial Times* poking out of a Hong Kong–branded tote bag, few Londoners would notice that Law is a leading member of the Hong Kong pro-democracy movement and the face of the almost 150,000 citizens who have fled CCP-ruled Hong Kong to the UK. But underneath his unassuming, affable manner is a steely resolve to help people understand and resist the distorted political picture being created by the CCP.

As Law explains, in a democracy citizens are granted freedom of expression, so that they can deliberate about who rules them and how. The media play a key role, scrutinizing government behavior and informing citizens about whether their representatives are acting in their interests. To be free, both citizens and the media need to be able to criticize the government. They need to be able to "hold values and make choices that the ruling party does not like."[21]

This freedom, Law recalls, was one of the reasons his family fled from the fear and repression of mainland China. First, people traffickers smuggled his father to Hong Kong by boat, so that he could look for work. Law arrived several years later, aged six. He vividly recalls being sent alone through the customs border, clutching a 50 renminbi note and a 50 Hong Kong dollar note—a moment that crystallized the difference between the territories. Growing up in Hong Kong, he quickly learned about other differences too, particularly the freedom of expression and freedom of the press Hong Kong citizens had enjoyed. Even under British rule, Hong Kong newspapers could openly criticize the government. People could say what they thought without fear of being denounced by their neighbors or family members.[22]

"Public interest journalism" in democracies means that journalists should hold governments accountable by reporting on their policies, so that citizens can be more informed about how they are being ruled. But the CCP's understanding of the role of the press is very different. For them, public interest journalism requires journalists to "love the Party, protect the Party and serve the Party," while instilling patriotism and "correct thinking" among the population.[23] The news media should practice "positive journalism"—reporting government successes and praising it for its achievements while self-censoring anything that reflects poorly on the party or the state.[24] Outlets that dissent from the party line, or question its decisions, are suppressed. Critical journalists are tried and imprisoned. Their confessions, sometimes made under duress, have been aired on state media as a warning to others.[25]

As a Hong Kong citizen, Law witnessed firsthand how his city's "proud history of press freedom" was eviscerated by the CCP. The CCP shut down previously independent news outlets such as Apple Daily, and arrested its directors. It co-opted others, such as Cable TV News and Radio Television Hong Kong, by installing new owners and editors, who then pushed out the CCP propaganda line. Independent reporters were coerced into self-censorship by a combination of physical abuse and arrests by Hong Kong police and online attacks from armies of pro-CCP trolls. Those who continued to produce critical reports were accused of being "foreign agents." This makes it harder for citizens to access news about what is really happening in their city beyond the parallel reality that CCP-controlled news presents.[26] The former British overseas territory was eighteenth in Reporters Without

Borders' World Press Freedom Index in 2002—just one place below the United States and above the UK itself.[27] It came in 140th in 2023.[28]

Chapter 2 explained how Russian state news outlets have had to adhere to an overarching "strategic narrative"—a story explaining the purpose of the government's war against Ukraine. In this story, Russia has been fighting to defend ethnic Russians in Ukraine against a fascist Ukrainian government, as well as fighting a patriotic war against the "collective West," which wants to destroy Russia. In a similar way, state-controlled media in Hong Kong are now required to adhere to the CCP's overarching "strategic narrative" about its political purpose. The story is that the CCP has saved the country from a "century of humiliation" by imperial powers, and since it founded the People's Republic of China in 1949, its enlightened governance is guiding the Chinese people (and increasingly the world) toward a brighter and more prosperous future. It has largely eradicated poverty and overseen decades of economic growth, for which it is the envy of the world. The Chinese people are free, prosperous, and happy with how responsive the government is to their needs. It is a Chinese "Make Our Country Great Again" narrative, with the CCP—and recently Xi Jinping— as the hero. The lead villain of the story is the United States, which is lambasted for destabilizing the international system, for failing to respond to the needs of its citizens, and for not being a real democracy at all.[29]

The CCP has been promoting this narrative with considerable success at home through its monopoly over domestic Chinese media and extensive censorship. Where possible the party directly censors any information that might present it negatively. Through its Golden Shield project, tens of thousands of censors have near total access to citizens' online communications. Armed with sophisticated censorship software, they filter out any information Beijing chooses—references to China being a dictatorship, references to pro-democracy protests in Hong Kong, even references to the children's character Winnie the Pooh as citizens were drawing unfavorable comparisons between his appearance and Xi Jinping.[30] References to censorship are themselves censored.[31] Once terms are removed they are rarely reinstated. In effect, the Chinese internet functions like the "Newspeak" curated by the Ministry of Truth in George Orwell's dystopian novel, *1984*.

Undesirable terms are erased from existence, shrinking language to the terms approved by the Chinese state.

The CCP's censorship efforts are especially strong on issues that would portray them negatively if citizens were fully aware of them. Law recalls his first moment of peaceful activism, surreptitiously attending a Hong Kong memorial in 2011 for victims of the 1989 Tiananmen Square massacre. The killing of thousands of student protesters in Beijing by the People's Liberation Army (PLA) was heavily covered by the free press in Hong Kong at the time. But ever since the incident the CCP has sought to erase memories of it from existence, be it in the news, in books, on search engines, and across social media. During the COVID-19 pandemic it even managed to pressure the US company, Zoom, to shut down online meetings commemorating the event.[32] Today, to stand in downtown Hong Kong and narrate to passersby an alternative history of China to the CCP's official version is to be guilty of the criminal offense of "historical nihilism." Bystanders hearing the alternative account are directed to a government website and instructed to denounce their fellow citizens for doing so.[33] Citizens must self-censor or face the consequences.

Self-censorship is also integral to the CCP's approach to news. The CCP reportedly provides a daily list of what topics state media must cover, and what topics they must not cover under threat of punishment.[34] But when editorial guidelines on a given topic are not clear, journalists and editors say they self-censor content that would portray China negatively, either through awareness of the government's agenda, support for it, or fear of repression.[35]

In the internet age, however, censorship is unlikely to be total. To get its narratives to dominate public discourse, China uses two further methods described by the political scientist Margaret Roberts as *friction* and *flooding*.[36] *Friction* works not by overtly censoring information. Instead, the Chinese government simply makes it more difficult to access information it wants to hide. Its Great Firewall bans websites and social media platforms, throttles the speed of certain websites, or prevents undesirable search terms from appearing. This means citizens need to make an extra effort to access sensitive information, be it through the use of Virtual

Private Networks (VPNs) or other workarounds. Only committed citizens will bother to do this, especially in an age of information overabundance.[37]

Alongside creating *friction*, the CCP *floods* the internet and social media with content that distracts the audience from what the government does not want them to see.[38] For instance, online criticism of China's repression of Uyghur Muslims in Xinjiang is drowned out by content emphasizing how great Xinjiang is as a tourist destination and how many people have been lifted out of poverty in the region.[39] This is done via all available channels, from legacy television and radio news to posts on social media apps and citizens' smartphones. As the prominent propaganda theorist, Jacques Ellul, explains, to be effective, "propaganda must be total."[40] It is not just a few slogans here, or a few news articles there. It works when it encircles the individual, surrounding them by all possible routes, utilizing all available forms of media.[41]

In the short term, this approach makes stories that the CCP wants people to read easier to find and stories that it wants to hide harder to find. But the more important effect may be long term. Psychologists have found that stories that are told more often are more likely to be remembered and believed.[42] Stories told more rarely are more likely to be forgotten.[43] The more successful the CCP is at promoting its preferred narratives, and silencing those it dislikes, the more widely believed its parallel reality is likely to become, domestically and internationally. So when a dissident like Nathan Law explains how Chinese authoritarianism is a threat to democracy worldwide, the CCP wants citizens to instinctively reject this as a misrepresentation of reality.

CHINA'S NEWS CONTROL GOES GLOBAL

China cannot control news and information internationally in the same way that it can domestically. This has not stopped it from trying to control as much as it can. Ever since its US$6.6 billion investment in external propaganda in 2009 as part of its "Going Out" policy, China has expended far more effort and investment in trying to control international news than any other country.[44] Reports have estimated that China spends US$7 billion to $10 billion per year on external propaganda as it tries to extend its methods of domestic influence to the international arena.[45] In contrast, the US public diplomacy budget was only about $670 million in 2014, and its state news budget for outlets such as Voice of America was only $800 million in 2020.[46] France's budget for France Medias Monde—the organization running its international news—was 263 million euros in 2018, and 259.6 million euros in 2022—a significant real-term decrease.[47] BBC World Service's budget was approximately £300 million between 2015 and 2020. But in 2022 the British government announced a £33 million budget cut to the BBC's international news and stated the BBC would cease radio broadcasting in ten languages, including Chinese, Hindi, Arabic, Bengali, and Persian—languages covering half of the world's population.[48] While liberal democracies have been cutting funding to their international news outlets, China has been expanding.

China's investment is strongly motivated by the perception that Western news outlets still dominate the international news agenda and that they present China too negatively. The CCP wants audiences to view China more positively, as a benign, well-governed state that always acts in the interests of its people and the international community. To achieve this, Xi Jinping has outlined a vision of a "new global media order" in which journalists support the party's interests and act as "state propaganda auxiliaries."[49] In this system, Xi asserted in 2016, "wherever the readers are, wherever the viewers are; that is where [China's] propaganda reports must extend their tentacles."[50]

However, because the CCP cannot control worldwide information flows, and because its state news faces competition from well-established liberal democratic news outlets, it has had to adjust its strategy when using news to influence international audiences. There are five main elements of its global news offensive:

1. **Cosplaying Neutrality:** creating news outlets imitating providers like the BBC but that never criticize China or the CCP.
2. **"Borrowing Boats":** paying for space in foreign publications to promote CCP narratives.

3. **"Buying Boats"**: taking ownership stakes in foreign media outlets to gain coverage and influence.

4. **Building Infrastructure:** building media and communications infrastructure through which to channel pro-CCP content.

5. **Spamming Social Media:** spreading the CCP's news and censorship regime via Chinese and Western platforms.

In pursuing these five areas the CCP is trying, among other things, to convince people across the globe that it is building the world's most responsive democracy.

COSPLAYING NEUTRALITY

The most overt weapons in China's international news offensive are its state media outlets, particularly CGTN, the *Global Times* and *China Daily* newspapers, China Radio International (CRI), and the international news agency, Xinhua. These outlets produce CCP narratives and disseminate them directly to international audiences. They practice the same "positive journalism" expected of Chinese domestic news, publishing persistently positive, at times utopian, news about China and the CCP's achievements. Having researched Chinese state news for several years, we have not found a single state news article that criticizes China or its government.

These outlets have taken the lead in promoting China's claims to be the world's most effective democracy. An important way they do this is to mirror the discourse of the United States. When Nathan Law appeared at the US-hosted Summit for Democracy in 2021 criticizing China for being undemocratic, Chinese state news released a slew of articles on why China was the real democracy and the United States was not. They did the same during the second Summit for Democracy in March 2023. When US politicians and think tanks allege Chinese human rights abuses, CCP state media allege US human rights abuses.[51] Notably, Chinese state news articles almost exclusively compare Chinese "democracy" with the United

States, but not with the thirty or so countries that score higher on indices of democracy than the United States does because that would make the comparison less favorable.[52]

In case audiences do not find these arguments about the superiority of Chinese "democracy" credible, Chinese state news also disseminates the CCP's fallback argument: whether a country is a democracy depends on what its people think.[53] As evidence, Chinese state news cites surveys that have shown consistent majorities of Chinese citizens agreeing that they live in a democracy. In June 2022 the *Global Times* enthusiastically cited a survey indicating that 83 percent of Chinese citizens say their country is a democracy, whereas only 49 percent of Americans say the same about their own country.[54] Even if audiences do not find polling results from authoritarian China credible, the CCP has a further fallback position: that the Chinese Communist Party is the representative of the Chinese people, so it implicitly has the authority to dictate whether China is a democracy or not.

Using Chinese state news to promote the claim that China is more "democratic" than other countries is a key part of the CCP's project to "Tell China's Story Well." But just telling a convincing story is not enough. As thinkers as far back as Aristotle have realized, narrators themselves must be credible for their stories to be believed.[55] To promote successfully its parallel reality in which China is a democracy, not an autocracy, and an upholder of human rights rather than an abuser of them, China must tell its story more credibly than the "Western" media outlets it sees as dominating international news. One way to do this is to try to make its international state media outlets adopt the style and format of liberal democracies' most respected outlets.

For instance, CGTN tries to present itself as a staid, detached observer of international news, similar to BBC World—something we found while comparing its coverage of the 2020 US presidential election with Russia's RT.[56] The election was the ideal event to look at how CGTN covered international politics, because US democracy faced its sternest challenge in more than a generation. Cities across the country had experienced rioting all summer following the killing of a black man, George Floyd, by the

Minneapolis police. Donald Trump was running for election for a second term and had, for months, stoked fears of election fraud, while overseeing a disordered COVID-19 pandemic response that saw the world's most medically advanced nation experience one of the world's worst outbreaks. Far-right groups threatened insurrection if in their view the election was "stolen" by the Democrats—a threat later put into practice with the Capitol riots on January 6, 2021. Commentators worldwide speculated on whether the United States was on the brink of civil war, just as they did before the 2024 election, in which Trump was voted back into power.

In these circumstances, it would have taken little effort for CGTN to portray China's leading geopolitical rival as weak, divided, and undemocratic. This is certainly what Russia's RT did. In the five weeks leading up to the 2020 election, RT produced dozens of articles amplifying unsubstantiated claims about electoral fraud. The Russian state's principal international news outlet took every opportunity to broadcast footage of protests, to magnify America's culture wars, and to give the impression of a country fast descending into chaos.[57]

But CGTN chose not to do this. When we analyzed CGTN's output leading up to the election—its news articles, opinion columns, video reports, and social media posts—we found that it took a very different approach to RT. It did report on disorder in the United States, on the United States's high COVID-19 rates, its handling of the pandemic, and its economic travails, but it did not seek to discredit the US election. It rarely reproduced Trump's claims about electoral fraud—and when it did so it emphasized the lack of evidence supporting them. It did not question the validity of the electoral system. It even published articles on how the US government was successfully maintaining the integrity of the process. One CGTN piece noted "How the city of Denver manages to run its election effectively."[58] Many of its articles were explainers about how the US Electoral College worked, the significance of the US Supreme Court, what the opinions of different groups of voters were, and how citizens in swing states perceived the candidates. Video footage of interviews with citizens provided balanced airtime to Democrats and Republicans. These were put together in a similar style to CNN and BBC "vox-pops," with a well-presented interviewer talking to citizens in the street about their views on the election.[59] It was as if CGTN was working to uphold the scrupulousness of the US electoral system.

The style of CGTN's coverage was also plain and measured; without hyperbole or humor—more BBC than Fox News or RT. It largely ignored the campaign's major scandals, such as the Trump campaign's accusations about Biden's mental fragility and corruption accusations against Biden's son, Hunter, preferring to report on policy issues such as COVID-19 and the economy.[60] Overall, CGTN's news reports provided informative, neutral, if relatively monotonous and monochromatic, coverage. Audiences would have learned little about the scandal and drama, but neither were they told who to vote for. It was the sort of coverage one might expect from a politically neutral news outlet.

However, CGTN's neutral, balanced façade slipped whenever articles compared the United States with China, which CGTN was often keen to do (almost a fifth of its 515 articles on US politics during the campaign made comparisons with China).[61] In these articles, CGTN's function as a propaganda arm of the Chinese state became explicit. CGTN's editorials or "op-eds" were especially vociferous. Ditching the measured tone of the outlet's election coverage, they tore into the United States for being a "failed state" and a "sham democracy," whose anti-China politicians were "liars" and "thieves."[62] Many op-eds were authored by pro-China international journalists, academics, and policymakers, to make the claims look more like authentic expressions of international opinion, even though they repeated the CCP propaganda line. These articles used crude binaries to compare the United States and China. The United States was poorly governed, hypocritical, a destabilizing power, undemocratic, with a failing political system. According to these CGTN articles, the United States misrepresents China, which—contrary to what US news media says—is a force for stability, is well-governed, has a successful political system, is an honest partner to others, and unlike the United States it is actually democratic.[63] Across more than five hundred articles and thousands of tweets that we analyzed, we did not find a single criticism of China nor did we find a single positive framing of the United States.

CGTN may be aspiring to gain credibility by copying the style and format of outlets such as the BBC. It may claim to be "committed to neutral, objective reporting."[64] However, beneath this semblance of impartiality it persistently promotes the CCP's preferred political narratives. We term this the "surface neutrality" propaganda model: seemingly impartial on the outside but with a systematic political bias underneath.[65]

DISINFORMATION AND CHINESE STATE MEDIA

This political bias becomes more apparent—and the distance from democratic principles more pronounced—when CGTN and other CCP outlets are dealing with information that presents the Chinese state in a poor light. In these circumstances, the outlets either become apologists for the state or, in certain cases, publish blatant disinformation. During the COVID-19 pandemic, for example, China suffered significant reputational damage in the early months of 2020 for being the place where the virus was first discovered, and for suppressing information that could have limited its spread early on. Rather than investigate or question the government, China's international media initially chose to ignore or deny China's role in the genesis of the pandemic, emphasizing that the virus was naturally occurring and a challenge for the world to resolve.[66] As the pandemic developed, Chinese state media went further, promoting various unsubstantiated theories about COVID-19's origins. In March 2020, state media reported the foreign ministry spokesperson Zhao Lijian's allegation that COVID-19 only emerged in Wuhan because a US soldier had brought it over while competing in the World Military Games in October 2019.[67] Later articles claimed the virus really originated in India; others Italy.[68]

In response to the ongoing "lab leak" theory that COVID-19 was leaked deliberately or accidentally by the Chinese in Wuhan, Chinese media outlets began to propagate a competing conspiracy theory that COVID-19 really originated at the US military base of Fort Detrick. Fort Detrick had been the home of the US's biological weapons program after World War II, and was also used in the Soviet Union's Operation Denver (often referred to as "Operation Infektion") in the 1980s: a disinformation campaign that claimed HIV/AIDS was a US bioweapon created at the base.[69] The *Global Times* asserted that Fort Detrick was "Suspect No. 1,"and that it "needs to be investigated for COVID-19 origins."[70] Using its mirroring strategy once more, the CCP tried to deflect accusations of its culpability by making counteraccusations against its main geopolitical rival.

The CCP has also used China's state media to promote falsehoods on behalf of its allies. Although China's official line on the Russia-Ukraine war has often been cautious and noncommittal, China's international news outlets reproduced Russian propaganda from the outset of its full-scale invasion of Ukraine in February 2022. Despite the fact that Russia initiated the 2022 invasion and occupied and annexed Ukrainian territory, *China Daily* asserted that "US animosity towards Russia" was the "root cause" of the war, and named the United States as the "primary aggressor."[71] On the eve of the February 2022 operation, CGTN argued that "neither Russia nor Ukraine wants a war," but "the US is desperate for one" to solve its domestic issues and to profit from arms sales.[72] Chinese state media also repeated Russia's unfounded claims that the United States runs dozens of bioweapons laboratories across Ukraine, calling for the United States to disclose evidence, without subjecting Russia's claims to any critical scrutiny.[73] Meanwhile, in February 2022 the Chinese news outlet, Horizon News, inadvertently leaked instructions from the CCP ordering that news content should be censored if it is "unfavorable to Russia or pro-Western," and that outlets must only use hashtags promoted by Xinhua, CCTV (China Central Television), or People's Daily.[74]

Despite Chinese international news media's claims of being equivalent to democratic news media such as the BBC, and despite their adoption of the manner and tone of Western media outlets, analysis of their output shows that they are instruments of CCP propaganda. They may give audiences the impression of equivalence, but they are anything but democratic.

"BORROWING BOATS"

In 2017 the state-run Philippine News Agency published an editorial claiming that a ruling by the international tribunal at The Hague was "ill founded" because it determined that China had violated the rights of southeast Asian countries in the South China Sea. The ruling had been made in 2016, following a maritime dispute between China and the Philippines over historical rights to a body of water extending hundreds of kilometers south from Chinese territory. Within these waters, China had occupied and militarized a range of small islands, and repeatedly harassed fishing vessels from neighboring countries. The international maritime court found against China's incursions, ruling them illegal.[75] And yet this editorial in Philippine state news argued that the ruling was perverse. China had every right to assert its sovereignty across these waters, it argued, and to claim influence up to the CCP's self-defined "Nine-Dash Line."

The publication of the editorial was remarkable for at least three reasons. First, it was making an argument previously only put forward by the CCP, and in contravention of an international legal ruling. Second, the Philippines' state news agency was arguing directly against the Philippines' national interest, as it was the main injured party in the dispute. Third, it repeated verbatim an editorial from China's Xinhua—illustrating how far the CCP has progressed in getting its perspective repeated in other country's news media.

The editorial, unsurprisingly, caused outrage across the Philippines and was eventually taken down after multiple complaints. Many Filipinos were genuinely shocked—why was the Philippines' state news publishing the propaganda of its opponent in the dispute? Filipino journalists were less shocked. They had already expressed concerns that Philippine state media had been co-opted to produce Chinese propaganda, especially after President Rodrigo Duterte signed a Memorandum of Understanding regarding cooperation between Philippine and Chinese media outlets in 2016.[76]

Getting established foreign news outlets to publicize Chinese state media content has been a core part of Beijing's efforts to promote the CCP's narratives. Described by the party as "borrowing boats to reach the sea," it reflects Mao Ze Dong's older idea of "Making the Foreign Serve China."[77] The logic is simple. Getting coverage in other countries' news outlets is a way of accessing audiences who would not ordinarily read or watch China's international news. Second, when independent outlets reproduce Chinese news content, it looks less like state propaganda and more like it comes from a credible news source. If readers do not notice that the content is Chinese government propaganda, the CCP benefits. Alternatively, even if readers do notice, China's state media outlets gain credibility by association with reputable outlets in other countries. A win-win outcome for Beijing.

Many news outlets have gone along with this for a simple reason: money. The shift to digital news and advertising has put immense pressure on legacy media outlets throughout the world. So when Chinese state media companies offer to pay for their content to be reproduced by another outlet, or offer content for free, many companies acquiesce. In turn, the need to maintain the relationship with high-spending clients creates incentives for news outlets to tone down criticism of China—which again serves Beijing's propaganda aims.

China's "borrowing boats" strategy has been most successful with its news agency, Xinhua. Founded as the Red China News Agency in 1931 to promote CCP ideology and gather intelligence for the party, a massive spike in investment in the last fifteen years has transformed it into one of the world's major news agencies. In 2018, Xinhua claimed a network of more than ten thousand journalists, with thirty-two domestic and 180 international bureaus worldwide—rapidly approaching the Associated Press's 250 bureaus.[78] China has also had great success incentivizing outlets to publish Xinhua articles through content-sharing agreements, of which China had signed 221 by 2018.[79] From Spain to South Africa, Italy to Indonesia, each of these provides an opportunity for the CCP to promote its preferred realities to international audiences.

Just as CGTN imitates outlets such as the BBC and Al Jazeera, Xinhua's dry, factual style imitates established Western new agencies such as the Associated Press and Reuters. Xinhua has developed a number of advantages over these competitors, however. Because it is centrally funded by the Chinese state, Xinhua can offer its content far more cheaply than established agencies, and sometimes for free. For cash-strapped media outlets this creates a strong incentive to use Chinese content. By prioritizing areas less covered by Western news outlets, such as Africa, Xinhua has gained credibility for covering local news that other outlets miss. Its tendency toward positive coverage—particularly of partner countries' relationships with China—gains it credit in countries where audiences criticize Western outlets for covering their politics too negatively.[80]

Xinhua may present itself as the equivalent of Western news agencies, but it is fundamentally different because it is an instrument of the one-party state, and it continues to gather intelligence on the CCP's behalf.[81] As the head of Xinhua, Fu Hua openly stated in 2022 Xinhua has a "sacred duty" as the "vanguard of the Party press." Xinhua must "not depart even for a single minute from the vision of General Secretary Xi Jinping and the CCP Central Committee."[82] Xinhua does provide factual reports on a wide variety of news happening around the world, but many of its articles reproduce official CCP statements (such as its response to its maritime dispute with the Philippines), and it never publishes news that reflects badly on the CCP.

As well as using content-sharing agreements to seed Xinhua content into other countries' news outlets, China has had considerable success paying established media outlets to publish its state news. From 2011, *China Daily* paid many of the world's leading newspapers to reproduce an eight-page supplement called "China Watch." Obliging outlets included the *Washington Post* (US), the *Daily Telegraph* (UK), *Le Figaro* (France), *Handelsblatt* (Germany), *El Pais* (Spain), and the *Sydney Morning Herald* (Australia). As well as China Watch, the UK's *Daily Telegraph* readers could also log onto the newspaper's website and discover a section titled "People's Daily Online," which reproduced content from the CCP's official newspaper. Unerringly positive, each story lauded China's achievements, but without the critical scrutiny expected of a news outlet in a democracy. Not only that, the Chinese state content was available to readers for free, but the *Telegraph*'s own news was behind a paywall. For a time it was easier for readers to access CCP state news on a British newspaper's website than the newspaper's own content.[83] At its peak, China Watch published more than thirteen million copies in thirty daily newspapers across the world.[84]

Many leading outlets in liberal democracies have since canceled content-sharing deals with Chinese state news outlets due to growing concerns about China's influence. However, in many countries in the Global South, where financial pressures are even greater, there is still no shortage of boats for China to borrow. In Kenya, CGTN has had a regular one-hour show on Kenya Broadcasting Corporation's Channel 1 from 2300 to midnight during the week. Established news outlets in Thailand have reproduced Xinhua editorials falsely blaming pro-democracy protests in Hong Kong on "Western agitators."[85] The International Federation of Journalists in 2019 found that a third of countries they surveyed had content-sharing agreements with Chinese state news outlets. In several countries Chinese state media content was even reproduced without attribution—giving the Chinese state direct access to international audiences without it being clear that the content is state propaganda.[86]

As the Philippines discovered, the risk is that a country's media becomes an uncritical vehicle for pro-CCP news, sometimes directly contrary to that country's interests. And yet Philippine state media continues to host Chinese state news content. In October 2022, the Philippine News Agency published an article by a CCP official explaining how "the world can learn from China's unique model of democracy."[87] Other publications across the world continue to do the same. In March 2023, South African news outlet *IOL* published a Xinhua article describing China's socialist democracy as "democracy in its broadest, most genuine, and most effective form."[88] The CCP seems to have little trouble getting other countries' news outlets to promote its "democratic" credentials.

"BUYING BOATS"

As well as "borrowing boats" to spread Chinese state news, China "buys boats" too, by using its state run media companies to take ownership stakes in news outlets throughout the world. China now has a near-monopoly on Chinese language news across the globe, including an estimated one hundred Chinese media outlets in Europe.[89] In Australia, for instance, there used to be considerable variety in Chinese language news. Now almost every outlet reproduces the CCP propaganda line.[90]

However, when investing in local companies, the Chinese government does all it can to hide its involvement, to make those companies' content look less like state propaganda. China Radio International (CRI)—the Chinese state's leading international radio outlet—is a prime example. In 2015 *Reuters* found that CRI controlled at least thirty-three radio stations in fourteen countries, including in the United States, but it used front companies to hide its involvement.[91] The channels claimed to be producing "unfiltered real news"—yet none of them hosted any criticism of China. If CRI could not control companies directly, it would buy slots on foreign radio stations to air Chinese state-produced programs. In other countries, CRI has set up media production partnerships with local companies or leased entire radio frequencies to pump out pro-China propaganda.[92]

Journalists elsewhere have reported complete shifts in the editorial tone of newspapers after investment by Chinese state companies. Research in the Czech Republic found that the Chinese company CEFC bought a stake in Czech Empresa media, which gave CEFC influence over a collection of TV channels and publications. After the Chinese company gained its stake, analysts found that negative and neutral coverage of China disappeared from the outlets, and only positive coverage remained.[93]

Chinese state influence over media outlets throughout the world has had consequences for journalists who criticize China. In an infamous 2018 case, the journalist Azad Essa had his newspaper column for South Africa's Independent Media company canceled after he wrote an article criticizing China's treatment of Uyghur Muslims in Xinjiang.[94] Chinese state media companies held a 20 percent stake in the firm. For Essa, the explanation of the cancellation of his column was clear: "China is buying the African media's silence."[95]

BUILDING INFRASTRUCTURE

China has also invested heavily in the infrastructure through which news is distributed worldwide to make its state news easier to access than that of its international competitors. With considerable success, it has contracted Chinese commercial companies to supply media infrastructure across the Global South.

StarTimes is one of China's most successful media companies. The company claims to be "the most successful digital TV provider in Africa," with thirteen million subscribers in more than thirty countries.[96] Exploiting a gap in the market, the company has installed satellite television infrastructure in rural areas deemed unprofitable by rival companies. The company is especially proud of its "10,000 African Villages" project, which has installed digital television in ten thousand villages across the continent, at little cost to local citizens.[97] The company has certainly done much to improve communication infrastructure across a continent in desperate need of it, and it has contributed positively to economic development in the process.[98]

StarTimes's branding suggests it has a simple and benevolent motive: "to ensure that every African family can access, afford, watch and share the beauty of digital TV."[99] However, StarTimes is not just a benevolent commercial company that invests where Western investors fear to tread. Like many Chinese media companies it is technically private, but it also serves as a proxy for the Chinese state. As with other commercial media companies, StarTimes is expected to make a profit, but it is also supported heavily by the Chinese government and legally obligated to serve the CCP's political agenda. It may frame its 10,000 African Villages project as a benevolent initiative by an enterprising private company, but it was also a Chinese government development project, which StarTimes was contracted to implement.[100] The extent of internal CCP influence over the company is deliberately opaque, which is consistent with the CCP's role in other companies. As Richard McGregor, the former *Financial Times* China bureau chief, explains, the party has for decades exerted internal influence on Chinese companies while keeping this influence as covert as possible.[101] Other leading Chinese tech companies, such as ByteDance and Tencent, are understood to have internal party committees to scrutinize their decision-making.[102] But by keeping the party's influence as covert as possible, the successes of these companies can be framed simply as the operation of the free market. However direct the CCP's control is, the government and its private media companies work symbiotically: the projects grant China's government soft power and potential economic and political leverage; the companies generate profit and market share.

StarTimes's subscriptions are well-tailored to its target audiences. Local content in each country is mostly found on the cheapest subscriptions. Like China's state news outlets, extensive subsidy from the Chinese government enables StarTimes to undercut other providers. Its subscription packages in sub-Saharan Africa start as low as $4 per month; other companies' entry-level packages cost twice this.

The news content available from StarTimes also favors Chinese providers over Western providers. Accessing StarTimes's website (startimestv. com) in December 2022, we found that the only major international news services on its cheapest packages were CGTN and Al Jazeera—outlets that aim to present "non-Western" perspectives on international news. European-based international outlets such as the BBC, Deutsche Welle, France 24, and RT only became available on the second cheapest tariff. Still more expensive were American news channels such as Bloomberg, Fox News, and MSNBC, on the third most expensive tariff. CNN was not available at all. By privileging Chinese voices and content over Western news outlets, StarTimes makes it easier for audiences to access good news stories from Beijing about how well-governed the country is and how happy its people are. In turn it makes it harder for people to find critical stories about China or the CCP. This again serves the CCP's attempts to promote itself as a successful alternative model of "democracy."

SPAMMING SOCIAL MEDIA

China also uses Chinese and American social media platforms and smartphone software to enhance the spread and influence of the CCP's news narratives, and it restricts audience access to news it would prefer to silence. This has led to a series of controversies when investigations have revealed China's activities.

Over the last decade, a growing body of evidence has revealed the Chinese government's systematic repression of Uyghur Muslims in Xinjiang. Extensive victim testimony, investigative journalism, and leaked documents detail the arbitrary detention of over a million Uyghurs in internment camps, mass digital surveillance, the destruction of mosques, the banning of Islamic practices, and even forced sterilization.[103] Such evidence fundamentally undermines one of the CCP's key arguments about why it is "democratic": that its good governance is meeting the needs of *all* its citizens, not just the Han ethnic majority. Because of this, the CCP has embarked on aggressive campaigns to deflect and discredit the accusations.

China's state media repeat the CCP's frequent rebuttal that the Xinjiang accusations are the "biggest lie of the century," 'cooked up by the United States to serve its "vicious aim of containing China's development."[104] The CCP combines this with increasingly creative use of social media. One technique they used in 2021 was to flood social media with videos of ordinary Chinese people denying there were any human rights abuses in Xinjiang. Although these videos initially appeared to be spontaneous and organic, an investigation by ProPublica and the *New York Times* discovered that these were part of a coordinated campaign. Their investigation identified more than three thousand videos that were published near-simultaneously on YouTube and Twitter—platforms banned in China. The people in the videos each told a similar story: that they were upset by Donald Trump's secretary of state, Mike Pompeo, for accusing China of human rights abuses in Xinjiang, and they wanted to correct the record by explaining how good life was in the region. Many of the speakers not only made similar arguments but used identical phrases throughout their videos, making it clear that their responses were scripted, not spontaneous. Not only that, several of them were first identified on CCP-affiliated accounts and were spread on Twitter by a coordinated network of bots and inauthentic accounts.[105]

Parallel to these "real-person" videos, the CCP ran a lavish social media PR campaign, promoting #BeautifulXinjiang or #AmazingXinjiang as a fabulous tourist destination. Across Twitter, Instagram, and TikTok you could find color-saturated photographs of mountain villages and apricot blossoms, carefully choreographed videos of Uyghur dances, and heart-warming pictures of Uyghur grandfathers playing traditional instruments to happy, clapping children.[106] These campaigns to promote Xinjiang positively are relatively crude. An artificially generated grassroots campaign (also known as "astroturfing") in which citizens use the same phrases is easily outed as propaganda.

However, there are signs of a "Russification" of Chinese influence activities, whereby China is using social media in a more subversive manner, as Russia has done in recent years.[107] On social media the CCP is increasingly using methods that are closer to what Lenin referred to as "agitation": to seize on emotive issues to "rouse discontent and indignation among the masses" in democratic societies.[108] In mid-2023, Meta reported taking down over 8000 eight thousand accounts across fifty platforms and forums for being part of the "Spamouflage" campaign: a Chinese state-linked influence campaign estimated to involve over one hundred thousand accounts, which Meta describes as the "largest known cross-platform covert influence operation in the world."[109] Since being identified in 2017, Spamouflage has been known mainly for spreading large volumes of low quality content, spamming China's critics with abuse, and hijacking online conversations that portray China negatively.[110] But analysts have found the networks' messaging to be evolving into attempts to exacerbate polarization in US politics. According to a report by the Institute for Strategic Dialogue (ISD) in 2024, the Spamouflage network began to spread messages attacking Joe Biden, and to a lesser extent Donald Trump, in the months before Biden withdrew from the election campaign in favor of Kamala Harris. This included extensive use of AI-generated images that put Trump face-to-face with Biden, with captions such as "Civil War" and the "Collapse of American Democracy" emblazoned between them. Many images placed Joe Biden next to his son, Hunter, next to terms such as "drug use," "bribery," and "corruption." Other posts tried to convey the sense of crisis in US politics, whether it be epidemics of opioids, homelessness, or gun violence.[111]

As with many other Chinese social media campaigns, the ISD report notes that the posts received minimal engagement—they are "generating the usual level of returns (i.e., none)."[112] But they are certainly a long way from the more measured and neutral coverage we found on CGTN during the 2020 election.[113] While this suggests that the CCP is adopting influence techniques more typically associated with Russia, it also shows how the CCP may be tailoring its approach more extensively to different platforms.

As well as using social media to promote its preferred narratives, smartphone software is also used to extend the CCP's censorship regime internationally. In September 2021, the Lithuanian defense minister announced that if any citizens owned Chinese phones they should throw them away. This was because Lithuania's cybersecurity forces had discovered that Chinese phones manufactured by the Xiaomi Corporation had built-in software to identify and censor over 449 terms, including "democracy movement," "Free Tibet," and "Long Live Taiwan independence."[114] Further research identified an ever-expanding list of 1,376 search terms that could be censored, and this capability could be turned on and off remotely without the user being aware. Even if Xiaomi designed these censorship measures themselves, such examples show how the CCP's influence over Chinese technology companies enables them to restrict access to information worldwide.[115]

Chinese social media apps such as WeChat and TikTok provide the CCP with another way to influence international news. Owned by the Chinese company Tencent, WeChat was the world's third most popular platform in 2020, with 100 million to 200 million global users.[116] Multiple reports document how WeChat, like its domestic version Weixin, functions as an extension of the CCP propaganda and censorship apparatus.[117] "It is a really powerful weapon," Nathan Law told us. "You pay with it. Your contact details are on it. It is the super-connector of everything. Everything under one platform. It is impossible not to use it in China. And outside China, you still have to use it."[118] And all of this information is fully available for monitoring by the CCP, even for users on phones registered in other countries. While Law participated in pro-democracy protests in Hong Kong, US-based supporters of the protests had their WeChat messages censored and their accounts frozen.[119] Toronto's Citizen's Lab reported that in the first half of 2020 WeChat censored over two thousand keywords related to COVID-19, especially criticism of China's response. This included censoring the revelation that China had reported the existence of COVID-19 to the US government on January 3, 2020, even though it waited three further weeks to inform its own citizens.[120]

TikTok, ByteDance's immensely popular video sharing app, has also been found to have censored content. A leak of internal documents in 2019 found that TikTok censored terms such as "Tiananmen Square" and "Tibetan independence."[121] Researchers at the Australian Strategic Policy Institute (ASPI) have shown that the app censored posts with the #BlackLivesMatter hashtag and LGBTQ-related content. TikTok has also been caught "shadow-banning" content that used politically sensitive hashtags regarding Xinjiang. A more subtle form of censorship, shadow-banning involves reducing the visibility of certain users or content without making the user aware of this. A user may post content, assuming this is visible to other users, but the app prevents the post from appearing.[122] Concerns that China might use TikTok for surveillance, or to spread propaganda and disinformation, have also led to several countries imposing partial or total bans on the app. Indeed the list of countries that have partly or wholly banned TikTok, or threatened to do so, includes unlikely bedfellows: the United States and Russia, the UK and Afghanistan, India and Iran.[123]

Smartphones and social media platforms provide a more deniable form of CCP influence over the news and give them access to audiences that may not choose to access Chinese state outlets. Mobile phone providers and social media platforms may be private companies, but they are required by law to serve the CCP, including, since 2022, registering their algorithms with state regulators.[124] The platforms in turn give the CCP deniability. The government can deny having a direct influence on the platforms, safe in the knowledge that consumers cannot access the black-boxed software, algorithms, and internal decision-making processes that determine what news they can see and share. In practice, this means that China can simultaneously claim to be a world-leading democracy while its companies censor criticism of it on their hardware and software.

THE INTERNATIONAL IMPACT OF CHINA'S STATE NEWS

China's attempts to control the news worldwide are in many ways unprecedented. Its influence can be seen when a British citizen reads Chinese state media content in their daily newspaper, when a South African journalist loses their job because China does not like their content, or when a social media user in Canada has content censored by a country thousands of miles away. But how effective are these efforts to convince international audiences about the legitimacy of China's political system, or that it too should be considered democratic?

It is hard to say, and probably too early to tell. The significant expansion of the CCP's efforts to gain discourse power internationally is a relatively recent phenomenon. And it is only in the last few years that the party has embarked on a systematic media campaign to sell the superiority of its "democracy" to global audiences.

STRUGGLING TO ENGAGE AUDIENCES

To date the available research on the effects of China's international state news suggests that the CCP's massive media investments have "not bought China anything like the love it would like." China's state media is so endlessly positive about China that it is fairly straightforward for international audiences to recognize it as propaganda.[125] Audiences bombarded with endlessly positive stories can easily infer that this scarcely matches the real world. International audiences do not just find Chinese news to be propagandistic; they also find it dull. Its style is dry, it relies too much on official press statements, and it rarely breaks original news stories before other outlets due to the CCP's need to closely control what it publishes.[126] CGTN is "the most boring news program probably in the whole world," according to a leading Chinese podcaster.[127]

In areas of the world where China supposedly has achieved significant influence and popularity, local engagement with its media remains low. Gallup surveys indicate that only 1.2 percent of Laos's population watch China's channels. Only 0.7 percent of Vietnam's population watch CGTN, and only 7 percent of those say they trust it highly.[128] The global communications scholar, Dani Madrid Morales, tried to quantify the "agenda-setting" capability of Chinese state news outlets in Africa—that is, how often African news outlets reproduce news articles from Chinese outlets rather than other outlets. He found that when African news outlets reproduced international news, 63.8 percent of their stories came from French outlets such as Agence France Press, and 23.6 percent came from British outlets such as the BBC. Only 7.9 percent came from Chinese outlets like Xinhua, although interestingly this was more than the 4.7 percent of news reproduced from US outlets.[129]

Chinese state narratives do not dominate the news in most countries. Awareness of their efforts to control the news is growing, leading to street protests against the influence of the "red media" in Taiwan in the run-up to the 2020 presidential election.[130] Revelations of censorship on Chinese smartphones and social media platforms undermine China's claims further. None of this suggests that China is likely to have great success persuading other countries that it is a world-leading democracy.

PROMOTING DEMOCRACY OR DIGITAL AUTHORITARIANISM?

However, even if there is scant evidence that international audiences believe that China is a leading democracy, there is firm evidence that China has gained international recognition for the achievements of its political system. With the exception of liberal democracies in the Global North, many countries view China positively.[131] Authoritarian states and the Global South, in particular, respect that China's government has achieved decades of economic growth, lifted hundreds of millions out of poverty, invested vast amounts in infrastructure worldwide, and developed into a technologically advanced, stable society.

Meanwhile, numerous liberal democracies are experiencing a performance crisis. A Pew survey in 2019 reported that while overwhelming majorities support democracy as a system of government, 51 percent of people across twenty-seven democracies reported dissatisfaction with how their democracy is working.[132] A Cambridge University report in 2020 found that faith in democracy among eighteen- to thirty-four-year-old "millennials" is far lower than older generations, largely because of a perception of their "economic exclusion."[133] Chinese state news' persistent focus on economic performance makes more sense in a context where liberal democracies appear to be struggling to meet the economic needs of their populations. Meanwhile, a number of populist governments are eroding trust in democracy further by weakening democratic institutions, questioning the legitimacy of elections, and attacking independent media (see chapters 6 and 7). The more liberal democracies are seen to struggle to meet their citizens' needs, and the more their citizens distrust mainstream news media, the more credible the CCP's narrative of competence and economic growth becomes. This is what has given the CCP the confidence to assert that the "China model" meets citizens' needs better—and is therefore more "democratic"—than liberal democracy.

China's efforts to control and influence international news reinforce these arguments. It is now easier for audiences to get good news stories about the benefits of the "China Model" than ever before, and as we have shown, China is employing an increasing number of methods to minimize criticism of Beijing. Experimental research across nineteen countries, published in 2023, found that exposure to Chinese state media's relentlessly positive content can significantly strengthen audience beliefs that China's system delivers "growth, stability and competent leadership."[134]

Even if the impact of China's international news remains limited, its growing control over the hardware and software through which news is distributed worldwide can help the CCP influence the international news agenda. This helps Beijing focus global discussions about what constitutes effective government onto its recent strengths—economic performance and stability—rather than the promotion of individual human rights and freedoms. If China's interpretation of what constitutes good governance becomes dominant, a smaller rhetorical leap is needed to claim that such a system is more "democratic." The significance of this is not necessarily in convincing skeptical liberal democratic audiences that China is really a democracy. Rather, it is about priming people to discount the core values of liberal democracy when assessing the relative quality of governments worldwide.

China's "democratic" parallel reality is unlikely to invite anything other than incredulity in liberal democracies, but arguably these are not Beijing's priority international audiences. Countries in the Global South, with whom China is trying to strengthen political and economic relations, are far more important to it. So are authoritarian elites, to whom China is having growing success exporting the technologies that underpin its surveillance and censorship regime.[135] Countries such as Vietnam, Thailand, Cambodia, Uganda, Tanzania, and Zambia have adopted restrictive internet legislation that closely imitates China's.[136] More rulers are taking control of state news providers and co-opting independent news outlets to churn out pro-government content and silence criticism. The independent public broadcasting model of news, exemplified by the BBC, where news outlets produce news free of government editorial interference, is "on the brink of extinction" worldwide, being present in only eighteen countries.[137]

At the 2021 Summit for Democracy, US President Joe Biden's national security strategy said that the defining conflict in the twenty-first century was between democracy and authoritarianism. China portrays geopolitical reality differently. At times it denies it is trying to compete at all, claiming that it is only interested in partnership with others. But when it does acknowledge geopolitical competition, it frames it not as a contest between democracy and authoritarianism but as a contest between different models of democracy: an inferior one with "American characteristics" and a superior one with "Chinese characteristics."

Time will tell whether the CCP has much success persuading international audiences to accept this parallel reality. At the time of this writing, China's economic prospects look far more uncertain, raising questions about how perceptions of China will fare if its economy stagnates.[138] But China's decades of growth and development, its growing influence over international news, combined with the struggles of liberal democracies, have put it in a stronger position to promote its "democratic" credentials than ever before.

As the twenty-first century evolves, liberal democracies should not be complacent that their interpretation of democracy, and their open, pluralistic approach to news, will triumph. As Nathan Law reminds us from his exile in the UK, freedom of speech, freedom of expression, and freedom of the press can be easily undermined by political actors with the will to do so, and they can disappear if not properly defended. "When governments control access to information and are able to define the narrative and dictate what we know," Law explains, "we lose more than our freedoms. We lose the ability to see the world for what it is."[139] This gives self-interested governments the opportunity to propagate parallel realities. Dictatorship, if we are not careful, becomes "democracy."

4

A COUNTERFEIT PUBLIC SPHERE

Orbán's Hungary

Propaganda is the executive arm of the invisible government.

—EDWARD BERNAYS, *PROPAGANDA*

I n December 2022 one of the most popular Hungarian news outlets, *Origo*, published a series of exposés of other Hungarian news outlets whose independence and accuracy—*Origo* claimed—had been compromised by their funding from foreign organizations and governments (calling them the "Dollar Media"). The "Americans," one article reported, have "poured money into the Hungarian left-wing propaganda press."[1] Brussels was similarly guilty, having paid "millions to Hungarian left-wing propaganda papers."[2] Orchestrating this flood of foreign money, *Origo* claimed, was the billionaire philanthropist Gyorgy (George) Soros. Soros, the outlet asserted, "maintains an entire organization to produce articles attacking Hungary" and "controls 253 news sites with his people."[3] The funding, these *Origo* investigations said, demonstrated the outlets' "left-liberal," "globalist," "elitist" bias and revealed their desire to "impose the Brussels narrative on the public" and lead an "international smear campaign against Hungary."[4]

Origo's articles about the "Dollar Media" had all the standard hallmarks of investigative journalism. There were lots of financial figures, references to obscure people's names, their positions and the connections between them, and hyperlinks dotted throughout. They were republished across other national and local Hungarian news outlets.[5] Moreover, this *Origo* series was followed by another, led by the conservative daily newspaper, *Magyar Nemzet*, in spring 2023.[6] This series, again reproduced across national and local media, inflated the threat of the "Dollar Media" still further, alleging that the Soros-funded network was seeking a New World Order and the destruction of Hungarian sovereignty. "In this fight," András Szabó wrote in *Magyar Nemzet*, "there is the Jewish money from the West, and the American stock speculator Open Society Foundation (OSF) is the flag bearer . . . the money is constantly pouring out of the empire of the Soros network, similar to a hundred-armed octopus."[7]

Both series were remarkable in several respects. First, it is highly unusual for media outlets to investigate one another's funding and almost inconceivable that they would question one another's credibility simply because they receive money from foreign sources (on this basis most major commercial media outlets would have no credibility). Second, the articles are riven with questionable sources, incomplete evidence, conspiracy theories, and blatant anti-Semitic tropes. The anti-Semitic motif of the "hundred-armed octopus" funded by "Jewish money" has been used since at least The Protocols of the Elders of Zion in 1903. Plus much of the evidence of foreign funding the articles cite consists of grants by international foundations, for which anyone can apply, and which are listed openly on the foundations' websites.

Yet the most striking aspect of these articles is how they reflect a mirror image of the reality of Hungary's media environment. As this chapter shows, it was not this handful of news sites whose independence was compromised by their funding but Hungary's mainstream media—including *Origo* and *Magyar Nemzet* themselves. It was not these nonaligned online start-ups, financially reliant on subscriptions and donations, whose narratives were being dictated by those in authority, but the vast majority of Hungary's now pro-government media. And if any media outlets were being propped up by Brussels subsidies, then it was the very sites that leveled the accusations.

This inverted, parallel reality—of the "Dollar Media"—is just one of many that now populate Hungary's mainstream public and private news outlets. Every day, Hungarians are told that George Soros and his global network of media outlets and NGOs are conspiring to flood Hungary with migrants and engineer a coup, in collusion with US Democrats, the CIA, and the EU. Leaders such as the EU's Ursula von der Leyen are simply puppets receiving directions from global elites like the Bilderberg Group.[8] The United States has pressured Hungary to support Ukraine's fight against Russia in order to profit from the war.[9] The EU, and the United States (prior to Trump's re-election), are the new "Evil Empire," and are just as dictatorial as the USSR was in Ronald Reagan's day.[10] These broader narratives are coupled with narrower ones targeting specific individuals or organizations. Zoltan Varga, for example, the owner of one of Hungary's few remaining independent media companies, Central Media, has been labeled the "Red Baron" and repeatedly attacked in national and regional news outlets.

The prevalence of these false and distorted narratives is such that—based on various surveys—many Hungarians now believe them. In 2018, 38 percent of Hungarians said they believed that secret groups control world events in an attempt to establish a totalitarian world order; 44 percent agreed with the statement that "Jews want to rule the world," and 51 percent thought that George Soros planned to inundate Europe with refugees.[11] One rarely sees the dominance of such conspiratorial fictions across national and local media anywhere but in authoritarian dictatorships, because to sustain these narratives requires almost total control of the public sphere.

Such control was more feasible in the age of broadcast and print media, especially when Hungary was part of the Soviet Empire. For the four decades after 1949, the governing Hungarian Socialist Worker's Party's (MSZMP) wielded oppressive control over Hungary's news media. Despite the country's 1949 constitution ostensibly protecting press freedom, the party made it clear that the role of the media was to promote the government and its policies. Rather than being formalized in legislation, control was exercised informally, via meetings and phone calls between outlets and the government. For important news services, such as the Hungarian News Agency (MTI), editorial operations were "totally intermingled with those of the political authorities."[12] The result was a uniform national news agenda that never strayed far from the party line. Only in the 1980s, as the MSZMP's grip on the press loosened and a network of underground, clandestine "samizdat" publications grew, did Hungary see the emergence of two distinct news narratives, or a "double public sphere."[13]

Once Hungary shed Soviet control and embraced democracy after the Cold War, such totalitarian control no longer seemed politically and technologically viable, especially after Hungarians moved online. When the renowned German philosopher—Jürgen Habermas—originally conceptualized the "public sphere" in his seminal 1962 book, it was limited to print newspapers, magazines, radio, and television.[14] As the internet proliferated, this "sphere which mediates between society and the state" was transformed, and it now includes an almost infinite amount of media and communication.[15] Given the internet's open technological architecture and the opportunities to self-publish, it seemed inconceivable that a government could control this overcrowded, fragmented and frenetic digital space.

Yet Orbán's Fidesz government has managed to do it. An estimated 80 percent of Hungary's broadcast, print, and online news outlets are now pro-government.[16] Most Hungarians do not routinely come across news that criticizes Orbán or the state. Orbán has gained this control despite not using most of the tools used by authoritarian governments. By his fourth consecutive electoral term, his government had not arrested or imprisoned journalists. It had not (directly) closed down news outlets that were critical of the government. It had not (directly) censored content that attacked the government. In the internet age this is an astonishing, antidemocratic achievement, and it needs explanation.

There are other reasons it is important to examine how Orbán achieved state control of Hungary's public sphere. As well as eschewing the traditional tools of the dictator, Orbán has carefully disguised his party's autocratic takeover of the media. Whether he was neutering media regulation, subjugating public media, co-opting private media, or trying to dominate Hungary's social media, Orbán and his lieutenants have taken elaborate steps to obscure their party's involvement, like an embezzler hiding his money trail. This has allowed them to keep claiming, despite evidence to the contrary, that Hungary has a plural independent media, free of government interference, and that their brand of conservatism provides a democratic alternative to liberal systems. These claims do not fool everyone. They do not need to fool everyone. They do not even need to fool most people. They just need to allow Orbán to assert a patina of democratic legitimacy. By doing so, Hungary can stay in the EU despite breaching its rule-of-law requirements, Fidesz can access vast EU subsidies, and Orbán can deceptively declare his government to be democratic.

This is why the Hungarian model is so dangerous to democracies. Orbán and Fidesz have provided a template that other political parties can follow. They have achieved what the former UK prime minister, Boris Johnson, termed "cakeism"—in other words, having their cake and eating it too. Since 2010, the Orbán government's success in taking control of the country's public sphere has attracted support from other central European parties, such as Poland's PiS and Slovakia's Smer-SD. Donald Trump gave Viktor Orbán his "complete support" before Hungary's 2022 election, and he singled Orbán out for praise during the 2024 US election campaign.[17] So enchanted was the former Fox News anchor Tucker Carlson by Orbán's brand of conservatism that he presented a week's programs from Budapest.[18] Orbán has not shied away from this international conservative adulation, positioning Hungary as an "incubator" for the future of right-wing politics.[19]

In this chapter we show how Orbán has successfully constructed a counterfeit public sphere in Hungary through a strategic, sequential process of "media capture" since Fidesz regained power in 2010. It is based on primary analysis of articles published across multiple Hungarian news outlets—using Google and Microsoft Translate where necessary—and interviews with journalists from several of them (including *444, Átlátszó,* and *Direkt36*). It also draws from secondary analysis of research by academics, journalists, and civil society organizations who have documented the changes in Hungary's media environment over the last fifteen years.

Our approach to examining how Orbán has captured Hungary's media builds from Marius Dragomir's research and his team at Hungary's Central European University.[20] Dragomir experienced Hungarian government influence firsthand when Viktor Orbán labeled the university at which he worked the "Soros University" and forced it to relocate to Vienna (he now splits his time between Austria and Spain). "Four things have to be there to have a capture situation," Dragomir told us from his new office in Santiago de Compostela, Spain. These are control of regulation, domination of public media, indirect ownership of commercial media, and direction of public resources (for example, through the use of government advertising). If any component is missing, Dragomir says, you don't really have a fully captured environment.[21]

The best way to show how Orbán achieved these four steps, and how he has recently embarked on a fifth—dominating Hungarian social media—is via the people through whom he has done it. These loyal lieutenants have been crucial to his construction of a counterfeit public sphere, and without them the façade of an open, plural, democratic society would shatter. Each of these people played their part in the process of media capture.

First up is the regulator. For a democratically elected government to assert control of the public sphere, and do so legally and without official obstruction, it first needs to ensure that the law and regulations are amenable.

THE REGULATOR

In late 2021 Viktor Orbán nominated András Koltay as the president of Hungary's media and communications regulator—the NMHH—and its subsidiary media regulator—the Media Council—for a nine-year term. His predecessor, Monika Karas, conveniently resigned shortly before the 2022 election so that Orbán could decide on her successor. From a democratic perspective, an independent, neutral media regulator is necessary both for regulating the press and protecting it from government interference. Ostensibly, Hungary's Media Council was empowered to do just this.

Established by the Media Act of 2010, shortly after Orbán regained office (having served his first term from 1998 to 2002), the council has responsibility for overseeing press freedom and maintaining media diversity.[22]

Koltay had already served a nine-year term as one of five members of the Media Council, from 2010 to 2019, and therefore can justifiably be described as Orbán's most experienced media regulator. He has excellent credentials. Having trained as a lawyer, Koltay turned to academia, authoring books and articles on Hungarian media law, media freedom, and regulation, and on the development of media in Hungary since the end of the Cold War. It would be difficult to think of someone who, on paper at least, seems better qualified to understand the dynamics of media freedom and the limits of state power.

However, since 2010 Hungary's media regulator has consistently, and repeatedly, stood by while Orbán's administration has extended his government and his party's power over the public sphere. As Fidesz turned public media into a mouthpiece for government policy, the Media Council did not stop them. When friends of Fidesz wanted to take over newspapers, radio stations, or TV channels, the regulator waved them through (such as the merger of a publisher, Lapcom, radio network, Radio 1, and television company, TV2). When other companies not run by government allies sought to do the same, they were blocked (such as the proposed mergers of Springer and Ringier from 2010 to 2014, and RTL and Central Media in 2016). The council granted broadcast licenses to pro-Fidesz radio stations while obstructing or denying them to stations that were independent or critical.[23] It failed to make public media funding transparent, or to recognize that government advertising campaigns—even those that stigmatized migrants or denounced George Soros—counted as party-political propaganda.[24] When Hungary's leading media moguls suddenly donated all their media holdings to a foundation established by the government, it accepted the government's rationale that it was a matter of "national strategic importance in the public interest."[25]

This inactivity is not through lack of power. Indeed, the 2010 Media Act gives the NMHH and the Media Council stronger powers than other regulators in Europe possess. The council can, for example, intervene in decisions by the Hungarian Competition Authority (GVH), enabling it to allow or prevent media mergers and acquisitions. The Media Council also controls public broadcasting appointments and funding. The Media Council's chair can choose the senior figures at the public broadcaster, including the head of the national news agency. It can give or refuse radio and TV broadcast licenses. It can issue fines if it finds media output to be too unbalanced.

But since Koltay first became a council member, Hungary has fallen forty-four places in the World Press Freedom rankings (down to sixty-seventh worldwide in 2024), and many international organizations have expressed concerns about media freedom in the country.[26] In 2021 the Council of Europe's Commissioner for Human Rights accused the regulator of being "politically controlled" and said that this, combined with repeated state intervention, had "eroded the conditions for media pluralism and the freedom of expression" in the country.[27] In 2022 the International Press Institute reported that Fidesz had sought to "systematically erode press freedom" and had "unprecedented" control "over the country's media ecosystem."[28] In 2020 the European Commission stated that the "independence and effectiveness of the Media Council is at risk."[29]

Those who have tried to explain the failure of Hungary's media regulator to protect plurality or press freedom point not to the law itself, which is flexible and open to interpretation, but to the independence of the Media Council members who are responsible for policing it.[30] Thanks to provisions of the Media Act, these members have, since 2010, all been chosen by the Fidesz Party. For their critics, this means they are, at best, insufficiently critical of Fidesz, and at worst, party loyalists or apparatchiks.

Is András Koltay a party loyalist? In an interview for this book, Koltay was adamant that he had no political affiliations. "I absolutely know that I was never a member of any party," he said, "apart from the Youth section of the Communist Party before 1989, because we had to be a member."[31] None of his fellow council members have political affiliations either, as far as he knows. Yet, if independent, how does he respond to the many international criticisms of Hungary's media system, and to the country's precipitous fall down the press freedom rankings? On the rankings, Koltay takes issue with the methodology. "Most of the time I see that the method-ology is very, very plain and simple" and too subjective. "The answer always depends," he continues, "on who you ask." As for the critics, their perspec-tive is, he thinks, politically motivated because they are not sympathetic to the Orbán government.

Koltay comes across less as a hard-headed regulator than as an easy-going university professor—which he still is. Despite being president of the NMHH, with its 700-plus employees, and chair of the Media Coun-cil, Koltay still teaches and was leaving shortly after we spoke to oversee university exams. His answers reflect this academic, semidetached attitude toward regulation. For him, the radical changes in Hungary's media system between 2010 and 2020 simply represent a rebalancing. The system was, he believes, overly left-liberal in the 1990s and early 2000s, and it has since shifted to the right. If critics think the regulator should have prevented that shift then they are overestimating the power of the regulator, Koltay suggests. It is not capable of shaping the media landscape, Koltay says, "because it's an authority and has to react to what happens in the media." It is for government, he says, to make media policy. Anyway, if people are con-cerned about media plurality, they can go online, "where content is naturally diverse, and any possible government intervention is doomed to failure." From Koltay's description, the Media Council is quite a modest body, and one whose capacity to make change in a digital environment is very limited.

This attitude toward regulation fits with a philosophy that Koltay refers to regularly in his academic work—Isaiah Berlin's "negative liberty."[32] This notion posits that the actions of the state should not restrict the freedom of the individual. Going by this logic, it would appear as though Hungary's media regulator is trying, by its inactivity, to avoid limiting the freedom of the media. Such a conceptualization sits oddly with regulation, which by definition is premised on the idea that intervention is sometimes neces-sary. More important, it does not seem to take into account the role of the regulator to protect plurality and press freedom in the face of government attempts to undermine it.

Still, such a philosophy suits the Orbán government. As the regulator has stood by or endorsed Orbán's occupation of the public sphere, so his party has been able to assert that all their actions, and the actions of their supporters, have been legal and fair. As Viktor Orbán said of the landmark 2010 Media Act: "There is not a single passage in the law that does not correspond to the media law in E.U. countries."[33]

In this sense the regulator provides a convenient veil over the state's co-option of the media. This was immediately apparent in the aftermath of the 2010 Media Act when the governing party set about dismantling and then reassembling public media in their own image.

THE PUBLIC BROADCASTER

Balász Bende makes for a striking figure on screen. With his closely cut dark hair, goatee, barrel chest, and generous girth, he looks a bit like a bearded Kim Jong Un. These physical similarities with the North Korean leader extend to Bende's on-screen political rhetoric, which critics have written is "reminiscent of North Korean TV announcers."[34] Until 2022, Bende was presenting *Virag* (World) on Hungary's public service news broadcaster, M1. As with Tucker Carlson, with whom the Hungarian broadcaster has been compared, Bende would not just report global news but also provide his interpretation of events for viewers.[35] Unlike Carlson, Bende was doing this on a publicly funded channel that was required—by law—to be accurate and impartial.

Based on his TV appearances, it would be hard to interpret Bende's reporting as impartial. During the 2021 election he called on viewers to ensure that "the government does not fall into the hands of parties who hate everything Hungarian and Christian, and would rather turn our country into a country of immigrants, even out of revenge."[36] In 2022 he claimed: "The Hungarian left is also constantly in favour of prolonging the war as much as possible by sending weapons to Ukraine."[37] For Bende, Brussels is a mafia democracy, and an opposition group can be written off as a "Soros-brigade."[38] The presenter emphasizes that the ruling Fidesz Party has the Hungarian people's best interests at heart, whereas its opponents are foreign agents harming the nation. He says this on a channel that, legally, is supposed to provide "unbiased, accurate, in-depth, objective and responsible news service and reporting."[39]

Bende was not just a presenter but a senior figure in public media. He oversaw all foreign news reporting, on television, online, and through the national news agency, the MTI. He worked directly with the director of news, Zsolt—"the Pitbull"—Nemeth. And, as was discovered in 2020, his partisan style was not an aberration but was consistent with public media policy. We know this thanks to a leaked recording of a confidential meeting Bende held with the foreign policy section of the state media company, the MTVA, on March 25, 2019. Unbeknown to him, an attendee recorded the meeting and leaked it to a journalist at Radio Free Europe.[40] "Whoever is in charge," Bende told the assembled editorial staff, "must produce content according to the appropriate narrative, method, and direction, mostly about migrants and Brussels."[41] This followed the requirement the previous year, an election year, to find one hostile migrant story per day. Do not, the staff were told, use the word refugee; it evokes sympathy. As far as party politics was concerned, "This institution." Bende said, "does not support the opposition coalition."[42]

When the heads of public media were asked to respond to the leaked recordings, they slightly bizarrely said that they would not bow to political pressure, before saying they would continue to safeguard public media's independence.[43] These responses seemed especially inappropriate when, two years later, internal documents exposed how compromised the public news channels had become by their relationship with the governing party. Public service news journalists and editors were obliged, it transpired, to publish statements, headlines, and editorial content supplied directly from the Prime Minister's or Cabinet Office. "DO NOT," a senior editor at the public news agency wrote in all caps, "change the title of statements from governmental and pro-government organisations."[44] In some cases, "ministry press officers even dictated by phone what should be highlighted in the title and introduction, and what should be left out of the coverage of their bosses' statements," explains Zuzanna Wirth, who managed to get hold of the materials for *Direkt36*.[45] Certain subjects could not be reported, such as foreign news criticizing Hungary, or evidence about the decline of press freedom. Specific language had to be used, such as "the left" rather than "the opposition."[46] All political news was pre-prepared, like a ready-meal prepped for the public media microwave. This even though Hungarian law stated that public media services must be "independent from the State and economic operators" and have "professional autonomy."[47]

It took less than a decade for Hungary's public media to become a dictation machine for Orbán's governing party and their antimigrant, anti-Brussels, antiopposition narratives. The first thing Fidesz did, in 2010, was make public media's subjugation legal. Changing the law allowed them to bring all of Hungary's public media bodies together and create a new governance structure that Fidesz could control—the MTVA. Then they began sacking people: more than eight hundred in 2011 alone.[48] Employees who were willing to follow the new political agenda, such as Balász Bende, were kept on. New heads were appointed for each media service, some of whom were immediately criticized by the opposition as professionally unsuitable for having falsified news in the past.[49]

The replacement of staff was accompanied, close observers said, by a deterioration of the news. Some output became more tabloid (simplified and made devoid of most political content). Political news often just reproduced government statements without contextualization or opposition responses.[50] By 2015, when a new public TV news channel—M1—was launched, the bias was glaringly evident. During that year's European migrant crisis, a study found that 95 percent of the public TV airtime devoted to the Hungarian referendum on refugee quotas supported the government's position, and over 90 percent of these news items "were negative about refugees."[51] Three years later, just before the 2018 national election, another study found that "61 percent of public media news coverage was about the government, 96 percent of which was positive, while 82 percent of the coverage about the opposition was negative."[52] Yet despite a decline in quality and a rise in partisanship, funding for public service media rocketed. The Fidesz government increased its budget from 145m euros in 2010, to 225m in 2015, to 270m in 2019, not including additional funding from state advertising.[53] The new employees of public media were being well-compensated for their compliance.

After the second tranche of leaks emerged in 2022, it was becoming ever-more difficult to maintain the fiction that public media was fair or balanced. As a Fidesz-loyalist journalist wrote shortly after the election that April, it was unsustainable "that opposition politicians practically can't set foot [on Hungarian public TV]," that news pundits are exclusively from the ruling party, that news programs often just dictate official statements, while "the opinions of the opposition usually appear wrapped in the ruling party's refutations."[54] Although, if he and others were hoping to break up the charade, they failed. The journalist was quickly written off as an ex Soros-employee "overtaken by left-wing hysteria."[55] Balász Bende was quietly retired from the public broadcaster after the 2022 election "on health grounds," as his revealing instructions to editorial staff had exposed too much of the inner workings of public media for him to stay. He left the media entirely to keep cattle on a farm south of Budapest.[56] With Bende gone, senior figures at the MTVA did their best to shore up the pretense. When questioned by the European Commission early in 2023, the head of the MTVA, Daniel Papp, told them that Hungary's public media was "balanced and operates in line with professional standards and the relevant legal provisions." He dismissed criticisms of public media as efforts "to drag the public media on to the political stage with accusations and lies" and pointed out that the media regulator had found no evidence of imbalance.[57]

Whether Hungarians now trusted, or even watched, public media channels was not that important from Fidesz's perspective because their news was now being funneled across Hungary's media ecosystem. In perhaps the most strategic move in its transformation of public media, Orbán's government had given the national news agency (the MTI) exclusive rights to produce news for public broadcasters, and made its content free to other outlets in Hungary—similar to how China's Xinhua offers its news for free in content-sharing agreements with other countries (see chapter 3).[58] Hungary's commercial media companies, many of them suffering from declining revenue due to loss of advertising, could suddenly fill their news slots with free public media bulletins. Many found it difficult to refuse, but given the obvious bias in the agency's news, accepting this meant sacrificing any commitment they had to independence. In radio, outside Budapest, this policy was so successful that "news supporting government ideology is almost unavoidable for those who wish to listen to music or any Hungarian talk over the air."[59]

Having successfully subordinated public media to their will, Orbán and Fidesz moved onto their next target: co-opting much of Hungary's commercial media.

THE CASHIER

In January 2023, Lőrinc Mészáros sat in the sun in Marbella, Spain, watching his favorite football team, Puskas Academy, play the German team Karlsruhe in a training match. Alongside him were various business colleagues and club representatives, who had reportedly flown out with Mészáros on a private jet from Budapest.[60] Mészáros was president of the Puskas Academy, although he had loyally supported the Felcsut club most of his life—as a fan, club member, and sponsor—so he would have been pleased to see them win 1–0 that day. But Mészáros owed the club much more than his support. The club was where he became close to Viktor Orbán. Orbán, who grew up in Felcsut and went to school with Mészáros, shared a love of football and was equally enamored with the local team.[61] Their lives temporarily diverged after Orbán entered Hungarian national politics in 1989, and Mészáros stayed behind in Felcsut where he ran a local gas-fitting company. The business was profitable in the 1990s and early 2000s, although by 2006 orders were drying up and the company's value sank to less than US$39,000.[62]

Yet Orbán had not forgotten his childhood friend, or his local football team, and he made Mészáros president of the Felcsúti Football Foundation, which was set up to fund the club.[63] Soon after, the gas-fitter's fortunes began to change. When Orbán was reelected in 2010, Mészáros stood for— and won—the Felcsut mayoral election (despite previously having shown no political ambitions). At the same time he began to win public procurement contracts for construction work. This was not yet enough to make him super-rich, but it was enough to allow him to fund pet projects in Felc-sut (such as a new football stadium next door to Orbán's holiday home).[64]

Then, in the few years after 2015, Mészáros saw himself catapulted into becoming one of Hungary's richest people. So quickly did his fortunes rise that the Hungarian outlet, *Index*, calculated that if they continued to grow at the same rate, he would be the world's richest man by 2024.[65] As his fortunes rose, so did the range of his business interests. From owning one company in 2010—the eponymous Mészáros es Mészáros—by 2017 he had over two hundred companies.[66] No longer restricted to gas-fitting, he now oversaw a sprawling business empire including construction, hotels, banks, roads, water supplies, fertilizers, railways, school dinners, power plants, and media.

Despite the eclecticism of his companies, a consistent thread was running through Mészáros' newfound wealth—public money. This tsunami of income came from winning a huge number of publicly funded contracts: to build bridges, run ski resorts, construct hotels, or bottle mineral water. Many of these—a majority according to one analysis—were not openly contested.[67] In other words, Mészáros was simply gifted these tenders by the Orbán government. The money to fund this endless stream of public projects came partly from tax income, but also from the European Union. Because Hungary's economy was less developed than others in the EU, it qualified for significant EU investment funds. Between 2014 and 2020, Hungary received more—in relative terms—than Germany and Italy were given annually during the postwar Marshall Plan (1948 to 1952).[68] Mészáros was, at least, self-aware enough to acknowledge the source of his riches. Asked about his expanding assets in 2014, he replied that "God, luck and the person of Viktor Orbán must have played a role in me getting this far."[69] But it was the spectacular fall-out between Orbán and Lajos Simicska in 2015 that was to have the most profound impact on Mészáros's fortune, and determine the fate of much of Hungary's commercial media.

Lajos Simicska, another childhood friend of Orbán and member of Fidesz since its founding, had been Fidesz's Mészáros before Mészáros. He built a business empire off the back of a large number of public contracts, and he used funds from these businesses to assemble a pro-Fidesz commercial media consortium. After his election victory in 2014, Orbán no longer appeared to need his old friend, so he started removing Simicska's people from government and leveled a punitive advertising tax on his media assets.[70] Early the following year the pair's split erupted in public, with Simicska telling various journalists that Orbán was a "jerk" and a "dick" (although less politely) and that they were at war.[71] Simicska told one news outlet that, for Orbán, there are only three types of media: those that agree with government, those who criticize government, and those who are opposed to government. Orbán's intention, Simicska said, was to keep the first and "make the others impossible."[72]

The rupture with Simicska represented a critical moment in the creation of Fidesz's counterfeit public sphere. Until then Orbán's influence over Hungary's commercial media was similar to that in other liberal democracies. Although there was a dominant legacy media owner who supported the government—Simicska—this was not dissimilar to the role previously played by Berlusconi in Italy, or Murdoch in the UK and Australia. But in breaking with Simicska, Orbán took a gamble, one whose outcome would not fully bear fruit until after the 2018 election. Mészáros was a critical component in this gamble, even if chiefly as the cashier for Orbán's own ambitions.

Until the Orbán-Simicska rupture, Mészáros had shown scant interest in owning media companies. But shortly after the split, he and his companies suddenly began a media-buying frenzy. From owning no media companies in 2015, by late 2018 Mészáros had acquired 205 media titles. This included radio stations Karc FM and TV channels Echo TV. In some areas, such as local newspapers, he bought up virtually the whole market. Of Hungary's eighteen regional daily newspapers, serving every region of the country outside Budapest, Mészáros bought all but two (and those were owned by Viktor Orbán's close friend, Andy Vajna). The gas pipefitter from Felcsút had gone from no media assets to the biggest media mogul in Hungary within three years.

Then he gave it all away. In November 2018, Mészáros, and a clutch of lesser pro-regime media magnates, suddenly all decided to donate their media holdings—476 outlets in total—to a government foundation (called KESMA). Hereafter these outlets would be overseen by the foundation's board, initially run by the same man, Gábor Liszkay, who had run Lajos Simicska's outlets before 2015. The motivation for first buying and then donating all these media outlets was clearly not economic—each buyer lost whatever they paid for them—it was political. Orbán's Fidesz wanted greater control of political news in commercial media. So why go through this complicated process? Why not simply nationalize all of these outlets? As with public media, it was to provide a thin veil of democratic legitimacy. Engineer a takeover by the state and Orbán would just look like an old-fashioned autocrat. This way the process was not only obscured but the end result was much more effective.

Attila Bátorfy is an academic and investigative journalist, although his particular specialism is data visualization. When he realized how quickly Hungary's commercial media system was being transformed, he set about visualizing it.[73] The results are startling. Hundreds of media outlets, each symbolized by a circle whose color denotes ownership, flowed from their owners in 2015, first to a small band of oligarchs—primarily Mészáros— and from there to the government-established foundation. Out of five hundred Hungarian media titles in 2015, only thirty-one were allied with the government. Three years later, they were all either allied or closed. Speaking to Bátorfy at his home in Budapest, he compares the new media system to a "kind of army" protecting the government with an "arsenal around them."[74] This system, he explains, is far more effective for propaganda purposes than a small number of state media services because, from the public's perspective, the media in 2018 looks pretty much the same as it did three years earlier. The local newspaper has the same title and format and the usual information about sports, weather, and community events. The only significant change is in its political coverage, which has become entirely pro-Fidesz. This coverage is not just partisan support—as you might see in commercial newspapers the world over—it is partisan control, directed from the center. The political potency of this control was apparent the day before the 2018 election, when every regional newspaper owned by Mészáros and two other oligarchs—in other words every regional newspaper in Hungary outside Budapest—published the same front-page interview with Viktor Orbán, with the same picture and headline ("Vote For

Fidesz").[75] The beauty of this system is that for the most part the newspapers seem different and there is still competition, "but this competition is," Bátorfy says, "about how to please Orbán."[76]

Keeping the existing titles and formats of news outlets, while neutering their political independence, has proved a highly effective method of maintaining the misleading impression of plurality. The popular online news outlet, *Origo*, for example, was not always as slavishly pro-Orbán as it was by 2022. Until around 2013 it was an independent online news publisher owned by a subsidiary of Deutsche Telecom. But in that year, the former *Origo* journalist András Pethő remembers, things began to change. "We started to get messages from the CEO," Pethő tells us from his new position at *Direkt36*, that "there are stories that you shouldn't really pursue." At first Pethő ignored the pressure, but after the site published a series of his investigations into the State Secretary in charge of the Prime Minister's Office, he remembers, everything changed. Suddenly there was huge pushback and Pethő 's job quickly became untenable. He left *Origo*, along with many colleagues, and cofounded a start-up, *Direkt36*. From then on, the *Origo* editorial line became more muted until, in 2017, the outlet was bought by a Fidesz loyalist and soon became vitriolically pro-government. Following its "investigations" into the "Dollar Media" in late 2022, *Origo* joined other pro-government publications such as *Magyar Nemzet* in vilifying independent outlets. They accused one—*444*—of being a national security risk, and its editor of "betraying the nation."[77] *Magyar Nemzet* referred to independent outlets collectively as the "lügenpresse," a derogatory label Hitler used for the left-wing press in 1920s Germany.[78] These independent sites experienced repeated Distributed Denial of Service (DDOS) cyberattacks, making it impossible for users to access them for prolonged periods. Within Orbán's counterfeit public sphere, independent news publishers would be tolerated because they maintained an impression of plurality, but they would have to survive constant attacks on their credibility, honesty, and patriotism.

Orbán and Fidesz began their third consecutive term in 2018 knowing they controlled not only the political coverage of public media but most of commercial media too. The remaining news outlets—representing around a fifth of the market—were useful for allowing Fidesz to claim that there was still diversity in Hungarian media, even if they found their number diminished and their sustainability threatened. Orbán also now relied less on fickle oligarchs who might one day turn on him. Mészáros continued to accumulate wealth, although his interest in media properties waned. Instead, his companies constructed sewage works, roads, and hotels, often—as one of the remaining independent media outlets discovered— buying their raw materials from Viktor Orbán's father.[79] Meanwhile, Mészáros remained ready to invest in future media ventures, his burgeoning bank balance operating almost like an Orbán escrow account, available for use by the administration when needed.

By 2018, therefore, Fidesz had gained control of the media regulatory system, public media, and much of private media, in a way that obscured the authoritarian nature of the process. Hungary's regional newspapers could still assert that they had editorial autonomy. But in each case it was a front. All were in effect controlled from the center. But a part of Hungary's public sphere remained in which the party did not yet dominate and where critical voices could still be heard—on social media.

THE INFLUENCER

The concept, István Kovács said, came to him during a Facebook chat on New Year's Eve 2019.[80] At least this is how he tells the story, and it is a story he has told to many sympathetic Hungarian news outlets since then. Across the world, he said, social media was dominated by left-liberal perspectives. "Every time we open Facebook, Instagram, or even sit down in front of Netflix at home," he told at an interviewer at Mandiner, "left-liberal content pours in almost like a tsunami."[81] Despite research studies showing that this perception is unfounded, Kovács believed that this content was drowning out right-wing voices.[82] Somehow, Kovács thought, these conservative voices had to be amplified. What if he were to start an organization to support them and enhance their volume online?

To that end, Kovács launched the aptly named Megafon in the summer of 2020, to identify, train, support, and amplify conservative influencers on social media. This strategy was different from that adopted by US conservatives, who set up "free-speech alternative" sites such as Gab, Parler, and Truth Social. In contrast, Kovács chose to amplify right-wing voices on platforms already popular in Hungary, most notably Facebook, which was used by 7.5 million out of Hungary's 10 million population.[83] The initial invitation to apply, Kovács says, was quickly overcome with hundreds of registrations, "from high school students to retirees, from manual labourers to people with university careers behind them."[84] Megafon gave them four days' free training on how to build a profile online and create viral content, and offered them ongoing mentoring and support. It even built a studio where they could shoot videos and record podcasts to improve the quality of their content.[85]

There are two ways in which the exposure of social media posts can grow. One is organic—when a post is sufficiently engaging such that it is picked up and spread by people who see it before network effects take over and it spreads virally. The other is inorganic—or manufactured. For the most part this means bought—inflating the popularity of posts by paying the platform for traffic. Megafon focused on the second. It paid Facebook to increase the exposure of the posts of its right-wing recruits. This became apparent from early 2021, when it started artificially enhancing the popularity of posts of figures such as Philip Rákay, Dávid Filep, Dániel Bohár, and Dániel Deák, who were attacking candidates opposing Fidesz, accusing the left of being antivaccine, and lambasting the EU.[86] Most of these figures had already been featured on right-wing TV or news outlets but had yet to build large online followings. Philip Rákay, for example, had sixty thousand followers on Facebook. By buying traffic, Megafon was able to extend the reach of his posts to more than one million users.

Throughout 2021 Megafon ramped up its social media spending to boost the messages of its leading influencers. By the end of the year, three months before the national election, it had spent more than five hundred million forints (almost US$1.5 million) on Facebook—over a third of this in December alone.[87] It spent as much again in the four months to the end of April 2022, by which time Viktor Orbán had won his fourth consecutive election with yet another landslide. In total, since its founding, Megafon had spent over a billion forints (about US$3.2 million) on promoting Facebook posts, more than either Fidesz or the Hungarian government.[88]

The spending worked, in a way. Posts that would only have been seen by a few thousand were seen by more than a million. Right-wing, pro-Fidesz messages were all over Facebook before the 2022 election. Attila Bátorfy remembers being inundated with these posts, despite telling Facebook he did not want to see them. "Every time I see this content," Bátorfy told us, "I report to Facebook that I don't care about . . . [and to] stop showing me this kind of content. And it took almost three weeks before Facebook understood what I wanted."[89] Other Hungarians, less tech-savvy and politically responsive than Bátorfy, found their feeds dominated by right-wing conservative propaganda for months before the vote.

Despite its lavish spending, Kovács was steadfast in his claim that Megafon did not receive public funding. "Megafon is not a political party," Kovács told *Magyar Nemzet*. "In fact it is independent from them both organisationally and financially." It is merely a "grassroots, Hungarian initiative that serves the interests of the Hungarian people," whose funding comes from "private donations."[90] Yet, as a number of independent news outlets noticed, its funding was highly opaque, and its revenues were stunning for such a young company with so few sources of income. Within a few months of launch, it had received over a quarter of a billion forints from private individuals, only a tiny proportion of this coming from crowdfunding. "We needed some initial capital to start and develop the website," Kovács admitted to a pro-government magazine. "This was solved by me reaching out to some conservative businessmen and asking them to support our launch."[91] One news outlet, staffed by journalists who had fled progovernment news services, dug deeper. It concluded that "Megafon could very well have received public money" through a tangled web of government supported foundations and think tanks.[92] It asked the company for clarification and instead Megafon took legal action (which Megafon lost).[93]

Coincidentally, in the same year that Kovács launched Megafon, another young Hungarian, Csaba Pál, launched a "free speech alternative" site called

Hundub. The site, which was funded via offshore companies, was promoted by Hungary's right-wing press, and one of its first registered users was the prime minister, Viktor Orbán, himself.[94] As with similar attempts to create alternatives to mainstream social media platforms worldwide, Hundub did not take off and was shut down within a year.

Whether Megafon's money came directly from Orbán's government, or from conservative businessmen such as Lőrinc Mészáros, is less important than the fact that its funding was opaque. Like so much else in Orbán's counterfeit public sphere, it was intended to look like something it was not. It was meant to seem like an organic response to left-wing voices online—a popular conservative digital uprising. Yet it was nothing of the kind. Launched by the strategic director of a pro-Fidesz think tank—István Kovács—and bankrolled by undisclosed sources, it artificially inflated conservatives who had already gained public exposure through right-wing media channels. Still, it extended Orbán's media sovereignty to social media and provided a model that could be used both for future election campaigns and for the worldwide conservative movement. Kovács was bullish about its potential: "Our goals go beyond an election victory": "We want to change the entire Internet, the world we live in," and "the online space plays an increasingly important role."[95]

Kovács would not get very far with his ambition without funding, and without Megafon's promotion across pro-government outlets. In this sense Megafon, and social media generally, was simply another element in Fidesz's efforts to dominate Hungary's public sphere. Another element that had to be coordinated, directed, and managed. Such coordination could only be done from the center, by someone with oversight of all the pieces of media and communications machinery.

THE UPM

When the credits roll at the end of a movie, the first person named is usually the Unit Production Manager (UPM). To those outside the film business, this may seem odd. Why should the first credit go to the UPM—whose role is unfamiliar and name unknown—and not to the director, the writer, or the lead actor? The reason is that without the UPM the film would never have been completed. Once the film is underway, the UPM is responsible for almost everything. They manage the production spending, hire and run the crew, manage the shooting schedule, respond to crises, pay people, and make sure the film gets finished on time and (hopefully) on budget. When it comes to Hungary's media and communications, and the management of the country's counterfeit public sphere, Antal Rogán is the equivalent of Viktor Orbán's UPM.

Unlike Mészáros and Simicska, Antal Rogán was not a childhood friend of Orbán. Almost ten years younger than the leader of Fidesz, Rogán grew up in the far west of Hungary, close to the borders of Austria and Slovenia. Yet, like Orbán, he threw himself into politics from an early age, joining the youth wing of Fidesz and becoming a Parliamentarian at the age of just twenty-six in 1998. By 2006 he was working on Fidesz's election campaigns, and he was elected mayor to a district in Budapest. Over the following decade he made himself one of the best known, and infamous, politicians in Hungary. This was partly due to his second marriage in 2007 to the glamorous Cecilia Gaal (subsequently Rogán-Gaal). Becoming a celebrity couple, the pair made themselves staples of tabloid coverage— from their engagement to their extravagant wedding in the capital, to the announcement of her pregnancy.[96] Yet his infamy was also due to repeated allegations of corruption throughout his political career. Properties within his mayoral district were sold at heavily discounted prices.[97] In 2012, Rogán started a "Golden Visa" scheme through which foreigners who invested over a quarter of a million euros could gain Hungarian residency permits— permits then granted to various people who posed a "serious security risk."[98] And in 2015, a defendant in a major fraud trial accused Rogán of accepting a 10 million euro bribe.[99] Rogán denied these and other allegations and said he was unaware of any wrongdoing while he was mayor. One news outlet that tried to investigate him in 2016 found that "the closer we got to him, the faster his traces disappeared everywhere. Not only was it impossible to reach him, but his friends, colleagues, and business partners also denied knowledge or kept silent."[100]

It was the Orbán-Simicska split in 2015 that elevated Rogán, putting him on a path to becoming the second most powerful political figure in Hungary and the central node in Fidesz's media-communications network. Having fallen out with Simicska, Viktor Orbán needed to reorient his government's communications strategy, wresting Simicska's media empire from him and extending government control to other commercial media outlets. This not only meant coordinating various media takeovers by pro-Fidesz oligarchs such as Mészáros, but ensuring that these outlets remained economically viable. At the same time, Orbán needed to ensure that public media—along with friendly commercial outlets—continued to push consistently pro-Fidesz narratives. Doing this would require careful and constant attention. Orbán needed someone whose loyalty he could trust, someone capable of directing the counterfeit public sphere while disguising the government's role, but also someone politically unpopular enough not to represent a leadership threat. In October 2015 he appointed Antal Rogán to head up the Prime Minister's Cabinet Office, and asked him to lead a new National Office of Communication with responsibility for overseeing the government's media and communications strategy.

Rogán fulfilled his new duties with aplomb. In just over three years he had helped coordinate the takeover of the majority of Hungary's commercial media by friendly oligarchs, and their subsequent donation of those same media outlets to a state-supported foundation. He had organized Orbán's successful reelection campaign in 2018, and he had centralized control of government communications via the Cabinet Office and the National Office of Communications, so separate parts of government could not run their communications independently. It was through the strategic control of communications, most notably the rapidly expanding communications budget, that Fidesz could then subsidize supportive media outlets and bankroll government "information" campaigns, while simultaneously claiming the government did not interfere with press freedom or encroach on media plurality.

In performing this last role—funneling state funds to supportive media via advertising—the Orbán government can justifiably claim credit for exploiting a loophole in democratic media theory. In a liberal democracy, theorists have long claimed the media should be free and diverse—a marketplace of ideas where different perspectives can be discussed without government interference.[101] Yet as Attila Bátorfy and his colleagues have rightly pointed out, "this basic premise says nothing about the fundamentally distortive nature of advertising."[102] It has always been assumed that income from advertising comes from the market and not from the state, and therefore protects commercial media from government interference. But what if the government is the biggest advertiser? And what if the government deliberately uses its advertising spending to direct and discriminate against political speech?

This is just what the Fidesz government did. It made itself into the dominant advertiser in Hungary, and used advertising—both the content and the budget—for political ends. Most democratic governments advertise, and state advertising income is often considered a form of indirect subsidy to the press. In the UK, for example, local authorities are even obliged to advertise in local newspapers. But in Hungary, Orbán's Fidesz took it to an entirely different level. First, they increased the amount of government spending, from 6 percent of total advertising in Hungary in 2006 to 40 percent by 2020.[103] In 2020 alone, the government spent 128 billion Hungarian forints (US$370 million).[104] Second, they targeted the spending toward pro-government media and away from media they saw as critical. This was most blatant in 2015, when the government quickly sought to draw down its spending on Simicska's media outlets, and increased its advertising subsidies to outlets owned by other friends of Orbán. *Magyar Nemzet*, which in 2015 was owned by Simicska, saw its share of the government's advertising budget drop from almost 20 percent to close to zero within a year, whereas the freshly launched—and staunchly pro-Orbán—daily newspaper, *Magyar Idok*, saw its share rise from zero to almost 10 percent of government spending in a few months.[105] This massive shift cannot be explained by changes in newspaper circulation because *Magyar Nemzet*'s circulation was far higher than *Magyar Idok*'s.[106] This politically targeted funding was repeated across Hungary's media—print, TV, radio, and online. In 2020, 86 percent of the money the government spent on media went to pro-government outlets.[107]

As head of the National Office of Communications from 2015, Antal Rogán was responsible for determining where this money went, and these decisions rarely followed market, or public interest, logic. In 2021, for example, a dollop of it went to the media company owned by Cecilia Rogán-Gaal (by this time his ex-wife) and her business partner, to advertise on their tabloid website, Top World News. So lucrative was this advertising that, an investigation by Direkt36 and Telex discovered, the publisher reported revenues of close to 4 million euros in 2021, with a profit margin of 85 percent.[108] Not only did this level of profit far exceed more established sites with much higher audience numbers, many of Top World News's users turned out to be "purchased traffic," and the government's ads were being played alongside rehashed clickbait content spun from social media (such as, "Strange reason: this is why you shouldn't pee while showering, according to the urologist").[109] It is unlikely that a government communications campaign that sought to reach a maximum number of citizens alongside credible media content would have chosen to advertise on Cecilia Rogán-Gaal's site.

Centralized control of a vast communications budget is what enabled Orbán's government to maintain Hungary's counterfeit public sphere. Some news outlets became so dependent on state advertising that without it they would not survive. In 2017 there were twenty-six media brands where the share of state advertising exceeded 50 percent of all their advertising revenues.[110] Yet the advertising also served another purpose. It enabled the government to pepper the media—and public spaces—with pro-Fidesz propaganda. After Rogán took over the Cabinet office, the government ran a continuous cycle of information campaigns via the press and in poster campaigns, emphasizing the threat of migrants to Hungary, the dangers of George Soros and his left-liberal network to Hungarian sovereignty, and the menace of an overbearing EU. In the lead-up to the 2022 election, advertisements and posters appeared across Hungary with a picture of bombs falling and the line "Brussels sanctions are ruining us." The governing party was, in other words, equating EU economic sanctions against Russia with actual bombs like those Putin was dropping on Ukraine, and asserting that Hungary was being harmed by these as much as by its Russian neighbor. Luckily for the government, Hungary's tame media regulator—the NMHH—ruled that information campaigns like these did not count as pro-government propaganda, meaning that they could all be paid for from the public purse (and ironically by grants from the EU). Rogán's office spent 146 million euros on "government 'information' and 'consultation' with the people" that year.[111]

Over the decade following 2015, Antal Rogán's office accumulated more and more power. In addition to an ever-expanding role managing government communications, he was given control of the secret services, asked to oversee an anticorruption drive, to organize state sports events, and to run the government's audit office.[112] Orbán was clearly satisfied with the performance of his key lieutenant, but Rogán's ascent was also an indication of how control of Hungary's public sphere had become integral to the Orbán project. Determining the dominant national narratives, framing them in a way that bolstered Fidesz, and ensuring that criticism of them could be marginalized as antinational, "leftist" sentiment, had become central to the party maintaining and enhancing its power. Yet it also showed how much effort and attention such control required. As well as subsidizing much of Hungary's media outlets, Rogán was monitoring media output, surveilling the internet, and micromanaging political messaging.[113] The Cabinet office was channeling money to think tanks and research centers who could put forward "experts" to speak on almost any political subject, although these "talking heads" always spoke in support of government policy.[114] These think tanks and foundations were also in a position to give money to new initiatives, such as Megafon. Such a strategy mimics one adopted in Putin's Russia, where money is channeled to state-linked think tanks such as the Strategic Culture Foundation.[115]

As Rogán's power grew, his penchant for publicity dwindled. He appeared less in the press, and when he married for a third time in 2020, the wedding was held in secret and only announced the following year.[116] By direction or design, he appeared to be embracing his role as the backstage administrator, the UPM of Hungarian politics.

* * *

Rogán's Cabinet office and the National Office of Communication oversaw each of the elements of Fidesz's counterfeit public sphere: regulation, public media, commercial media, and social media. Without any one of these elements, and Rogán's central apparatus, the whole operation would be less effective, and the undemocratic nature of the system more likely to be exposed. A flexible media law, combined with a passive and compliant regulator, allowed the Fidesz government to assert that all its actions were legitimate and lawful. A cowed and submissive public media provided the party with conduits for its messaging, while allowing it to claim that public media remains autonomous and balanced. A co-opted commercial media, much of which had been corralled within a state-backed foundation, gave the government the means to disseminate its narratives through multiple different outlets to diverse audiences and insist that this represented evidence of media plurality. And, Fidesz discovered, it is straightforward— and quite cheap—to buy voices within social media, which have the added benefit of sounding like authentically held personal views. Together, these elements became inherent not just to Hungary's media but to its structure of governance and its ability to dominate the public sphere. They are also eminently replicable by illiberal leaders and parties in other countries, who want to maintain the outward appearance of democratic legitimacy while exercising oppressive control and perpetuating their power.

These elements were not assembled at once, but incrementally and iteratively. First, a new media law was introduced that made possible the subsequent appropriation of public media, and the cumulative acquisition—by willing frontpeople—of commercial media. When these frontpeople became too powerful or independent—as with Lajos Simicska—others were found to replace them, and the power of these successors were muted by the submission of their media assets to a public foundation. As the influence of legacy media on politics waned, the party turned its attention to social media, where it found it could simply pay to identify and amplify pro-government messages and voices, and do so deniably. As Hungarians migrate from open social media to less public messaging services such as WhatsApp, then no doubt the party will employ methods to populate these with its propaganda—as the Bolsonaros did so successfully in Brazil (see chapter 6). Orbán's control of Hungary's public sphere has been won by years of obsessive attention, money, and adaptation.

This, at least, is a positive sign for other democracies anxious about Orbán-imitators. If not all of these elements are present, and if the party in power does not devote continuous resources and effort to managing and evolving them, they will not achieve similar success. In Poland, for instance, the Law and Justice Party started in 2015 down a path toward media capture similar to that adopted in Hungary—making changes to media law, subduing public media. But the Polish party failed to replicate Fidesz's takeover of commercial media and was unable to dominate social media, leaving Poland's public sphere polarized rather than controlled.[117] This gave the opposition just enough political space to oust Law and Justice at the election in 2023.

There are also frailties in Hungary's counterfeit public sphere. For one, it relies on a perpetual flow of money. Money for contracts for Fidesz-friendly oligarchs, who can then spend it on acquiring or launching media. Money to advertise in pro-government "commercial" media so that it remains viable. Money for information campaigns. Money for public media. This money comes from public funds—sourced from Hungarian citizens' taxes, from the EU (the same "enemy" that the government demonizes in its information campaigns), and from foreign loans. Since 2010 Fidesz has sought these loans from East and West, including Russian loans for nuclear energy and Chinese funding for transport infrastructure. Were public funds to grow more scarce, or the EU to withhold its grants, or Russia and China to become less willing to provide loans, Fidesz would struggle to maintain the patina of democratic legitimacy of its manufactured public sphere.

The system also depends on the propagation of narratives that stoke public outrage and fear. These stories must tell of enemies with malign intent who are seeking to undermine Hungary's sovereignty, desecrate its culture, import crime and disease, overwhelm its citizenry, or overthrow its democratically elected government. These fabricated enemies are woven together by elaborate conspiracy theories in which left-liberals, globalists, or sinister international organizations such as the Bilderberg Group are said to be pursuing a dastardly master plan. But behind them all, cast as the ultimate *éminence grise*, the omniscient Machiavellian manipulator, is George Soros. Despite the ever-greater complexity, absurdity, prejudice, and malevolence of these false narratives and conspiracy theories, thanks to

Fidesz's dominance of media and communication these narrative realities are promoted daily and unashamedly in Hungary's mainstream media.

Once established, the benefits of this counterfeit public sphere to the government are manifold. Orbán's Fidesz has won four elections in a row, all by significant margins. Fidesz, and Orbán himself, have been able to avoid negative coverage, or damaging stories that could jeopardize their public support. Such stories are either not reported at all, or are reported in such a way that marginalizes them, or that shifts the blame onto someone else. Take, for example, the news about József Szájer that broke in December 2020. Szájer—the Fidesz-KDNP representative at the EU, close confidant of Viktor Orbán, and one of the original founders of the Fidesz party—was arrested in Brussels after climbing out of a window to escape a police raid on a "gay orgy" he was attending that contravened COVID-19 lockdown rules. Ecstasy was discovered in Szájer's bag.[118] In most free societies, and in most commercial news outlets—especially tabloid outlets—this would be newsworthy enough for a front-page splash. In Hungary, where Szájer was a senior politician, married to a prominent female Hungarian judge on the Constitutional Court, in a ruling party that campaigned on socially conservative Christian values, one would have expected it to lead the news for days. Yet many of Hungary's leading outlets hardly covered it. Tabloid outlet Bors did not report it at all. Metropol, *Magyar Nemzet*, and *Origo* published Szájer's personal statement, but then preferred to entertain conspiracy theories about the affair rather than focus on the arrest itself and its political implications. "Revenge from Brussels?," *Magyar Nemzet* asked, quoting a former head of operations at the information office as saying "József Szájer is certainly the victim of a secret service operation."[119] By ignoring the story and instead propagating a conspiratorial fantasy that distracted from the scandal, the pro-Orbán media once more showed their commitment to narrative, rather than material, reality.

5

THE *GODI MEDIA*

Modi's India

THE BALAKOT STRIKE

On Saturday February 23, 2019, at 10:31 P.M., the Republic TV news anchor Arnab Goswami messaged the CEO of India's Broadcast Audience Research Council (BARC), Partho Dasgupta. Goswami is India's most prominent news anchor—likened by some to Tucker Carlson, formerly of Fox News in the United States.[1] Goswami's text explained cryptically to Dasgupta that "something big will happen" regarding Pakistan. Suspecting a military attack, Dasgupta asked for clarification: "Strike? Or bigger?" Goswami replied that the action would be "Bigger than a normal strike" and that Indian people "will be elated" about it. With Prime Minister

Narendra Modi's Bharatiya Janata Party (BJP) languishing in the polls, Dasgupta suggested the timing was "good for the big man in this season. He will sweep polls then." He believed a military strike against India's traditional enemy, Pakistan, would be a vote winner.[2]

This WhatsApp exchange was leaked two years later during a police investigation into alleged manipulation of TV ratings, during which Dasgupta was imprisoned.[3] It reveals both how deep the relationship between Arnab Goswami and the Modi government had become by 2019, and how blurred the lines between his news outlet and the state. Thanks to his intimate government connections, the TV anchor apparently knew about the strike on Pakistan days before it happened. Goswami also had advance notice, according to the exchanges, of the Indian government's plan to revoke the special status of the Muslim-dominated state of Jammu and Kashmir.[4]

Sure enough, on Tuesday February 26 the Indian Air Force bombed Balakot in Pakistan, claiming it was a terrorist training camp. That night in the primetime debate he hosted on his channel, an ecstatic Goswami called it a "fantastic day" and one for "all of us to come together and celebrate." "The Pakistanis," he told his viewers, "have been shown their place." Not only was this the right thing for India to do, Goswami thundered, "But we should strike again, I really think we should."[5]

Goswami may have been India's most bombastically patriotic TV news anchor, but other channels were similarly tub-thumping. "Network anchors fell over themselves to outdo one another's displays of patriotism," recollects the journalist Salil Tripathi, "shattering any barrier that may have existed between a state-propaganda channel and a credible news network."[6] It later transpired that the strike did not kill three hundred terrorists as the government claimed (or even one); nor did it do any significant physical damage. This did not matter to the news channels, though. They were too busy playing martial music, streaming videos of Indian jets, and praising the Indian Air Force's courage and Modi's leadership. The truth about the attack was secondary to the channels' desire to praise what they called a "historic military victory for India."[7] "Jai ho!" one news anchor tweeted—let the victory prevail.[8]

After the strike, the BJP's popularity rose. Rather than the hung parliament that had been predicted before the attack, Modi's BJP secured a greater majority in the Indian parliament—the Lok Sabha—than it had won in 2014. "The Balakot effect," journalist Rajdeep Sardesai subsequently wrote, "was evident."[9]

THE *GODI MEDIA* PHENOMENON

National news outlets are well known for "rallying round the flag" in times of war; US news channels flew flags in the corner of their screens during the 2003 Iraq war.[10] So it was not entirely surprising that many outlets would celebrate India's attack on Pakistan, although their coverage was particularly jingoistic. But the intensity and frequency of such outlets' support for the Modi government is far from a one-off, and it represents more than just a temporary rally-round-the-flag effect. Nor was the early warning Goswami received a unique example of the closeness between Republic TV and the Modi administration. Indeed, it is symptomatic of a phenomenon that has become characteristic of much of India's mainstream broadcast media: they have become so slavishly supportive of Modi's government that they have come to be referred to as the "*Godi Media*"—literally lapdog media. A derogatory term coined by the former NDTV news presenter Ravish Kumar, it refers to media outlets that have abandoned any commitment they had to objectivity, balance, and truth in favor of producing staunchly pro-government news.[11]

The previous chapter described how Hungary's Viktor Orbán co-opted commercial news outlets, mainly through changes of ownership, and repurposed them to produce pro-government propaganda. The *Godi Media* are distinct from this because they have voluntarily chosen to be co-opted to serve the government's agenda, despite outwardly claiming editorial independence. They have made the positive choice to act as state propaganda outlets, rather than being directed or coerced.

As our analysis of Indian news coverage in this chapter shows, *Godi Media* outlets have struck a Faustian bargain with the government, consciously choosing to provide flattering, noncritical coverage, and to promote the government's strategic narratives. In return, they hope to gain access, patronage, and advertising revenue and to avoid censure—or worse—by the government. The government, meanwhile, enjoys a double benefit. The purported independence of these news outlets enhances their credibility as avenues for government propaganda. Any praise the government receives looks like it comes from an autonomous source rather than a state-controlled outlet. Moreover, because these outlets need to attract an audience, they package their output to maximize viewership. This means that the news broadcast on these channels is a far cry from the gray, somber, Indian state news output of the Cold War era. Rather, the channels produce provocative, noisy, colorful, sensationalist infotainment, which gets attention and is all the more effective as a vehicle for the government's messages.

Yet the rise of *Godi Media* has come at a steep cost to Indian politics and society. Rarely is the government closely scrutinized. Issues that make the government uncomfortable, or that reflect badly on the leader, are downplayed or ignored. Government critics, no matter how valid their case, are written off as ill-motivated or "antinational." Most dangerously, certain groups within society—especially Muslims—are demonized, and discrimination and violence against them is presented as justified and proportionate. The rhetoric of *Godi Media* is so inflammatory, some observers have said, that it could pave the way toward genocide.[12] This is especially troubling because of how dominant the *Godi Media* have become in India's news environment. Shortly before India's 2024 election, the cumulative share of the top four English-language TV news channels, each of which has been accused of being *Godi Media*, was 91 percent.[13] The viewership of the Hindi-language *Godi Media* news channels was even higher.[14] Even in the wake of the BJP's disappointing 2024 election result, in which Modi's party lost its outright parliamentary majority, the TV channels remained steadfastly devoted to the incoming BJP-led coalition.

In this chapter we explore the *Godi Media* phenomenon: how it emerged, its features, its consequences, and the extent to which it is becoming not just an Indian but a global phenomenon. It is based on original analysis of television footage on India's main TV news channels, focusing on Republic TV and Times Now, covering issues including the COVID-19 pandemic, the Farmers' Protests of 2020–21, and the Gyanvapi mosque dispute of 2022. Original interviews with leading Indian journalists reveal the underlying processes through which the *Godi Media* works and help corroborate what we have learned from analyzing outlets' English language output. We show how the *Godi Media* have helped construct a parallel reality that portrays India's response to COVID-19 as one of the world's best rather than one of its worst, in which ordinary farmers are misrepresented as separatists and terrorists, and in which the country's ruling Hindu majority is supposedly being repressed by the Muslim minority, even as the government disenfranchises that same minority. Finally, we show how one can now see elements of the *Godi Media* phenomenon across the globe, in authoritarian states and democracies, in Russia, the United States, France, and the UK.

To understand how this pro-government commercial media emerged, why it has become so dominant, and why it represents such a threat to democracy, one has to understand how these channels grew up, what drives them, and how they became so interwoven with Indian politics. Nothing illustrates how and why this happened better than the rise and rise of Arnab Goswami.

THE STORY OF ARNAB GOSWAMI

It was the terrorist attacks on Mumbai in 2008 that transformed Arnab Goswami's fortunes and set him on the path to becoming India's most influential newsmaker. Not that he had been unsuccessful before then. After a short stint in print journalism following his master's degree at Oxford University, Goswami joined New Delhi Television (NDTV) in 1996 and soon became one of its lead presenters. Always immaculately dressed, with a carefully parted full head of hair and bookish glasses, Goswami came across as India's equivalent to a 1970s BBC newsreader. His academic credentials were reinforced following his Visiting Fellowship at Cambridge University in 2001, during which he wrote a book lamenting the weakness of democratic governments in dealing with terrorism. This intellectual mien fit with NDTV's culture at the time, which was populated by the offspring of the Delhi establishment. Goswami's coworkers were the children of ministers, commissioners, ambassadors, and cricketers.[15]

Despite his family's pedigree—his father was a colonel in the Indian Army—Goswami said he never felt comfortable with this Delhi power elite. So when the opportunity came to start something new far away in Mumbai, he leaped at it. The powerful Jain family, owners of leading outlets, the *Times of India* and the *Economic Times*, offered him the chance to start a new TV news channel—Times Now. This was a heady period for Indian TV news. The country had previously had a public broadcaster, Doordarshan, which enjoyed a monopoly until the late twentieth century. But in the 1990s, cable and satellite news took off, and the government relaxed broadcast regulations. Between 2000 and 2008 the number of news channels jumped from ten to sixty-seven.[16] Times Now was one of them, and Goswami worked six or seven days a week through 2005 and 2006 to ready his new channel for launch.[17] Despite his efforts, initially the channel struggled to gain public attention in India's increasingly competitive and chaotic news environment. Within a few months of going on air, the channel's ratings were so poor in 2006 that Goswami was almost replaced as editor.

Then came the Mumbai terrorist attack, in which ten members of the Pakistan-based Islamist extremist group, Lashkar-e-Taiba, attacked multiple locations in Mumbai over three days, killing 175 people. It had an electrifying effect on the nation and on Goswami. He saw this as his moment to seize public attention. "I started [broadcasting] at about 10 o'clock," he recalled later, "and went on for three-and-a-half days. I remember going home only once and must've slept for an hour in that entire period."[18] He vented his frustration with Delhi's liberal establishment on-screen, haranguing his guests and the "human rights brigade" who prevented harsher responses to terrorism, advocating for these killers "to be dealt with professionally."[19] His antagonistic and impassioned performance, along with that of other correspondents who got caught up in the national frenzy, attracted widespread disapproval and even calls for greater broadcast regulation. But Arnab Goswami was unapologetic. The TV anchor had found his voice.

Over the next six years, Goswami turned himself into a national figure. From being Arnab Goswami, the Times Now presenter and debate host, he became simply *Arnab*. His primetime debates, which deliberately pitted people with radical views against one another, became daily national talking points. Arnab captured public attention by breaking news conventions and norms—disrespecting public figures, expressing his own opinions, emoting and shouting, always shouting. And as more and more channels began to imitate his methods, he and his channel changed journalism in India.

Despite its belligerent style, prior to 2014 Times Now could justifiably claim to be holding the government to account. From 2011, Times Now championed the India Against Corruption campaign. This followed the Commonwealth games and 2G mobile scandals, which implicated Indian politicians in corrupt financial and contractual practices. In 2012, after the shocking Narbiya gang rape and murder, Goswami called for a "national awakening" and defended students' right to protest and their calls for greater safety on the streets.[20] At every opportunity, Arnab would highlight corruption and scandals and associate them with established politicians and journalists. He distanced himself from the Delhi media, referring to them disparagingly as the "Lutyens media" (Edwin Lutyens having designed the government buildings of colonial New Delhi). A 2014 promotional video for Times Now proclaimed that Arnab had independence and integrity, unlike the corrupted Delhi news houses: "In an independent journalist, integrity isn't merely an embellishment," a female voice intones, "it is the sum total of character. Arnab Goswami on the Newshour at 9."[21]

Times Now's claim to be performing its role as a "Fourth Estate," holding the government to account, ended when Narendra Modi was elected in 2014. Modi and his BJP party instigated the change, although it was Arnab and other media outlets who chose to embrace it. That year's election campaign began as normal. Arnab, as the leading news personality in India, secured interviews with all the leading politicians, including Rahul Gandhi and Narendra Modi. In the Gandhi interview he was characteristically confrontational, making the Congress leader look casual, unprepared, and complacent.[22] Then he interviewed Modi, and his whole manner changed. Modi, speaking in Hindi, immediately went on the offensive, attacking the media for criticizing him and for protecting the Gandhi family, even criticizing Arnab and Times Now for "emotionally blackmailing him."[23] Arnab responded quietly, almost as though he was cowed by Modi's more forceful approach toward the media. When I am elected, Modi appeared to be saying, I will treat the media differently and my government will not look kindly on critical voices.

That was indeed the approach that Modi took when he assumed office. Throughout his tenure, Modi avoided direct contact with the press, failing to give a single press conference in the next ten years.[24] When Modi did speak to the media, it was in carefully prepared set piece interviews. His first, after becoming prime minister, was in 2016—again with Arnab Goswami. But by now the shift in Arnab's method was palpable. The usually pugnacious anchor pliantly congratulated the prime minister on "a fantastic speech" to the US Congress with "a lot of humor." He lauded the leader's economic record: "you have managed to grow the economy at 7.5 percent when the global economic climate is very bleak," and remarked on his phenomenal rate of activity, "you keep a terrifying pace. The number of meetings you hold, people say your officers find it hard to keep up."[25] As a promotional exercise for the Indian leader, it was hard to surpass.

For Arnab, 2016 was also the year he outgrew Times Now. Bristling at the constraints imposed by the Jains, he wanted more ownership, greater editorial control, freer rein. So, again, he left to start a new news network, becoming the founder, owner, managing director, editor in chief, and lead news anchor of Republic TV. On his own news network Arnab could be as loud as he wanted, as dictatorial as he wanted, and as editorially independent as he wanted.

Sure enough, the volume of Republic TV was even higher than at Times Now, and Goswami ran his news room "like a durbar" (a medieval court).[26] Despite his editorial freedom, he chose not to challenge the governing BJP. Instead, Republic TV's news agenda turned out to be strikingly similar to, and supportive of, the Modi government's agenda. An analysis of all 1,779 of Republic TV's debates in its first three years found that they were "consistently biased" in favor Modi's government and the BJP's policies and ideology. These debates also avoided issues that might reflect poorly on the government's record—such as education and health—focusing their criticism on the opposition instead. Remarkably, Republic did not host "even one debate that we could classify as being in the opposition's favour."[27]

Although Republic TV led with this pro-government agenda, its success soon spawned multiple imitators. Times Now, which replaced Arnab with two similarly obstreperous anchors, Rahul Shivshankar and Navika Kumar, became similarly admiring of Modi and supportive of the BJP's agenda. The Hindi-language news channels were more sycophantic still—Zee News, Aaj Tak, Sudarshan News, among others. Often, they would compete to be first to champion the administration. As a former Times Now employee we interviewed put it, Arnab may have been antiestablishment until Modi came to power, but he was now instrumental in turning the media into the government's first line of defense.[28] Though not officially state media, the leading TV news channels became an integral propaganda arm of the state.

THE FAUSTIAN BARGAIN: WHY THE *GODI MEDIA* EMERGED

To understand why Republic, and so many other Indian TV news outlets, became so supportive of the government, it is necessary to understand how the *Godi Media* phenomenon works.

At the core of the phenomenon is a Faustian bargain between news channels and the government. In the original play by Christopher Marlowe, Dr. Faustus traded his soul with the devil in exchange for knowledge and power. For Indian TV outlets, the deal is that the outlet voluntarily sacrifices any commitment it might have to objectivity or to scrutinizing the government, and instead promotes the government's preferred narratives. In return, the government gives the outlet access, funding, and support (or refrains from penalizing them).

This is not the first time that the Indian news media had consistently supported the government. When Doordarshan held a monopoly, it was expected to act as a channel for government communication. Later, when the broadcast market opened up in the 1990s, the ruling Congress Party continued to enjoy strong support, as three of our interviewees—all Indian journalists—told us.[29] Equally, the Gandhi family was treated like Indian royalty for decades, and criticism of them by the press was kept muted or off-limits. Indeed, research with journalists across India indicates that many accept and even embrace political bias as part of the job. "[I]n this business," a journalist told researchers in 2016, "you have to write the wishes of the employer on your forehead, if you can't do it, you have to get out."[30] Those who own or invest in India's news media, especially at the local level, are as likely to be doing it for political as for economic reasons. As Kalyani Chadha and Michael Koliska write, "while the involvement of businessmen and politicians in regional news channels might be underpinned to some degree by commercial considerations, it is principally directed by their desire to have a voice and to garner support for particular political and economic agendas."[31]

Under the Modi administration the relationship between media and government has become even more transactional. Since the BJP took office, access to the prime minister, senior ministers, government information, and government institutions has become dependent on coverage. Previous administrations would still give access to journalists who criticized them; the BJP does not.[32] This approach emanates from the top. Narendra Modi has given interviews to Republic TV, India Today, Times Now, and Aaj Tak.[33] He has given no interviews to journalists or channels who take a critical stance.[34] Other ministers take their lead from the prime minister. Similarly, journalists are no longer allowed easy access to government buildings to speak to officials. They need a pass, or the explicit invitation of someone within the department.[35] When Modi goes on official foreign trips, rather than take a coterie of journalists from leading publications, he takes none—or only those known to provide positive coverage. Journalists report that information from the prime minister's office is doled out via WhatsApp, like gifts or currency, to those journalists most in favor with the leadership.[36] As one interviewee told us, "What is political news nowadays? It is which reporters get the WhatsApp message first from the PMO [Prime Minister's Office]. The most important journalist gets the WhatsApp message at 9:01. The second most important at 9:02 and so on. That journalist then has to pass on the message immediately, as delivered to them. If they don't, then they may not receive the next WhatsApp message."[37]

The exchange of positive news for political access explains why Arnab Goswami learned about the Balakot attack days before it happened: the BJP knew he would use it as the government wanted. Likewise, Republic TV journalists gained access to Kashmir because the government knew they would self-censor anything that conflicted with the government's claims about the region. This "symbiotic relationship," as one interviewee put it, rewards favorable media with scoops and helps the government's strategic narrative dominate.

In addition to access, pro-government news outlets can benefit from greater government advertising revenue. Over the last two decades Indian media have become increasingly dependent on advertising. Many channels rely on advertising for more than 70 percent of their revenue.[38] As the government is a key source of advertising revenue, there is a strong incentive to produce pro-government content.[39] Criticize the government and channels risk losing that revenue.[40] Similarly, conferences and events have become an important supplement to media organizations' income. A keynote speech by the prime minister or a senior minister will guarantee good attendance and sponsorship. Nonattendance will have the reverse effect. The government knows this and uses it as leverage.

News outlets that are especially supportive, and have high audiences, are given greater license and ministerial support than others. Despite strong calls, for example—by opposition politicians and members of the military—for an inquiry into the leak of information about the Balakot strike, the government did not set one up. When Arnab Goswami himself was arrested in November 2020, accused of abetting the suicide of an architect, the minister of home affairs and the information and broadcasting minister both rushed to condemn the arrest as an "an attack on individual freedom and the 4th pillar of democracy."[41] Critical journalists and news outlets have not received similar government support.

However, the reasons these channels support the government so strongly go deeper than funding and access; they reflect a fundamental shift in power between the media and the state. The Modi government believes it does not need institutional media as previous governments did. Like other populist rulers worldwide, Modi presents himself as having a direct relationship with the people rather than one that needs to be mediated through traditional media outlets (as with AMLO—see chapter 7).[42] Yet unlike leaders of the past, he can produce and distribute his own mass media and do so on a wide range of platforms. By the time of the 2024 Indian election, he had more than 97 million followers on X (formerly Twitter), 88 million on Instagram, almost 50 million on Facebook, and more than 22 million subscribers to his YouTube channel. The Modi app, "NaMo," boasts more than 10 million Android downloads, and he has a website (www.pmindia.gov.in.) that contains all his speeches, news updates, and footage from his events.

Yet the Modi government's ability to communicate directly with the public goes beyond his personal social media followers. In 2024 the BJP claimed to have 180 million members, through whom it could disseminate its messages and relay news.[43] Millions of these party members act as digital foot soldiers to the party, especially in the lead-up to elections. During the 2024 campaign, these BJP digital warriors were managing a reported five million WhatsApp groups. This gave Modi a combination of centralized and decentralized control. He could post messages directly from one of his accounts, or send them from campaign command to "any remote place across the country . . . [in] 12 minutes, down from 40 minutes a few years ago."[44] Equally, individual digital administrators could use their local knowledge to drum up BJP support and get out the vote. The BJP called their 2024 election operation the "Shankhnaad campaign," shankhnaad being the sound of a conch shell being blown, as it was—in Hindu tradition—as a war trumpet.[45]

Given the scale and reach of the BJP's social media operations, one begins to understand why the Modi government has come to see news outlets as one element within its communications strategy rather than the cornerstone. News coverage remains critical for setting the public's agenda on the BJP's terms and for producing political content that can be shared online, but the party can also produce its own news, and news outlets no longer control how their stories spread among the public. In India, it is as likely that people will see news on their phone as on a TV screen at home. A recent report found that one-in-three urban Indians with internet access "do not watch linear TV at all," preferring YouTube and Instagram Reels (TikTok being banned since 2020).[46] Indians are prolific users of mainstream social media. There are more WhatsApp users, more YouTube users, and more Instagram users in India than in any other country on the planet.[47] More than half a billion Indians use WhatsApp regularly—greater than the next six countries combined.

News outlets that want to be heard among the din of social media therefore need to shout loudly. Those that want their political content to be endorsed, promoted, and shared on social media or WhatsApp need to recognize both the power of Modi's BJP as a source of news, and the power of its 180 million members to spread it. One can therefore see why many outlets have embraced their own instrumentalization by the BJP government. Support Modi and his party and they gain access, income, and popular approval online. Criticize Modi and the BJP and they court exclusion, impoverishment, and denunciation on social media. This shift in power away from traditional media is not particular to India. A similar tilt can be found across the globe, and it has given leaders including Donald Trump (USA), Jair Bolsonaro (Brazil), and Reccep Tayip Erdogan (Turkey) the opportunity to bypass legacy media and communicate directly with the public.[48] However, the shift is particularly acute in India, and it helps explain the extent of the *Godi Media* phenomenon.

Although other news channels and outlets had reservations about Arnab Goswami's approach to news—there is no shortage of Arnab critics in

India—they could see how well it worked.[49] Republic TV, like Times Now before it, topped the news channel ratings (TRPs) from launch. Arnab had access, revenue, and license from the government (sometimes overt, other times not). As a consequence, his approach became an archetype for how to do news successfully in India that is now dominant across Indian television news, even after the 2024 election.

What is Arnab's formula for success? What are the key ingredients that make it work, and at the same time make it so dangerous to democracy?

THE *GODI MEDIA* FORMULA

Based on our analysis of more than a hundred hours of televised footage of Republic TV, Times Now, and other pro-Modi outlets, corroborated by our interviews with leading Indian journalists, the formula for the *Godi Media* model consists of five key ingredients: theatricality, loudness, feeling, nationalism, and populism.

Ingredient number one: Theatricality. Enter Arnab's news channels and you will find yourself in a carefully constructed world where everything is planned and everyone has a predetermined role. At center stage is Arnab himself—the Master of Ceremonies, the host, the showman. Arnab—literally and figuratively—anchors the channel and controls its tone, its tempo, its stories, and its players. People who appear on one of his channels, as guests or during debates, are his dramatis personae. Each is intended to play a character—normally in vivid, clashing tones. There are the villains, the heroes, the fools or jesters, hand-picked and conducted by Arnab himself and his team. The studio is the command center. Since Times Now's coverage of the Mumbai attacks in 2008, the news has been directed from the studio rather than by events on the ground. The audience knows in advance what they are going to get: not just in terms of format but in terms of narrative, framing, and personalities. They are told (repeatedly) that it is news. But despite being dramatic it is in many ways the opposite of *news*; it is standardized, scripted, and predictable.

Ingredient number two: Loudness—of both *sound* and *vision*. Arnab's shouting has become synonymous with his brand, and when he is quiet he receives concerned emails asking if he is unwell.[50] His debates are even louder, and with the host and guests yelling over one another only the most simplistic arguments can be heard. If the yelling leads a guest to stomp off set, all the better. As a former employee of Times Now told us in an interview, participants "throwing off their mikes and leaving the studio" makes for "good TV." Moreover, the controversy generated by the channel often leads other channels to follow Goswami's stories.[51]

The visual loudness is similarly jarring. Multiple on-screen headlines flash across the screen, using discordant primary colors, bold and capital letters, alongside repetitive expressions of urgency (LIVE & BREAKING, BREAKING NEWS, NOW). Live video sits within all these hyperactive graphics—occasionally one feed, but more often two, three, or more. Each showing related but distinct footage of the same news story. As the Times Now journalist explained to us, when other channels would send one correspondent to cover a story, Arnab would send five—all of them expected to come up with different angles and insights.[52] Switching to different correspondents gives the story the feeling of movement and dynamism, which mirrors the techniques and visual grammar of television drama. When Arnab then draws the audience back to the studio for his evening debate, there are literally sparks dancing at the bottom of the screen—intended to whet anticipation about the incendiary discussion to come. The channel acts as though it is in a perpetual fight for your attention, forever having to raise the volume to keep you watching.

Ingredient number three: Feeling. When Arnab launched Times Now in 2006, he—rather than the marketing team—came up with the channel's tagline: "Feel the news." In Arnab's model, news channels do not report dispassionately or objectively. Their job, he believes, is to immerse themselves in the story and take sides. "I'm not neutral," he told an interviewer in 2020, "I'm absolutely not neutral. I detest the concept of neutrality in journalism."[53] For Arnab, explicitly taking sides demonstrates authenticity, frankness, and integrity. "Feeling the news" goes beyond the anchors expressing their views, however. It encompasses how each story is presented. Emotive language indicates how the audience should feel. Pounding background music is used to convey seriousness and weight, and the cloying melodies normally found in soap operas are used to communicate sadness.

Ingredient number four: Nationalism. For Arnab, nationalism is inherent to doing journalism. "Being a nationalist," he said in 2020, "is a prerequisite of being a journalist."[54] From this it follows that all Indian journalists should prioritize the national interest. "I believe," he said on another occasion, "all journalists should be for India. Simple."[55] He wears his own nationalism overtly and touts it constantly on screen. He presents his voice, and that of his channel, as the voice of the nation—hence his perennial slogan "The nation wants to know."

Yet the nationalism espoused by Arnab and other *Godi Media* outlets is of a particular type. It is not the civic, *swaraj* nationalism of Mahatma Gandhi, associated with India's push toward self-rule and intended to promote tolerance among all Indian communities. It is a narrow form of ethnic nationalism, associated with the Hindu-nationalist Hindutva movement.[56] Embodied by Modi and the BJP, Hindutva ideology conflates Indian national identity with Hindu identity. Ideologically it underpins a political project to ensure Hindu dominance of Indian society and culture, to the exclusion of India's other ethnic groups. In equating the nation with a single ethnic group, it has been described as a "Hindu supremacist," "Hindu fundamentalist," and even as a fascist ideology.[57] To its adherents, it is a project to restore Hindus' rightful place at the center of Indian society.

In Republic TV's coverage, the BJP and Modi himself are framed as the embodiment of this interpretation of the Indian nation. This produces a political logic whereby what the Modi government does is considered to be in the national interest, and opposition to it or criticism of it is considered to be against the national interest. This nationalism is combined with promoting a cult of personality around Modi as a uniquely popular and visionary leader.[58] From our analysis of coverage in 2021–22, Republic TV commentary is unswervingly adulatory of Modi. When Modi speaks, he is "incisive," "cuttingly accurate," and his speeches are "power-packed." His leadership, Republic TV states, is "unwavering." Even after an unexpectedly inconclusive 2024 election result, superlatives follow all of Modi's speeches and actions.

The flip side of exalting Modi and the BJP at any opportunity is the aggressive demonization of government critics and any group perceived as acting against the interests of the Hindu nationalist regime. This Hindu nation is, the news repeatedly claims, under constant threat from terrorists, anarchists, separatists, and from a dishonest, self-interested establishment. Throughout 2021 there were forty-nine Republic TV debates on terrorism, plots, or conspiracies. To watch Republic TV is to inhabit a place in perpetual fear of the "Other." The Other can be an Islamic terrorist cell, a Kashmiri militant, a Pakistan-funded plot, a Maoist insurgency, Khalistani separatism, or a global conspiracy against India. The opposition are demonized as terrorists, "Pak-sympathizers," and even "urban-Naxalites" (an incongruous reference to a rural Maoist insurgency in West Bengal in the 1960s and 1970s).[59] Anyone who opposes or criticizes the Modi regime is framed as a potential threat. Hashtags of Republic debates we analyzed capture this call to alarm: #TerrorLobbyExposed, #ConspiracyAgainstIndia, #PurgeTheEnemy, #GlobalKhalistanPlot, #NationVsForeignHand, #IndiaExposesGlobalPlot, #IndependenceFromTerror, #IndiaVsGlobalTerror.

The importance of nationalism to the *Godi Media* formula is shown by Arnab's brief attempt to whip up a "Nationalist Collective" in January 2021. In response to the Farmers' Protests during that period, Goswami announced the creation of "a committed group of Indians who will preempt and fight every attempt at targeting the Nation."[60] "Yesterday," he wrote in an open letter, "it was rioters in the name of farmers. Tomorrow, it will be Maoists and Maoist-terrorists, and the day after, it could be radicalized terrorists or any other such group." *We* must therefore, he said, "collect together and fight *them*" (italics added). The sole aim of the Collective would be "to put India first"; it would be "an Instrument in the Defence of the Nation," Arnab frames these supposed threats to the nation as "antinational elements," "complicit with India's external enemies like Pakistan," abusing the "liberties and rights *our* democracy gives *them*."[61] The campaign was Goswami's attempt to blame the recent revelatory WhatsApp leak— where he had secretly exchanged messages with the government about the forthcoming Balakot strike—on sinister dark forces. However, the political intervention of a news anchor to start a new nationalist social movement is an astonishing departure from the role previously expected of news anchors in democracies. As the executive editor of the independent Indian news site News Laundry put it to us, rather than being the watchdogs of the state, the *Godi Media* have become the attack dogs of the state.[62]

Ingredient number five: Populism. Like other populists worldwide, Arnab separates India's political world into a "pure people" and a "corrupt elite."[63] Prior to launching Republic TV, he claimed that "we will truly be the voice of the people"; a "people's movement."[64] This, he claims, is then proven by the channel's popularity, which has consistently led the ratings. By framing the channel as representing the will of the people, he implies that to challenge the channel's perspective is to oppose the people. Set in contrast to the people are the elite. These are, for Goswami, India's political dynasties, Congress politicians, and the Delhi media houses. These are variously called "the Lobby," "the Lutyens Club," the "Khan Market gang" (a shopping district in Delhi), or another label Goswami claims to have coined, the "Tukde-Tukde" gang (meaning those who want to divide the country). As if to demonstrate the closeness between Goswami's agenda and the Modi regime, Modi himself used the "Tukde Tukde gang" label against the opposition Congress Party in parliament in February 2022.[65] The anchor expressed his delight at this in his Republic TV debate two days later, at one point standing up and shouting over other speakers at the top of his voice that he was "guilty of a moment of pleasure" when the prime minister used his chosen populist slur.[66]

These five ingredients are the essence of the *Godi Media* formula. They have been developed and honed over the quarter of a century that Arnab has been in television. Since 2008 they have served him very well. His channels have come to dominate television news and the wider Indian news landscape. So successful have they been that you can find Arnab replicas across Indian TV news. Indeed, there are now so many channels using these ingredients that News Laundry began a series calling out the most inflammatory and misleading *Godi Media* coverage—calling it BloodLust TV.[67]

IS THIS A PROBLEM?

So what? Why should we care that this model has become so dominant? For decades of the twentieth century, Indian TV was controlled by the Doordarshan's broadcast monopoly. These new, boisterous, jingoistic channels could be seen just as an overdue reaction against the stifling colorlessness of Indian news previously. Equally, Arnab and his clones could be dismissed as entertainment rather than news, as distractions from the real business of politics, as sideshows, even as carnival acts. Yet we should care because these channels have become integral to politics in India. They show how commercial media can embrace their own co-optation by government and how their unremittingly positive coverage reduces citizens' ability to hold the government to account. They have become fundamental to the success of the Modi government's ethno-nationalist project, but their coverage can also lead to the justification of systematic prejudice and the normalization of mass violence against ethnic minorities.[68] These consequences can be seen in our analysis of the COVID-19 pandemic, the 2020–21 Farmers' Protests, and the rise in tensions between Hindus and Muslims in India.

COVID-19

The COVID-19 pandemic revealed how the *Godi Media*'s coverage could reduce the Indian government's accountability toward its people. At several points in the pandemic, the Modi government received scathing international criticism for its response. In March 2020 it imposed a lockdown with only four hours' notice, which led to a mass exodus of millions of newly unemployed workers back to their villages, provoking concern that this was spreading COVID-19 more rapidly across the country. However, rather than criticize the Modi government, India's TV news channels preferred to blame religious minorities for the disease's spread, specifically blaming the Muslim group Tablighi Jamaat for its annual religious gathering in Delhi.[69] The Hindi-language news channel ABP accused the group of being "the human bomb which can explode Coronavirus numbers."[70] Zee News asked if Tablighi Jamaat had "betrayed the nation" by holding its conference.[71] These outlets framed any criticism of the government's crisis response as political, arguing that the patriotic thing to do was to avoid challenging the Modi regime's efforts. A debate titled "Lockdown negativity gang strikes again" describes critics of Modi's policies as "creeping opportunists" in the pay of the USA, who must be "called out as liars."[72] Disapproval of Modi's policies was seen to be, at best, unhelpful, and at worst, anti-Indian.

By early 2021, despite the chaos and confusion of the early pandemic, the BJP and the news channels were exalting Modi's handling of it. As the prime minister received his first dose of the Covaxin vaccine, Arnab expressed how proud he was of him, and of how "he has ensured that India truly is ready to be COVID-free."[73] This closely echoed the government line. A BJP press release hailed its own leadership as a "proud and victorious nation" in the fight against COVID-19, thanks in large part to Modi's "able, sensible and visionary leadership."[74] Modi himself claimed at the World Economic Forum that India had "saved humanity from a big disaster by containing corona effectively."[75]

Then, only weeks later, India experienced one of the world's deadliest second COVID-19 waves. The outbreak itself was not the government's fault, emerging due to a new variant of the virus. However, once again the Modi administration failed to acknowledge the gravity of the situation until it was too late. In March the health minister, Harsh Vardhan, announced that India was in the "endgame" of the pandemic.[76] In April, Narendra Modi himself continued to hold mass campaign rallies in West Bengal, and let hundreds of thousands of Hindus participate in the Kumbh Mela in Uttarakhand, even as COVID-19 numbers spiked.[77] Meanwhile, images spread worldwide of corpses floating down India's rivers, and of countless bodies being burnt in improvised crematoria. By May there were reported to be more than 222,000 deaths, and more than twenty million COVID-19 cases.[78] The international press accused the Indian government of "arrogance," "recklessness," and "demogoguery."[79] An editorial in the *Lancet* said that "India squandered its early successes in controlling COVID-19."[80]

Despite this, TV news outlets repeated their position that the government should not be criticized, because to criticize government policy would be to undermine national unity. The opposition, Republic TV claimed, was playing politics with people's lives, and ignoring India's vaccine successes. Now was a time, Arnab argued, for politicians to #UniteAgainstCOVID, not for criticism of the BJP (#NoPoliticsNowPlease). "COVID-19: Time for India to Unite, Not to Settle Political Scores" was the theme of a typical Republic TV debate. But as the most popular YouTube comment in the thread stated, "It's not Politics—its Accountability of [those] in power."[81]

THE 2020–21 FARMERS' PROTESTS

The Farmers' Protests of 2020–21 provided further evidence of how far the *Godi Media* was willing to go to align itself with the administration, even if this meant misrepresenting and demonizing the same public they claimed to represent. The protests began in response to three new farming laws that sought to deregulate the food market and remove guaranteed minimum pricing. Farmers saw them as a fundamental threat to their livelihoods and communities. After two months of peaceful protest had provoked minimal political response, the farmers escalated. In November 2020 they called for *Delhi Chalo*—a march on the capital, asking the public to join them in a nationwide shutdown—250 million people, almost one in five Indians, joined the strike on November 26. Tens of thousands of farmers walked or drove to Delhi. Stopped by police at the city limits with water cannons, tear gas, and trenches, they blocked roads and set up camp.[82]

Until this point, the mainstream media—most notably the TV news channels—had largely ignored the protests.[83] Now they were impossible to ignore. But as the leading TV news outlets turned their cameras onto the protests, rather than trying to explain the farmers' cause they searched for evidence to undermine it. Republic TV and Times Now claimed the protests were instigated by political forces and that the farmers were "props."[84] On November 28 Zee News went further, claiming that many of the farmers were actually Khalistani separatists—referencing the Khalistani movement that had sought an independent state in Punjab.[85] The Khalistani accusation was then repeated by prominent BJP politicians, and in turn amplified by TV news outlets.[86] By December, broadcasters were routinely claiming that the protests were riddled with extremists—Khalistanis, Maoists, Naxalites, terrorists, and "antinationals."[87]

These claims seemed strange to reporters who were actually with the farmers; they found no signs of extremism and no reason to doubt their genuine anger at the farm bills.[88] The Editors Guild of India even issued a Media Advisory notice expressing its concern at the labeling of farmers as extremists "without any evidence or proof."[89] To the farmers themselves, the claims were not just bizarre but deeply offensive. They started to refer to the outlets as the fake or "Godi media." "Don't cover us, you are fake media," one protester's sign read, accompanied by the logos of Republic TV, Zee News, and Aaj Tak.[90] "Godi media is not allowed here" read another. Journalists started to be yelled at and chased away.[91] In their desperation to support the Modi government's policies, news channels had convinced many people that rather than being their voice they were their enemy.

ETHNIC NATIONALISM AND THE RISK OF SECTARIAN VIOLENCE

Godi Media threaten to do the most harm to India's fragile plurality and peaceful diversity in their aggressive promotion of the BJP's Hindutva agenda, and in their normalization of sectarian violence and justification of Hindu discrimination against Muslims. The Hindutva movement promises, in essence, to Make India Great Again, with Modi the inspirational leader who will make it happen.[92] But the key difference with similar "Make a Country Great Again" projects worldwide is that to make India great again is to make Hindu India great again. The strategic narrative driving the movement mythologizes Hindus as a downtrodden group, enslaved over a millennium by Buddhists, Muslims, and later the British

Empire.[93] The Hindutva movement aims to reverse this alleged subjugation, despite Hindus representing more than 80 percent of India's population and being represented by the party of government.

These themes regularly feature in our analysis of *Godi Media* channels, which frame Hindus as disrespected, discriminated against, and misrepresented. Debate topics on Republic TV and Times Now ask "Is being Hindu a disadvantage?," "What is Hinduphobia and why is it important?," "Hinduphobia alive and real," and "Hindus under attack."[94] These debates emphasize alleged discrimination against Hindus, but we found no debate that centered on discrimination against Muslims. Some anchors, such as Arnab, go as far as lauding Hindutva and claiming it is inherent to Indian nationality. "Hindutva means the way of life, the philosophy, the culture and the tradition" Arnab said at the start of one of his primetime debates in 2021, "and I think that it is a beautiful tradition; a beautiful philosophy, a beautiful way of life."[95]

In contrast, Muslims were presented as villains, aggressors, and terrorists. An analysis of forty-four debates on these channels between 2014 and 2018 found that Muslims were invariably described using antagonistic terms, and Hindus were routinely portrayed as victims. They portray Hindus as "hated, jobless, at a disadvantage, denied rights," while Islam "has a free run, is replete with brutality, sickening depravity, rage and terror."[96] This invective mirrors the rhetoric of politicians—illustrating again the symbiosis between the BJP government and the *Godi Media*. NDTV's "VIP hate speech" tracker claimed to have identified a 1130 percent rise in hate speech by officials in the eight years following Modi's 2014 ascent to power, with more than 80 percent of these instances attributed to BJP politicians.[97] During this "hate pandemic," Muslims were variously described as "bigoted and violent oppressors of Hindus," as "unpatriotic, loyal to Pakistan, terrorists, sexual predators, love jihadis, cow-killers, child breeders and infiltrators."[98]

The impression of Muslims as a threat to Indian society is reinforced by a series of media-concocted scandals that have accused them of various forms of "jihad." Muslims are, these channels purport, waging "bureaucratic Jihad"—taking over government bureaucracy. They are also waging "love jihad" and compromising Indian marriages with "triple talaq." "Love jihad" was the claim that Muslim men were seducing Hindu women in order to convert them and grow the Muslim population in India. "Triple talaq" asserted that Muslim men in India were divorcing their wives simply by saying "talaq" three times. Twenty-six debates from 2014 to 2018 on Times Now and Republic TV focused on these topics.[99] These claims, which were not substantiated in the coverage, alleged an ethnic group-wide conspiracy to out-breed and marginalize a majority population, resembling the "Great Replacement" and "White Genocide" narratives told by far-right groups in Europe and the United States.

To these the *Godi Media* added "COVID jihad": spreading COVID-19 deliberately, and more specifically, "Thook jihad" or "spit jihad."[100] This was the contention that Muslims were spitting on other people's food, or even at other people, to infect them. Aman Chopra (another Goswami simulacrum) spent an hour of his News 18 program playing videos showing people—all apparently Muslims—spitting on food or utensils. Closer inspection revealed these to be untrue—none of them were doing so.[101] But it was used to generate outrage, "to not only show Muslims as profane and uncivilized but also as full of hatred towards Hindus."[102]

Manisha Pande is the executive editor of News Laundry and the host of its show "Newsance"— "your weekly dose of all the insanity that passes off as news on TV." Her insightful and acerbic observations about Indian TV news have become essential viewing for concerned citizens and media watchers. Speaking to us for this chapter, Pande expressed her fears about the consequences of this escalating demonization of Islam. Before the riots of 2022 and the protests of 2021, there had already been months of "Muslim-blaming" for COVID-19, Pande said, with *Godi Media* channels "claiming that COVID would not have come to India were it not for Muslims." This vitriol encourages abuse of, and violence toward, Muslims. "It is all about division. Vitriolic rhetoric has become normalized. You can openly say almost anything [against Muslims] now."[103] Her comments are supported by reports from human rights groups. Amnesty International recorded "181 incidents of alleged hate crimes in the first half of 2019, the steepest rise in such incidents since 2015."[104] And in 2022 Human Rights Watch reported that "Attacks against religious minorities were carried out with impunity" under the BJP regime.[105]

THE CONSEQUENCES OF GOING GODI

The *Godi Media*'s rhetoric toward Muslims is not only inflaming communal tensions but also having geopolitical consequences. On May 26, 2022, Nupur Sharma, the BJP spokesperson, appeared on the evening primetime debate on Times Now to speak about the ongoing controversy around the Gyanvapi mosque. The controversy concerned a bitter debate about whether the mosque rests on the site of a former Hindu temple, and therefore should be reappropriated as a site for Hindu, rather than Muslim, worship. This was similar to the decades-old Ayodhya dispute, in which India's Supreme Court finally judged in 2019 that the site of the Babri mosque, destroyed in a Hindu nationalist rally in 1992, should be repurposed as a Hindu temple.[106] The debate contained the typical back and forth shouting—along with derogatory remarks about religious groups and Islam. In this instance, the official spokesperson Sharma chose to insult the Prophet Mohammad.

Initially, the anchor, Nikita Kumar, hardly reacted; nor did Times Now's audience, the channel, or the government. Why would they? They were already accustomed to these sorts of debates and comments. However, a few days later there was a reaction. On Friday June 3, demonstrations broke out in response to the comments in Kanpur, Uttar Pradesh. These escalated to violent clashes with police, and more than six thousand people were arrested.

The dispute then went international. Two days later, Qatar, Kuwait, and Iran told India's ambassador's they too were outraged by Sharma's comments. Saudi Arabia and the UAE followed shortly afterward. Having taken no action to this point, the BJP then decided to suspend Sharma, calling her a "fringe element." But she was not a fringe element. Her comments were similar to many that she and others had made—and been encouraged to make—on these channels. They are littered throughout our analysis of *Godi Media* TV debates. However, the outlets appeared unable to see that their incendiary rhetoric was inflaming communal violence and provoking geopolitical responses. To emphasize the dangers of this, the

Editors Guild of India wrote an open letter to India's media on June 8. Some television channels, it said, are "deliberately creating circumstances that target vulnerable communities by spewing hatred towards them and their beliefs." These channels, it went on, "were seemingly inspired by the values of Radio Rwanda whose incendiary broadcast caused a genocide in the African nation."[107] The representatives of India's newspapers were literally warning that TV news debates could lead to mass killings. Yet the very next day, on his debate at nine, Arnab was back on his soapbox, claiming that Hindus were the victims of discrimination. "What about Hindu sentiments? Do they matter?," he asked rhetorically. "Are Hindus expected to soak it in, be tolerant about it, and carry on?."[108]

* * *

India's *Godi Media* has now reached the stage where there are enough outlets, with sufficient dominance of the Indian news ecology, to manufacture a parallel reality. In this parallel reality, the Modi government's handling of COVID-19 was a great success, it is guiding the economy to ever greater heights, and it is leading India to a more powerful and respected position on the world stage. The only threats to this rosy future come from the self-interested machinations of "the Lobby" in Delhi, from terrorists and extremists, and from the "Pakistan-backed" Muslim minority. Whatever is actually happening in the world, the news is made to conform with this picture. It is no coincidence that this parallel reality conforms closely with how the Modi government wants Indians to see the world.

There are limits to the persuasiveness of this parallel reality. It works at demonizing the Muslim "other," at inflating jingoistic patriotism, and at obscuring government mistakes. Yet in the 2024 election it did not manage to convince enough people of being something that went against their direct experience. So divorced had the *Godi Media*'s coverage become from people's economic circumstances that many voters discounted its partisan claims. Modi failed to gain the 400-plus seats he desperately craved for a supermajority in parliament, and he had to settle for a coalition government.

Moreover, this parallel reality does not come without resistance. Some independent outlets are willing to criticize the government, such as The Caravan, The Wire, and News Laundry, even though such criticism is becoming more dangerous (in 2020, two hundred journalists were physically attacked and sixty-seven were arrested across the country).[109] During India's second COVID-19 wave, a few outlets issued rare censure of the Modi regime for "bungling" its response, for being "missing" in action, with one even suggesting India was a "failed state."[110] The Farmer's Protests show how the *Godi Media* can provoke public resistance, especially when their coverage grossly misrepresents the reality on the ground. Despite this, *Godi Media* outlets derive credibility by styling themselves as purveyors of the news and falsely claiming independence. As Manisha Pande told us, "the problem is, that amongst many in India, news is trusted. It is seen as a source of what is happening in the world. So, if the channels tell them a Muslim is a snake, people believe he is a snake."[111] This residual credibility, no matter how inflammatory or misleading news content may be, is at the root of the *Godi Media* phenomenon. Taking advantage of that credibility is the very reason governments are using news channels to help them dictate reality today.

GODI MEDIA GOES GLOBAL

Although the *Godi Media* model pioneered by Arnab Goswami evolved within India's diverse and noisy media landscape, it is not just an Indian phenomenon. The raucous, cacophonous, nationalistic style may be less prevalent elsewhere, but one can now find Arnabs across the broadcasting world, from autocracies to democracies. As chapter 2 showed, Russia has no shortage of bellicose and patriotic news anchors, such as Vladmir Solovyev, whose state news talk shows and radio phone-ins combine state propaganda with his rants about the Russia-Ukraine war.

Still, it is not that surprising to find anchors and channels so willing to align themselves closely with an autocratic regime—although even in

Russia the carnivalesque ultra-nationalism is distinct from the gloomy, dull Soviet news broadcasts of the Cold War.[112] More surprising is the growth of Arnab-like presenters in democracies. These are different from Goswami in that they may back opposition politicians and parties rather than the government. Yet at the same time they share an attitude, style, and a commitment to manufacturing their own reality that is similar to the Republic TV anchor. Indeed, Arnab has frequently been likened to Tucker Carlson in the United States, and Republic TV with Fox News, the channel where Carlson made his name.[113] Like Arnab, Carlson flaunts his lack of neutrality, gives long opinionated lectures, peppers his programs with emotive and inflammatory claims and language, and adopts a populist and ethnic nationalist agenda.[114]

Similar to Goswami, Carlson claims to be defending a downtrodden majority ethnic group, although in Carlson's case it is white Christian Americans he is defending—"legacy Americans" as he calls them. As an in-depth *New York Times* investigation of Carlson and his Fox News primetime show found in 2022, for him it is the white male majority who are discriminated against, disrespected, and attacked (a claim he has made in more than six hundred episodes).[115] Like Goswami, Carlson tells his viewers that they "inhabit a civilization under siege," although in this case the barbarians at the gate are immigrants, refugees, and nonwhites. Like Republic TV, the cause of this, the real villains, are "they"—the established "ruling class" as Carlson calls them, but in Carlson's case "they" are the Washington elite, along with the mainstream media, liberal celebrities, academics, and tech giants. Apparently "they" are not interested in the nation or its people; they are purely self-interested. And, just as in India, a host of other TV anchors have adopted elements of Carlson's approach, including other current and former presenters on Fox News—Jesse Watters, Sean Hannity, and Laura Ingraham—and those on NewsMax and OANN.

In reproducing this ethno-nationalist rhetoric, anchors such as Arnab Goswami and Tucker Carlson appear to merge with the populist politicians (Modi and Trump) that they promote. The anchors, just like the politicians, claim to channel the popular will and assert that they represent the fears and aspirations of the *true* citizens of their nations. It is little surprise, therefore, that there is frequent speculation that both anchors might run for political office—with *Time* magazine describing Carlson as "the most powerful Conservative in America."[116]

The merging between news anchor and politician is just as evident in Europe. Despite regulation that obliges broadcast impartiality, there has been a growth in nationalist, opinionated anchors and emotive news channels. In France, news anchor Eric Zemmour used his ultra-nationalist, polemical role on CNews as a springboard for his unsuccessful candidacy for the presidency in 2022. In the UK, the blending of news anchor and politician has become even more common. A bevy of conservative politicians, for example, have also worked as news presenters on the new right-wing channel, GB News. This includes the founder of the Reform Party, Nigel Farage, the then-Conservative Party Chairman Lee Anderson, and the Conservative ministers Jacob Rees-Mogg and Esther McVey (see chapter 7).[117] The emergence of the news anchor as a hyperpartisan political figure is a long way from the staid, neutral, softly spoken archetype that populated broadcasting in the late twentieth century.

Why do we see the rise of this new model of news across the world? A model that reverses traditional perceptions of the role of the news. A model in which news anchors do not try to inform viewers about what is new or even true, but who seek to confirm and enhance their audiences' existing politics, prejudices, and paranoias.

It is partly down to market competition. The last two decades have seen a flourishing of new TV channels and news outlets, thanks to how easy and cheap technology and distribution have become. The explosion of news in India has been greater than in most countries (there are now 383 news channels in India), but it is symptomatic of a much broader expansion.[118] The United States, for example, has more than forty broadcast news outlets, and more online. These rely on advertising revenue to survive, and to gain this they need public attention. In such supercompetitive markets you have to shout to be heard, and fight for exclusive content and access. If a government chooses to take advantage of this—and numerous governments have—it gains leverage to shape and distort the news agenda.

It is also down to cost. Manufacturing news stories is far cheaper than reacting to them, especially if the storyline and the format remain much the same. When keeping afloat from one day to the next is your chief concern, as it has become for many news outlets, reducing your costs is a strong incentive. This is one of the reasons that in India and elsewhere news outlets deliberately focus on one or two stories a day, rather than multiple ones. As our interviewees told us, *Godi Media* channels such as Republic choose a couple of stories that are designed to fit a simple, repetitive master narrative.[119] The stories rotate the same cast of "folk devils"—be it immigrants, Muslims, terrorists (loosely defined), global elites, or the Deep State—and describe an ongoing moral panic about the threat they are meant to pose to the nation. They venerate a single hero—typically the leader—as the embodiment of the nation, and its savior. Sticking to this story enables news to be produced at a relatively low cost, while achieving high audience figures. And by producing slavishly pro-government content, it ensures government advertising and patronage.

It is also a consequence of the shift in power away from legacy media. Neither the Modi government, nor many other governments around the world, feel they need print or broadcast media as they once did. Social media gives them channels through which they can communicate directly with the public and reach their supporters unedited and unfiltered.

Finally, *Godi Media* can only survive if there is a public appetite both for this form of news and the populist anchors who promote it. Right now there appears to be an appetite for both. The public proclivity for authoritarian personalities as heads of state—as seen in the rise of the populist strongman—seems to extend to strongman TV news anchors.[120] Strongmen who are defined as those who are willing to defy convention, eschew political correctness, welcome conflict, and offer simplistic solutions to the complexities of contemporary life (such as explaining that all problems can be blamed on religious or ethnic minorities, antinationals, separatists, the political opposition, or globalists).[121] According to the Pew Research Center, 48 percent of Indians and 50 percent of Hindus want a Leader with a Strong Hand in preference to a Democratic Form of Leadership.[122] For enough viewers, anchors such as Arnab Goswami seem to be on their side, ready to explain to them why they are right to believe what they believe, and desperate to warn them that their way of life is under threat from a host of enemies.

The result is news that deliberately does not seek to reflect reality. News that does not seek to inform, educate, and challenge audiences. News that seeks to present the world in a way that the government of the day wants and that panders to the prejudices of the audience. News that provides guaranteed drama and conflict, but with all the uncomfortable and critical news filtered out. News that takes a strong view not just on what is right and wrong, but on who deserves to be considered a citizen and who does not. News that deliberately seeks to polarize society. News that normalizes state violence, domestically and internationally. News that threatens democracy.

* * *

In the summer of 2022, Gautam Adani, a close friend of Narendra Modi and among the world's richest people, acquired just under 30 percent of the broadcast news channel NDTV. Adani had not previously shown much interest in media, making most of his vast fortune from government contracts for Indian energy and infrastructure. But in advance of Modi's national election campaign for a third term in 2024, Adani suddenly decided he would make a hostile takeover bid for one of India's only remaining independent TV news channels. This was the channel at which Arnab Goswami began his TV news career. The channel where he presented himself as a measured, scholarly news anchor, before morphing into the brazen and boisterous *Arnab* of later years. After Goswami left, NDTV maintained this more reserved air and—unlike Goswami—it criticized rather than championed Modi's administration when it won power. In return, the channel and its journalists found themselves ostracized, harassed, and intimidated. "India is going through an aggressive variant of McCarthyism against the media," one of the channel's founders, Prannoy Roy, told Reuters in 2018.[123] By the end of 2022, Adani had managed to acquire almost two-thirds of NDTV, making him the largest shareholder. His ambition, he said, was to build an international media house comparable "to the *Financial Times* or Al Jazeera."[124] Despite the new owner's nod to the importance of media independence, it was not long before the news channel softened its approach to politics and the BJP. It screened an adulatory documentary about Modi himself, mollified its adversarial political coverage, and upped its output of celebrities and crime.[125] It eschewed news that jeopardized the reputation or popularity of the government or its friends, leading to an exodus of editorial personnel. More than a dozen senior NDTV staff resigned, Bloomberg reported, "over directives to avoid storylines that entangle government allies."[126] By the time the 2024 election campaign kicked off, the reconstruction of mainstream broadcast news was complete. It was all *Godi Media* now.

6

MASS DELUSION

Bolsonaro's Brazil

---

*In a world that has really been turned upside down, the true is a moment
of the false.*

—GUY DEBORD, *SOCIETY OF THE SPECTACLE*

C hairs lay overturned and strewn around the marble floor. Long, high
windows looking out across the Three Powers square were shattered.
As Mulatas, a Brazilian modernist mural that stretched across the
third floor mezzanine of the Presidential Palace, had been stabbed multiple
times. The desk of Juscelino Kubitschek, the Brazilian president who established Brasilia, had been turned on its side and used as a barricade. It was
Monday morning, January 9, 2023, the day after all three of the buildings
that signify Brazil's separate governing powers—the executive, the legislative, and the judiciary—had been wrecked. Trashed by a marauding mob of
yellow- and green-shirted protesters.

Yet the damage was not structural. There had been no attempt to blow
up the buildings or to topple the pillars propping up the Congress. Moreover, the vandals ransacked the capital on a Sunday so the buildings were

mostly empty. President Luis Inácio Lula da Silva, known as "Lula," had been inaugurated the week before and was down near Sao Paulo seeing the effects of the recent flooding. The former president, Jair Bolsonaro, on whose behalf the protestors claimed they were acting, was in Florida and about to be admitted to hospital with stomach pain. If this was an insurrection, it was an insurrection as conceived in a teenage bedroom—naïve, emotional, and attention-seeking, without any realistic expectation of revolutionary consequence.

Indeed, to see the events of January 8 as an attempt to overthrow the existing government misunderstands their rationale and significance. It was a spectacle: a performative insurrection to be live-streamed across YouTube, Instagram, Twitter, Telegram, TikTok, Facebook, Gab, Parler, and Kwai. For many of these *bolsonarista* protesters, the virtual had become real. This was best described by the French philosopher and filmmaker, Guy Debord, back in 1967: "The spectacle," Debord wrote, "cannot be understood as a mere visual excess produced by mass media technologies. It is a worldview that has actually been materialized. It has become an objective reality."[1] When a protester filmed himself appearing to defecate in the Presidential Palace, he was demonstrating his literal and metaphorical disdain for Brazil's democratic institutions—via Twitter.[2] The act would have been pointless without the opportunity to record and share it via social media.

Calling January 8 a spectacle does not reduce its importance. It highlights the extent to which large sections of Brazilian society were submerged in spectacle by 2023 and suffering from what the *New York Times* journalist Jack Nicas called "mass delusion."[3] This mass delusion did not happen overnight. Nor did it date from October 30, 2022, when Lula da Silva narrowly beat Jair Bolsonaro in the second round of the Brazilian election—a result the *bolsonaristas* believed was fraudulent. This mass delusion was the product of years of conscious effort, much of it driven by Bolsonaro's government. It was the result of thousands of false narratives manufactured by those working within the state to delude the public and disseminated through a multiplicity of new media channels. Neither was this mass delusion just about the result of the 2022 election; it was also about the legitimacy of Brazil's democratic process, the integrity of its governing institutions, the probity of elected members of Congress, the welfare of the Amazon, and the competence of the government's COVID-19 response. It was a consequence of a whole disinformation ecosystem that had been built over the previous decade and had helped to create a parallel digital reality, now inhabited by much of the Brazilian population.

This chapter is about how that ecosystem was constructed, how it worked, and why its significance goes far beyond Brazil. It is based on evidence and findings from a series of inquiries and investigations into "fake news," "antidemocratic acts," and "digital militias" conducted by Brazil's Congress, Supreme Court, and police between 2019 and 2023. The inquiries sought to expose the disinformation ecosystem established by the Bolsonaros and their supporters before the 2018 election and during their administration. Their evidence is jaw-dropping, but also scattered, inconsistent, and incomplete. In this chapter we draw together all the available documentation and combine it with a detailed study of contemporary Brazilian news reporting, supplemented with original social media research. Piecing together each of these jigsaw pieces, and guided by interviews with people who lived through these events, we explain how the Bolsonaro regime engineered such a sprawling (dis)information ecosystem and what its implications are for democracies elsewhere.

BRAZIL'S LOVE OF SOCIAL MEDIA

Brazilian society is unusually susceptible to submersion in alternative realities, in part due to its enthusiastic embrace of social media. By the 2022 presidential election, Brazilians were spending more than three and a half hours a day on social media—mostly via smartphones.[4] Almost an hour of this was on WhatsApp, which has become the default method of communication in Brazil and is used by 80 percent of the population.[5] Unlike in the United States, the Meta-owned app is used not only for chatting with friends but for work, politics, religion, and sharing news.[6] Poorer Brazilians are especially dependent on WhatsApp and its sister services, Instagram and Facebook, because Meta subsidizes access to them. Meta's partnerships with Brazilian telecoms providers allow someone to keep using its apps even when their fixed data allowance—their *franquias*—runs out. In 2018, two-thirds of Brazilians had a *franquias* plan, making a significant number reliant on Meta's services.[7]

The content Brazilians share mainly consists of videos, images, and memes. Brazil's mass media has long been mainly visual—popular print newspapers never really took off.[8] More Brazilians use YouTube than any other country except the United States and India, and over half of the population use Instagram.[9] Add to this their fondness for TikTok, and another Chinese video sharing service called Kwai, and you get an idea of how hooked Brazilians are on social media. In fact, the average Brazilian regularly uses nine different social media platforms—more than people in any other country.[10] When coupled with Brazilians' fast-declining trust in legacy media, and with more than half saying they consciously avoid the news, social media has become the country's de facto public sphere.[11]

What Brazilians see on social media depends on who they follow, and many follow influencers. Brazilians are twice as likely to follow an influencer as the global average (44 percent versus 22 percent), and surveys suggest they are more swayed by what influencers say than anyone else in the world.[12] This is why the principal 2022 election candidates, Lula and Bolsonaro, vied for endorsements from footballers (such as @NeymarJr: 204m Instagram followers—who endorsed Bolsonaro), YouTubers (such as @FelipeNeto: 45m YouTube subscribers—who endorsed Lula), and singers (@Anitta: 64m Instagram followers—who endorsed Lula) over endorsements from traditional media outlets. Gone are the days when Roberto Marinho, the founder of Brazil's broadcasting behemoth TV Globo, could inflate the candidacy of Fernando Collor de Mello in the 1989 presidential election and frame a youthful Lula as the candidate of "disorder, fanaticism and insanity" and see Collor win.[13] When it comes to entertainment, fashion, sports, fitness, beauty, news, and politics, Brazilians now look to one of the five hundred thousand Brazilian influencers on social media for guidance.[14]

This makes for a chaotic, crowded, and raucous digital public sphere, which has given Brazilian politics a particular tone, style, and form. But digital politics in Brazil did not emerge fully formed when most Brazilians adopted smartphones in the 2010s. It evolved over three decades as the internet developed. One figure who shaped both Brazil's digital public sphere and its political information ecosystem was a self-styled philosopher and mystic called Olavo de Carvalho.

THE SPLENETIC STANDARD-BEARER OF
BRAZIL'S NEW RIGHT

Olavo de Carvalho began his career as a journalist in the mid-1960s. Similar to other twenty-somethings at the time, he flirted briefly with communism before turning against it and, with the zeal of the convert, becoming convinced that communism was the source of the world's evils. By the mid-1970s he went freelance. Alongside his journalism he went on a two-decade intellectual odyssey, studying and self-publishing books on an eclectic range of topics including astrological symbolism, universality, Gramsci, and Aristotle.[15] At the same time, he experimented with mysticism and Sufism, even being appointed a *muqaddam* (a religious official or teacher).[16] By the 1990s he was a regular commentator in Brazil's mainstream press, —including in Bravo!, República, Época, and O Globo—and was gaining a reputation as a formidable right-wing polemicist.[17]

Carvalho was frustrated by the constraints of traditional media and its closeness to those in power, and in 1998 he started blogging. In 2002 he launched an online publication—*Midia Sem Mascara* (Media Without a Mask)—in which he published contributions from conservative writers who railed against corruption in Brazil's government and mainstream media.[18] Over the next few years, whenever new self-publishing tools emerged, Carvalho exploited them. When the social media site Orkut launched in 2004, two of the first political forums focused on Carvalho's works. After YouTube launched in 2005, he started uploading interviews and commentary. In 2006, he began his own radio show—suitably titled *True Outspeak*.[19] For Carvalho, every new media platform was a fresh way to publicize his ideas, grow his audience, and attack established media and left-wing politicians. He was a strange mix of cyberjunkie, soothsayer, and Rush Limbaugh.[20]

The idea that the established media exerted malign control of the public agenda was fundamental to Carvalho's critique of the existing political system. For Carvalho, Brazil's postwar left had successfully adopted the ideas of the Italian communist philosopher Antonio Gramsci.[21] Marx's predictions of communist revolution had failed, Gramsci wrote in the 1930s, because Marx had underestimated the importance of culture.[22] If the left wanted to win power, it first had to win the culture war. This, Carvalho thought, the left had achieved in Brazil after the military dictatorship ended in 1985. Seventeen years later, Lula da Silva's first election victory was the inevitable outcome of the left's cultural dominance. The established media (mostly communists according to Carvalho) then perpetuated the left's power by manufacturing consensus around topics such as human rights, global governance, and climate change. By Carvalho's rationale, only by undermining the established media and its associated culture warriors (notably at universities) could the right regain power and recenter society around the conservative values of family, nation, and religion.[23] Similar ideas have been adopted by the populist right worldwide.

Once one understands Carvalho's worldview his dyspeptic attitudes and behavior become more explicable.[24] His enthusiastic embrace of digital media platforms was a way of avoiding and denigrating traditional media outlets. The credibility he gave to outlandish theories and global conspiracies came from his inherent distrust of the mainstream media. He was sympathetic with claims that the world may be flat, that a Bilderberg-type clique was seeking to establish a New World Order, that climate change is a hoax, that vaccines kill you or drive you mad, that the Inquisition was a Protestant myth, and that homosexuality was incompatible with democracy.[25] Mainstream media narratives, he believed, were deliberately invented or distorted to promote liberal, universalist values. He was similarly scathing toward intellectual elites and citizens for spreading and believing these ideas in two of his most popular books: *The Collective Moron* and *The Least You Need to Know Not to Be an Idiot.*

He justified his often expletive-laden, scatological language by arguing that to respond diplomatically to his "enemies" would be tantamount to collusion. A "delicate response," he wrote, "would be complicit with the intolerable."[26] In his Manichaean and paranoid *weltanschauung*, the only way to break the stranglehold of cultural Marxism was to bring down the whole liberal democratic system and the Western intellectual elites upholding it. In this sense, Carvalho was South America's equivalent to the American political insurgent Steve Bannon.

Without social media and the other digital tools that emerged in the early twenty-first century, Carvalho would have remained a marginal, maverick, iconoclastic figure. Especially after he decamped to rural Virginia in 2005 with his collection of plaid shirts, smoking pipes, and shotguns.[27] As he learned to take advantage of these new digital tools, he gained a following in Brazil as a trenchant critic of Lula's PT (Worker's Party) government, and a key proponent of Brazil's New Right. Among those who discovered Carvalho's online screeds were Jair Bolsonaro's three older sons—Flavio (#01), Carlos (#02), and Eduardo (#03). Flavio, a state deputy in Rio de Janeiro, was so taken with Carvalho's ideas that he traveled to Richmond, Virginia, in 2012 to present the ideologue with a medal (all recorded on YouTube, of course).[28] The Bolsonaro boys then introduced Carvalho to their father, Jair, who was similarly smitten, and Carlos streamed discussions between the right-wing guru and the president on YouTube in 2014.[29] It was the Bolsonaros' embrace of Carvalho's philosophy and methods that would provide the strategic rationale and direction for the construction of a parallel information ecosystem once they were in office.

Still, in 2014, both Carvalho and the Bolsonaros were niche figures. It almost certainly would have remained this way but for a series of disturbances that exploded across Brazilian politics between 2013 and 2018. On Thursday June 6, 2013, two thousand people blocked traffic on one of Sao Paulo's main roads, *Avenida Paulista*, protesting against the rising price of public transport. Two weeks later these protests had spread to 140 cities and involved 1.4 million people.[30] Transport prices drove the protests initially, but they quickly became a means of expressing Brazilians' broader frustrations with the state of their country: from anger about excessive government spending (notably on the 2014 World Cup and the 2016 Olympics) to concerns over police violence, the economic downturn, and resentment with media monopolies.[31] The following year the *Lavo Jato* (Car Wash) scandal reignited the protests. *Lavo Jato* started as a police investigation into a money-laundering operation above a petrol station (hence the name), but as can happen when investigations "follow the money," it ended up exposing a vast network of corrupt politicians and industrialists. So extensive was the corruption that the operation lasted almost seven years and led to the imprisonment of senior figures from across politics and industry.[32] Protests continued sporadically through 2015 and 2016.

These public protests would not have been so widespread and persistent without digital tools. People learned about the protests via smartphones and Facebook, monitored them via Twitter, filmed them using Instagram and YouTube, and discussed them on WhatsApp.[33] This digitally empowered activism was nurtured by online movements such as Vem Pra Rua (VPR) (Come to the Streets) and Movimento Brasil Libre (MBL) (The Free Brazil Movement). Groups like VPR mainly sought greater government accountability, but groups like MBL wanted to shift public sentiment to the right, toward figures such as Jair Bolsonaro.[34] Those who founded and incubated these movements, such as Carla Zambelli, would go on to become central figures in Bolsonaro's disinformation ecosystem.

Jair Bolsonaro was well-placed to benefit from this burgeoning antiestablishment and anti-PT sentiment, which came to be called *antipetismo*. Ever since he was elected to Brazil's Lower House in 1990 Bolsonaro had been considered a peripheral, slightly preposterous figure. He ignored the issues that engaged his colleagues. Instead, he lauded past military dictatorships, pushed for higher military pay, and even advocated for civil war. On social issues he was so unashamedly conservative that mainstream media would give him airtime just to attract attention and provoke outrage.[35] He was like an embarrassing, bigoted uncle: someone guaranteed to make a racist, misogynistic, homophobic comment.[36] So marginal was he to the political establishment that from the public's perspective he was not compromised by *Lavo Jato*. When swathes of his colleagues faced corruption accusations, he was left relatively untainted.

To benefit from this populist surge, Bolsonaro had to convince people that voting for him was the best way to express their contempt for the political establishment. He needed to be viewed as the answer to the frustrations of Brazil's agrarian landowners, the aspirations of Brazil's free marketeers, the social conservatism of its Christian evangelicals, and the *antipetismo* of ordinary Brazilians. For this he could not rely on the traditional media as they had long written him off as a noxious, comic anachronism. "I cannot have a contrary opinion," he said of the press back in 2011, "because I am considered prejudiced."[37] Instead, he would need to depend on digital tools and social networks. For this he would have to rely on his second son—#02 or *Zero Dois*—Carlos Bolsonaro.

THE "BEAST" OF THE BOLSONAROS

Carlos—or *Carluxo*—was a professional politician before he even reached adulthood. At age seventeen his father pressed him to stand as councilor in Rio de Janeiro against his mother (with whom Jair had recently separated). Carlos, who idolized his father (later having his father's face tattooed on his right arm), stood and won. His inauguration was just after his eighteenth birthday. With little time to develop his own ideology, Carlos's political views closely paralleled his father's, if anything going even further to the right. To address poverty and homelessness, Carlos proposed giving social welfare payments only to those who agreed to be sterilized.[38] He spoke out against LGBTQ education in schools and fulminated against the increasing influence of what he called the "Gay dictatorship."[39] He defended gun ownership and the liberalization of gun laws. Yet Carlos was always more concerned about his father's career than his own. From the beginning he cast himself as his father's protector. Whenever his father was criticized he would leap to his defense—a frequent occurrence given Jair's outlandish views. This placed Carlos on constant alert for critics and detractors. The magazine *Veja* would later write that Carlos sees "enemies around every corner," has a "difficult" temperament, and is "sensitive to conspiracy theories."[40] He became a sworn enemy of Brazil's big media outlets, believing they were institutionally leftist and systematically biased against his father. He referred to Brazil's most respected political newspaper *Folha de Sao Paulo* as the "sickle of Sao Paulo"—a reference to the hammer and sickle of the Soviet flag.[41]

Relatively reserved in public, Carlos was—in his father's words—a "beast" online. Anyone who dared criticize his dad would face a volley of abuse from him. But beyond Twitter outbursts, Carlos had a broader fascination with the power of online tools and a natural talent for exploiting them politically. It was this talent, especially his "genius" on social media, as one opponent put it, that made him instrumental in creating the parallel information architecture that helped his father win the 2018 election.[42]

Carlos's digital strategy to get Jair Bolsonaro elected took almost a decade. It began when he set up a Bolsonaro family website and started his father's YouTube channel in 2009, having been running his own since 2007. A Jair Bolsonaro Twitter account followed in 2010, and a public Facebook page in 2013. On each platform, he tailored content to grow his and his father's profiles. He combined softer posts about their family holidays, to temper his father's irascible reputation, with harder posts that asserted his conservative credentials. Over time Carlos became more familiar with different digital tools and how to mobilize online supporters to take down political opponents. By 2014 his online efforts helped quadruple his father's vote in the legislature, at which point the Bolsonaros announced that Jair Bolsonaro would run for president in 2018.[43]

As the Bolsonaros grew their father's online presence, they experimented with different techniques. In 2016, they used the municipal elections in Rio de Janeiro, in which Flavio was standing, as a sandbox for testing methods they would subsequently use in 2018. Watching the campaign play out online, three researchers in Rio's NetLab discovered thousands of automated accounts (bots) and cyborg accounts (part bot, part human) that were frantically promoting the Bolsonaros or attacking their opponents.[44] Some of these were "campaigner bots," political cheerleaders who amplified pro-Bolsonaro messages. Others were "inciting agents," firestarter bots whose job was to provoke, assault, and inflame.[45] According to the researchers, the inciting agents were also "synthetically promoting and testing narratives" with distinct voter groups on issues such as sex education, LGBTQ rights, the communist menace, and moral disorder.

Using the 2016 election as a laboratory helped Carlos and his brothers develop a formidable digital arsenal of "trolls, bots, cyborgs, sock puppets" to support his father's 2018 presidential campaign.[46] As well as automated accounts, each Bolsonaro brother had millions of volunteers and supporters across multiple social media platforms. Nor were these followers passive. They were loud, active, and organized. Some assigned themselves military ranks of lieutenant or general and sorted themselves into brigades, battalions, and commands.[47] Some of them were trained in the language and philosophy of the culture wars via YouTube classes hosted by Olavo de Carvalho himself.[48] They were, effectively, a *bolsonarista* digital army.

David Nemer, an academic ethnographer, discovered how effective this online organization was when he joined various pro-Bolsonaro WhatsApp groups before the 2018 election.[49] Participants in the groups appeared to be organized in a pyramid structure. At the top of each WhatsApp group of up to 256 people were four or five influencers. They would post a regular diet of pro-Bolsonaro content, attacks on Bolsonaro's critics, and allegations about his PT opponent. At the next level were the group admins who would endorse and promote the posts. At the final level were everyday Brazilians who were presented with an endless stream of unidirectional propaganda. In each group there were thousands of posts per day—many of them images or videos.[50] Estimates about the total number of these groups ranged between 20,000 and 300,000.[51] These groups were the ideal incubator in which to put Olavo de Carvalho's culture war ideas into practice at scale.

The Bolsonaros' digital army was also boosted by Brazilian business leaders who were desperate to stop the left-wing PT from regaining power and were prepared to bankroll anyone who could prevent it.[52] A cabal of business leaders gave a small fortune to digital marketing companies Yacows and Quickmobile to flood Brazilian WhatsApp groups with scandalous, shocking, and false messages about Bolsonaro's opponent, Fernando Haddad. The companies did this by acquiring databases of foreign mobile numbers, using these to join masses of WhatsApp groups, and then using them to spread automated partisan messages.[53] Many messages claimed that Haddad was corrupt—one showed a photo of a criminal gang and claimed (falsely) that Haddad had received $R68 million from them for his campaign.[54] Then there was the infamous fabrication that claimed the PT were sending baby bottles with penis-shaped teats to nurseries as part of a "gay kit" to normalize homosexuality.[55] Absurd as these claims sound, a survey shortly after the election found that the majority of Brazilians believed many of them.[56] This illegal practice was exposed ten days before the second round of voting in 2018 by the journalist Patricia Campos Mello from *Folha de Sao Paulo*, but it was too late to change voters' minds or the result.[57]

During the campaign Carlos almost never left his father's side. After Jair Bolsonaro was stabbed, Carlos even took over his personal social media accounts. After the election, Jair Bolsonaro credited his second son for his victory. "It was really his media that got me here," he said afterward.[58] Even the elected president's official campaign manager, Gustavo Bebianno, acknowledged the contribution of Carlos's social media efforts: "without him, the campaign would not have developed so well."[59]

ELECTED TO OFFICE

Jair Bolsonaro came to office buoyed by a digital wave of *antipetismo*. But beyond his supporters' dislike of the PT, there was little that unified them. There were a mixture of gun-owning rural landowners, who favored the protection of their gun ownership rights and the further agricultural development of the Amazon; free market advocates, who bridled at the PT's social welfare policies; and evangelical Christians, who were upset by the progressive social reforms enacted since 2010. To these he added the burgeoning ranks of ordinary Brazilians revolted by political corruption who wanted to "drain the swamp." Although these groups had coalesced in the 2018 election, there was no reason to believe they would not fracture after it. This was made more likely, the Bolsonaros believed, by the strength of the forces arrayed against them. Most significant, they believed the institutional left—led by Brazil's mainstream media and supported by a liberal Congress and a progressive Supreme Court—would try to stymie them at every opportunity. To oppose these forces they would need to be able to take down their opponents, counter mainstream media narratives, and weaken the institutions that obstructed their agenda. This would require keeping their disparate base united, harnessing the digital movements that brought them to office, and ensuring that their own political narratives outperformed those of mainstream news outlets. During their four years in office, this is exactly what the Bolsonaros and their fellow Carvalhists sought to do.

It was the Catalan sociologist Manuel Castells who put forward a network theory of power. In a "networked society," Castells wrote in 2011, "It should not surprise us that . . . social power is primarily exercised by and through networks."[60] Led by Carlos, the Bolsonaro movement put this network theory of power into action. Between 2018 and 2022 they built an intricate networked information ecosystem that enabled them to disparage and discredit Jair Bolsonaro's critics, undermine Brazil's democratic institutions, and promote false and distorted narratives. A system that was later called—by the judge Alexandre de Moraes—a "criminal organization."[61] The system comprised a vast network of news sites and YouTube channels, coordinated authentic and inauthentic social media accounts, had armies of bots and social media influencers, and had a daily audience of millions of Brazilians. It was geographically dispersed, involved elected representatives and civil servants, and encompassed public and private initiatives. Its diverse funding methods were sometimes open, sometimes opaque. In its scale and efficacy, it showed how far a democratically elected executive can go if it wanted to create a parallel information universe.

Initially it looked like Carlos would develop this disinformation machine from a senior position within government, potentially as the secretary of communication (Minister of Secom).[62] However, this was blocked by Gustavo Bebianno, Jair Bolsonaro's minister of the general secretariat, on grounds of nepotism. Instead, Carlos would shift into the background, from where he would develop a parallel, shadow operation run via social networks.

THE MACHINERY OF DISINFORMATION

A fuller understanding of the scale and complexity of this parallel information ecosystem has emerged over the course of the administration and its aftermath. It comes from the testimony of those who were victims of government orchestrated virtual lynchings, from a vast body of evidence submitted to multiple inquiries, and from police raids and investigations. Although the system relied on social media and digital networks, it was driven by what David Nemer refers to as "the human infrastructure of fake news."[63] The inquiries and investigations identified four main elements to the system: a political nucleus, an operations component, a dissemination network, and a funding strategy.

STRATEGIC NUCLEUS

At the center of the operation was a strategic nucleus. This was made up of a small core of people who set up and executed the operation's strategy and managed the various networks. Carlos led this core team, working closely with his brother Eduardo (son #03). Eduardo is a couple of years younger than Carlos and has greater personal political ambitions, seeing himself as the natural successor to his father. It was Eduardo who made himself the bridge between Brazil and the United States' "alt-right," meeting regularly with Steve Bannon and maneuvering (unsuccessfully) to become Brazil's ambassador to the United States.[64] The brothers employed a small executive team—three long-standing supporters: Tercio Arnaud, José Matheus, and Mateus Diniz—who worked out of an office on the third floor in the Presidential Palace (the *Planalto*).[65]

They were joined in January 2019 by Felipe Martins, appointed as international advisor to the president at the tender age of twenty-nine, who had only two years of government experience. Although Martins lacked government experience, he had shown himself to be highly effective online. By 2018 he had become known, Globo reported, as one of the main online recruiters for "Bolsonarist" and "Olavist troops."[66] So ideologically purist was he that he was called "Roberat," a reference to France's revolutionary Jacobin, Robespierre.[67] Martins was also a conduit to Olavo de Carvalho himself, having previously worked with the belligerent polemicist. Indeed, Carvalho was effectively another member of the team, posting daily from rural Virginia, proposing his preferred political agenda, policies, and personnel—even though the Bolsonaros did not always agree with them. It was this strategic nucleus that became infamous as the *Gabinete de Odio* (the Office of Hate). Together they devised the information strategy, monitored political developments, and decided which people, organizations, and issues to target.[68]

OPERATIONS

The operationalization of the political nucleus's strategy had public and private dimensions. The public dimension used the authority, facilities, and personnel of state, beginning with the president himself. Carlos Bolsonaro retained access to his father's social media accounts, enabling him to speak with the authority of the president.[69] His father supplemented this by posting prolifically on Twitter himself, live-streaming weekly on YouTube or Facebook, and publishing photos on Instagram.

Beyond the president, the Bolsonaros knew they would need a cadre of compliant government ministers to promote their narratives. Working in concert with Olavo de Carvalho, they recruited a clutch of key ministers in the departments of foreign affairs, education, and communications who shared their political perspectives and their commitment to the culture wars—notably their enmity with the established media, their unsparing social conservatism, and their conspiratorial conviction that an international cabal of communists wanted to take over Brazil.[70] For example, they appointed Ernesto Araujo as Minister of Foreign Affairs, who had recently published a blog calling the PT a "terrorist party" and saying that "Globalism is the economic globalisation that came to be piloted by cultural Marxism. It's an anti-human and anti-Christian system."[71] "This guy is a genius!" Olavo de Carvalho exclaimed when he read the blog, "He has to be Foreign Minister."[72]

The president and his Carvalhist ministers could put forward narratives that promoted Bolsonaro and attacked his critics, but these needed to be disseminated on social media. For this the *Gabinete de Odio* recruited Parliamentary advisors and civil servants across most of Brazil's twenty-six states. An investigation by Facebook in 2020 found that employees from the offices of Eduardo, Flavio, and Jair Bolsonaro were using duplicate or fake pages to "create fictitious personas posing as reporters, post content, and manage pages masquerading as news outlets." "About 883,000 accounts followed one or more of these Pages," Facebook reported, "and about 918,000 people followed one or more of these Instagram accounts."[73] This was happening across Brazil. Take, for example, the State of Caera in the northeast. Despite being more than 1,800 kilometers from Brasilia, six Parliamentary aides working for two Caera delegates would regularly fly in for meetings on the third floor of the *Planalto*. These aides would then return to Caera, where each managed multiple social media pages and profiles (mostly under pseudonyms) and maintained membership in numerous WhatsApp groups. Across these they would publish, according to later testimony, coordinated attacks on individuals, videos lambasting Brazil's Supreme Court, and disinformation.[74]

The public dimension operated in parallel with a carefully constructed private dimension. Without this, most of the output could be written off as state propaganda. This private dimension included a panoply of loyal news sites, YouTube channels, social media influencers, and WhatsApp power users. Some of these were motivated by *antipetismo*. Some were ideologically driven adherents of Brazil's New Right. Others were financially motivated. Cheerleading for the government could be highly lucrative, especially because the *Planalto* gave privileged access and exclusive material to sites that showed themselves to be slavishly supportive and uncritical of Bolsonaro. Some of these sites had close ties to the administration. *Gabinete de Odio* member Felipe Martins, for instance, was deputy editor of one (Senso Incomum).[75] Others had no clearly identifiable ties (such as *Jornal de Ciudade*). The format of the sites mimicked the design and tone of large news outlets, even if they were built overnight and staffed by a handful of volunteers. Thanks to evidence gained by the police and inquiries, we know that many of these outlets acted in a coordinated way.

This is how it would work. A "news" story would be published on one of these sites—given to them directly from the *Planalto* or taken directly from content produced by the Bolsonaros. An article about chloroquine and COVID-19, for example, would be published by *Jornal de Ciudade*. The site, based in the soybean city of Campo Grande in southwestern Brazil, published articles written by dozens of unpaid contributors, some authentic, others invented.[76] Within minutes the article would be republished on multiple other "news outlets" in the network—sites such as Portal Novo Norte and Terra Brasil Notícias.[77] Once they were circulating across multiple sites, they would gain the appearance of breaking news. Once this happened, links to the articles were posted by supportive influencers and bot networks. Even if these articles were later fact-checked and found to be false, they had gained widespread exposure. A 2019 research study by computer scientists at Northwestern University found that articles published by *Jornal de Ciudade* were the most popular across right-wing WhatsApp groups prior to the 2018 election.[78]

Working in tandem with the news sites were the YouTube channels. YouTube was fundamental to this alternative information ecosystem because YouTube videos could be shared on other platforms and WhatsApp. As one researcher put it: "In an analogy to drug trafficking, it's like the apps are the message runners ('aviõezinhos') and YouTube is the crack house. The centre of production is YouTube and to run the logistics of these industrial disinformation products, they enter the networks and the apps."[79] During the Bolsonaro years there was a heterogeneous mass of YouTube channels on Brazilian politics. Some mimicked broadcast news programs—complete with musical intros, swooshing headline graphics, and smartly dressed presenters in faux newsrooms. Foco do Brasil was one of the most popular of these, with almost three million YouTube subscribers by the end of Bolsonaro's presidency. Just like TV broadcast news, Foco do Brasil would stream 20+ minute programs daily, with a constant diet of pro-Bolsonaro items. Some of these it was fed via WhatsApp, courtesy of Tercio

Arnaud in the *Planalto*.[80] For other programs the YouTube channel was given special access to the president. Other newly formed YouTube news channels would edit together clips from Bolsonaro's live-streams, footage broadcast in the Senate and Chamber of Deputies, and video from the Supreme Court.[81] These news clips would then be spread via social media. For this the Bolsonaros would rely on the third, and most important, element of the disinformation ecosystem—the dissemination network.

DISSEMINATION

If Bolsonarist news and attacks on his critics were to spread across Brazil's social media, they had to be popular. If this popularity did not occur organically, it would need to be manufactured. For this the Bolsonaros relied on a network of online influencers and bots. The Bolsonaros themselves were leading influencers, each with millions of social media followers by the time Jair was elected. But to reach as many Brazilians as they could, they developed a series of concentric influencer networks.

Around a dozen accounts formed the hub of the network. Some of these were well-known social media figures who had grown mass followings on YouTube, Twitter, and Instagram, such as Bernardo Küster and Leandro Ruschel. Others were elected representatives who were diehard Bolsonaro loyalists, such as Carla Zambelli or Filipe Barros. What they all had in common was their devotion to Olavo de Carvalho. Küster even visited Carvalho in early 2019 and toured his house.[82] Combined with the Bolsonaros, these dozen or so accounts could directly reach well over ten million people. Coordinated publication could reach millions more. This corresponds to a phenomenon seen elsewhere on the internet—the networked power law—whereby most accounts have very few connections but a small number of influencer accounts have a vast number. These then act as superspreaders. For instance, researchers in the United States found that during the COVID-19 pandemic almost two-thirds (65 percent) of the antivaccine content published on Twitter and Facebook in 2021 was attributable to just twelve people. This equated to more than eight hundred thousand posts during a six-week period in February–March 2021.[83] As long as the Office of Hate's hub network acted in concert, it could generate significant reach across Brazil's information environment.

News and attacks on Bolsonaro's critics were amplified further by legions of bots. The Bolsonaros had already discovered the electoral value of these in 2016, and by the time they were in power they could regularly command hundreds of thousands of automated accounts. These bot armies could be sourced domestically or rented from abroad—including from Russia, China, and Israel, at a cost of $R15,000–20,000 (US$3,000–4,000), according to evidence cited in a report for Brazil's Supreme Court.[84] The inquiry revealed that more than a quarter of Jair Bolsonaro's Twitter followers in 2019 (1.5m of 5.4m) were bots, as were an even greater proportion of Eduardo's.[85] One indication that these were bots was "the almost simultaneous dissemination" of identical texts across multiple Twitter profiles in many different states. Another was the way in which these social media profiles would suddenly stop tweeting about one political issue, or against one political target, and then—all at the same time—start tweeting about another.[86] Once pro-Bolsonaro narratives had been published across multiple pop-up websites and inauthentic social media profiles, spread by influencers and inflated by legions of automated accounts, these could be reheated and reshared by conservative online movements. Some of these were the same movements that had grown online since 2013, such as MBL, Brasil Conservador, and Avanca Brasil.

THE "FAKE-NEWS KINGPIN"

The Bolsonaros could not have managed this sprawling parallel information ecosystem from one office in the *Planalto*, particularly not the private dimension. They needed help in the coordination, the direction, and the funding. They found this in the form of a failed priest from Rio de Janeiro, Allan dos Santos. Allan dos Santos has the look of a Jesuit missionary, with a domed balding head, dark graying beard, and intense eyes framed by rectangular glasses. Having enrolled in a seminary as a teenager, he abandoned his religious ambitions in his twenties, but if anything his spiritual conviction had become more militant and adversarial. In the early 2010s he enrolled in Olavo de Carvalho's online classes and quickly became a devotee. Learning from Carvalho's methods, dos Santos started a website in 2014, called Terça Livre (Free Tuesday). Initially the site published just one weekly show that was freely available every Tuesday, but it was soon producing daily news, interviews, opinions, and courses—all from a Carvalhist position. From 2016 Allan dos Santos began evangelizing for Bolsonaro as president and offered his services to the family.[87]

By December 2018, barely a month after Bolsonaro's election, the former seminarian had moved from his garage office in Porto Allegre to a grand house in an expensive quarter of the capital, Qi 19 on Lago Sul de Brasília, a short fifteen-minute drive from the *Planalto*. It was at this house that dos Santos started convening meetings—some of them with officials and elected representatives, others with Bolsonaro supporters and online influencers.[88] While there he set up high-level WhatsApp groups with senior members of government—including the advisor to the president, Colonel Mauro Cesar Barbosa Cid—to discuss communications. Terça Livre had a studio in the house, so dos Santos could film interviews, produce online content, and monitor Brazilian politics there. At one stage the outlet had fifty employees.[89] From this mansion in Brasilia, therefore, Allan dos Santos was able to bring together the public and private dimensions of the Bolsonaro's shadow communications operation and coordinate the publication of attacks on Bolsonaro enemies.

This was the machinery of the Bolsonaro "disinformation ecosystem" as it came to be known. Headed by a strategic nucleus, supported by a web of public and private digital publishers, and disseminated by a network of political influencers, automated profiles, and conservative online movements. Thanks to this parallel information ecosystem, millions of Brazilians, most of whom were getting their news via social media and WhatsApp, were exposed to the same pro-Bolsonaro content, but this identical content appeared to come from multiple different sources and seemed to be endorsed by masses of other social media users.

FUNDING STRATEGY

This vast, constant, hyperactive parallel information system was not free. The ministers, delegates, Parliamentary advisors, and civil servants were paid for by the state, but the private aspects of the network needed money to fund the production of "news" (the staff, the studios, the equipment) and its dissemination (via influencers, bot armies, and fake social media profiles). The money came from two main sources: wealthy businessmen who sympathized with Bolsonaro's politics and believed he would benefit them commercially, and from digital advertising paid for either by commercial companies or by the Brazilian government.

One of these businessmen was the investor Otavio Fakhoury. Fakhoury's involvement started in 2015, when he was at a protest in favor of the impeachment of the president Dilma Rousseff. At the protest he noticed a man filming—Paulo Eneas—and asked him what he was doing. Eneas was, he said, gathering footage for his blog, Critica Nacional. Fakhoury offered to support and grow the blog, and over the next few years he bought equipment, rented office space, and invested R$30k–40k a year in it.[90] By 2020, Critica Nacional was a long way from being a blog. It had the appearance of a professional news site. Its masthead had changed to "national and international political articles and analysis," and it had become a key member of the "Bolsonarist 'Jacobin' network."[91]

Fakhoury was one of a coterie of Brazilian businesspeople identified by the Supreme Court's investigations as a funder of the Bolsonaros' parallel information ecosystem. Another was the retail magnate Luciano Hang. Hang owns one of Brazil's biggest department stores—Havan. In photographs he is almost always captured wearing Brazil's national colors—green and yellow. When he gave evidence to the COVID-19 inquiry, he was dressed in a fern green suit, a canary yellow tie, golden yellow shoes, and striped green and yellow socks. Hang's financial support for the Bolsonaros began before the 2018 election, when Havan spent an estimated R$12 million on bulk messaging via WhatsApp to support the campaign. This support continued, the inquiries found, once Jair Bolsonaro was in office, funneled covertly through Hang's offshore accounts.[92] Beyond

Hang and Fakhoury, Supreme Court and police inquiries identified a syndicate of retail entrepreneurs, construction barons, gym owners, and import-exporters either giving money to outlets directly, or indirectly via offshore companies, willing intermediaries or support-in-kind.

However, the easiest way to fund the parallel information ecosystem was through advertising. All these businesses advertised, and as long as these websites and channels had users, they could legitimately argue that by paying for ads on their sites they were simply trying to reach consumers. The Bolsonaros could do their bit to boost user numbers by giving them privileged access to the *Planalto*, by giving them interviews with the president and ministers, and by giving them exclusive information. They could also promote the channels via their influencer network and bots.[93] *Gabinete de Odio* member, Tercio Arnaud, admitted to Brazil's Supreme Court that he would pass on undisclosed presidential information and videos to bloggers.[94] Similarly, the president's advisor, Colonel Mauro Cesar Barbosa Cid, would channel messages and material to and from Allan dos Santos, who would act as "a kind of representative for other YouTube channels."[95] In this way propaganda sites and channels like Folha Politica could earn approximately R$100,000 (US$20,000) per month.[96] Terça Livre's YouTube channel alone earned about R$180,000 from digital advertising in the last six months of 2020.[97] So lucrative was digital advertising for pro-Bolsonaro sites that new networks such as Pensa Brasilia sprang up that appeared to be entirely financially motivated.[98]

More controversially, it was discovered that the government was paying for advertising on these sites, as well as increasing subsidies to media outlets that were unstintingly supportive of Bolsonaro.[99] After Fabio Wajngarten was appointed to head the government's Ministry of Communication in April 2019, he explicitly discouraged advertisers from giving money to media outlets—like *Folha de Sao Paulo*—which were critical of the government. At the same time he sought to protect ultra-*bolsonarista* news services like *Jornal de Ciudade* when they were threatened by advertising boycotts.[100] Similarly, Carlos Bolsonaro leapt in when Banco de Brasil threatened to boycott *Jornal de Ciudade*, accusing them of trying to suppress "alternative media."[101]

THE DISINFORMATION MACHINERY IN ACTION

Had this machinery been used simply to promote the Bolsonaro administration in a positive light, it would not have been dissimilar from what governments have done in the past. There is a long history of governments promoting themselves through whatever means necessary. Moreover, the Bolsonaros could have argued that they were trying to counterbalance the systematic criticism of Jair Bolsonaro by mainstream media over many decades. But the parallel information ecosystem did not limit itself to positive promotion. In fact, its primary focus was attack, not defense. Attacks on political opponents, rivals, and critics. Attacks on democratic institutions, especially the Supreme Court and the press. And attacks on anyone telling stories that reflected badly on Bolsonaro or his administration. Moreover, the machinery did not limit itself to publishing factual information; rather it deployed whatever information served its purposes, however false or misleading. It produced and disseminated, a police investigation subsequently wrote, "fraudulent news, false reports of crimes, violations of confidentiality, threats and crimes against honour (slander, defamation and libel)" and attacked individuals with the aim of achieving "ideological, party-political and financial gains."[102]

ATTACKS ON INDIVIDUALS

Our most detailed understanding of the impact of the *bolsonarista* digital militias comes from the testimony of its victims. Many were politicians who served in Bolsonaro's government but fell out of favor or were targeted for factional reasons. These were intended as "reputation killings," in the words of one victim, aimed at forcing the person out of office, crushing their credibility, or shaming them into silence.[103]

Joice Hasselmann, a journalist, politician, and social media influencer, was initially a member of Jair Bolsonaro's party, before falling out with the president. Shortly after their split, Hasselmann found herself the subject of a cascade of vicious attacks online. These spilled offline at the end of November 2018 when Hasselman received—at her home—a severed pig's head, a blond wig, and an accompanying note that read: "You will suffer and you will die."[104] Hasselmann chose not to run away but to investigate what happened to her. In an astonishing presentation to the CPMI Fake News Inquiry, she laid out in visual detail the methods and content of the operation against her—including images of social media posts. "A target is chosen," she told the inquiry, "An attack is planned and there even is a calendar setting out the date of the offensive and who is responsible for it."[105] Then the virtual jackals are set on their prey.

These campaigns escalated once Jair Bolsonaro took office. Often the targets were within the government itself. The first minister to be targeted was Gustavo Bebianno, the minister of the general secretariat who had blocked Carlos's appointment as head of the ministry of government communications. Weeks later, Bebianno was dealing with questions about the diversion of campaign funds when suddenly Carlos accused him of being a liar on Twitter. Carlos followed up his tweet by leaking an audio recording of Bebianno that Carlos asserted supported his claim. His posts were then succeeded by a flood of attacks directed at the minister on social media. Jair Bolsonaro did not step in to defend him and a short time later asked him to leave. Bebianno did not blame the president for his dismissal. "I was fired by Carlos Bolsonaro," he said later. It's "that simple."[106]

After Bebbiano, General Carlos Alberto dos Santos Cruz, Hamilton Mourau, Nereu Crispim, Rodrigo Maia, and Sergio Moro all found themselves targeted by digital militias. Despite the damning evidence Hasselman gave at the CPMI Fake News Inquiry, the attacks continued. The following spring, as COVID-19 spread rapidly through Brazil, the health minister, Luiz Henrique Mandetta, recommended that people socially distance and take other preventative measures to avoid the disease. Although such recommendations were common worldwide, Jair Bolsonaro had taken a starkly different approach, calling COVID-19 a "little flu" and telling people to continue as normal. Mandetta's stance infuriated the Bolsonaros and precipitated a ferocious online campaign against the health minister. A subsequent investigation by the DFR Lab discovered how this campaign started and how it spread.[107] A news story was published on one of the pro-Bolsonaro sites, Agora Paraná, falsely alleging that Mandetta had agreed to government advertising contracts with mainstream media companies in return for positive personal coverage. Once published, the article was reposted on other pro-Bolsonaro news sites in the network, and on multiple Facebook pages. The Bolsonaro influencer ecosystem then tweeted links to the articles, and these were disseminated around WhatsApp. Shortly after, on April 16, 2020, Jair Bolsonaro fired the health minister. Joao Doria, a governor who criticized Jair Bolsonaro's early handling of the pandemic, was similarly rounded on by the online brigades. In addition to a torrent of abuse, Doria received death threats and messages on his phone "saying that his home would be invaded." His house had to be protected by the civil defense force. He ascribed the threats to Carlos's digital militias.[108]

Similar virtual lynchings happened to almost anyone who crossed the Bolsonaros, diverged from the government line, or was not sufficiently "Olavist." For those outside government, the hate machine could be just as ruthless. Patricia Campos Mello, the journalist who revealed that pro-Bolsonaro groups were illegally financing bulk WhatsApp messaging before the 2018 election, described how she was constantly abused online and off—at the instigation of the Bolsonaros themselves. Following encouragement from the president, "Thousands of memes circulated on the internet in which my face appears in pornographic montages," she said in 2021, which were followed by threats of rape and violence.[109] Some of these were disseminated via WhatsApp groups run by two of Jair Bolsonaro's sons.[110]

ATTACKS ON INSTITUTIONS AND PROCESSES

These attacks on individuals were motivated by political infighting, factionalism, paranoia, dogma, and revenge. But they were also part of a broader project to undermine public trust and confidence in Brazil's democratic institutions and processes; driven by Olavo Carvalho's ideas that reestablishing conservative ascendancy over "cultural Marxists" required a dismantling of the political establishment. This could be seen, for example, by the persistent attacks on Supreme Court judges. It did not necessarily matter which judge was being attacked, just that their integrity and objectivity was being questioned. In autumn 2019, for example, Dias Toffoli was being targeted. Then, abruptly, the same social media profiles that had been targeting Toffoli started going for another judge, Gilmar Mendes, after Mendes altered his position in favor of releasing Bolsonaro's nemesis, Lula, from prison. Cue a sudden spate of calls on social media to impeach Mendes. Once these calls cohered behind a hashtag—#ImpeachmentGilmarMendes—eleven key *bolsonarista* influencers, including Allan dos Santos, adopted it and pushed it to their millions of followers.[111]

The smearing of individual judges was coupled with persistent online condemnation of the Supreme Court and other democratic institutions, including Congress and the institutional news media. At every opportunity the Bolsonaros' network questioned their honesty, impartiality, and patriotism. They also engineered attempts to turn their digital hate campaigns into real-world offensives against these institutions. A study of the role of social media in the Brazilian protests in March and April 2020, for example, found an increasing number of posts earlier in the year calling for national street protests on March 15—the five-year anniversary of protests pressing for the impeachment of the former president, the PT's Dilma Rousseff.[112] Many of these posts had hashtags such as #dia15porbolsonaro and #somostodosbolsonaros (we are all Bolsonaros). On the day itself the hashtag #bolsonaroday was posted 1.2 million times and became one of Twitter's trending topics. More than half of these posts, the researchers found, were published by bots or automated profiles. Some of these were posting up to 1,200 posts per day, compared to fewer than ten for an average human account.[113]

These digital efforts were rewarded. By early March there were pro-Bolsonaro demonstrations being planned across Brazil from the middle of the month. Then COVID-19 struck. A week before the protests were due to kick off, Jair Bolsonaro—in an uncharacteristically cautious speech—suggested postponing them until the pandemic had died down. This, along with rising infections, deterred many from turning out, although demonstrations still went ahead in Brasilia and elsewhere. Their tone was less pro-Bolsonaro than vehemently anti-Congress and antijudiciary.[114] Contemporary reports described banners calling for military intervention and for a return of Institutional Act Number 5 (AI-5): the decree during Brazil's military dictatorship that gave the military almost unchallengeable powers, even over Brazil's constitution. Calling for its return was tantamount to calling for an end to democracy in Brazil.

Although the president had initially discouraged attendance at the March 15 demonstrations, he could not resist enthusing about them on social media, and he went out to join them on the day. He did the same the following month, actively inflaming the protesters even more. "The era of the swindle is over," he shouted from the back of a truck amid the demonstrators on Sunday April 19. "It is now the people in power."[115] "Enough of old politics," he said to supporters who carried signs pressing for the closure of the Supreme Court and military intervention. The president was, observers remarked, actively encouraging a coup.[116]

There was not a coup attempt in the spring of 2020, despite Jair Bolsonaro's encouragement, although the Supreme Court established an inquiry into these "Anti-Democratic" acts to establish who was really behind them. They concluded that Allan dos Santos and his network had played a central role in fomenting the demonstrations. This conclusion was based in part on evidence collected from a raid, conducted by the Federal Police, on dos Santos's lavish Brasilia house in which they discovered documents that "pointed to strong indications of the existence of a criminal organisation aimed at promoting various conducts to destabilise and . . . destroy the Legislative and Judicial Powers." This included resources whose objective was "to train people capable of acting professionally in political and cultural change" and "to materialise popular anger against governors/mayors [with the] Intermediate end: take to the streets; [and the] Last end: overthrow the governors/mayors." This was engineered, the Supreme Court inquiry wrote, by a "virtual network of supporters who act systematically to create or share messages that have as their final motto the overthrow of the democratic structure of Brazil."[117] It was to break up these virtual networks and stop social media being used to instigate the end of Brazilian democracy that the Supreme Court, led by Justice Alexandre de Moraes, later sought to remove accounts and posts from X, prompting an outraged Elon Musk to accuse de Moraes of being an "evil dictator," and Lula's government "an oppressive regime."[118]

By July of 2020 Allan dos Santos could see that the authorities were closing in on his operation, and he fled to the United States, helped out of the country by none other than Eduardo Bolsonaro.[119] His departure did not stop his activities, however. Like Olavo de Carvalho, Allan dos Santos continued publishing material from the United States, and doing what he could to coordinate further antidemocratic acts.

PROMOTION OF FALSE NARRATIVES

In addition to the attacks on individuals and institutions, there was a third element of the disinformation ecosystem that was arguably the most damaging of them all. This was its production and dissemination of false narratives. It was the production of these narratives that, among other things, convinced large sections of the Brazilian population that COVID-19 was not harmful, that the administration was taking good care of the Amazon and its Indigenous peoples, and that the country's electoral processes were corrupted and broken.

COVID-19

In 2020 Jair Bolsonaro became known as the leader most closely associated with COVID-19 denialism—even more so than Donald Trump.[120] He persistently downplayed the harm of COVID-19, pushed false cures such as chloroquine, and claimed actions taken to reduce the spread of the virus by regional governors and mayors were harmful and politically motivated. The parallel Bolsonarist information system was well-suited to communicating this false and misleading information. Not only were people primed to distrust the Supreme Court and Congress, but there was a virtual army ready to distribute the president's allegations and claims. This was especially true of WhatsApp groups and Telegram channels where Jair Bolsonaro's videos, tweets, and posts could be seeded and promoted by the wide network of *bolsonarista* digital militias.

Immediately after Bolsonaro gave his March 2020 COVID-minimization speech, urging people to ignore the virus and live their lives as normal, a research team led by Felipe Soares saw a spike in disinformation across the five hundred Brazilian WhatsApp groups they were studying. These posts explicitly connected anxiety about coronavirus and policies like social distancing to political affiliation. State governors who countered Bolsonaro's claims were "leftists" or "communists." Congress and the Supreme Court's efforts to push further health measures were part of "a macabre plan to overthrow our President."[121] On Telegram, Paulo Fonseca and his colleagues discovered users telling each other that mainstream outlets like Globo were killing people by questioning the efficacy of chloroquine. Despite having 14,000 channel members, they found no one there who accepted the findings of mainstream science about the supposed cure, and a general consensus that critics of chloroquine had malign intentions and should be considered murderers. Fonseca and his colleagues call this "patriotic science," or a version of science that they categorize as "institutionalized ignorance."[122]

The impact of the president's "patriotic science" across Brazil's virtual networks was profound. Research has found that many people's knowledge about COVID-19 was strongly influenced by their support—or lack of support—for the president.[123] Based on their knowledge, lots of Brazilians chose not to social distance, conform to health guidelines, or seek treatment when they became ill. According to the World Health Organization, 699,917 people died of COVID-19 in Brazil.[124] This represented a higher mortality rate than all but four other countries worldwide.[125]

THE AMAZON

Roraima is Brazil's northernmost state, its top half squeezed between Venezuela and Guyana. Originally inhabited entirely by Indigenous Amazonian peoples (the Yanomami), since the 1970s there has been an influx of migrants, many of them in search of minerals and gold. In January 2023 an unusual sight sprang up in the state's capital Boa Vista—tented field hospitals. The emergency hospitals, normally only used in wartime, were treating hundreds of desperately ill Yanomami women and children, many of them suffering from severe malnutrition or poisoned by toxic river water.[126] In recent years many more Indigenous peoples had already died, killed by illegal miners, mercury poisoning, starvation, or COVID-19.[127] The deaths were so numerous, and many so avoidable, that Lula's newly elected government said it should be called a genocide.[128]

For most Brazilians, the news about the Yanomami came as a terrible shock. In part because their government had ignored, distorted, or blocked news about what was really happening in the Amazon for the previous four years.[129] Any stories that did emerge—of rampant deforestation, uncontrolled fires, illegal mining, and violence against Indigenous peoples—were dismissed as concoctions by leftists and self-interested NGOs. Instead, the Bolsonaros used their parallel information networks to manufacture the perception that the Indigenous peoples welcomed mining and industrial development, that Jair Bolsonaro was protecting and preserving the Amazon, and that the president was defending the Amazon from predatory international organizations and NGOs that were trying to take it from Brazil.

These false claims by Bolsonaro and his ministers were distributed across the *bolsonarista* network. In one speech Jair Bolsonaro claimed, "We are committed to this richest and most sacred piece of land in the world [the Amazon]. It is no wonder that other countries are increasingly trying to win the information war so that we will lose sovereignty over this area." The speech was edited and republished on Folha Politica where it was watched more than a million times.[130] The same was done with speeches and interviews by his sons and compliant ministers. A research project by

InfoAmazonia found four hundred such videos on YouTube that were then republished across the *bolsonarista* network.[131] These four hundred videos together had more than seventy million views.

Thanks to the breadth of their virtual news network, the Bolsonaros and their supporters were able to present a parallel reality about one of the most important environmental regions on the planet. "We see an infrastructure for the production and dissemination of false information . . . from the government itself," said Debora Salles, the director of Brazil's NetLab. As a consequence, they were able to cover up the acceleration of deforestation, the escalation of illegal mining—and the violence that went with it, including the mass deaths of many of Brazil's Indigenous people.[132]

ELECTORAL FRAUD

Once the digital architecture of a parallel reality has been constructed, it can be used to distort or discredit almost anything, including electoral defeat. And so it was with the Bolsonaros' system. Jair Bolsonaro had questioned the integrity of Brazil's electoral process since well before 2018, presumably as an insurance mechanism in case of loss. But before the 2022 election his questions escalated exponentially. In YouTube videos, livestreamed events, even meetings with ambassadors, Bolsonaro regularly claimed that Brazil's electronic voting system was open to fraud.[133]

As with so many other false narratives he and his network propagated, he used his lack of evidence of fraud as a strength. In a contortion of Karl Popper's scientific method, the president told voters that although it was possible to say there was currently no evidence of electoral fraud, that did not necessarily mean there was no electoral fraud. It simply meant there was no evidence *yet*. "Prove to me," Bolsonaro challenged his detractors, "that Brazil's electronic voting is not fraudulent—in the meantime I will assume it is."

As the presidential election approached in 2022, the false narratives continued to pour out of the administration and spread among the population, despite Congressional and Supreme Court inquiries, police investigations, journalistic exposés, and persistent and detailed fact-checking and debunking. Bolsonaro's opponent Lula was, it was variously claimed, a corrupt, anti-Christian alcoholic, who had links to organized crime and drug dealers, and who had previously commissioned murders. He and his party, alleged influencers and elected representatives, encouraged sexual depravity and pedophilia, planned to persecute Christians, shut down churches, and were engaged in wholesale vote-buying.[134] Nor was this avalanche of disinformation only one-way. Supporters of Lula had concluded that attack was the best form of defense, and they were now posting lurid and distorted claims about Jair Bolsonaro.[135] "The electoral campaign takes place in the midst of the acute crisis of disinformation," independent fact-checking agency, Lupa, wrote, "which has jumped from an epidemic to a pandemic." "There is," they continued, "a reality and a parallel reality."[136]

Lula da Silva won the 2022 election. Just. He received less than 2 percent more than Jair Bolsonaro in the second round of voting (50.9 percent versus 49.1 percent). In the National Congress, many of those who had participated in the Bolsonaros' disinformation ecosystem were elected to office, including Eduardo Bolsonaro. Bolsonaro's outspoken loyalist, Carla Zambelli, was elected too, despite startling video footage of her threatening a man with a gun and pursuing him into a cafe on the day before the second round of the presidential election.[137] Given the constant shouts of election fraud, and the deterioration of Brazil's digital public sphere, it is unsurprising that many Brazilians did not believe the outcome. A poll published in early January 2023, after the January 8 Brasilia riots, found that only 56 percent of Brazilians thought that Lula had won.[138]

THE END OF THE *BOLSONARISTAS*?

When Jair Bolsonaro was elected in 2018, he lacked the powers of an authoritarian leader. He was constrained by institutions such as the Supreme Court and Congress. He lacked a party structure through which he could assert hierarchical control. He could not censor or shut down independent media. He did not even have a substantial state broadcaster or enjoy the political backing of Brazil's mainstream news outlets. Yet despite this, he and his sons, led by Carlos—*Zero Dois*—were able to build a parallel information infrastructure using the new platforms of digital communication. With this parallel infrastructure they were able to produce alternative realities, give these realities the patina of credibility, and disseminate them to millions of Brazilian citizens.

They could never achieve narrative dominance, especially given the continuing importance of Brazil's legacy media, but they could ensure there were always multiple conflicting narratives, and that these narratives incited frustration, anger, and tribalism. They could also use their digital militias to assail their critics, and to try to discredit and silence any narratives that cast them in a bad light. For this they developed a well-honed strategy. Publish an allegation against the target in an obliging news outlet. Republish the same allegation across multiple other compliant outlets across their network. Inflate the popularity of the story via their web of influencers and bot armies. Give it further credibility by featuring it on supportive YouTube news and debate shows. Rinse and repeat.

This alternative news ecosystem would have been far less successful without the tools and authority of the state. The Bolsonaros and those they aligned themselves with (notably Olavo de Carvalho and his disciples) took advantage of the machinery, personnel, finances, and authority of government to enhance the reach of their narratives. This meant using the office and influence of the presidency, enlisting elected representatives, parliamentary advisors, and officials, and channeling advertising money and government contracts to supplicant media. Marrying public funding with their private network of websites, influencers and administrators made their pro-government narratives look less like propaganda and more like news. This "news" would never convince everyone, but that did not matter. It only had to convince enough people to keep Bolsonaro in power—and it nearly did.

The Bolsonaros showed how far it is possible to manufacture a digital disinformation ecosystem, as long as you are prepared to wreck democratic processes and institutions and destroy individuals' lives and reputations in the process. Their digital slash and burn approach was accompanied by an upsurge in political violence, a collapse of public trust in democratic institutions, and an escalation in social fragmentation. In the three years from January 2019, political violence in Brazil rose by 335 percent. This equated to 1,209 attacks on politicians, with forty-five political leaders killed in the first six months of 2022.[139] Shortly before the 2022 presidential election, 78 percent of Brazilians said they had little or no confidence in the country's Supreme Court, and only slightly more had confidence in the election regulator.[140] And, following the election, almost eight in ten Brazilians believed their country was more fragmented than in the past.[141]

Olavo de Carvalho died on January 24, 2022, of COVID-19 related illnesses. This despite his claims that COVID-19 did not exist and that it had been made up by the state as a means of political control. Brazil's digitally empowered New Right had lost their talisman and lodestone. The new president, Lula da Silva, also set about trying to introduce new laws to limit the spread of disinformation online. Although the parallel information system was diminished, it was not extinguished. Brazil's public remained as reliant on social media for their news and information as they were before. Political influencers continued to post on Twitter and YouTube, as well as on more "free-speech friendly" services such as Telegram, Gab, and Parler. And the *bolsonaristas* were armed and ready for future political battles.

7

THE GOSPEL TRUTH

AMLO's Mexico

If anyone says to you, "Look, here is the Messiah!" or, "There he is!" do not believe it. For false messiahs and false prophets will appear and perform great signs and wonders to deceive.

—MATTHEW, CHAPTER 23: 23–24

I t is 7 A.M. on Wednesday morning, June 30, 2021. The Mexican president, Andrés Manuel López Obrador—nicknamed "AMLO"—walks up to a podium in the National Palace to deliver his daily early morning press conference. Dressed in a plain, dark gray suit, white shirt, and red tie, he issues a friendly "*buenos dias*" to the attending journalists as he approaches the lectern. He is flanked by the Mexican flag and a giant screen on which he sometimes delivers PowerPoints to inform the watching masses on television and YouTube about his regime's achievements. The room becomes silent; he begins to speak.

AMLO's morning press conferences or *mañaneras*—also a slang term for an early morning sexual encounter—often last two to three hours. The president conducts them almost every day, including on weekends. Unlike his predecessors, who relied on spokespeople rather than addressing journalists themselves, AMLO answers journalists' questions directly. Like all populists—although he generally represents the political left—a key part of his brand is being seen to communicate directly with his people. In a calm, engaging style he delivers a lecture about his regime's achievements, then fields questions, first from regime-friendly journalists in the front rows, and then those from less favored outlets further back. Sometimes he gets regime officials to deliver briefings, but as the leading actor in this production, he never leaves the stage himself. There may be a supporting cast, but this is AMLO's spotlight, his news, unfiltered. Once he is finished, the veteran politician has set the news agenda while his fellow politicians are still waking up or indulging in "executive time." Through the mañaneras, AMLO dominates the news. He *is* the news.

Looking over his pulpit at the rows of journalists sitting before him, the president knows his marathon press conferences are a key element of his popularity. AMLO's government claims ten million Mexican citizens watch them every day.[1] But he has also developed a reputation for castigating journalists when they question the veracity of his statements: many of whom receive a torrent of online abuse as a result. His daily diatribes against the "disinformation media" come despite analysts documenting him issuing tens of thousands of misleading or false statements as president.[2] But this morning he has decided to ramp up his criticism of the news media, announcing that the mañaneras will have a new weekly segment, "*Quién es quién en las mentiras de la semana?*" ("Who is who in the lies of the week?"). According to AMLO, its purpose is "not to slander anyone" but to "consolidate democracy" by making known "the lies that are spread in conventional media," so that Mexican citizens are "less susceptible to manipulation" and so that "the truth always prevails."[3]

AMLO steps to one side and invites his presidential spokesperson, Ana Elizabeth García Vilchis, onto the stage. She explains how the government is responding to the "malicious and negligent use of information" by "the media." Like her boss, García Vilchis claims that the segment is not intended "to persecute or censor journalists." She continues with a smattering of examples of the week's news, some of which do appear to be misleading. But according to observers, the segment itself is "littered with inaccuracies," as AMLO's mañaneras often tend to be.[4] Almost immediately García Vilchis contradicts the claim that the section will not persecute journalists, lambasting the spread of falsehoods by "these media outlets and the so-called opinion leaders" who "commit abuses by issuing threats, insults, slander and even incitements to violence" against the president and the government.[5] Toward the end, she highlights the "Pinocchio of the week"—singling out a journalist she believes has, like the mendacious wooden puppet, told the week's most blatant lie. Criticizing the journalist for posting information with insufficient evidence, she explains threateningly that "We are going to remember . . . and we are going to remind the people of Mexico who he is": an ominous statement in a country where more journalists were murdered in 2022 than any other.[6] Having successfully named and shamed the journalist, she offers the floor back to her leader with a satisfied "That's all, President."[7]

Earlier that week AMLO had said that he "doesn't claim to be the owner of absolute truth."[8] Yet here he was at his daily conference, directing his spokesperson to pass judgment on what he saw as true and real in Mexican news. For his critics, AMLO was flagrantly attempting to make himself the primary source of truth for Mexicans, despite the tens of thousands of documented falsehoods he had issued while in office. But in AMLO's parallel reality, he is Mexico's truth. There is no need to use the "*prensa fifí*" or "snot-nosed media"—just tune in to the mañaneras to get your truth directly from the president. Anything contradicting his interpretation of reality reflects a conspiracy by "conservative" elites to thwart the will of the Mexican people, among whom he retained widespread popularity throughout his presidency.

As president of Mexico between 2018 and 2024, AMLO was the archetypal example of a leader trying to position himself as the "unfiltered" source of what is true. As leader he was one of a generation of populists who portrayed themselves as messianic figures, promising to save "the people" from their elite "enemies."[9] For such leaders, the scrutiny of established new outlets is unwelcome. For them the ideal media channel is simply a conduit to deliver their Word directly to the masses. If news outlets do try to filter, mediate, or question the leader, they dismiss them as "fake news" and incite their disciples to attack the unbelievers, many of whom are then forced to self-censor, hide, or simply put up with a deluge of abuse. Simultaneously these leaders use alternative media channels, old and new, to disseminate their gospel to their congregation.

In this chapter we explain how a range of populist leaders have tried to take control of the news agenda, evade media scrutiny, and undermine journalistic independence, as they have sought to establish themselves as the primary source of truth in their societies. Our main focus is AMLO, Mexico's left-wing populist leader, and how he used his mañaneras to promote his version of reality to Mexican citizens and discredit those who questioned it. It combines primary analysis of hundreds of hours of these mañaneras with analysis of news content used by other populist leaders, including Narendra Modi's radio shows, Donald Trump's use of Truth Social before his reelection in 2024, and Conservative politicians' use of GB News in the UK. As we will show, democratic leaders are increasingly adopting more autocratic approaches to news as they seek to ensure that *their* truth comes to be accepted as *the* truth, regardless of how far it deviates from material reality.

MY WORD IS GOSPEL

AMLO's mañaneras received relatively little attention worldwide compared to the public statements of the fellow populist Donald Trump. Although Trump may be the highest profile exponent of contemporary populism, in so many ways AMLO got there first. In 2006, while Trump was managing his property empire and presenting the fifth season of the hit TV show *The Apprentice*, AMLO had narrowly lost the Mexican presidential election, claimed that he only lost because of election fraud, participated in mass protests against the result, and staged his own inauguration as Mexico's "legitimate President" in front of one hundred thousand supporters.[10] Like Trump, this did not stop voters from electing him president subsequently. By the time AMLO was voted into power in a landslide in 2018, he had amassed thirty years of experience positioning himself as the antiestablishment candidate, standing up for ordinary Mexicans against a corrupt, "conservative," "neoliberal elite" that had dominated Mexican politics for decades. This included the PRI (Institutional Revolutionary Party) who had led a single-party system in Mexico between 1929 and 2000, and successive conservative administrations that followed, led by the National Action Party (PAN).

Many leaders, from Kim Jong Un to the Saudi Royal Family, emphasize their eliteness, claiming to stand above the people while still representing them. Other governments adopt a "technocratic" approach, focusing on stable, competent governance. But "populists" such as AMLO approach politics differently. As Cas Mudde, Cristobel Kaltwasser, and others have set out, populists seek legitimacy by framing politics as a struggle between "the people"—whom they claim to represent—and an "elite" who they claim is thwarting the popular will.[11] Left-wing populists traditionally rail against economic elites, accusing them of enriching themselves at the cost of ordinary people. Today's right-wing "national" populists attack economic elites too, but specifically "globalist" elites who they see as profiting from globalization while neglecting the economic well-being and cultural identity of a given country's natives. AMLO's populism combines both elements.

Successful populists convince their followers that they represent the people, although they are often elite figures themselves. Not AMLO. He had an austere upbringing and was raised by his shopkeeper parents in the agricultural Tabasco region of Mexico. He maintained a modest lifestyle as leader. As the mayor of Mexico City from 2000 to 2005, he lived in a small house in a nondescript neighborhood, drove an old, battered Japanese car, and worked long hours. While Trump was known during his first term for beginning his day with several hours of "executive time," AMLO developed a long-standing reputation for working sixteen to eighteen hour days. His mañaneras, which he began as mayor of Mexico City, routinely began at 6.15 A.M.[12] He was a master at employing the "plain folks" mode of propaganda—when a leader seeks to gain support from citizens by claiming that he or she is an ordinary citizen like them.[13] As president he cut his salary by 40 percent and promised to sell Mexico's presidential airplane—finally selling the Boeing 787 Dreamliner, with its marble trim interior, to

Tajikistan in April 2023.[14] On becoming president he refused to live in the presidential palace, *Los Pinos* (The Pines), turning it into a museum. These gestures, combined with his lifestyle, gave him a credibility many populists have lacked when they claim to genuinely represent ordinary people. So effective was AMLO in cultivating an image of a humble man representing the poor that he was termed the "Mexican Messiah."[15]

"Messianic populism" takes populism to the next level. Many populists try hard to frame everyday political issues as showing that "the people" are being stymied by "the elite." But some are sufficiently effective at convincing people that they will deliver them from their elite enemies that they develop a cultlike, divine status, regardless of their ethical conduct.[16] AMLO, Jair Bolsonaro (Brazil), Narendra Modi (India), Donald Trump (USA), and the Philippines' "macho messiah" Rodrigo Duterte have all been exalted as messiahs by their followers, many of whom believe that they are or were divinely appointed to save the nation.[17] AMLO denied being a messianic figure when asked, simply arguing that he was at one with the people. Modi has been described by the BJP officials as "God's divine gift to India" and the "messiah of the poor," an idea Modi has been happy not to contradict.[18] Trump has tried to embody messianic status more flagrantly, blurring political and religious rhetoric to boost his support. At a rally in March 2023, he announced in Old Testament tones: "In 2016, I declared: I am your voice. Today, I add: I am your warrior. I am your justice. And for those who have been wronged and betrayed: I am your retribution."[19]

The ideal situation for the messianic populist is to have a direct communication channel to the population so the leader can speak to the people unfiltered, unedited, and unchallenged. The information environment in the digital age is ideal for messianic populists. Social media provides leaders with a platform to communicate directly with their followers with little or no mediation.[20] But today's messianic populists effectively combine social media with older forms of communication to channel their Word directly to their congregation. Trump likes political rallies. Modi likes radio. AMLO liked live-streamed press conferences.

By the time YouTube was launched in 2005, the "Mexican Messiah" had already conducted hundreds of mañaneras as mayor of Mexico City.

His mayoral mañaneras were less adversarial than those he conducted as president—closer to a (pre-Trump) Whitehouse press conference where AMLO fielded questions from reporters. The press pack, longtime Mexico expert George Grayson writes, were mostly sympathetic to AMLO's agenda in those days, partly because his administration invested heavily in addressing the city's challenges, including urban regeneration, reducing crime, and improving housing, education, pensions, and welfare provision. Some behaved, according to Grayson, "as if they were communicants receiving truth from the master." In turn, AMLO was far more convivial with the press than when he became president.[21]

AMLO left the mayorship with approval ratings of over 80 percent, and he ran for president in 2006. He lost to Felipe Calderon of the conservative National Action Party—which under the then-president Vicente Fox had attempted to disqualify AMLO from running for office. AMLO lost by just 0.5 percent, and then lost the 2012 presidential election to the PRI's candidate, Enrique Peña Nieto, by just under 7 percent. In both cases AMLO questioned the result—perhaps understandably in a country with a documented history of election fraud.[22] In each case the electoral authorities did identify irregularities and agreed to recounts in some constituencies, but they determined that the irregularities were insufficient to change the outcome.[23]

As successive conservative governments failed to address Mexico's decades of inequality, economic stagnation, organized crime, and corruption, AMLO's popularity grew. Opponents tried to replicate the mañaneras but lacked his charisma and commitment. By 2018, even some of Mexico's conservative news outlets started to cover AMLO positively and toned down accusations that he was a socialist, like Hugo Chavez of Venezuela, who would bring Mexico to economic ruin.[24] AMLO also became more astute at using social media in the 2018 campaign. He used it to present a softer, human side, posting unassuming Facebook videos of him playing baseball and giving fireside chats to reinforce the "plain folks" impression he had always conveyed so effectively.[25]

In 2018, at the third attempt, AMLO won an emphatic victory as head of the MORENA party he founded in 2012, leading the *Juntos Haremos*

Historia ("Together we will make history") coalition. He did make history. He won 54.71 percent of the popular vote against 22.91 percent for his nearest challenger; a landslide by Mexican standards—indeed any standards. Voters had tired of rulers who repeatedly promised economic and security reforms but failed to deliver. In a stark illustration of these security concerns, an astonishing 130 politicians were killed during the year-long campaign.[26] AMLO had finally won power with his promise to end corruption and institute a "Fourth Transformation" in which Mexico would be ruled for the poor rather than the elite.[27] This time he accepted the result.

Having used the mañaneras so effectively as mayor of Mexico City, AMLO reinstated them as president. But times had changed. AMLO became president in what was dubbed the "post-truth era" or the "age of populism," in which a host of leaders were building popular support by attacking established news media rather than courting them, and disregarding factual truth rather than adhering to it. The growing use of social media as a news source meant that leaders could communicate with their followers more directly than before. Their congregation could attend their sermons without relying on "mainstream media" to filter, challenge, or criticize the leader's Word. The communication environment had changed, and AMLO's mañaneras changed with it.

AMLO still needed established media outlets to convey his version of the truth to Mexican citizens, but his presidential mañaneras were far more adversarial. He lambasted journalists who questioned or criticized him, accusing them of being part of a lying, corrupt, out of touch elite, conspiring with the conservative opposition to undermine his regime.[28] Journalists targeted by AMLO then typically received waves of online assaults by his loyal followers, including death threats.[29]

AMLO's critics blame his rhetorical attacks on journalists for an increase in violence against them during his administration.[30] The first three years of AMLO's presidency saw thirty-six journalists murdered— a 50 percent increase compared to the two previous administrations, and 1,945 attacks on the press—an 85 percent increase.[31] A direct link between AMLO's verbal assaults and the abuse that followed cannot be proven. But for Mexico's press, experiencing more attacks every day, the link was clear.

An open letter from leading Mexican journalists in December 2022 called on the president to tone down his rhetoric, arguing that "almost all of the outpourings of hatred towards journalists are incubated, born and disseminated from the presidential palace."[32]

THOU SHALT NOT BEAR FALSE WITNESS

The *Who Is Who in Lies of the Week* segment of the mañaneras demonstrated how far AMLO was willing to go to delegitimize his critics. For this reason, it is worth studying in more depth. Drawing on our observations from the dozens of *Who Is Who* segments available online since the weekly segment began in June 2021, we identified five key themes that regularly recurred: falsification, editorial critique, ad hominem slurs, ridicule, and conspiracy theorizing.

In the first, and most common theme, falsification, AMLO's spokesperson identified tweets or news articles that were displayed on the large screen at the mañaneras. These were typically emblazoned with *"falso"* across the front in red letters, and the spokesperson, Ana Elizabeth García Vilchis, explained why—in the president's view—the content was false.

The second theme is critical analysis—similar to how a media owner might take apart an editor's news judgment. AMLO's spokesperson dissected the week's news agenda, indicating where they thought media outlets had devoted too much attention, and where too little. In one instance, they complained that the press was both underreporting AMLO's achievements in reducing inequality and focusing too much on reporting organized crime—as though the government's editorial preferences ought to be factored into decisions about what news media outlets should cover.[33] They then suggested that to get more accurate figures all the journalists needed to do was to take figures from the government website, implying that journalists should simply trust this without question rather than scrutinize it or investigate on their own.

If they could not determine that an article was false or misleading, AMLO and his spokesperson reverted to personal attacks. Journalists

who criticized the regime were "conservatives" who "lie to confuse readers."[34] On November 3, 2021, García Vilchis took exception to a World
Justice Project report that placed Mexico as one of the five most corrupt countries in the world, out of a sample of 139 states.[35] Rather than
explaining why the figures were wrong, she tried to discredit its authors,
claiming that the data was not credible because the organization was
US funded; the experts it consulted lacked academic credentials, and
the institutions involved were "opponents" of AMLO's government.[36]
At other times they simply tried to undermine the journalist's integrity.
One segment aired a video about the mansion owned by a leading news
anchor, Carlos Loret De Mola. The video said that he did not admit
where he got the money to afford the mansion and claimed it was harming the local environment.[37] But it made no reference to the content of
the journalist's news whatsoever.

Sarcasm, humiliation, and humor were also key elements of *Quien es
Quien*. García Vilchis would jokingly accuse outlets that published the
same misleading information of "synchronized swimming": "we are
thinking of registering them for the Olympics in the synchronized swimming category, they will surely be gold medallists."[38] "Sorry, it makes me
laugh," smiled García Vilchis as she alleged sarcastically that the "super
reliable sources" in Mexico's press had underrepresented the number of
welfare centers the government had opened.[39] When trying to debunk
articles suggesting Russia could eventually acquire sanctioned aeronau-
tical parts from the sale of the presidential plane to Tajikistan, García
Vilchis chose memes spread by the Russian embassy as her way of ridicul-
ing the proposals.[40]

Conspiracy theorizing was also integral to *Quien es Quien*. Almost every
time AMLO and his spokesperson named a journalist, they framed the
individual and their publishing organization as part of a broader conspiracy against the regime. A false or misleading tweet was apparently typical of "the media" and "the opposition" generally.[41] As with populist news
anchors such as America's Tucker Carlson or India's Arnab Goswami (see
chapter 5), AMLO and García Vilchis used the pronoun "they" to describe
a vague, shadowy opponent conspiring against the people's interests. But

unlike the bombast of Carlson and Goswami, AMLO and his spokesperson's delivery was far calmer. Almost whispering, with a wry smile, AMLO explained slowly and plainly on May 18, 2022: "It is important to know how *our* adversaries lie and slander in *their* desperation, why *they* would want the corrupt regime to return." "*They* miss corruption." "*They* got used to the fact that the people did not exist, and now that the people are the protagonists of this story, it bothers *them* a lot" [emphasis added].[42]

Part of the reason these conspiratorial claims resonated with AMLO's supporters is that Mexico had a long history of media capture by the government and its business allies. The single-party PRI government had a near monopoly on print and television news from the 1940s to the 1990s, and a close relationship between government and the press had long been maintained by an extensive system of bribes, subsidies, and concessions.[43] This history gave AMLO a sympathetic audience when he claimed that viewers who want "the truth" should ignore the *prensa fifi* and go directly to him and his government instead.

The problem is, research has shown that the content of AMLO's mañaneras was often untruthful. Whereas AMLO the mayor developed a reputation for dodging difficult questions, AMLO the president developed a reputation for fabricating answers. His go-to catchphrase was "I have other data," but he usually would not cite any. When questioned in a 2019 mañanera about official government figures showing an increase in the frequency of murders during his administration, AMLO denied the increase had taken place, said his own government's figures were wrong, and said "I have other information."[44] When questioned in a 2021 mañanera about why he disagreed with official poverty figures, he simply said he had his own method of measuring well-being, and did not elaborate.[45] During the COVID-19 pandemic, AMLO infamously encouraged citizens to continue to hug each other despite scientific evidence of how proximity helped the virus spread.[46] At one mañanera he brandished amulets he said he was wearing to ward off the virus.[47] In his first three years as president, the SPIN think tank counted more than 61,000 false or misleading AMLO statements—eighty-eight per press conference on average, and twice Donald Trump's rate during his first term as the US president.[48]

Even though AMLO was willing to field multiple questions from the attending press, it is debatable whether the mañaneras were as dialogic as they appeared to be. According to Jorge Muñoz and Pablo Aguirre, the mañaneras were heavily structured in his favor.[49] AMLO mainly fielded easy questions from carefully positioned journalists close to the podium. Some of these were accused of being phony reporters, planted there to ask AMLO easy questions on his preferred topics.[50] His answers to these questions took twelve minutes each on average, denying airtime to reporters who scrutinized the government more robustly or raised more challenging issues.[51] Reporters from the major newspapers and TV channels were positioned further back, and AMLO offered them a platform far more rarely. In this way the press conferences were carefully orchestrated to enable AMLO to deliver his sermons directly to his audience, while limiting his critics' ability to question him.

Despite sustained criticism from Mexico's press, the mañaneras remained popular throughout AMLO's presidency. In October 2019, 69 percent of Mexican citizens approved of them, and until December 2021 disapproval of them never exceeded 25 percent.[52] Regardless of how often AMLO distorted reality, a poll by El Financiero in 2021 found that 50 percent of young Mexicans felt better informed because of the mañaneras.[53] Few leaders are willing to engage in such a labor-intensive way to dominate the news agenda, but for AMLO they were instrumental in his efforts to become the primary source of truth for Mexico's citizens.

IF YOU QUESTION MY WORD YOU ARE A HERETIC

AMLO's mañaneras showed how leaders could use direct communication to position themselves as the primary source of truth and reality for the masses. His news, his agenda, and his framing dominated the news. For his followers, his "truth" was Mexico's truth. His version of reality *was* reality. But to become the dominant source of truth in democratic societies, dominating the news agenda is usually not enough. The leader must ideally limit the ability of unbelievers to counter the leader's version of reality. There are two major problems for today's would-be political messiahs. First, independent news outlets will scrutinize the leader's version of reality and challenge it if it is false or misleading. Second, the social media platforms they rely on to communicate directly with their followers can take down the leader's content when it violates their policies on disinformation, hate speech, and incitement to violence—if they choose to do so.

To undermine the legacy media's ability to scrutinize the government's version of reality, today's messianic populists adopt two major strategies: attacking their critics rhetorically and evading them. AMLO prefers to attack. Few know this better than the veteran reporter Carlos Loret De Mola.

Carlos Loret De Mola was one of Mexico's highest profile journalists both before and during AMLO's presidency. An award-winning television presenter on Televisa and a former war reporter, De Mola's 9.6 million X followers in January 2024 almost matched the 10.4 million followers of AMLO himself.[54] In 2020 De Mola set up *Latinus*, a digital journalism platform, to investigate crime and corruption. From this platform, De Mola published in January 2021 an exposé detailing the opulent lifestyle of AMLO's eldest son, who reportedly lived in a $1 million home in Houston, Texas.[55] For De Mola, investigating the wealth of political elites was a legitimate piece of public interest journalism in a country with a history of corruption.

AMLO, who had so successfully built his brand on his austere lifestyle, was furious. For him the article was a hatchet job intended to discredit him by a wealthy journalist who was part of the power elite himself. He went on the attack. To discredit De Mola, during his next mañanera AMLO published on his giant screen a breakdown of De Mola's income alongside his own. In the process, critics alleged, he likely violated the country's tax laws and De Mola's constitutional right to data privacy.[56] He lambasted De Mola as a "bully" and a "mercenary," who was concocting scandals because he "continues to be at the service of the mafia of power."[57] AMLO had issued these criticisms hundreds of times as president. But for his detractors, targeting a journalist like this went too far, especially since five journalists had been killed in Mexico in the previous month.[58] De Mola released a video saying that the figures were inflated, that they contained income from a company he no longer worked for, and that AMLO had endangered him and his family by revealing them. But AMLO doubled down. He showed the same income graph at a mañanera three days later. Asking rhetorically why De Mola earns so much, AMLO stated that is because De Mola is paid "to attack me, to weaken us" and to "strike, not only at the government, but at the transformation project that millions of Mexicans are carrying out to put an end to Mexico's problem: corruption."[59] For investigating his son's lifestyle, AMLO accused De Mola not just of trying to undermine his reputation. He smeared De Mola as a corrupt enemy of the entire Mexican people—live in front of millions of citizens. As a wealthy, elite journalist, De Mola was the ideal figure for a populist such as AMLO to rail against. But more important, De Mola was a heretic. He dared to question the Mexican Messiah's version of reality. Heretics must be punished.

Verbally attacking journalists has predictable consequences in a country where they already face the threat of violence. Carlos Loret De Mola knew this all too well. He was the third generation of journalists in his family, after his father Rafael Loret De Mola, and his grandfather Carlos Loret De Mola Mediz. In November 2023 Carlos's father, Rafael, reported on his YouTube channel that his house had been broken into. An AMLO critic himself, he often posted videos on his YouTube channel criticizing AMLO's regime, referring to him as "Mr Rotten Head." As Rafael surveyed his remaining possessions, which were strewn about his house, he noticed a knife stabbed into his desk. The knife, Rafael reported, impaled a note that simply said "AMLO."[60] This dramatic death threat was far from his first after over half a century as a Mexican journalist. But for Rafael this was even more personal. His father, Carlos Loret De Mola's grandfather, and another journalist were killed in a car accident in 1986. Ever since, Rafel has maintained that the crash was a state assassination because of his father's criticism of the regime.[61] His grandson, AMLO's current antagonist, was just ten at the time.

AMLO's attack on Carlos Loret De Mola was one of thousands of diatribes against the news media by his administration. Much of the violence against journalists was documented by press freedom organizations, such as the think tank, Article 19.[62] By mid-2023, the group had documented more than three thousand attacks on Mexican journalists during AMLO's tenure.[63] About half of these consisted of intimidation and harassment by public officials and just under half were committed against journalists reporting on political corruption.[64] Despite calls by Article 19 and other press freedom organizations for AMLO to cease his vitriol, AMLO demurred. Instead, he used World Press Freedom Day in May 2023 to accuse Article 19 of being an instrument of US foreign policy "nourish[ing] a coup" against his administration.[65] In doing so he used a tactic more often associated with dictators rather than democrats: he accused his critics of being foreign agents who were plotting his regime's downfall.

AMLO's attacks demonstrate the zeal with which today's messianic populists attack the legacy news media. As George Grayson writes, messianic populists position themselves as having a "monopoly on truth." Their narratives are not to be debated, just disseminated, because "they hold promise for the political salvation of the destitute." The messianic politician defines the law as "the will of the people" as he or she interprets it, and their Word defies mediation or moderation.[66] Because of this, messianic populists tend to reject the notion that the press should act as the Fourth Estate, holding them to account in the public interest. Instead, they believe their authority as truth-tellers comes from a direct mandate from the people. As a result, they and their supporters respond swiftly and aggressively when journalists dare to question their version of reality.

PUNISHMENT BY THE RIGHTEOUS

In his mañaneras, AMLO named and shamed specific journalists who disagreed with his version of reality. But many democratic leaders prefer not to do this themselves because it looks too authoritarian. For today's aspiring political messiahs, however, there is an alternative: to incite their online followers to attack their critics, covertly boosting these attacks with bots, trolls, and other manufactured activity. The leader's legions exert their righteous indignation on the detractors, and the whole thing looks like a spontaneous, democratic expression of the popular will.

Jorge Ramos is another veteran journalist who experienced AMLO's wrath for questioning his version of reality. Well-known across Central and South America, Ramos was a leading news anchor at Univision, the leading US Spanish language television network, which broadcasts in sixteen other countries in the region.[67] Taking US citizenship in 2008, Ramos had won eight Emmys for his journalism, published over a dozen books, covered every major US news event "since the fall of the Berlin Wall," and managed to question a remarkable range of leaders, from Barack Obama to Cuba's Fidel Castro.[68] In 2015 he was temporarily ejected from a press conference by Donald Trump for asking him unprompted questions about Mexican immigrants, who Trump had previously described as "criminals" and "rapists."[69] In February 2019, he and his team were temporarily detained by the Venezuelan president, Nicolas Maduro, who was unhappy with Ramos's robust questioning.[70] He has a knack for asking questions leaders do not want to answer.

Now, in April 2019, Ramos attended one of AMLO's mañaneras, and questioned him about Mexico's crime figures. The president and the journalist sparred over their interpretations of the murder rate. Ramos cited the government's official figures, which indicated that there were more murders under AMLO's regime than in previous administrations. AMLO disagreed with Ramos, claimed that his own government's official figures were wrong, and that he "had other data" that apparently showed the murder rate declining. Both got increasingly agitated; AMLO with Ramos's persistent questioning, and Ramos with AMLO's evasive answers. Following the exchange, AMLO reflected on an interview he had seen in which the presenter suggested that Ramos was a good journalist because he questioned the president so robustly, but that many other journalists at the mañaneras were not because they were too passive. Disagreeing with this, AMLO offered his own interpretation: that the press pack were "prudent," because "if you cross the line, you know what happens to you. But it's not me, it's the people."[71]

AMLO's comment was quickly picked up by the world's press, who interpreted it as a threat.[72] In many ways it was more significant. He had acknowledged something many leaders prefer not to admit: that their popularity gives them the power to incite a storm of online abuse toward their critics, and that this is an efficient way to coerce them to self-censor. AMLO showed he knew that if he took exception to how a journalist questioned him his followers would rain fire and brimstone down upon them. Moreover, because the abuse would appear to come from authentic citizens online, it would seem like an organic, spontaneous expression of popular dissent rather than something incited by him.

Mexico's press already knew how this works, though. In April 2019, the chief editor of the *Reforma* newspaper, Juan Pardinas, received death threats and was "doxed" (had his addressed publicly revealed) after being criticized by AMLO for a report on the increased security arrangements at the president's home. A social media campaign with the hashtag #NarcoReforma spread on Twitter, insinuating that *Reforma* had links to organized crime, with commenters suggesting that the newspaper's facilities should be burnt down with the editor inside.[73] The conversation thread underneath the YouTube live-stream of the mañaneras was filled with invective against journalists who asked challenging questions.[74] Abuse of female journalists was often sexually explicit, echoing the abuse of female journalists in India, where journalists that criticize Modi are referred to as "presstitutes," and female journalists who criticize the government regularly receive rape and death threats.[75] All it took was to question AMLO's statements and a storm of abuse followed.[76]

As Mexican journalists knew all too well, this abuse did not just create pressure to self-censor: there was a very real risk that some would interpret it as a justification for offline violence. In December 2022, the high-profile Mexican news anchor Ciro Gomez Leyva narrowly survived an assassination attempt, saved by bulletproof glass as armed gunmen shot at his car.[77] The following morning, AMLO expressed relief that Levya survived, "because he is a journalist, a human being, a leader of public opinion and damage to a personality like Ciro generates a lot of political instability."[78] But just the day before, AMLO had rhetorically attacked the journalist himself, claiming that by listening to journalists like Leyva "you can even get a tumor in your brain."[79] Rather than acknowledging the potential link between aggressive rhetoric toward journalists and the attacks that follow, AMLO veered into conspiracy theory, hinting that the attack on Leyva might have been staged to discredit his government. One could not easily prove a link between AMLO's attacks and the violence that followed.[80] But for many of Mexico's press, AMLO's rhetoric was partly responsible, because it set an example that journalists could be attacked with impunity.[81]

AMLO's status as a messianic figure provided an even stronger motivation for his acolytes to persecute those who questioned him. For true believers, to challenge the leader's version of reality is heresy. The "near deification" of the leader leads supporters to respond "to even the mildest criticism of them with the vehemence of those whose religious faith has been mocked by a blasphemer."[82] Not only that, there is no need for a leader with a cult following to explicitly instruct their followers to persecute the leader's critics. They can issue their threats in coded language and maintain deniability, knowing that those with faith do not require direct instruction—the righteous will persecute their enemies, believing that they are doing their leader's will. AMLO admitted this himself; all the press had to do was to "step out of line" and his loyal followers would do the rest.

TRUE BELIEVERS?

What was less clear in AMLO's Mexico was how far the online abuse journalists experienced really was an authentic expression of the popular will, or whether it was augmented by covert manipulation. Investigative journalists and academics have identified government campaigns to manipulate social media in dozens of countries across the world, from Argentina to Zimbabwe, from Australia to Yemen.[83] As chapter 6 detailed, in Brazil Jair Bolsonaro's government faced investigation for operating its "Hate Cabinet," which coordinated harassment and abuse campaigns against journalists and public figures who criticized the regime. In India, investigative journalists and whistleblowers have alleged that the BJP's "IT Cell" have paid citizens to troll Modi's critics and flood their accounts with abuse (see chapter 5).[84]

AMLO appeared to benefit from coordinated, inauthentic, social media manipulation himself, although whether his regime was directly involved is unclear. A 2019 study from Signa Lab explained in detail how automated accounts amplified attacks on AMLO's detractors. First, MC or "Master of Ceremony" accounts emerged at about 8 A.M. during the mañaneras, introducing content that was intended to go viral.[85] These messages were then disseminated at high volume by a chorus of automated "choir bots," which tweeted up to 8,500 times per week, most of which were retweets. Troll accounts, which tweeted about two hundred times per week on average, spread the MC's content, adding their own criticism of the journalist in question. Then authentic citizens, supportive of AMLO, reproduced this content, although they only produced a fraction of the content that the choir bots did.[86]

AMLO denied the government's involvement, stating that "we do not have bots."[87] Indeed, he may have benefited from pro-regime business people or other political actors organizing such campaigns on his behalf. In one mañanera, he called on social media companies to restrict the use of bot networks, and not without reason. His predecessor, Enrique Peña Nieto, benefited from a well-documented army of "*Peñabots*," which were used to flood Twitter and Facebook with pro-government messages and smears against his critics.[88] This covert manipulation can make government narratives look more popular—and their critics' narratives less popular—than they really are.

For leaders that do use social media manipulation, it is especially important that genuine citizens participate. This enables governments to deny their involvement, and it makes the abuse journalists receive look more authentic and democratic. Meanwhile the leader can stay above the fray, and the whole thing can be used to reinforce an exaggerated sense of their popularity, increasing their cult following further. Their preferred version of reality becomes more widespread, and their critics know they must self-censor or face a torrent of abuse.

DENYING MY CRITICS

AMLO's approach to news was unique in an important way. He was willing, day after day, to stand up for hours and face questions from the press, something even the most democratic of leaders have rarely had the time or willingness to do. He did submit himself to critical scrutiny, albeit on his terms. His fellow populists have been far less willing to be challenged by outlets that might question or criticize them. So as well as attacking the news media, they have tried to evade outlets that might contradict their versions of reality.

India's prime minister, Narendra Modi, is another leader with a humble upbringing who has deftly crafted an image of himself as a messianic leader who channels the popular will. Like AMLO, he was touted as the world's most popular elected politician, at least until his party, the BJP, lost their majority in the 2024 election.[89] The big difference between AMLO and Modi is that Modi engages with the press as little as possible. At the time of writing, he has never answered questions at a press conference in India after a decade as prime minister, whereas AMLO has conducted over a thousand.

Modi can evade press scrutiny because technological advances mean that there are more ways for leaders to communicate directly with their audiences than ever before. Social media is the most obvious example. But the proliferation of new, and often partisan, digital news channels gives leaders the option to appear only on sympathetic outlets. It is quicker, easier, and cheaper than ever for leaders to create and stream their own content. Many leaders have their own social media teams, but all they really need to do is hold their phone up and press "record."

By combining these tools, leaders such as Modi can bypass the traditional gatekeepers of the Fourth Estate and limit access to news outlets that might question or criticize them. Modi has used Google Hangouts to interact with voters during election campaigns, and used Twitter to accuse his opponents of being corrupt and out of touch.[90] In 2015 he set up his own "NaMo" app, a Twitter-like platform replete with pro-regime propaganda, although its few million followers are dwarfed by the over a hundred million followers Modi has on more established platforms. Modi also favors older broadcast media, using radio addresses, phone calls to citizens, and even holograms to address political rallies in over a hundred locations simultaneously in the 2014 Indian elections.[91] But in power his favorite conduit to deliver his Word to the masses is radio, specifically his monthly show, *Mann Ki Baat* ("Speaking from the Heart").[92]

Part national address, part sermon, *Mann Ki Baat* is a half-hour audio show produced by Modi's team and broadcast on national radio and online. In the decade after he came to office in 2014, he released over a hundred shows, almost one a month. His office boasts that over a billion citizens have tuned in at least once, and that it is a "transformative force in Indian governance, embodying the principles of participatory democracy, inclusivity, and social change."[93] A think tank directed by senior members of Modi's BJP party lauds the show for having "transformed the country's mindset" because of its "powerful and inspiring messages coupled with a practice of open dialogue."[94] These are impressive claims for a show with only thirty minutes of heavily scripted content per month.

Yet *Mann Ki Baat* is integral to Modi's populism. Through the show he claims to channel the popular will directly, stating that his words are "an expression of the feelings" of "millions of Indians."[95] The show's webpage says that the show involves him "interacting" with his people, who he refers to regularly as "friends" or "family members," positioning himself as a warm, paternal figure. Outside the broadcast itself, the show allows some interaction—users can post comments or post requests for new policies, like religious devotees queueing to receive alms from their master. To celebrate the one hundredth show, the government invited people to submit ideas, theme tunes, and a logo that the show could use. These tightly controlled interactions enable leaders like Modi to claim that broadcasts such as this represent a more direct and participatory form of democratic political communication. But *Maan Ki Baat* involves little interaction in reality—it more often involves a lecture from Modi vaunting his regime's achievements and describing success stories about Indian entrepreneurs, interspersed with Modi's personal anecdotes, occasional recitals of his poetry, or comments about yoga. No one can question Modi's pronouncements during the broadcast or challenge his claims. On *Mann Ki Baat*, Modi is in control. He is on send, and his citizens are on receive.

For populists such as Modi, broadcasts like *Mann Ki Baat* make strategic sense. Combined with social media, they allow leaders to communicate their narratives unfiltered and to evade the scrutiny of news publishers who might challenge them. Unsurprisingly, the press criticize Modi for refusing to engage with them. To placate his critics, Modi sometimes publishes a prerecorded interview by a regime-friendly journalist. A technique more often associated with autocrats, but increasingly popular among democratic leaders, it gives leaders greater control over the mediation process and creates the misleading impression that they are open to scrutiny.[96]

Messianic populists have moved beyond simple evasion of news publishers. They avoid media scrutiny not just as a political strategy or electoral tactic but on principle. The messianic leader claims to embody the people's will. They see their Word as *the* news, the gospel; something that should not be questioned. It is not just that they do not *want* the press to mediate what they say. They do not believe their messages *should* be mediated by journalists or moderated by social media platforms. Like televangelists, what they want most is a conduit to channel their gospel directly to their audience. They define truth. They dictate it.

This is a key reason why messianic populism is a troubling political phenomenon. It can seem democratic: leaders can argue that their direct engagement with citizens is more democratic than more distant opponents, and they often have genuine popular support. But such leaders are asking citizens to consent to an authoritarian approach to communication. They see open debate, criticism, and freedom of the press not as necessary elements of democracy but as threats to be countered or evaded.[97] Their approach to truth is not based on the liberal-democratic idea that citizens should engage in open discourse and debate, which will allow the truth to win out over lies. It is instead based on a more religious, autocratic approach to truth: that the truth is what those in authority say it is. Citizens should have faith in their leader and accept their words uncritically, however far they deviate from material reality.

MY PLATFORM, MY WORD

On January 8, 2021, Twitter, Facebook, and YouTube banned Donald Trump. Having done relatively little about the tens of thousands of falsehoods he had issued during his first term, the platforms finally suspended his account because his encouragement of the protesters at the January 6 Capitol riots constituted incitement to violence.[98] Instantly, Trump lost his megaphone. Twitter especially had been the main way he communicated with his base and gained the attention of mainstream media.[99]

Observing events further north, AMLO might have been expected to show little sympathy. After all, he railed against conservatives and even called Trump a "neofascist" while campaigning for president.[100] But, like Trump, AMLO often used social media to speak directly to the people, and he knew that Mexico had no regulations in place to stop the platforms doing to him what they had done to Trump. Reflecting on the platforms' decisions, he asked rhetorically: how can such companies act like an "all-powerful," "omnipotent" "Spanish Inquisition" on freedom of speech? "Yes, social media should not be used to incite violence and all that," he admitted, but "this cannot be used as a pretext to suspend freedom of expression."[101]

AMLO had raised an issue that troubles today's messianic populists, and any government willing to spread misleading or false information: what happens if you are denied access to the platforms you rely on to communicate with your followers? News distribution online—at least outside states such as North Korea—is dominated by a small group of platforms (including Google, YouTube, Facebook, WhatsApp, Instagram, and X) who can take down leaders' content if they choose to do so. It is hard to become a society's primary source of truth if the platforms can silence you at will.

One answer is to move to a platform where content moderation is more lax. Following Trump's ban, AMLO posted a Facebook message inviting his followers to join him on Telegram, as Jair Bolsonaro had in Brazil.[102] But AMLO also suggested a second solution: to create Mexican state social media channels to preserve Mexican citizens' freedom of expression. The press speculated about what they might be called: "Facebookóatl" perhaps, or "Twitterlopochtli," drawing on the names of gods from Aztec mythology.[103]

AMLO's national social media channels have not yet been created, although he is not the only party leader who has considered creating an alternative platform. With one eye on politics and the other on profit, Donald Trump created his own platform, Truth Social, in October 2021.

After the Capitol riots, Truth Social provided Trump with a safe space to deliver his gospel directly to his congregation during Joe Biden's term of office. In the absence of the presidency itself, it was Trump's "bully pulpit"; the platform on which he could share his views without mediation or moderation. The site offered his most loyal followers the chance to join him in the Promised Land. The "alt-right" and "far-right" sections of his base had spent years in a long march across the web in search of platforms that would uphold their interpretation of free speech, from platforms like Reddit, 4Chan, and 8Chan, to Discord, Telegram, Gab, Parler, Gettr, and Rumble. With Truth Social, Trump promised that their exile could end. The new platform would give them a permanent home where they could commune with their leader free of what they saw as the stifling censorship of mainstream social media:

> I created TRUTH Social and TMTG (The Trump Media and Technology Group) to stand up to the tyranny of Big Tech. We live in a world where the Taliban has a huge presence on Twitter, yet your favorite American President has been silenced. This is unacceptable. I am excited to send out my first TRUTH on TRUTH Social very soon.[104]

During this period, the site itself was largely indistinguishable from Twitter before its rebranding as X, with a blue "T" logo rather than a bird. Users had the usual options to comment, like, and repost content. A sidebar listed trending hashtags and suggested topics to follow. But while the site visibly resembled mainstream social media outlets, its content was similar to other platforms associated with the pro-Trump "alt-right." Conspiracy theories abounded, and the most commonly shared links were to mainstays of the US's right-wing news ecosystem—One America

News Network (OANN), NewsMax, Breitbart, Fox News, Rumble, and Telegram.[105] Truth Social's unique selling point was Trump's presence on the platform. "TRUTH SOCIAL IS MY VOICE, AND THE REAL VOICE OF AMERICA," he exclaimed in March 2024.[106] Trump used the platform similarly to how he used Twitter—to rant about opponents, repeat claims of election fraud, post clips of his speeches, and highlight content portraying him favorably and his opponents unfavorably. On Truth Social, he always knew that his posts would not be flagged or removed if they contained disinformation. He also used the site to bolster his messianic credentials as he campaigned for reelection. This included reposting in January 2024 a video titled "God Made Trump," which portrayed him as a divinely appointed figure with a mission to return America to prosperity.[107]

Trump's disciples framed Truth Social as a broad church for anyone concerned about free speech: a "big tent, an open and free network to be able to assert your First Amendment rights," according to his son, Donald Trump Junior.[108] However, research into the site's content moderation practices during this early period suggested that it was better described as an echo chamber for like-minded Trump supporters to receive his Word unfiltered, rather than a site for genuinely free expression. It immediately faced accusations of censorship when its initial terms of service stated that users were not allowed to "disparage, tarnish, or otherwise harm, in our opinion, us and/or the Site."[109] Early users found that the site would reject usernames critical of the site or of Trump himself. The site shadow-banned references to topics that would discredit Trump, including coverage of the January 6 Committee, investigating Trump's involvement in the Capitol riots. Early on, the site even shadow-banned some conservative content, including criticism of US support for the war in Ukraine, and some pro-gun material.[110] Ironically, the initial terms and conditions also railed against excessive use of CAPITAL LETTERS in posts.[111] For a platform stylized as TRUTH Social, it was a surprising edict, especially given that its founder still used them liberally himself.

The branding of Trump's site as "Truth Social" neatly captures how leaders can try to present themselves as *the* authority on what is true and real in their societies. "Truth" is the term used to describe posts on the site, and reposts are "ReTruths"—which dilutes the concept of truth to whatever a user says at a given moment. In this way the site trades in authenticity rather than veracity. At a time when people can be praised for sharing *their truth*—their authentic, honest perspective—Trump's "truths" are "what he really thinks," regardless of its resemblance to material reality.

There is an Orwellian twist to this conceptualization of truth, though. A key characteristic of authoritarians is how they pervert the meaning of everyday concepts to serve their purposes—as Russia has done with the concept of "war" (see chapter 2) and China has done with "democracy" and "human rights" (see chapter 3).[112] Trump's use of the term "Truth" on Truth Social perverts its meaning as "something factual" in two ways. On the one hand, Truth Social's use of "truth" resembles the old Soviet newspaper *Pravda* ("Truth"). That is, "truth" is what authority figures (in this case Trump himself) want people to believe. Whether the leader is democratically elected or not, this approach to truth is inherently authoritarian, as it asks citizens to accept whatever the leader says as true, however honest or reliable.[113] But the site's twist on the term "truth" goes further, reducing it to mere "opinion" or even "content." This strips the concept of meaning and importance. A "shitposter" posting abuse to provoke other users, a conspiracy theorist, and someone giving their opinion on the latest baseball game are all posting "truths" on Trump's platform.

Hannah Arendt wrote that the result of repeated political lying is not necessarily that lies end up replacing the truth. Rather, that people will distrust the truth of any statement, in the process losing "the sense by which we take our bearings in the real world."[114] The use of "truth" on Truth Social suggests something even more disconcerting—a communication environment not just where people do not know what is true but that they do not *care* what is true. In that situation, why not choose your government's perspective over another country's, the most entertaining leader over their more boring competitor, or simply whichever version of reality you find most profitable or appealing? Trump's insight about this helps answer a question that confounds his critics: how he managed to win reelection in 2024 despite his frequent disregard for factual reality.

Whether Truth Social helped Trump get reelected is debatable. Its estimated two million active users in early 2024, and Trump's six million followers were a fraction of the seventy-six million who voted for him that year. Winning the endorsement of the X owner, Elon Musk, who used his control of the platform to flood his two hundred million followers' feeds with pro-Trump messaging, provided far greater volume and reach. In its first two years, Truth Social filed a net loss of US$31.6 million, raising questions about its future viability, even though it was valued at US$7.85 billion at the end of its first day on the stock market in March 2024.[115] But however limited the platform's success was during Trump's interregnum, it served as an effective pulpit. Even if his followership was limited, his posts were picked up by news outlets and amplified across mainstream social media. But it also enabled Trump to gather together his congregation in a partisan echo chamber where they were less likely to come across counterarguments or criticism from other users. Their leader's Word was communicated directly, and he knew it would not be taken down. It is a prototype of how leaders can avoid platform content moderation, subvert the meaning and importance of truth, and position themselves as the primary source of reality for their followers.

SPREADING THE WORD

The ongoing popularity of Trump, Modi, and AMLO has shown how populist leaders in democracies can retain mass support regardless of whether their narratives correspond to material reality. By attacking their critics, bypassing the Fourth Estate, and setting up direct communication channels with the masses, they can create a news environment in which it is easier for their narratives to dominate. This is more straightforward in democracies where media freedoms remain limited (Mexico was ranked 128th on 2023's Press Freedom Index and India was ranked 161st).[116] Observing their successes, governments in more liberal democracies are imitating populist approaches to the news in the hope that their governments' versions of the truth come to be accepted as *the* truth.

On March 11, 2023, the UK's news broadcaster, GB News, televised a prerecorded interview with the chancellor of the exchequer, Jeremy Hunt, about the government's upcoming budget statement. The self-consciously right-wing populist outlet (it promotes itself as the "People's Channel") had struggled to gain market share since its inception.[117] Early on, several of its broadcasts suffered technical difficulties, and it faced an advertising boycott and multiple staff resignations due to its overtly partisan, and at times conspiracist, approach to news.[118] Having weathered these early setbacks, the viewing numbers of the UK's "Fox News" were improving, and it was being rewarded with an exclusive interview with the government's second most powerful politician to discuss the country's future economic direction.[119]

The interview was relatively benign, in a cozy, warmly lit room with shelves of identical old books in the background. Hunt sat comfortably with his red budget briefcase strategically positioned on the mantelpiece next to his head, and received little challenge from his two questioners. Viewers quickly realized why. He was being interviewed by two other current Conservative members of Parliament, married couple Esther McVey and Philip Davies, who had taken on second jobs as presenters on the channel in addition to their full-time jobs as government politicians.

The presenters made little effort to hide their affiliation. McVey's responses to Hunt's answers were friendly: "I think we all agree with that," she said at one point, offering little pushback to the chancellor's responses. Despite being the presenter, McVey explained that as a Conservative government "*we* have to make sure that *we* don't spend what *we* haven't got"—repeating a campaign message her party had used since at least 2010. Before asking a question about rumored rises in corporation tax, she described it as a "horrifying thought," showing her agreement with the chancellor's tax-cutting preferences before even asking the question. "That's why you and I are Conservatives, Phil," the chancellor responded later, "because we believe in bringing tax rates down." Hunt jokily referred to the presenters as the "dynamic duo" as they laughed together. Much of the interview came across as a relaxed chat between friends and colleagues about what it means to be a Conservative, in which news presenter and politician merged into one.[120]

As a mature liberal democracy scoring relatively highly on media freedom (twenty-sixth on the World Press Freedom Index in 2023), the UK has stronger media regulations than most countries.[121] Broadcasters are answerable to an independent regulator, Ofcom, which requires them to present a range of political viewpoints, and politicians are not usually allowed to be news presenters unless "editorially justified." But here sat a Conservative finance minister being interviewed by two Conservative MPs about a Conservative budget. "Really hard hitting journalism there," the most liked commenter on the interview's YouTube feed noted sarcastically.[122]

Unsurprisingly, Ofcom determined that the program violated impartiality guidelines for failing to provide viewpoints other than those of the ruling party.[123] It was one of several cases against GB News at the time. The channel has been dubbed "Tory TV" for its repeated violation of impartiality guidelines and its employment of several Conservative politicians while they were still serving in parliament.[124] It takes an act of Orwellian doublethink to accept that government politicians cosplaying as news presenters to interview fellow government politicians could realistically be considered "impartial" news or "independent journalism." But the channel's defense stretched credulity further, claiming that it had not violated broadcasting guidelines because the content of "GB News" is not actually "news." Instead, it claimed that its politician presenters were anchoring "current affairs shows" rather than "news bulletins," a regulatory loophole the channel used to justify employing Conservative politicians as presenters.[125]

Sending government politicians to be interviewed on GB News by their colleagues was part of a broader pattern of evading independent scrutiny by successive Conservative administrations, as they attempted to ensure that their news was mediated on their terms. Earlier in Rishi Sunak's premiership, his home secretary, Suella Braverman, was criticized for denying the BBC and the UK's centrist and left-wing newspapers access to her visit to Rwanda to conduct diplomacy in support of the government's controversial immigration policy to ship a fraction of the UK's failed asylum seekers there.[126] The Boris Johnson government had previously done the same, and it had also blocked centrist and left-leaning outlets from attending a Downing Street press conference.[127] Johnson's government boycotted programs on the BBC, ITV, and Channel 4 on which ministers received more challenging questions, and in one especially embarrassing moment Johnson hid in an industrial fridge to avoid questioning by an ITV reporter during the 2019 election campaign.[128] This avoidance of the press has not been limited to the political right, though. The US president Joe Biden was criticized for having done only eighty-six media interviews in the first three years of his presidency, compared to the three hundred by Trump in his first term.[129]

The legality of the Conservative administration and GB News's use of politicians as news presenters remained under dispute at the time of writing. The opposition Labour politician, David Lammy, was also under investigation by Ofcom for presenting a radio phone-in on London-based LBC radio. However, Lammy's phone-ins typically involved callers with a wide range of views, and he relinquished the role when appointed the foreign secretary after the Labour Party won power in 2024.[130] Whatever the outcome, having members of the government presenting the news and interviewing each other about their own policies is self-evidently undemocratic, as it prevents the government's actions from being subjected to independent scrutiny. There can be no such thing as independent media if the government *is* the media. George Orwell's acclaimed novel *Animal Farm* concludes by showing how those who claim to promote freedom from oppression can end up resembling the oppressors themselves: "The creatures outside looked from pig to man, and from man to pig, and from pig to man again; but already it was impossible to say which was which."[131] Or in the case of GB News, "the audience looked from politician to journalist, and journalist to politician, and it was impossible to say which was which." The more successfully a government achieves this, the more they are able to position themselves as the authoritative source of truth and reality in otherwise democratic societies.

* * *

From the start, 2024 was touted as one of the most important years for contemporary democracy. Over half of the world's population, across over fifty countries, would vote to determine whether their leaders would stay in power. One leader who did not seek reelection was AMLO. Respecting Mexico's constitution, which limits presidents to a single six-year term, he left office with personal approval ratings of over 60 percent—a figure about which most democratic leaders could only dream and that would have seen him easily reelected.[132] As Luis Rubio explains, his rule began with promise, a vast personal mandate, and valid objectives—to address Mexico's "ancestral evils" of "inequality, poverty and lack of growth."[133] He received justified praise for successfully improving the economic situation for working class Mexicans. He raised the minimum wage to 85 percent above inflation, invested in a range of infrastructure projects, and visited local communities across Mexico that had previously been neglected by state authorities.[134] After well over a thousand mañaneras, the man dubbed the "Mexican Messiah" perhaps worked harder than any other leader to position himself as the primary source of truth and reality for his people.

Yet for his critics, AMLO demonstrated an approach to news that undermines democracy. For messianic populists like the veteran Mexican leader, the process of establishing ground truth in society does not stem from deliberation between citizens or independent verification: truth and reality are whatever the leader says they are. Such leaders claim authority based on faith rather than reason—they want people to accept that their Word is gospel and denounce any who disagree. If audiences consent to this—and many in the world currently do—it gives leaders enormous power to propagate parallel realities, a power usually sought and acquired by autocratic leaders (and cult leaders) but increasingly coveted by democratic ones.

A key norm—an established practice—through which liberal democracy is traditionally maintained is that governments accept (however reluctantly) the scrutiny of independent news outlets from across the political spectrum. But as this chapter has shown, democratic leaders are undermining this norm by avoiding outlets that might criticize them and by providing patronage to sycophantic outlets. Through communication technologies old and new, they are creating their own platforms and channels so they can control the mediation process and beam their version of reality directly to their followers.

As a result, the news environment in a growing number of democracies is becoming less democratic and more authoritarian. If political access is only open to pro-government outlets, news providers may feel compelled to tone down their criticism to gain access. If journalists are coerced into self-censorship through fear of abuse, government actions will not receive adequate scrutiny and press freedom will be undermined.[135] The more democratic politicians get used to fawning, sycophantic news coverage on their chosen platforms, the less willing they will be to accept critical scrutiny in the future. The Fourth Estate will weaken even further, and news providers will be less able to question the government's version of events, even if it deviates wildly from material reality.

The question is, how can news organizations that are still committed to presenting reality accurately respond to governments' attempts to subordinate them and become the primary source of truth for citizens? How can established news providers maintain relevance and regain trust when they can be circumvented and attacked with impunity? How can news organizations help foster a shared understanding of reality when it seems more difficult than ever for citizens to discern, let alone agree on, what reality is?

8

THE TRUTH-SEEKERS

Verifying Government Narratives

If the mind is to emerge unscathed from this relentless struggle with the unforeseen, two qualities are indispensable: first, an intellect that, even in the darkest hour, retains some glimmerings of the inner light which leads to truth; and second, the courage to follow this faint light wherever it may lead.

—KARL VON CLAUSEWITZ, ON WAR

AL AHLI HOSPITAL, OCTOBER 17, 2023

It was 6 P.M. and Alex Murray was already in his cycling gear ready to set off home to south London. Before leaving, he stopped at his desk to check how things were. Looking across his social media feeds he could see lots of online chatter about an explosion, apparently at a hospital in northern Gaza, although its location and cause were not yet clear. Murray quickly realized he was not going home anytime soon. So he sat down and tried to figure out what had happened.

Murray is speaking to us over coffee in early November 2023, just outside the BBC's New Broadcasting House in central London.[1] Mostly bald, with a round face and large, black rimmed glasses, he looks a little like Penfold from Danger Mouse, except in a puffer jacket and white trainers. He is describing a night, three weeks earlier, when he and his colleagues sought to verify the explosion at the Al Ahli Hospital in Gaza at 6:59 P.M. local time on Tuesday, October 17, 2023. Murray has been at the BBC for almost two decades, spending most of that time sifting through and verifying content sent in or posted online by the public. He remembers material from London's "7/7" terrorist attacks, the Arab Spring, the Syrian conflict, the 2015 London attack in Leytonstone (where the bystander shouted, "You ain't no Muslim bruv"), and the Bastille Day lorry attack in Nice in 2016. As he speaks, Murray bounces from one news event of the last twenty years to the next, as though he has lived through them—which, in a way, he has, if mostly vicariously. He is now a "Verification Lead" within the recently launched BBC Verify.

On the night of October 17 there was, initially, little information about the explosion. They needed to identify source material fast. Then they found a photograph of an ambulance with Al Ahli on the side, and they could see burning in the background. Al Ahli Hospital looked like it had been hit, although there were simultaneous reports of casualties at Al-Shifa Hospital. They also thought there may be a third hospital, but they quickly learned that "the Baptist hospital" referred to Al Ahli. They scoured the photo for clues. Was it real? Was it current? Was the ambulance definitely at Al Ahli? The image was not yet cached on Google, suggesting it was new. Then a video was discovered, shot from a high angle down into a courtyard. There were distinctive features within the image and video: the shape of the buildings, the size of the courtyard, the palm trees. They compared these against other photographs and video of Al Ahli Hospital they had sourced. Generally, they will use a triangulation approach with images, searching for three distinct and identifiable features before being confident of the location. In this case, it was a fourth element that convinced them. They could see that the reflections of the blaze were tilted, and realized this must be because of rooftop solar panels—which could be found on earlier photographs of the hospital. The identification of the location was combined with reverse image searches, satellite mapping, and online cross-checks. By 9:30 P.M. that evening, Murray and his colleagues were sure there had been an explosion at Al Ahli Hospital, and that the images and video they had found online were real. They knew the *where* and the *what* of the explosion. The *who* would have to wait for further investigation. The story then led the BBC's 10 P.M. news.

Verifying the explosion at Al Ahli Hospital in Gaza was not an academic exercise but one of immense political importance. Hundreds of people were reported dead, and within hours protests had erupted in Ramallah, which then spread across the Middle East. The protesters believed Israel had bombed the hospital in contravention of International Humanitarian Law, but Israel vehemently denied it. Following the explosion, Arab leaders canceled their meeting with President Joe Biden the next day in Jordan. Biden had unexpectedly decided to travel to the Middle East, at some personal risk, hoping to act as a peace broker in the Israel-Hamas conflict. Instead, by just meeting with Benjamin Netanyahu, it looked like the United States was siding solely with Israel—something Russia and China used for propaganda advantage, contrasting what they characterized as US warmongering with their own search for peace and prosperity.[2]

BBC Verify launched in May 2023. Murray is a member of one team within the operation—the verification team. His job is to identify material requiring verification—videos of explosions, images of terrorist attacks—and assess them as quickly as possible. He can then add them to the BBC's Digital Online Verification Engine (or DOVE) library of checked material, accessible across BBC News (despite its official title, DOVE is actually named after its inventor—Daniele Palumbo—Palumbo meaning "dove" in Italian). There are about a dozen people in the verification team, working alongside four other teams within Verify: fact-checking, data analysis, open-source intelligence, and disinformation. They can also call on the skills of BBC Monitoring, which monitors media output globally and has been housed in New Broadcasting House since 2018. In total, Verify has around sixty specialists who spend their days assessing the truthfulness of digital content.

THE NEED FOR VERIFICATION

As information disorder escalates, and governments try to assert greater control and influence over the news, a new generation of *truth-seekers* has emerged. These truth-seekers share similarities with previous generations of journalists and reporters, but they are also quite distinct. As with the so-called "muckrakers" in the United States at the turn of the twentieth century, who invented the practice of investigative journalism, so the new truth-seekers are reinventing journalism in the twenty-first century. Using skills more often associated with the military, police, and private detectives, they pore over digital images and videos, trying to establish whether they are true or false, real or manufactured. For them, the process is as important as the outcome because they need to show how they reached their conclusions, and why they think they are right. This new generation is trying to provide a bedrock of shared facts about online content—a digital ground truth for news. Given the state of our digital information environment—which has quickly become an epistemological junkyard of false claims, artificially generated images and text, and hyperpartisan bickering—the need for such truth-seeking could not be more evident.

In this chapter we explain how these truth-seekers emerged and, through original interviews with the BBC Verify team and senior journalists and executives in the organization, documents how they operate. Analyzing and detailing the experiences of fact-checkers and OSINT (open-source intelligence) analysts in a range of countries, we show how far these truth-seekers can challenge governments and leaders whose narratives deviate from material reality. We also show that the future of these truth-seekers is highly uncertain because their work can undermine the legitimacy of governments and political leaders who propagate falsehoods for political gain. This makes the truth-seekers dangerous and vulnerable to attack. As Hannah Arendt wrote: "Throughout history, the truth-seekers and truth-tellers have been aware of the risks of their business; as long as they did not interfere with the course of the world, they were covered with ridicule, but he who forced his fellow-citizens to take him seriously by trying to set them free from falsehood and illusion was in danger of his life."[3]

This is the contemporary political and epistemological minefield in which BBC Verify launched, although its constituent parts have a much longer history.

THE EVOLUTION OF BBC VERIFY

On Boxing Day 2004 a vast tsunami engulfed coastlines across the Indian Sea. The waves, and the devastation they wrought, were captured in countless grainy photographs taken using phones that had only recently been equipped with cameras. Many of these photographs were sent to the BBC. Matthew Eltringham, a rangy, balding, slightly owlish-looking figure, was a BBC news editor when the photos started to come in. This was not, Eltringham thought then, a one-off but a portent of the future. As people's ability to capture images and video on their phones grew, he believed, so would the quantity of potential news material and the sources from which it could be gathered. Capturing the news would no longer be the preserve of professional journalists and "Big Media"; it would be "produced by regular people."[4] It would be democratized. Eltringham therefore pitched the idea for a center—or hub—for "user-generated content" (UGC) at the BBC. His senior colleagues were unsure but said he could run a three-month pilot over the summer of 2005.

Before the pilot period had ended, during rush hour on July 7, 2005, four suicide bombers detonated their explosives in central London. Just after 10 A.M. that day, well before the UK government acknowledged that these were terrorist attacks, BBC News received images and testimony from the public about the bombings (sent to "yourpics@bbc.co.uk"). Although the UK government was yet to make a statement, the BBC could already see—from the images and their metadata—where and when the bombs had exploded.[5] Some of the photographs would later come to define that day in the public mind—including a haunting image of passengers walking down a dark train tunnel toward the light. "7/7," as the day came to be known, convinced the BBC that Eltringham was right that the corporation should collect and verify news material gathered by the public.

But until a Tunisian street seller—Mohamed Bouazizi—set himself on fire on December 17, 2010, and sparked a wave of revolutionary protest across north Africa and the Middle East, the role was still considered relatively marginal to professional newsgathering. The Arab Spring, as the protests came to be known, demonstrated that news production was fast becoming as much about gathering and verifying media that other people had captured as it was about capturing media themselves. It also became increasingly apparent that news material gathered from the ground often did not tally with official versions of events. Alex Murray remembers speaking to a contact in Syria in 2013. According to the authorities, there were no protests in the contact's city. But Murray was speaking live to the man in Homs, and he could hear rapid gunfire in the background. "Where are you?," Murray asked. "At the front of the protests," his contact said, "trying to avoid being shot."[6]

It was the growing consciousness of disparities between statements by those in authority and material evidence that subsequently convinced James Harding, head of BBC News from 2013 to 2018, to pilot a fact-checking project within the BBC (called Reality Check), running parallel to the UGC hub, in 2015. By 2017 this too had become permanent.[7] Accompanying Reality Check and the UGC hub were the BBC's data analysis team and BBC Monitoring—the latter having been incorporated within BBC proper in 2014 when the BBC took over funding of the World Service.

Therefore, when BBC Verify launched in 2023, it was—at least in part—a coordination and rebranding of activities the BBC had been doing for almost twenty years. However, it was also more than that. It was an acknowledgment that the media and communications environment had been transformed. It was a recognition of the limits of the BBC's own newsgathering operation. It was a restatement and reassertion of the BBC's journalistic ambition—to serve the public and speak truth to power. Combining all the elements of verification would enable the BBC to coordinate its investigations and take advantage of its skills, networks, and experience. As Eltringham said when we interviewed him: "Together, BBC Verify was more than the sum of its parts."[8] And most important, it was a commitment by the BBC to pursue that increasingly controversial and much misunderstood goal—to seek out truth.

THE RISE OF TRUTH-SEEKING

The BBC was certainly not the only organization to recognize the need to verify media content in our disordered and chaotic digital information environment. The year before Eltringham proposed a user-generated content hub at the BBC, the Annenberg Public Policy Center at the University of Pennsylvania had established the first dedicated independent fact-checking organization, FactCheck.org.[9] Fifteen years in the making, the center grew out of growing despair with the distortions and inventions of US political advertising (such as the infamous "Willie Horton" weekend passes ad during the 1988 bitter Bush-Dukakis presidential campaign, which used racist stereotypes to paint Dukakis as soft on crime).[10] A spate of other fact-checking organizations followed Factcheck.org, but as with the BBC's UGC hub, it was not until after the Arab Spring in 2010–11 that fact-checking mushroomed. By 2015 there were 151 active fact-checkers globally, and by 2020 just over four hundred.[11] In the United States most were associated with existing news organizations such as the *Washington Post* or the Associated Press. Internationally they were more likely to be stand-alone or linked to a university or civil society organization.[12] As the 2010s wore on, certain countries found themselves blessed with a surfeit of fact-checkers—India with thirty-one by 2023.[13] Some others—Russia, Kuwait, and Vietnam—had none.

As the number of fact-checkers grew, they became more self-conscious about their methods, standards, and impact. Fact-checkers started to compare their techniques and processes, with the first international conference at the London School of Economics in 2014. To codify their values and establish a more formal community, in 2015 the Poynter Center in the United States designed a set of principles for fact-checking and formed the International Fact-Checking Network (IFCN).[14] By 2023 this had 118 signatories.[15] When COVID-19 struck in 2020, fact-checkers created the #CoronaVirusFacts alliance to share reports about conspiracy theories and misinformation.[16]

The explosion of fact-checking across the globe in the last fifteen years can be seen as a natural response to the glut of information published online. As the quantity of publicly accessible information has accumulated, so has the need to distinguish between what is credible and what is not.[17] It is also a reaction to the "interpretive turn" in journalism since the late twentieth century, as Lucas Graves shows in his valuable book on fact-checking. Fact-checkers are pushing back against news publishers' shift toward opinionated and partisan news. In this sense they can be seen as a reform movement—aiming to revive and enhance journalism's core democratic role.[18] In the late 2010s, fact-checking became an urgent palliative response to the proliferation of disinformation online and to efforts to distort elections and referenda. Fact-checkers were encouraged by social media companies like Meta at this stage. Having been blamed for enabling disinformation, the tech platforms saw independent fact-checking as one way of addressing it, and of mitigating the waves of public opprobrium and political pressure they were receiving. It was also a way the platforms could avoid becoming what Meta's chief executive, Mark Zuckerberg, referred to as "arbiters of truth."[19]

Alongside the growth of the fact-checkers came the emergence of the OSINT movement. Taking advantage of the abundance of media available online, and the accessibility of data analytics tools, Eliot Higgins and others started investigating conflict, crime, and corruption. Higgins and his growing collective of online sleuths at Bellingcat looked for the sources of weapons in the Syrian conflict, the perpetrators who shot down Malaysia Airlines flight MH17, war crimes in Syria and Ukraine, and the poisoning of Alexei Navalny (as it turned out, the Russian government was instrumental in all of these).[20] Even more than the fact-checkers, the OSINT movement quickly became networked and collaborative and experimented with new digital methods—building a knowledge base of digital forensics techniques. Like the fact-checkers, they saw themselves as a response to some of mainstream media's flaws, and they believed their essential purpose to be truth-seeking. "Their main driver," academics Nina Müller and Jenny Wiik write, "is idealism, the wish to make a change and to serve a social good."[21]

Yet in the ocean of digital mis- and disinformation, how do these new truth-seekers decide what to focus on? What selection criteria do they use? Ask journalists, and their answers are remarkably reminiscent of public interest journalism.[22] The job of fact-checking, as they see it, "is primarily to evaluate the accuracy of statements by public figures and institutions."[23] OSINT researchers sound similarly idealistic when asked, and they are even more focused on challenging those in power. "We are all going against government narratives" and exposing their methods and distortions, Benjamin Strick from BBC Africa Eye explains.[24] But unlike traditional journalism, these truth-seekers' work is less about reporting and more about assessing. A fact-check results in a conclusion: this claim was true, false, or misleading, with some margin for interpretation. An OSINT investigation normally identifies a culprit. Because their targets are political, the offenders are frequently governments, politicians, and political parties. Because of this, many governments, politicians, and political parties see these truth-seekers as adversaries.

THE VULNERABILITIES OF THE TRUTH-SEEKERS

In some senses these new organizations and collectives hew closer to the liberal ideal of a Fourth Estate than traditional news institutions. They self-consciously and explicitly seek out the truth, they endeavor to distinguish it from falsehood, and they aim to tell truth to power—for example, by messaging politicians directly and publicly via Twitter or its rebrand, X. Some of them have been embraced by legacy media, awarded journalism prizes, and referred to as members of "the press," such as Bellingcat, which won two News Emmy Awards in partnership with CNN in 2021. Equally, some governments—when it suits them—will treat them as regular journalists and news publishers. Yet they are also quite distinct from legacy media institutions and are more fragile and vulnerable.

For one thing, they are not "institutions" at all. At least not in the sense that they have endured over time, share equivalent processes, structures, and hierarchies, and perform "similar jobs that occupy a central place in the society and polity."[25] Most have sprung up within the last decade and are run as loose collectives or start-up NGOs. As such, they do not automatically enjoy the same privileges as news institutions: the access, the recognition, the legal protections, and the tax breaks. Many of those working in these organizations do not consider themselves to be journalists. Nor do they employ the same economic model. Rather than fund themselves through advertising or subscriptions, they mostly rely on grant funding, public support, or income from training. More than a third of Bellingcat's budget, for example, comes from running workshops.[26]

This new species of truth-seeker has also not built up the organizational infrastructure of legacy media companies. They rarely have settled job titles or publishing routines, seldom develop bespoke production systems or custom-built technologies, and lack distribution networks. Instead, they lean heavily on technology platforms for their tools, content, distribution, audience, engagement, and in some cases, their income. In a 2022 survey of 525 open-source researchers, Bellingcat found that three of the top four most popular OSINT tools were produced by Google.[27] When fact-checkers decide what to check, the chances are it will be something posted online that is going viral. We reviewed all the fact-checking posts by Factcheck.org in the six months from July to December 2023 and found that more than half of their fact-checks (73 of 127) were of claims posted on social media, whereas just over four in ten examined political claims made elsewhere, be it in speeches, political debates, or televised political adverts. When truth-seekers publish their findings, they know that most people will discover them via mainstream social media: TikTok, Facebook, Instagram, X, and a handful of other services. In late 2024, Factcheck.org had more than eight hundred thousand Facebook followers; Bellingcat had a similar number on X. Moreover, if their findings are to have real impact, they need these same mainstream tech platforms to take action—label false posts, limit the spread of disinformation, sometimes remove posts entirely.[28] Although most of these verifiers do not rely on advertising income earned via the tech platforms, they have often received money from them. Meta claims to have invested more than US$100 million in fact-checking from 2016 to 2022, although only part of this went to third-party fact-checkers.[29] This multidimensional reliance on the platforms makes these truth-seekers vulnerable. Should the platforms decide not to label posts, for example, or choose to reduce their financial commitment to information integrity (as Meta did in 2025), this will undermine the truth-seekers' ability to achieve their aims.

The truth-seekers' reputations are also precarious. A fact-checking organization is only as good as its last fact-check, or as credible as the person doing the fact-checking. If someone within a fact-checking organization is found to be partisan, or is acting unethically, it overshadows the whole organization's work. When an investigation by Buzzfeed discovered that the chief executive of Snopes was copying articles from reputable news sources and publishing them on the site under his own byline, or an invented byline, political sources rubbished the whole site's credibility. "Everything Snopes has ever reported regarding me has been boilerplate bullshit," Roger Stone, the Trump ally found guilty of making false statements to Congress, told Buzzfeed after reading its exposé.[30] Similarly, open-source investigations frequently seek to identify a culprit. If they identify the wrong one, or their evidence is unconvincing, they lay themselves open to derision.

These vulnerabilities are compounded by their intrinsically oppositional stance. It is hard to be conciliatory when telling someone they have not told the truth. And because politicians dislike being exposed as liars, fabricators, or mythmakers, they and their supporters often fight back. Sometimes they do this using similar methods to those used against legacy media, but increasingly they are adopting new and creative approaches as well.

POLITICIANS AND PARTISANS VS.
THE TRUTH-SEEKERS

Mohammed Zubair and his *Alt News* cofounder, Pratik Sinha, have consistently exposed false and misleading narratives promoted by India's ruling BJP party. After the 2019 Balakot air strike on Pakistan, *Alt News* showed that the shrouded bodies in an open grave that were published online were not—as was claimed—terrorists killed in the strike, but Pakistanis who had died in the 2015 heatwave.[31] In 2020, Zubair and his colleagues demonstrated that India's Muslims were not intentionally spreading coronavirus by licking utensils; that protesters against the 2019 Citizens' Act were not paid to protest; and, in the same year, that students at Jamia Millia Islamia University were not to blame for clashes with police.[32] For exposing these falsehoods, the Indian fact-checking service has been regularly targeted by India's government, mainstream media, and police. "We are repeatedly showing how a false narrative is being created [by the BJP]," Sinha told *Rest of World* in 2021. "This is why I think Alt News became a target."[33] *Alt News'* most effective truth-seeking has exposed how the Modi government and its media allies have demonized Muslims in their pursuit of a Hindu nationalist agenda.

In June 2022 Zubair was arrested. A few days before his arrest he had shared a clip from Times Now in which Nupur Sharma, the BJP's national spokesperson, made Islamophobic remarks (as discussed in chapter 5). Zubair's arrest was ostensibly for a satirical tweet he posted in 2018, but by bringing attention to Sharma's comments, he had provoked the BJP's ire. Zubair spent a month in prison, and the official harassment continued even after his release. Further police charges were filed against him, and the head of a *Hindutva* group alleged he sexually abused other inmates while in jail, a claim dismissed by Zubair.[34]

The harassment and imprisonment of Zubair made it harder for him to do his work, but it also raised his profile and drew domestic and international attention to *Alt News*. By 2024 Zubair (@zoo_bear) had almost a million followers on X. He and Zinha were reportedly among the favorites for the Nobel Peace Prize in 2022. Modi's government's persecution of Zubair had—in the short term at least—the opposite effect to the one intended. Conscious that such autocratic methods can backfire, politicians and their partisan supporters have tried to undermine these new truth-seekers in other ways.

In February 2023, a class action lawsuit was filed against four US organizations whose primary purpose is to expose and diminish disinformation online. The action alleged that these four organizations—the Stanford Internet Observatory, Graphika, DFRLab, and the Center for an Informed

Public—collaborated closely with the US government "to monitor and censor disfavored viewpoints on social media" in what was, the filing states, "probably the largest mass-surveillance and mass-censorship program in American history."[35] The alleged wrongdoing of these organizations was to seek to identify, and limit the spread of, false content about the 2020 US election and around the COVID-19 pandemic—working where necessary with government officials, the intelligence agencies, and the tech platforms. The "disfavored viewpoints," the legal action claimed, were from the political right. The organizations' 2020 election project (the EIP) even "admits that it focuses on speech from the 'political right'," the filing asserts. This is not quite correct. Actually, the project found that "Influential accounts on the political right . . . were responsible for the most widely spread incidents of false or misleading information in our dataset."[36] In other words, it had not focused on speech from the political right. It had focused on false claims and discovered that most of these were made by those on the political right—as other researchers have corroborated.[37]

The organization behind the legal action, America First Legal (AFL), was run by Stephen Miller—Trump's senior advisor, and after the 2024 US election, the White House deputy chief of staff for policy and homeland security advisor. AFL's stated mission was to turn "the legal tables on the radical activist left," which it claimed was "using its power inside and outside of the government to destroy our country."[38] America First Legal was therefore using the courts to try to incapacitate some of the leading counter disinformation organizations in the United States—and it worked. By the summer of 2024 the Stanford Internet Observatory's funds had been exhausted, the university had run up "huge legal bills," and the Observatory was shuttered, with some of its research shifted to other parts of the university.[39] It did not continue the election integrity work it did in 2020. Other members of the 2020 Election Integrity Project persisted in their work but against a background of rising legal costs and constant political attack.[40]

Truth-seekers are also liable to assault by state media or pro-government news publishers. Bellingcat has found itself a constant target of Russian state media. RT and Sputnik have used almost any excuse to publish articles questioning the credibility of Eliot Higgins and his open-source intelligence collective, often using the same language as fact-checkers and OSINT investigators. In 2016 RT published a YouTube video "Debunking 'arm chair blogger' Bellingcat." An RT article in 2018 claimed: "Despite mainstream glory, questions raised about Bellingcat authenticity and Skripal poisoning case."[41] In the absence of any evidence, the Russian state outlets would claim that Bellingcat was part of the "Deep State," working with the United States or UK intelligence ("Is Bellingcat being played by the CIA?"), or just resort to comic stunts.[42] After Russia's attempted assassination of Sergei Skripal in Salisbury (UK) in 2018, the agents responsible told RT they had only gone to the city to visit its cathedral (which they apparently did in two separate visits on two consecutive days). Shortly afterwards, RT sent Bellingcat a gift of a chocolate cathedral.[43]

GOVERNMENT AS FACT-CHECKER

Should politicians and partisans want to undermine these new truth-seekers, they could not find a better way than India's BJP government. In 2019, Modi's second administration established a fact-checking unit to check the accuracy of information published about the Indian government.[44] Two years later it passed a law—the Information Technology Rules (2021)—to reduce the spread of fake news on social media and increase platform accountability for online harms. It then amended this law, in 2023, such that if the government's own fact-checking unit determined something published about the government was "fake, false, or misleading," then the platforms were obliged to take it down—without due process, and without clarification of what constituted "fake, false, or misleading" content. Should the platforms refuse, they could lose their legal protection, making them liable for anything published on their services—something the platforms have long sought to avoid.[45] The Editors Guild of India said it was "deeply disturbed" by this amendment that, "in effect," gave the government "absolute power to determine what is fake or not."[46]

Soon after the amendment was made, regional authorities started setting up their own fact-checking units. In October of that year, the state government of Karnataka invited proposals from companies to run its "Information Disorder Tackling Unit," which would not just fact-check but analyze the dynamics of mis/disinformation and educate the public about its dangers.[47] Tamil Nadu's government followed Karnataka's lead, and others were expected to do so shortly afterward.

India's BJP was not the first government to set up a state-sponsored fact-checking unit. The Malaysian government set up Sebenarnya.my in 2017 (Sebenarnya means "in reality"). The Thai government set up an Anti-Fake News Center in 2019 after the Singaporean government had established "Factually." Each of these would, in the words of legal scholar Lasse Schuldt, produce "official truths" on behalf of their respective governments.[48] Similarly, the Brazilian government set up Brasil Contra Fake in 2020, and the Ethiopian government established Ethiopia Current Issues Fact Check the same year.[49] Indeed, one could point to a trend in the establishment of state-run fact-checking units. These are in addition to the fact-check and disinformation initiatives of state-sponsored broadcasters, such as CGTN's "Reality Check." Not only do these initiatives make judgments about truth and falsehood, they emphasize the "constant and omnipresent threat to public order" represented by fake news, justifying government takedowns, punishments, and arrests.[50]

Immediately before India's 2024 election its Supreme Court blocked the government from enacting the legislation that would force platforms to take down content that the government had decided was fake, until it could examine its constitutionality. The ruling came after the law was challenged by the stand-up comedian Kunal Kamra and editors of India's newspapers and magazines, who were outraged by the power the law gave the state to arbitrate truth. Following the election, Bombay's High Court judged that elements of the law were indeed unconstitutional and should not be enacted.[51] Despite this, the government's fact-checking unit continued to assess the truth or falsehood of news about the government, and Modi's new administration looked into how to reverse the High Court judgment.

THE UNSUSTAINABILITY OF TRUTH-SEEKING

Even without political leaders' and parties' efforts to undermine the new truth-seekers, there are good reasons to believe that many of them are unsustainable in their current form. They are financially precarious, their political purpose is being compromised by their dependence on the large tech platforms, their audience reach is limited, and they are highly susceptible to politicization.

A study of verifiers from more than fifty countries across the Global South found that funding was the biggest worry for almost all independent verifiers, especially those not integrated into an existing news organization. Many are run more like NGOs than publishers, relying mostly on grants, which tend to be short-term and intended for specific projects, and donated by organizations from outside their own country. "Funding is very difficult to come by," Mahoshadi Peiris of Factcheck.lk in Sri Lanka explains. "We constantly search for grants."[52] This is equally true of funding from technology platforms, which has until recently driven much of the increase in independent fact-checkers. Some of these tech companies have said they remain committed to supporting verification, but they also slashed costs after the COVID-19 pandemic, including their spending on what they call "integrity."[53] When, in 2025, Meta announced that it would end its fact-checking partnerships in the US and reconsider the future of the program, it removed 'a very significant source of funding for the ecosystem globally' and jeopardized the sustainably of many of these nascent organizations.[54]

Fact-checkers' reliance on the platforms also makes them vulnerable to the ideological proclivities of their owners. When self-declared "free speech absolutist," Elon Musk, took over Twitter in 2022 (rebranding it to X in July 2023), he sacked thousands of internal content moderators and external contractors, both to cut costs and to reduce the platform's role in monitoring speech.[55]

Reliance on the tech platforms has also drawn some verifiers away from their original mission—to check the veracity of what politicians, political parties and governments say. Fact-checkers who were part of Meta's partnership program were obliged to focus on false content that was going viral, whatever the subject matter, based on the assumption that, by affecting more people, viral content would be more harmful. This could mean chasing an invented story about school bullying or about a consumer product withdrawal—in other words, debunking popular, but for the most part not political, false information.[56] At the same time, according to these same partnership rules, Meta would not label false statements by local politicians as untrue for fear of censoring political speech—reducing the fact-checkers' incentives to verify what politicians said. Therefore, as Vinhas and Bastos found in their research on fact-checking across twenty-seven countries, "The rules undergirding the partnerships prevent fact-checkers from performing a core component of their mission, which is to hold politicians to account."[57]

Some verifiers have raised even more existential concerns. What if they expose something as false but this goes unseen by those who most need to see it? The most viral political disinformation can spread millions of times, but many independent fact-checkers' viewing figures are in the thousands or tens of thousands.[58] Or, what if even those who see the fact-check ignore it? Research on political fact-checks suggests that partisanship plays a big role in whether people take any notice.[59] Moreover, when it comes to politics, most people believe what they choose to believe, regardless of the evidence.[60] This seems to be borne out by the persistence of false beliefs in the United States and Brazil. In the United States, despite dozens of legal rulings and official reports providing no evidence of fraud in the 2020 election, by 2023 three in ten Americans still believed Biden's victory was fraudulent.[61] Two months after Lula da Silva's victory in the 2022 Brazilian election and following the January 8 riots in Brasilia, four in ten Brazilians did not believe Lula had actually won. "It's just not getting better," Tai Nalon, cofounder of the Brazilian fact-checking organization Aos Fatos, told the *New York Times*.[62]

This reluctance to believe the verifiers is more pronounced on the political right, especially in the United States, where counter disinformation activities have been politicized as partisan efforts to suppress conservative views.[63] An analysis by the Duke Reporters' Lab in 2017 found that conservative writers were unlikely to cite fact-checks, and if they did, they would do so critically, or use sarcastic quote marks ("fact-checking").[64] This attitude has since become pervasive on the US right. "Seven-in-ten Republicans say fact-checkers tend to favor one side," a 2019 Pew Center survey discovered, "compared with roughly three-in-ten Democrats."[65] Not only do those on the right dismiss US fact-checkers as biased, they accuse them of being censors and government propagandists. "What [fact-checkers] try to pass off as a public service," Mike Howell from the right-wing Heritage Foundation wrote in 2022, "instead seems to be public relations for their favored regime's message."[66] "In reality," Jacob Siegel wrote in the conservative magazine, the *Tablet*, in 2022, "America's new public-private 'Ministry of Truth' mainly serves the interests of the tech platforms and Democratic Party operatives who underwrite and support the fact-checking enterprise."[67]

For Americans on the right, these new truth-seekers are not defending democracy, they are pursuing an insidious left-wing campaign against conservatives. Truth-seeking itself is now seen as a partisan act rather than a necessary practice in the new information environment. In 2023, The Republican-dominated House Judiciary Committee—chaired by Trump champion Jim Jordan—launched an investigation into fact-checkers and the tech platforms that support them, accusing them of censoring right-wing voices online.[68] After taking over Twitter, Elon Musk stopped working with fact-checkers, amplified misinformation, and—as with conservative commentators—referred sarcastically to "fact-checkers" as well as calling them "huge liars and incredibly biased."[69]

Fact-checkers became similarly politicized in Brazil and the Philippines, in part because of their partnerships with the tech platforms, especially Facebook. As soon as the social media superpower announced it would be using recommendations from these organizations to reduce the spread of certain posts, the fact-checkers were called leftist censors. In Brazil, before the 2018 election, a 229-page pdf was distributed online with fact-checkers' names and contact details.[70] From then on, they were harassed online relentlessly, egged on by Bolsonaro and his coterie.[71] Rodrigo Duterte was similarly keen to politicize and disable the fact-checkers in the Philippines, telling Facebook that it should not accept the claims of those who were—in the government's view—biased against it.[72] Once labeled partisan, it becomes much easier for Duterte, Bolsonaro, Trump, and other political leaders to reject any fact-checks or exposés by the new truth-seekers as politically motivated.

Struggling to find sustainable funding, buffeted by the vagaries and proclivities of the tech titans, plagued by self-doubt about their efficacy, and dismissed as politically partisan by their key audiences, it is unsurprising that the explosive growth of fact-checking plateaued. An annual fact-checker census by the Duke Reporters Lab found that, having grown rapidly from eleven sites in 2008 to 424 in 2022, the growth in fact-checkers then slowed "to a more trudging pace."[73] Following the reelection of Narendra Modi for a third term in India in 2024, and Donald Trump for a second in the United States, combined with the rising investments in state-news by the Chinese and Russian governments, the challenges facing the verifiers are only likely to grow.

THE NEED FOR A NEW MODEL OF VERIFICATION

For verification to be sustainable, and for it to help ground our digital information ecosystem more strongly in reality, it needs a different model. It needs a model that combines financial stability and institutional weight, a model that is underpinned by public purpose and political independence, one that couples depth of experience with extensive reach, and that is imbued with a sense of moral responsibility and fairness. Fortunately, just such a model exists, and has for over a century. It is called Public Service Broadcasting (PSB). The values of PSB, as outlined by the body whose job it is to promote its sustainability—the European Broadcasting Union (EBU)—map directly to the values associated with verification. Public Service Broadcasting (or Public Service Media—PSM—as it is now generally called) ought to be characterized, the EBU states, by its universality, independence, diversity, excellence, accountability, and innovation.[74] In theory, public service media organizations ought to act as "the cornerstones of democratic societies" and provide the glue that connects citizens to one another and to reality. Who better to carry out and evolve the practice of verification?

Of the more than a hundred public service media organizations globally, the BBC is arguably best-suited to invent a PSM model for digital verification. For one thing, the BBC invented public service broadcasting. John Reith, the tall, forbidding, Presbyterian Scotsman who founded the British Broadcasting Company in 1922—that "Wuthering height," as Winston Churchill called him—believed from its outset that it should serve a public purpose. "The B.B.C. should be a public service not only in performance but in constitution," Reith wrote in his autobiography, "but certainly not . . . as a department of State." This purpose was then formalized by Parliament in the 1920s, and underpinned by Royal Charter in 1927.[75] The organization's independence from government did not emerge fully formed at birth but was shaped over its hundred-year history—during domestic political battles (over the 1926 General Strike and representation of the Irish Republican Army or IRA in the 1980s) and foreign conflicts (including the Suez Crisis, the Falklands, Afghanistan, and Iraq). The BBC has always had a close relationship with the UK government, but it has never been a creature of it. Indeed, Prime Minister Margaret Thatcher "conducted a covert war against BBC," and Tony Blair berated the corporation for a "real breakdown" in the distinction between news and commentary before the Iraq War.[76] Rather, the BBC and the British state have perpetually performed what the writer Charlotte Higgins calls a "curious dance" and a "delicate waltz"—in which tensions between them wax and wane according to circumstance and need.[77] Over its long lifetime, the BBC has repeatedly demonstrated its value to democracy worldwide, having been "avidly followed by people hungry for truth but trapped in oppressive states," as Jean Seaton, the BBC's official historian, puts it.[78] At the end of the twentieth century Kofi Annan, the UN General Secretary from 1997 to 2006, called the BBC's international broadcasting "perhaps Britain's greatest gift to the world this century."[79] Thanks largely to its charter obligation to "provide impartial news and information to help people understand and engage with the world around them."[80]

The institutional weight, global reach, and historic reputation of the BBC give it the ability—should it choose to use it—to corroborate government statements, challenge political narratives, and investigate the records of political leaders. We saw this in China in 2021 when the BBC reported on the "vast and secretive system of internment camps in the Xinjiang region," in which there was "mass surveillance, detention, indoctrination, and even forced sterilisation." According to firsthand accounts, the BBC said, within these camps there was "evidence of an organised system of mass rape, sexual abuse and torture."[81] We have seen this in Russia, where the BBC investigated close links between Putin's intelligence services and organized cybercriminals, tracking down hackers from the "Evil Corp" group who were on the FBI's Cyber Most Wanted list.[82] In Iran, when the official report was published on the death of twenty-two-year-old Mahsa Amini in police custody in 2022, BBC Persia managed to speak to her father live on air. "It is a lie," he told them about what authorities claimed, "the short footage they showed me [of her] was all edited and censored."[83] In 2023, the BBC published a documentary about Narendra Modi titled *India: The Modi Question*. The documentary questioned the official history of the Gujarat riots in 2002, in which more than one thousand Muslims were killed, and whether Modi, as chief minister of the state, was complicit in the violence.[84] Each of these stories challenged a government narrative, exposed state-sponsored crimes and injustices, or revealed the checkered past of a political leader. That they were published by the BBC made them more dangerous for each of the governments concerned because the BBC has a commitment to impartiality, ingrained public trust, and international reach.

EFFORTS TO DISCREDIT THE BBC

Conscious of the dangers posed by BBC reporting, contemporary governments and political leaders have actively sought to discredit it and stop it from doing its job. They have done this by claiming that the BBC and its journalists represent a threat to other countries' sovereignty and security, by questioning its accuracy and reliability, by fabricating and inflating public anger about the broadcaster, and by framing its criticisms as neocolonialist.

"Do I look like a threat?," the BBC's Sarah Rainsford asked an airport official when he said she would be denied entry to Russia indefinitely "for the protection of the security of Russia."[85] Given she had been reporting from Russia for more than two decades without incident, Rainsford was understandably perplexed by the sudden change in her status. She was followed out of the country by Andrei Zakharov, a BBC investigative journalist in Russia who had tracked down a member of the Evil Corp hacking group. Zakharov, as with other journalists within Russia, was designated a "foreign agent" who was undermining Russia's national security.[86] Similarly, in China, authorities alleged that BBC journalists were actually government operatives, pushing false narratives on behalf of the UK state. John Sudworth, a senior BBC China correspondent, earned the wrath of the Chinese government when he questioned their version of the origins of COVID-19, and later reported that the Communist authorities were employing forced labor in Xinjiang. State international broadcaster CGTN wrote that Sudworth, and journalists like him, are not just guilty of "poor reporting," they "are no longer working as journalists at all, but as foreign agents, spreading disinformation on behalf of their governments."[87] Sudworth left China with his family in March 2021, saying there had been "an intensified propaganda campaign targeting not just the BBC but me personally."[88] By this time the Chinese government had also banned the BBC from broadcasting in China. Russia did the same in March 2022, its foreign ministry saying that the BBC "was being used to undermine the internal political situation and security in Russia."[89]

Governments are using their own state media and diplomats to assert that the BBC is unreliable, inaccurate, and that it publishes in bad faith. "A typical report by Biased Broadcasting Corp," tweeted Zhao Lijian, a spokesperson for the Chinese Foreign Ministry about the BBC's coverage of Xinjiang in 2019.[90] "The BBC's so-called investigative journalism is more like an 'Oscar' drama written and performed according to a script," said China's Global Times the following year.[91] CGTN went further in 2021, writing that "the BBC is a dogmatic, ideological institution with long complicity in information warfare" that is trying "to manufacture consent for Western confrontation against China."[92]

A third state-led approach to delegitimize the BBC has been to manufacture public outrage. In February 2021, shortly after banning the BBC from broadcasting in China, the CCP conducted a coordinated social media campaign to give an impression of popular outrage about the BBC. The campaign was led by accusations of inaccuracy and bias by "[CCP] diplomatic accounts, Chinese state media, pro-CCP influencers and patriotic trolls."[93] The BBC's internment camp stories, one Chinese Embassy spokesperson commented, are "nothing but a latest example of the anti-China forces slandering and attacking China's Xinjiang policy."[94] These comments were amplified and accompanied by others on "hundreds of websites and social media accounts and [in] thousands of comments across state-affiliated news sources." These accounts were all claiming that the BBC was unreliable, inaccurate, and systematically biased against China. Many claimed that the BBC was consciously distorting and darkening the images used in its reports on China—literally painting the country in a dark light. They called this the BBC's "gloom filter"—a "special grey filter" intended to make images of China "look dull, lifeless and sad."[95] The BBC denied this.[96]

A fourth tactic has been to claim that the broadcaster is pursuing imperialist or colonialist aims. When the BBC released its documentary on Narendra Modi in 2023, the Indian government rushed to implement emergency legislation to prevent it from being broadcast. Three hundred prominent Indian figures, including a former foreign secretary and former home secretary, signed a letter claiming the BBC was acting like a colonial power and promoting an "imperialist agenda." Under the title "Delusions of Imperial Resurrection," the letter accused the BBC of "unrelenting prejudice" and of "*mala fides*" (bad faith), and concluded: "It is time to let the BBC know that India does not need colonial, imperialistic, somnambulistic outsiders . . . to teach us how to live together in unity."[97] China's CGTN responded with a similar tone to the BBC's reporting on Xinjiang, writing: "The BBC constantly frames itself as an impartial and neutral arbiter of facts and truth with an arrogance that its reporting is above criticism. Such an attitude is not different from Britain's prejudice in its imperialist era."[98]

These attacks on the BBC and its journalists share common themes. Each casts the BBC as a tool of the UK government, bent on an ideological mission rather than performing a news function. Its critical reporting is, therefore, not valid journalistic scrutiny but politically motivated, equivalent to foreign interference or subversion. The BBC's institutional longevity and global reputation mean it can probably withstand these efforts to delegitimize and discredit it. However, if it is to do this successfully, both within the UK and internationally, it needs domestic backing. Such support is under threat, especially—and counterintuitively—from the UK government itself.

UK GOVERNMENT WAGES A WAR OF ATTRITION AGAINST THE BBC

It was a mild Monday morning in London in late January 2024, and the Conservative Secretary of State for Culture, Media and Sport—Lucy Frazer MP—was doing a round of media interviews. Dressed in a bright purple dress with a sun-drenched photograph of the UK Parliament behind her, she told ITV's Good Morning Britain that "Audiences across the board have lost trust in the impartiality of the BBC to some extent."[99] From there she continued onto Sky News, where she was more forthright, saying that "I think that on occasions it [the BBC] has been biased." Speaking to Times Radio that morning she extended her comments: "Audiences," she said, "are feeling like impartiality and the BBC is on a downward trajectory."[100] And on she went to Conservative-friendly GB News, telling its audiences, "Trust in the impartiality of the BBC, unfortunately, is going down."[101] Pressed on what evidence the UK government had of BBC bias, Frazer told interviewers that her conclusions came from audience research, conducted by the UK media regulator Ofcom. The statistics she cited were indeed from Ofcom research, but her claims about them were misleading. The figures were not representative of the public, and they did not show that BBC impartiality had dropped over time.[102] Moreover, they represented perceptions of the BBC rather than actual evidence of partiality; perceptions that had been shaped by successive UK governments and culture secretaries.

At a time in which governments around the world are pushing their strategic narratives and trying to take control of the international news agenda, one would have thought the UK government would be grateful for the fact that the world's most trusted broadcaster was British. One might have expected that it would nurture one of the UK's premier instruments of soft power and international influence. That it would treasure the BBC's stature and position, and do its utmost to bolster and enhance these. The UK government may not have the capacity to spend the billions each a year that the CCP is spending on "Telling China's Story Well," but it could still try to strengthen the corporation's existing capabilities, protect its reputation, and emphasize its distinctiveness from state media such as CGTN and RT. The BBC World Service alone has a weekly audience of more than three hundred million, and bureaus in fifty-eight countries around the world.[103] Instead, successive UK governments have repeatedly questioned the impartiality, integrity, and purpose of the BBC, while at the same time slashing its funding. It would not be excessive to say that successive governments have waged a war of attrition against the UK's leading public broadcaster.[104]

Between 2007 and 2024 the UK had seventeen different secretaries of state for culture, media, and sport, spanning Conservative, Labour, and coalition governments. Eleven spent less than eighteen months in the post. Despite their short tenures, most of them found time to disparage the BBC, particularly on their perception of its lack of impartiality. Jeremy Hunt—as culture secretary—said he thought the broadcaster was institutionally biased.[105] Sajid Javid—as culture secretary—said the BBC's flagship Today program was "very very anti-Tory."[106] Oliver Dowden—as culture secretary—said the BBC lacked "diversity of thought."[107] Nadine Dorries—as culture secretary—said that there was a "lack of impartiality" at the BBC.[108] And this is just what the culture secretaries said. Other

Conservative politicians were less diplomatic. In 2023, Jacob Rees-Mogg told journalists that the BBC simply "is not an impartial broadcaster."[109] His colleague and then deputy chairman of the Conservative Party, Lee Andersen, called it a "safe haven for perverts," after allegations of criminal misconduct were published about Huw Edwards, a leading BBC news presenter.[110]

These politicians—Andersen excepted—generally combined their criticisms of the BBC with positive platitudes about how the broadcaster is a national treasure, a crown jewel, and one of the most respected news services in the world. However, the denigration has an effect. In 2023, more than 70 percent of British citizens thought the BBC was high-quality, accurate, and trustworthy, but only 60 percent thought it was impartial.[111] This despite the BBC's director general, Tim Davie, making a commitment to impartiality his "number one priority" when he took the post in September 2020. Impartiality, he said then, is "the very essence of who we are. It is the bedrock of why people come to us."[112] In the digital news environment, this is also a fragile principle on which to base the BBC's future.

Never widely understood, the concept of impartiality has become increasingly muddled as people gain greater access to alternative media perspectives. When it comes to news, impartiality has become associated with what the journalism scholar Jay Rosen calls "the view from nowhere." Such a view, Rosen argues, hides the fact that no one is fully impartial, that everyone has a degree of subjectivity, and not to be transparent about your partiality is disingenuous.[113] The BBC, for example, has been accused of multiple—and often conflicting—biases: in its political partisanship, its coverage of the EU, its metropolitanism, its elitism, its liberal tendencies, its closeness to the establishment, its self-censorship, and its bias by omission. For some it is insufferably left-wing and politically correct; for others it is suffocatingly conservative and consensual. In part this reflects public confusion with the nature and purpose of impartiality. Richard Sambrook was the director of BBC News from 2001 to 2004, and he wrote a report on impartiality for the Reuters Institute. As a concept, he told us, impartiality is "deeply misunderstood." "Impartiality is a *process*," he said, "which, if done right with properly weighted views and properly evidenced, leads to better journalism."[114] Such nuance is lost when politicians repeatedly accuse the BBC of bias and partial reporting.

Moreover, although these politicians may well believe that the BBC is partial, it is difficult to divorce their criticisms from political self-interest. Tirades against the BBC play well, especially with more partisan sections of the public, and thanks to the BBC's actual commitment to impartiality, they can be made without fear of negative blowback. The British politician who has played this political double game most adeptly is Boris Johnson—London mayor, cabinet minister, and then prime minister from 2019 to 2022. Johnson owes much of his national celebrity to the BBC, which included him as a guest star on much-loved BBC entertainment programs including "Have I Got News for You," "Top Gear," and "EastEnders" (on which he had a walk-on part in 2009). However, as an ambitious politician he rarely missed an opportunity to gain political capital with his Conservative base by belittling the corporation. "Statist, corporatist, defeatist, anti-business, Europhile" he wrote about BBC newsrooms in 2012, "and, above all, overwhelmingly biased to the left." BBC London was, he said, his "chief opponent" when running for election as mayor.[115] The following year he was berating their coverage of Margaret Thatcher's funeral: "they played Ding Dong the Witch Is Dead on taxpayer-public radio" while BBC Two broadcast "Boris Johnson: The Irresistible Rise."[116] He continued to snipe after he joined the Cabinet ("the most left-wing audience I've ever seen," he complained of the Leaders' debate in 2017), but he reserved his real political ire for the election campaign of 2019 and his first months as prime minister.[117] During the campaign he consciously sought to avoid speaking to the BBC, while at the same time saying he was considering scrapping the Licence Fee—the charge British households pay to fund the corporation.[118] In office he banned ministers from speaking to the BBC's flagship radio news show, The Today Program, and started a "People's Prime Minister's Questions" on Facebook. When the director of BBC News at the time, Fran Unsworth, met with members of Johnson's team (Dominic Cummings and Lee Cain) in Downing Street in February 2020, they told her that having their ministers appear on The Today Program "is not worth it, you're not fair on us. Anyway, we don't need you."[119]

The BBC might well weather these political slings and arrows, but not the economic diminution that goes with them. Since 2006, when the BBC's status was "reclassified to the central government sector" and its License Fee reclassified as a tax rather than a service charge, the government has treated the BBC—when it comes to its financial status—more like a government department than an independent broadcaster. This means it has acted as though the BBC's budget is part of the central government's expenditure, told the BBC it will have to pay for things that go far beyond the broadcaster's remit, and—when relations are strained—threatened the BBC's future funding. In mid-October 2010, for example, officials from the secretary of state's office telephoned the director general and chair of the BBC and told them the government had "a shopping list" of things it now wanted the BBC to pay for, including the World Service, BBC Monitoring, and a new local TV news initiative.[120] Then, in 2015, the government informed the BBC that it would be paying for all License Fees for the over-75s (at a cost of around £600 million). Nor could the broadcaster be confident of its future income. In 2022 the culture secretary, Nadine Dorries, announced on Twitter that "This licence fee announcement will be the last." It was time, she said "to discuss and debate new ways of funding, supporting and selling great British content."[121] What these new ways were we never discovered, Dorries resigning from her position after Boris Johnson was ejected from office by his party.

By the early 2020s the BBC reported that its UK services had experienced a "30 percent reduction in income" over the previous decade.[122] It could now only spend a fifth of the amount on content as Netflix. Losing a third of its income meant constant and painful cuts, domestically and internationally. In 2022 the BBC announced that the World Service would be cutting almost 400 staff, with another 130 going in 2025.[123] Alongside staffing cuts, in 2023 it even merged its TV world news service with its domestic TV news channel. Viewers in Asia and Africa would find themselves watching news about very unfamiliar—and distant—people and events, such as the tribulations of British TV news presenters Philip Schofield and Huw Edwards. The merging of these two BBC TV news channels "has to have been really damaging," Richard Sambrook told us.[124] It certainly would not raise the credibility of the broadcaster globally. But for many senior politicians the BBC cuts were still not enough. Some made it clear that they wanted the BBC to be a more attenuated service, relying on subscriptions, donations, and advertising—similar to its US cousin, PBS. Such a service would not be universal, would have significantly less reach—at home and abroad—and would not provide a model for the reinvigoration of Public Service Media. The incoming 2024 Labour government forestalled further World Service cuts with £27 million in extra funding, although the corporation warned that it was losing the battle against much better endowed state-funded news services.[125]

PUBLIC-SERVICE TRUTH-SEEKING

When pressed for an example of the BBC's lack of impartiality, Frazer came up with just one: its coverage of the Al Ahli Hospital explosion. "It did make an error," Frazer told ITV, "an error it accepted, in relation to the bombing of the hospital, for which it apologised." This was not an error with regard to verification, it was in reference to a live two-way shortly after the explosion happened, in which the BBC correspondent Jon Donnison said: "It's hard to see what else this could be really given the size of the explosion other than an Israeli air strike or several air strikes." The Israeli government also reacted strongly to the correspondent's error, posting on the official government X account that the BBC was guilty of a "modern blood libel."[126] The BBC apologized for Donnison's speculation shortly after the broadcast.

BBC Verify never came to a conclusion about who was responsible for the Al Ahli explosion. "We have never said," Alex Murray tells us, "that the flash you see in the Al Jazeera video hits the hospital." The verification team could not source enough evidence on which to base a solid finding. They decided it was not possible to make any firm claims based on pixelated footage taken miles from the hospital. This is why, Murray says, "We were very, very cautious about who was responsible. We were completely vanilla." This caution can mean that BBC Verify looks slow, restrained, and slightly plodding. It also means that when it verifies something, it is verified. Those in the Verify team are acutely aware that they need to have high levels of confidence before they publish. If we say it, Murray says, "then everyone else is gonna say it." So, he continues, "If we say it and it's wrong," not only does the BBC's reputation take a hit, "that's a Parliamentary inquiry!"[127]

In our world of fake news and digital disinformation, it is a truism to say that we need more help figuring out what is true and what is false, what is trustworthy and what is deceptive. Individually, we do not have the time, the tools, the skills, or the resources to evaluate all the news and information we see and hear. We need truth-seekers who have the ability and inclination to do this. Organizations such as Bellingcat, Airwars, Full Fact, and Aos Fatos have pioneered new ways of *truth-seeking*. These and some of their contemporaries in the field of verification are likely to thrive and grow, and some will become integral to existing news publishers. And others will fold because they cannot find adequate funding or because they are marginalized and suppressed by antagonistic governments and political parties. Many countries will therefore be left with sparse and anemic fact-checking NGOs and open-source intelligence networks floundering for project funding and ignored or mocked by those they most need to convince.

For these verifiers to survive and become a part of democratic information ecosystems across the world, they need to be financially sustainable, nonpartisan, and free from government control. They need, in other words, structures and principles like those of Public Service Broadcasting institutions. Although there are plenty of flaws with the PSB model, it has shown itself to be central to the health of modern democracies. As these democracies are being destabilized by political polarization and information disorder, who better to help them recover stability than Public Service Broadcasters? Yet, if they are to do this, they need reinvention. They need new capabilities and capacities to evaluate and assess digital news and information so they can provide their publics with factual ground truths, if only to stop us falling into an abyss of unknowing. And who better to lead this reinvention than the organization that originally invented Public Service Broadcasting?

In May 2023, when the BBC established BBC Verify as a new, multilayered, integrated model of verification, it was drawing together and re-purposing assets that already existed in the organization more effectively. But at the same time it was signalling a bigger ambition—to reform the way in which news is produced. If people do not know whether to trust what they see, they need to know where it came from, who gathered it, for what purpose, and whether it has been tampered with. They need, in other words, to be taken on a journey with the news producer. When we met her, the head of BBC Verify—Lindsay McCoy—referred to this as "assertive impartiality"—where the public can see how the process of impartiality works.[128]

Whether the BBC can provide such a model of verification for the reformation of Public Service Broadcasting is, however, uncertain. The corporation remains under perpetual assault—from commercial media organizations, political partisans (on all sides), foreign states, and from the UK government itself. In October 2024, the former UK prime minister, Liz Truss, openly stated that conservatives "need to be prepared to defund state media" to prevent the left from "winning the argument" on a range of issues.[129] However, without a sustainable model for verification, there is a danger that we will come to rely almost wholly on unchecked government narratives. Or worse, we will rely on government narratives checked by government fact-checkers and government-run open-source intelligence operatives.

Shortly after the Al Ahli explosion, the Israeli Defense Force (IDF) published a number of fact-checks and OSINT analyses. The blast, the IDF claimed, was caused by a malfunctioning rocket fired as part of a salvo by Palestinian Islamic Jihad in the direction of the hospital. A key piece of evidence they cited was a video of "Raw Footage" taken from Al Jazeera, in which it said: "A rocket aimed at Israel misfired and exploded at 18:59—the same moment a hospital was hit in Gaza."[130] The assertion—coupled with the footage—spread quickly across social media and was eventually watched more than five million times. It was followed up with a convincing-sounding, fifteen-minute-long OSINT analysis by an IDF spokesperson debunking Hamas's claims as "a lot of fake nonsense," and saying the group had been "given a free ride to fake" by "journalists who did not do their jobs."[131] The Israeli claims and analyses were enough to stop many news organizations from assigning responsibility to Israel. Some went further and said that the evidence indicated that the Palestinian rocket was responsible.[132] US President Joe Biden, meeting with Benjamin Netanyahu the day after the explosion, said he thought the evidence showed "the other team" were to blame.[133]

It was not until a few days later that a detailed investigation by Al Jazeera and the *New York Times* found that although Israel's theory of a malfunctioning rocket could not be discounted its evidence was flawed. The explosion in the night sky on which the IDF claim was initially made could not have caused the explosion at Al Ahli. Triangulating footage from a range of locations, forensic investigators concluded that the missile "appears to have exploded above the Israeli-Gaza border, at least two miles away from the hospital."[134] Similarly, Al Jazeera concluded that the flash in the sky was "consistent with Israel's Iron Dome missile defense system intercepting a missile fired from the Gaza Strip and destroying it in mid-air."[135] The evidence Israel had used in its OSINT analysis was not right. But by this time the political conversation had moved on.

9

BACK TO REALITY

"Any advice for dealing with a QAnon parent who thinks WW3 will
happen during the inauguration?"
"Do they have weapons?"
"Yep. A lot of them."

GREG JAFFE AND JOSE REAL, "LIFE AMID THE RUINS OF QANON"

In early 2021, the *Washington Post* journalists Greg Jaffe and Jose Del Real reported a story about "Tyler," a twenty-four-year-old man living near Minneapolis, whose mother had armed herself and stocked up on ammunition, canned food, camping equipment, and a water purifier in anticipation of Joe Biden's inauguration. Over the previous months, Tyler's mum had become a QAnon believer, and she was convinced that the 2020 US election result was fraudulent. She anticipated weeks of civil unrest, after which—she believed—Donald Trump would emerge victorious and be inaugurated the rightful president.[1] Seeing her posting increasingly extreme and outlandish content, and following several attempts to disabuse her of her beliefs, Tyler faced a decision: whether to cut himself off from his mother entirely or try to find another way to pierce her parallel reality. This dilemma was not unique to Tyler; Jaffe and Real discovered families across America torn apart by their beliefs about the 2020 election, no longer able to speak to each other, and convinced that their relatives were not just wrong but dangerously deluded.

These false narratives about the integrity of the 2020 election were largely driven, researchers at Harvard University have shown, by political elites and their news media allies: primarily Donald Trump, the Republican National Congress, and major US news channels such as Fox News. "The efforts of the President and the Republican Party," Yochai Benkler and his colleagues write, were "supported by the right-wing media ecosystem," with "Fox News and talk radio functioning in effect as a party press."[2] News outlets did this despite knowing that there was no evidence to support the claims. Their duplicity was exposed by emails and messages released in 2023 as part of the legal action taken by Dominion Voting Systems against Fox News. These revealed that Fox News anchors Tucker Carlson and others invited election deniers onto their shows and let their claims stand despite knowing they were not true. As Carlson wrote to Laura Ingraham in November 2020: "Sidney Powell [Trump advisor and regular Fox News guest] is lying by the way. I caught her. It's insane."[3] In other words, these parallel political realities about the election were deliberately concocted and spread by political leaders, their parties, and supportive news outlets. And with great success. Three years later, polls showed that approximately 30 percent of Americans, and two-thirds of Republicans, still believed the election was fraudulent.[4] And even if other voters did not believe this, enough were sufficiently willing to discount Trump's repeated attempts to overturn the outcome to vote him back into power in November 2024—"history's greatest comeback!," the Israeli prime minister, Benjamin Netanyahu, effused.[5] Within days, articles once more started appearing about families splitting apart, irreconcilably divided over whether Trump was America's chief villain or its savior.[6]

Nor is it just in the United States where families and friends have been torn apart by the parallel realities spread by political leaders and compliant news outlets. Since Russia's full-scale invasion of Ukraine in February 2022, journalists have reported on dozens of Ukrainians whose Russian relatives appeared to be living in a parallel reality about the war. Alexander Serdyuk, a Russian living in Lviv, Ukraine, told journalists that he had cut off contact with his mother in Russia because whenever they spoke she would parrot Putin's narrative that Russia is not attacking Ukrainians, but instead that Ukrainian fascists are attacking their own people.[7] A Uyghur woman, Jewher Ilham, has explained how she became unable to relate to her Chinese friends when talking about the human rights abuses Uyghurs have faced in Xinjiang because they say that she has been brainwashed.[8] Across the world, as patients in intensive care wards were dying of COVID-19, doctors and nurses reported how some patients—even while gasping for breath—were insisting that the virus did not exist or that its harmful effects had been hugely exaggerated.[9] Several world leaders played central roles in the spread of these misleading claims early in the pandemic. Brazil's Jair Bolsonaro, for example, said COVID-19 was just a "little flu" and the crisis was a "media trick." AMLO's government in Mexico ran official adverts in early 2020 saying "COVID-19 is not an emergency situation" and "COVID-19 is not serious."[10]

Nor is it just families and friends being polarized by these parallel political realities. As Morgan Marietta and David Barker found in their study of polarization in US politics, *One Nation, Two Realities*, once ordinary citizens recognize that others hold contrary perceptions of reality, they can disengage from them and treat them with disdain, causing an already divided society to polarize further.[11] In the United States, Marietta and Barker write, it is increasingly hard to find points on which the political left and right agree, with citizens divided "not just on climate and racism, but on the origins of sexual orientation, the consequences of vaccines, immigration, the national debt, minimum wage increases, gun control, the prevalence of violent crime and false convictions, the degree of threat from terrorism, and too many other examples to list."[12]

Influential media figures consciously emphasize and endorse this divide. As deceased conservative "shock jock" Rush Limbaugh told his listeners in 2009, "We really live, folks, in two worlds . . . We live in two universes."

"One universe," he continued, "is a lie . . . Everything run, dominated and controlled by the left here and around the world is a lie. The other universe is where we are, and that's where reality reigns supreme."[13]

The consequences of these parallel realities extend far beyond silence and separation. Because of them, people refuse to accept election results, object to complying with medical guidance, reject vaccinations, assault their political opponents, trash government buildings, and join insurrections. Without a collection of shared facts on which to base political opinions, reasoned debate becomes impossible. Once people live in separate realities, they struggle to communicate with one another or to find common ground. It is similar to the Monty Python "Argument" sketch, in which a man walks into an office where you can pay to have an argument, but all his interlocutor does is deny everything he says, even that they are having an argument at all. Except that real life is not a comedy sketch.

Yet, many leaders, parties, and governments now see the creation and dissemination of these parallel realities as integral to their political success. AMLO relied on his daily live-streamed press conferences (mañaneras) to channel his version of "the truth" directly to the Mexican public for two-plus hours a day. Jair Bolsonaro exploited social media to disseminate his political messages, post unfounded claims of election fraud, and belittle his opponents. Narendra Modi's popularity has been sustained and enhanced by the raucous support he receives from TV news anchors like Arnab Goswami, who acclaims Modi's Hindutva agenda and dismisses BJP critics as a corrupt *Tukde-Tukde* gang. For Arnab Goswami in Russia read Vladimir Solovyev, and in the United States read Tucker Carlson. In Hungary, Viktor Orbán's election victories rely on manufactured news narratives about enemies at the gate—George Soros, the globalists, and the Jewish International. While in Brazil, the Bolsonaros fabricated a host of adversaries including cultural Marxists, leftists, and imperialist NGOs.

Although these leaders' and governments' approaches to convincing the public of their narratives vary, they each see the importance of news in propagating them. Across the countries we studied, we identified fifteen

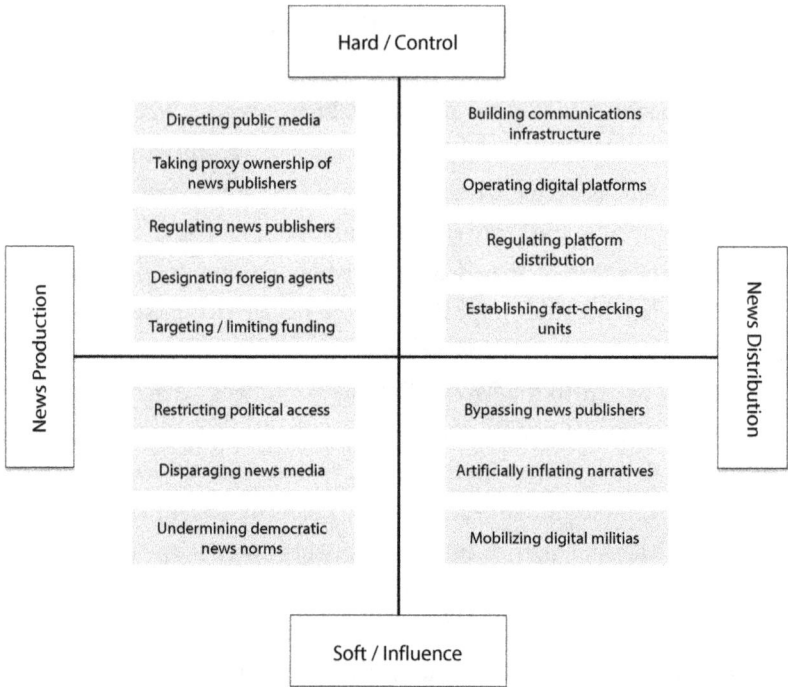

FIGURE 9.1 Methods governments are using to control and influence the news.

Note: The graphic illustrates the main news control and influence techniques we identified as being used by governments during our research. It is not intended to be exhaustive of all the methods governments use to influence the news.

methods—some older, some newer—that governments are using to control and influence the news (see figure 9.1). Each method, in different ways, undermines the democratic ideal that news should make citizens better informed and enable them to scrutinize those in power, and therefore each contributes to producing a more authoritarian public sphere. Some are *hard*, and involve exerting direct control, such as taking proxy ownership of news outlets. Others are *soft*, and involve exerting influence more indirectly, such as disparaging "mainstream" news outlets, or mobilizing digital militias to harass them. Some focus on the outlets and processes of *news production*; others focus on *news distribution*, be it by infrastructure, platforms, or users. Broadly speaking, authoritarian states such as Russia and China have more freedom to use control-based methods, and democracies with stronger checks and balances are more likely to rely on indirect methods of influence. But just as our case studies sit on a spectrum from autocracies to liberal democracies, so each government draws on a range of direct and indirect methods, depending on their objectives and the affordances of their political systems.

China's CCP has focused on long-term, structural investments, growing its international news networks, dominating Chinese-language news globally, taking ownership stakes in foreign news outlets, paying for news to appear in international publications, and offering access to its news at minimal cost to promote its brand of "positive journalism" across the Global South. In contrast, Russia has increasingly turned inward: its government has asserted control of domestic news outlets and directed them to paint a dark and menacing picture of the world for Russian citizens, while adopting dehumanizing, genocidal rhetoric to justify the military's actions in Ukraine. Both Viktor Orbán's Fidesz in Hungary, and Narendra Modi's BJP in India, have managed to co-opt domestic news channels while maintaining a patina of democratic legitimacy. They have done so by leveraging the tools available to all democratic governments—regulation, money, and political access—but taking them to the extreme. In different ways, Modi, Bolsonaro, and recent Conservative administrations in the UK have tried to circumvent "mainstream media" by denying some outlets political access and using alternative platforms instead, undermining norms that previously enabled news institutions to hold governments to account. Modi and Brazil's Jair Bolsonaro have cultivated digital militias capable of amplifying government narratives, attacking news outlets, and mobbing critics. With the exception of the UK, each of these leaders adopts the mantle of the messianic populist whose word should be accepted as gospel. No one has exemplified this better than Mexico's Andrés Manuel López Obrador (AMLO) as he sermonized directly to his citizens, without filter, every day.

To these leaders, whether the alternative realities they conjure resemble material reality or are supported by empirical evidence is relatively unimportant. What matters more is to communicate a compelling narrative that identifies their friends and enemies and explains why they are the solution to their country's problems. Disregarding factuality in favor of storytelling, these leaders are engaging in what the political scientists Emanuel Adler and Alena Drieschova call "truth subversion" politics. They are undermining the importance of facts and rational argument and flooding the public sphere with messages designed to agitate and divide.[14] Prioritizing polarization over consensus, they often govern ineffectively because on any given issue their priority is not to find the best policy but to discredit and demean their enemies.

The harmful effects of truth subversion on domestic politics extend to the international system. The more national governments attempt to impose self-serving narratives that disregard factual reality, the more the world will fragment into sovereign realities in which "our nation's truth" subordinates "the truth." In such a divided world, communication between countries becomes less frequent and less constructive. As dialogue frays, miscalculations become more likely and the risk of disputes increases. Multilateral diplomacy is less likely to succeed—or even begin. Countries stop adhering to international agreements because they assume others will renege on them. Reducing carbon emissions, agreeing on shared responses to pandemics, signing arms control treaties, addressing antimicrobial resistance, and fighting organized crime, maritime piracy, and international terrorism all become more difficult. If people cannot agree on "what *is*," how will they be able to agree on what "*ought* to be?"[15]

Equally, it becomes tougher to make the case for liberal democracy, especially in a world in which every country claims that their political system is democratic. In this sense, Francis Fukuyama's much-criticized assertion of "The End of History"—when he proclaimed the political triumph of democracy following the end of the Cold War—was correct, in a way.[16] Democracy did win, at least in narrative terms. In the decades following the Cold War, more and more countries would hold elections and claim to be democracies. By 2024 more than half of the world's adult population would find themselves voting in "democratic" elections, including citizens in Belarus, Russia, Iran, and North Korea. Even though the results of elections in these countries were predetermined, their respective governments assert democratic legitimacy. Even in China, an authoritarian one-party state, the government declares the political system to be democratic—and not just democratic but the world's leading democracy (as discussed in chapter 3). The former US president Joe Biden framed the twenty-first century's key geopolitical conflict as being between democracy and autocracy, but at the narrative level it is more likely to resemble a conflict between different interpretations of democracy: democracy with American characteristics, democracy with Hungarian characteristics, democracy with Chinese characteristics.

There is no guarantee that liberal democracy will win this narrative struggle. Even if countries do not go as far as adopting the "China Model" of "democracy", citizens may still find the idea of sacrificing political freedoms in exchange for economic growth appealing. South Korea, Taiwan and Singapore achieved much of their twentieth-century economic growth under autocratic governments. Narendra Modi's popularity in his first decade as India's prime minister, despite his government's growing authoritarianism during that period, suggested that many Indian citizens might be willing to prioritize economic opportunity over political freedom (although they then punished him in the 2024 election after his government had failed to deliver enough of those opportunities).[17] And in the United States in 2024, surveys indicated that voters' belief that Donald Trump would manage the economy better than Kamala Harris outweighed their concerns about his authoritarian tendencies.[18]

HOW SHOULD LIBERAL DEMOCRACIES RESPOND?

How should societies respond to governments' increasingly authoritarian approaches to news? Can political actors arrest the corrosion of the democratic public sphere and reverse the spread of parallel realities?

It would be trite to suggest that such vast shifts in global consciousness can be changed by simple tweaks in public policy. However, by rethinking and reframing the problems that liberal democracies face, it should be possible to reduce the risks of an increasingly authoritarian public sphere and its destructive consequences. In practice, this means stopping three things and reviving a fourth. It means stopping seeing these problems through the frame of disinformation. It means no longer characterizing news as an instrument of warfare. It means no longer making narrative the primary way of understanding political reality. And, it means reviving respect for the "Constitution of Knowledge."

STOP FRAMING THE PROBLEM AS DISINFORMATION

In the initial stages of the COVID-19 pandemic, medical experts approached COVID-19 as a respiratory disease, and therefore they assumed that a solution was to manufacture more ventilators. Then, as countries rushed to acquire new ventilators, they realized they did not have enough hospital beds, so they built more hospital beds. Then they realized they did not have enough nurses and doctors to staff them, which was far more difficult to address. Over time medical researchers learned that COVID-19 was a systemic illness, whose effects reached far beyond the respiratory system, weakening the heart, brain, kidneys, nervous system, digestive system, seemingly exploiting any weakness a person had when infected with it.

The way we understand and address the pathologies of the digital information environment may be similar to our approach to COVID-19 early in the pandemic. The most visible symptom of disease may be disinformation, just like the most visceral symptom of COVID-19 was respiratory distress. As medical authorities were fond of saying early in the pandemic, there was an "infodemic" of misinformation and disinformation about the virus as people (and many leaders) turned to folk wisdom, quack medicine, and conspiracy theories in response to the fear and uncertainty brought about by the virus.[19] But like COVID-19, the etiology of the information disorder we currently face is far more systemic. Treating the most egregious symptom—disinformation—is just one element of an effective response. It may be an important element—ventilators keep people alive—but framing the problem as disinformation not only ignores deeper issues with the digital public sphere but distracts attention from dealing with them.

We see this in the emergence of the cottage industry—dubbed "Big Disinformation"—that has developed to deal with the spread of false and misleading content online. This burgeoning sector searches for solutions to the disinformation dilemma—from regulatory responses to algorithmic fixes, from legislative initiatives to media literacy programs. The hope is that reducing the amount of disinformation in the public sphere will restore public trust in information, prevent people from falling for conspiracy theories, and limit foreign states' ability to interfere in democratic processes or undermine social cohesion.

This misdiagnoses the problem. Of course there is a vast quantity of disinformation and misinformation in the digital public sphere, and it makes sense to try to reduce it, especially if it is intentionally harmful. But there are exponentially greater amounts of *all* information. Look for any sort of information, and you will find much more of it than in the analogue past. This is because we have shifted from a world of information scarcity to one of information abundance.[20] Thinking that information disorder can be "solved" by simply identifying and removing any false or misleading information online is like thinking that pollution can be solved by taking waste out of the ocean with a teaspoon. Especially since there is not only hyperinflation of information but also hyperinflation of sources. Everyone is now capable of publishing news and information, and most people can publish from any one of a handful of their multiple online profiles.[21] On top of this, the methods of information verification (and distortion) are available to everyone—to the journalist, the open-source intelligence (OSINT) analyst, the conspiracy theorist (hence the term "truther"), the state propagandist, the PR agency, as well as your Average Jo. It is hardly a surprise, therefore, that there is a broader crisis of legitimacy, in which people are finding it harder to know who or what to trust. The digital public sphere is already an epistemological junkyard, and it is becoming more so as the tools of AI come into common use.

Anxiety about the credibility of information online, and whether the tech platforms are doing enough to limit it, is motivating calls for governments to limit platform power and to regulate the digital environment. But as we have shown throughout this book, many governments are part of the problem. Many of the most prominent false and misleading narratives in the public sphere come from governments, leaders and political parties.[22] Many of them are "weaponizing" terms like "fake news" for political gain, and using them to dismiss news that is embarrassing, uncomfortable, or incriminating.[23] So, although there is a role for government in addressing the information disorder we currently face, relying on politicians and political parties to be arbiters of truth, or expecting governments to present an authoritative picture of reality, risks putting a counterfeiter in charge of the central bank.

We need to think beyond trying to "solve" disinformation and consider how to forge a more democratic public sphere in the face of information abundance, platform power, and growing government intervention. Part of this is to reexamine the role governments should or should not play in regulating public speech. Laws rushed through to stop "fake news" are unlikely to produce a more democratic information environment.

STOP WEAPONIZING NEWS AS INFORMATION WARFARE

If there are problems with responding to the spread of parallel realities by focusing solely on reducing disinformation, another comes from approaching the issue through the lens of information warfare. Across the world, a growing number of domestic political parties, leaders, and national security establishments are approaching news as an instrument of war—something they believe is being weaponized by their competitors for geopolitical gain.[24] National security doctrines employ an ever-expanding range of terms to capture this idea of a global struggle for influence, including "information war," "political warfare," "cognitive warfare," "narrative warfare," "psychological warfare," "public opinion warfare," and the recently fashionable "foreign information manipulation and interference" (FIMI).

Approaching the spread of parallel realities through the lens of information warfare is understandable because this is what authoritarian states are doing. Russia and China both approach international news as an instrument of political warfare: in Russia's case mainly to subvert democratic societies and erode support for Ukraine, and in China's case to promote its political system as superior to that of the United States. Both are propagating parallel realities—Russia claiming that its war in Ukraine is liberating Ukrainians from fascism rather than colonizing them, and China claiming that it is the world's leading democracy and a defender of human rights (see chapters 2 and 3). Neither country draws a clean distinction between war and peace. Instead, they see themselves as being in a state of permanent conflict with their Western adversaries. The first task of the commander, the military philosopher Karl von Clausewitz writes, is to understand "the kind of war on which they are embarking; neither mistaking it for, nor trying to turn it into, something that is alien to its nature."[25] If information has indeed been "weaponized," and one's adversaries recognize no boundaries between war and peace, surely it makes sense for liberal democracies to approach the information environment this way too?

Perhaps. The problem is that the integral part that news plays in maintaining the health of democracies risks being fatally compromised when news is reduced to an instrument of political warfare. News in democracies is vital for establishing a shared foundation of reality and for keeping citizens informed. The more strongly news is viewed as just another "munition of the mind" to gain political advantage over perceived adversaries, the more its democratic purpose is lost from view—domestically and internationally.[26]

By viewing the news through a national security lens, liberal democracies also risk accelerating the shift to a more authoritarian public sphere, in which the pursuit of truth is subordinated to the national interest. Democracies would be approaching the news as they do in wartime, where governments use national security arguments to justify pressuring news outlets to self-censor information that would undermine "national unity" or "social cohesion." These arguments are commonly used by authoritarian states to suppress dissent, but they are now being employed by a growing range of democracies. India (see chapter 5) is one of many countries that have introduced national security legislation against "fake news" and been accused of using it to censor information that presents the Modi regime negatively.[27] More and more states are creating their own fact-checkers, arguing that national security dictates that the state needs to decide what is true. Countries that do this are taking a step closer to dictatorship in a literal sense: the state gets to dictate reality.

If democratic states accept the characterization of the public sphere as a conflicted space, in which news and information are used as weapons, that means accepting that we are in a continuous state of warfare, in which government manipulation and distortion of the news is justified on a permanent basis. In such a "forever information war" news is no longer reporting; it is propaganda.

STOP PRIORITIZING NARRATIVE ABOVE ALL ELSE

In the 1980s and 1990s, narrative theorists argued that there are two modes of thought and communication, which Jerome Bruner called the narrative mode and the logico-scientific mode.[28] In communication they are analogous to storytelling and rational argument. Bruner was writing after decades in which, in the West at least, rationalist, empiricist approaches to governance had been dominant. The ideal was that governments would engage in "evidence-based policy-making," finding solutions based on empirical evidence that would make societies more productive and improve well-being. Bruner's point was that humans are not just cold-hearted rationalists, as orthodox economists have argued, and that narrative is also fundamental to how humans think and communicate. As this idea got more popular, more and more fields began to focus on the value of narrative communication, including business, law, medicine, politics and war. As narratives, or stories, seem such an intuitive way to communicate—the main form of communication through which children learn—many came to see them as the most important form of communication.[29] The solution to terrorism became to "tell better stories." The solution to business profitability was to "tell better stories." The way to win in war or politics was to "tell better stories."[30] In the process, the importance of evidence and rational argument started to become marginalized, especially in political communication.

As discussed in the introduction, narratives are constructed by creating a plot, which explains how events play out over time, in order to convey a central idea.[31] A simple political narrative, for example, might involve a politician who uses their humble background, their charitable behavior, and their consistent political record to convey the idea that citizens should vote for them. Or, in today's polarized times, a politician might tell citizens a story about how their country is being destroyed by their political opponents, neoliberal globalists, hateful fascists, corrupt mainstream media, Big Tech censors, "woke" elites, or a cabal of Satanic pedophiles (insert your preferred enemy). The point of the story is to portray the leader as a national savior or a political messiah: the only one who will vanquish the enemy and make our country whole again. Or it might be a story, as in Russia, where citizens are told it is their patriotic duty to support Russia's "special military operation" in Ukraine because it faces a range of enemies trying to destroy it (again insert your preferred adversary—NATO, "LGBT brigades," Satanists, British special forces, Jews, Poles, Ukrainian fascists). According to narrative theory, these stories are not necessarily convincing because their constituent parts are logically coherent or verifiably true but because they possess "verisimilitude"—in other words, people find the overall story *plausible* based on their existing knowledge of the world. Stephen Colbert famously called this feature of narrative "truthiness"—the story *seems* true, regardless of whether it actually is.[32] An effective storyteller convinces the listener that they have gained more understanding of the world, even if the story bears little correspondence with observable reality. As Bruner writes: "Great storytellers have the artifices of narrative reality construction so well mastered that their telling pre-empts momentarily the possibility of any but a single interpretation."[33]

Approaching political communication as if adherence to a narrative is the only thing that matters lowers the standards against which the validity of political communication is assessed. All that matters is "does this content fit the overall story I want to tell," rather than "is what I say verifiably true?" This approach can be used to justify the use of false or misleading information as long as the message fits the "strategic narrative" a political actor thinks the audience will find believable. An archetypal example of this came during the 2024 US election, when Donald Trump's running mate, J. D. Vance, amplified a false claim that Haitian immigrants were stealing people's pets in Springfield, Ohio, and eating them.[34] When challenged, Vance admitted that he knew the claim was almost certainly false, but that he was justified in amplifying it because it focused the media on an issue that they would have otherwise ignored. "If I have to create stories," Vance said, "so that the American media actually pays attention to the suffering of the American people, then that's what I'm gonna do."[35] For Vance, promoting his overarching strategic narrative that immigrants are harming America was sufficient moral justification to just make stories up.

As we have shown throughout the book, this philosophy has been adopted by political actors in various political systems worldwide. They are engaged, they believe, in constant battles for narrative supremacy, regardless of the truth. For the CCP in China, news must above all else fit the strategic narrative that the CCP is competent and is meeting people's needs. For Russia, news about its war against Ukraine must fit its strategic narrative that Ukraine is fascist and committing genocide against its own people. For the populist leaders Viktor Orbán, Narendra Modi, AMLO, Jair Bolsonaro, and Donald Trump, the news must fit a strategic narrative in which they are the only thing that stands between their people and imminent destruction. For these leaders, fashioning parallel realities is justifiable to maintain the coherence of their strategic narratives. And as the news remains a key source of authoritative storytelling about how the world really is, it is an obvious medium for these political actors to influence, through direct control if they can and indirect influence if they cannot.

News outlets that are not directly state-run can choose whether to adopt this narrative-led approach, selecting news in a way that supports whatever story their preferred party or leader wants to tell, or they can adopt an approach based more on empirical evidence. Choose the former and, as the journalist Peter Oborne puts it, they "say goodbye to the truth" because their version of reality is dictated by political fealty first and objective reality second.[36] But choose the latter, and—depending on where they are located—news outlets may find themselves unable to do their jobs for lack of funding, lack of access, and constant harassment. Moreover, they will find that by choosing the evidence-led approach they are unable to reach a large segment of citizens who have already been convinced that their reporting is biased and politically motivated.

Giving narrative reality primacy is doubly problematic because of the surreptitious way stories persuade. Rather than openly inviting citizens to consider how the evidence measures up to one's claims, as argument does, storytelling aims to engage and enthrall and to discourage critical thought.[37] Effective storytelling involves "transporting" audiences into the story world, populated with characters with which the narrator hopes they will emotionally identify (positively or negatively). The idea is that while immersed in this story world (a bit like when one loses the passage of time while reading a good book or watching a good movie) the narrator can persuade the audience through stealth, rather than openly stating their argument and the premises on which it is based.[38]

The more dramatic a story is, the more emotionally engaging it is likely to be. Because of this, political actors will often exaggerate the plots and characters of their stories and overemphasize the political stakes. This is why messianic populists draw so strongly on dystopian themes, describing how their enemies seek to annihilate them and how their countries are falling into the abyss, so that they can cast themselves as the hero riding to the rescue. Few leaders exemplify this more strongly than Donald Trump—who decried "American carnage" at his 2016 inauguration, told his supporters that "if you don't fight like hell, you're not going to have a country any more" just before the 2021 Capitol riots, and claimed in a 2024 campaign speech that "if we don't win this election, I don't think you're going to have another election in this country."[39] This rhetoric may be engaging, but it is also dangerous. The more apocalyptic political narratives get, the more likely they are to lead to conflict. In his book *Why War*, Philip Smith explains that cultures that tell apocalyptic stories to themselves, accentuate the presence of good and evil, and emphasize the role of heroes and villains are more likely to go to war.[40] In contrast, cultures that frame issues with greater nuance are less conflict prone.

This is not an argument for elevating technocratic, rationalist thinking in politics and communication above all else. We recognize that politics and news will always involve storytelling. We are arguing that there is a need for political communication to combine narrative and rationalist modes of thought, rather than only pursuing whatever content fits one's narrative, regardless of the evidence. We need to bring rational argument and reasoned debate back into news and political communication. If we want to prevent the further erosion of the democratic public sphere, we need truth to get in the way of a good story.

REVIVE RESPECT FOR THE CONSTITUTION OF KNOWLEDGE

Finally, ensuring that political narratives are more strongly grounded in material reality means reviving respect for what the author and journalist Jonathan Rauch calls the "Constitution of Knowledge." Over much of the last century, Rauch explains, the liberal democratic conception of news has been underpinned by the idea that its purpose is to communicate verified truths about what is happening in the world. However, the idea that verified truth is desirable or even knowable is under attack worldwide, as political actors are deliberately subverting the expert-led institutions that liberal democracies rely on to create knowledge. These institutions—journalism, academia, scientists, the legal profession—have long-established norms and practices of truth-seeking. There are plenty of journalists and news outlets that routinely fail to live up to these norms and practices, but for those that do, information should be examined, properly sourced, peer-reviewed, and independently verified before being accepted as established knowledge.[41]

One can recognize people who uphold the norms and practices of these institutions, according to Rauch, as they will correct their mistakes, issue retractions, and more generally act as if "lying and making stuff up is a firing offense."[42] Those who adhere to the Constitution of Knowledge accept that their views should and will be challenged. They embrace verification rather than trying to convince people to accept their word without question. They do not try to avoid criticism by only talking to friendly news outlets or journalists. They accept the importance of independent scrutiny rather than trying to eradicate it. They do not try to infiltrate otherwise independent news outlets with government politicians. They do not attack others who challenge their version of reality, or label them as enemies of the people. These are things political actors do when they want to deny the truth, avoid scrutiny, and propagate their own versions of reality. Donald Trump admitted as much when asked why he kept attacking the press. "You know why I do it? I do it to discredit and demean you all, so when you write negative stories about me no one will believe you."[43]

Leaders across the world are attacking the very idea that objective, verified truth is either important or attainable, and promoting other forms of truth instead.[44] The authoritarian leaders and populist politicians we have analyzed seek to replace *verified* truth with *authoritative* truth—convincing people that the truth is whatever those in authority say it is. "Better to get your news directly from the President," Lamar Smith, a Republic congressman from Texas, said on the House floor, shortly after Trump began his first term as president. "In fact," he added, "it might be the only way to get the unvarnished truth."[45] Audiences who accept this literally give their leaders the power to dictate reality—to argue that two plus two equals five, and have the audience believe it. This promotion of *authoritative* truth over *verified* truth has not just come from the political right. As chapter 7 showed, Mexico's left-wing leader, AMLO, presented himself as the font of truth in government, despite issuing tens of thousands of recorded falsehoods and systematically attacking established news outlets on a daily basis.

Our concern about this is not driven by partisanship. A leader seeking the authority to dictate what is true represents a fundamental threat to democracy whether left-wing, right-wing, conservative, socialist, or nationalist.

The importance of verified truth to the liberal democratic public sphere is also being undermined by the growing prominence of other forms of truth: *subjective truth* and *tribal truth*.[46] Russia demonstrates how these combine. By propagating multiple, often contradictory narratives, it tries to discredit the notion of verified, objective truth altogether. Instead, it argues for *subjective* truth—that everyone's narrative is just as valid as any other. Like an ongoing *Choose Your Own Adventure* story, this invites citizens to pick whichever version of reality suits them. But what Russia is ultimately aiming for is *tribal truth*: that is, that in the absence of being able to tell what is true, people will simply choose to believe whatever their tribe believes. It wants people to accept the government's official version of reality in which Russia is a force for good, that it has been fighting a patriotic war to free Ukrainians from oppression and to prevent its Western allies from destroying Mother Russia.[47] In an information environment in which it is harder than ever to determine the truth, why not believe the version of reality to which one's in-group subscribes?

Whether democracies can resist a shift to a more authoritarian public sphere depends on whether they can revive and reinvent the institutions that can establish and verify the truth of what is happening in the world. Central among these are independent news outlets and truth-seekers. As Hannah Arendt writes, "when a community has embarked on organised lying on principle," as many political actors now have, the truth-teller "become[s] a political factor of the first order."[48] The fact-checking and OSINT industries represent two early attempts to create an alternative model for verification more suited to our digital news and information environment. Public service broadcasters such as the BBC could play a key role in developing and sustaining this model. Yet even these nascent attempts to create new ways of verifying reality are in danger. They are being undermined by governments that fail to understand their significance, and they are attacked by governments who want their own version of reality to be beyond question. If democracies fail to support news publishers who independently pursue and verify facts, they risk falling prey to storytellers, mythmakers, and fabulists.

Without concerted action to counter these trends, we risk a more authoritarian world in which countries prioritize their own sovereign "truths" over universal ones, in which independent sources of news and information become ever weaker, and in which citizens live in different—often contradictory—realities. In such a world nationalism and tribalism are more likely to spiral, with misunderstanding and conflict the result. To avoid such a world means protecting and promoting independent news, reviving respect in the "Constitution of Knowledge," and holding to account leaders who offer convenient narrative fictions rather than inconvenient truths. If societies can resist the allure of parallel realities, they will be better able to improve social cohesion, reach consensus on the challenges they face, and work with rather than against each other.

ACKNOWLEDGMENTS

This book is the product of many conversations. First, our own. These began during a project to compare how Russian and Chinese state news outlets covered the 2020 US election, but then quickly expanded to consider the myriad ways governments are trying to wrest control of news across the world. As we watched politicians and parties figuring out how to take advantage of the digital media and communications environment, we were astonished to see their efforts lead on to electoral shocks, attempted coups, wars, and invasions. Making sense of what they were doing was only possible thanks to the help and insights of many people along the way.

We would like to thank our editor at Columbia University Press, Philip Leventhal, for his enthusiasm and guidance from the outset. We would also like to thank the production team, especially our proof-readers, for their thoroughness and professionalism. Thanks also go to our anonymous reviewers, whose enthusiastic comments and incisive feedback were invaluable as we refined the manuscript.

The book would not be what it is without the contribution of the many people who talked to us formally and informally across the world. In particular we would like to thank people who kindly agreed to be interviewed, including those who agreed to speak from war zones or from countries where media freedoms are under threat. We would also like to thank our colleagues and students at King's College London and the Royal Military Academy Sandhurst, with whom we discussed and refined many of our ideas. We are particularly grateful to Chloe Autran, whose research and language support on Brazil and Hungary was immensely helpful.

We are indebted, too, to those who kept us on track through their reassurance during more challenging moments. Thanks must go to our families and friends for their patience, support and, at times, distraction from the challenges in making sense of the realities the book describes.

NOTES

1. NEWS AS REALITY

1. James Markham, *Voices of the Red Giants: Communications in Russia and China* (University of Iowa Press, 1967).
2. Anna Christensen, "Pravda Publishes Picture of Andropov to Dispel Health Fears," *UPI*, November 8, 1983, https://www.upi.com/Archives/1983/11/08/Pravda-publishes-picture-of-Andropov-to-dispel-health-fears/2751437115600.
3. Alexander Amerisov, "A Chronology of Soviet Media Coverage," *Bulletin of the Atomic Scientists* 42, no. 7 (1986): 38–39.
4. John Perry Barlow, "A Declaration of the Independence of Cyberspace," 1996, https://www.eff.org/cyberspace-independence.
5. George H. W. Bush, "Address Before a Joint Session of the Congress on the State of the Union," January 28, 1992, https://www.presidency.ucsb.edu/documents/address-before-joint-session-the-congress-the-state-the-union-0.
6. Jean Baudrillard, *The Gulf War Did Not Take Place*, trans. Paul Patton (Indiana University Press, 1995), 72.
7. Piers Robinson, "The CNN Effect: Can the News Media Drive Foreign Policy?," *Review of International Studies* 25, no. 2 (1999): 301–9.
8. BBC, "France Launches World TV Channel," December 6, 2006, http://news.bbc.co.uk/1/hi/world/europe/6215170.stm.
9. Daya Thussu et al., *China's Media Go Global* (Routledge, 2018).
10. Alina Mungiu-Pippidi, "How Media and Politics Shape Each Other in the New Europe," *Romanian Journal of Political Science* 8, no. 1 (2008): 72. See also Anya Schiffrin, ed., *Media*

Capture: How Money, Digital Platforms and Governments Control the News (Columbia University Press, 2021).

11. Walter Lippmann, *Liberty and the News* (Dover, 2010), 39, 16.

12. Herbert Gans, *Deciding What's News* (Constable, 1980), 5.

13. Michael Schudson, "The Politics of Narrative Form: The Emergence of News Conventions in Print and Television," *Daedalus* 111, no. 4 (1982): 97–112.

14. Schudson, "The Politics of Narrative Form," 98–99.

15. Linus Hagström and Karl Gustafsson, "Narrative Power: How Storytelling Shapes East Asian International Politics," *Cambridge Review of International Affairs* 32, no. 4 (2019): 387–406.

16. Thomas Colley and Carolijn van Noort, *Strategic Narratives, Ontological Security and Global Policy: Responses to China's Belt and Road Initiative* (Palgrave MacMillan, 2022).

17. Jelena Subotić, "Narrative, Ontological Security, and Foreign Policy Change," *Foreign Policy Analysis* 12, no. 4 (2015): 610–27.

18. Mark Galeotti, *The Weaponisation of Everything: A Field Guide to the New Way of War* (Yale University Press, 2022); and Tzu-Chieh Hung and Tzu-Wei Hung, "How China's Cognitive Warfare Works: A Frontline Perspective of Taiwan's Anti-Disinformation Wars," *Journal of Global Security Studies* 7, no. 4 (2022), https://doi.org/10.1093/jogss/ogac016.

19. Timothy Frye, *Weak Strongman: The Limits of Power in Putin's Russia* (Princeton University Press, 2021).

20. NORC, "New Survey Finds Most Russians See Ukrainian War as Defense Against West," NORC at the University of Chicago, January 9, 2024, https://www.norc.org/research /library/new-survey-finds-most-russians-see-ukrainian-war-as-defense-against-west.html; and Levada Center, "Russians' Perceptions of Changes in Various Spheres in the Outgoing Year 2023," February 7, 2024, https://www.levada.ru/en/2024/02/07/russians-perceptions -of-changes-in-various-spheres-in-the-outgoing-year-2023.

21. Luke Harding, *Invasion: Russia's Bloody War and Ukraine's Fight for Survival* (Guardian Faber, 2022).

22. Anne-Marie Brady, *Marketing Dictatorship: Propaganda and Thought Work in Contemporary China* (Rowman and Littlefield, 2008).

23. Reporters Without Borders, "China's Pursuit of a New World Media Order," 2019, https:// rsf.org/en/rsf-report-chinas-pursuit-new-world-media-order.

24. Manuel Castells, *Communication Power* (Oxford University Press, 2013).

25. Silvia Tieri and Amit Ranjan, "Covid-19, Communalism, and Islamophobia: India Facing the Disease," *Social Identities* 29, no. 1 (2023): 62–78.

26. Tom Phillips, "Mexico Media Say President's Attacks on Journalists Are 'Invitation to Violence'," *Guardian*, December 21, 2022, https://www.theguardian.com/world/2022/dec/21 /mexico-journalist-safety-andres-manuel-lopez-obrador-amlo.

27. Jerome Bruner, "The Narrative Construction of Reality," *Critical Inquiry* 18, no. 1 (1991): 1–21.

28. Bruner, "The Narrative Construction of Reality," 13.

29. Barack Obama, *Dreams from My Father: A Story of Race and Inheritance* (Three Rivers, 2004).

30. Donald Trump, *The Art of the Deal* (Ballantine, 1987).

31. Ireneusz Karolewski et al., "Carl Schmitt and Democratic Backsliding," *Contemporary Political Theory* 22 (2023): 406–37.

32. Carl Schmitt, *The Concept of the Political* (University of Chicago Press, 1986), 26.

33. Schmitt, *The Concept of the Political*, 27.

34. Karl Popper, *The Logic of Scientific Discovery* (Routledge, 2002), 316.

35. Jennifer Hothschild and Katherine Einstein, "Do Facts Matter? Information and Misinformation in American Politics," *Political Science Quarterly* 130, no. 4 (2015): 587.

36. Philip Wiener, ed., *Charles S. Peirce: Selected Writings* (Dover, 1966), xx. See also Jonathan Rauch, *The Constitution of Knowledge: A Defense of Truth* (Brookings Institution, 2021).

37. Jürgen Habermas, *The Structural Transformation of the Public Sphere* (Polity Press, 1992).

2. WAR IS PEACE: PUTIN'S RUSSIA

1. Amnesty International, "'Children': The Attack on the Donetsk Regional Academic Drama Theatre in Mariupol, Ukraine," 2022, https://www.amnesty.org/en/documents/eur50/5713/2022/en/; and Lori Hinnant et al., "AP Evidence Points to 600 Dead in Mariupol Theater Airstrike," Associated Press, May 4, 2022, https://apnews.com/article/russia-ukraine-war-mariupol-theater-c321a196fbd568899841b506afcac7a1.

2. Amnesty International, "'Children': The Attack on the Donetsk Regional Academic Drama Theatre."

3. TASS, "Azov Battalion Militants Blow Up Mariupol Theater Building—Defense Ministry," March 16, 2022, https://tass.com/world/1423275.

4. Katie Polglase et al., "Anatomy of the Mariupol Hospital Attack," *CNN*, March 17, 2022, https://edition.cnn.com/interactive/2022/03/europe/mariupol-maternity-hospital-attack/index.html.

5. Barbie Nadeau, "Russia Says Injured Pregnant Woman Is a Crisis Actor. She's Actually a Pregnant Blogger," *The Daily Beast*, March 10, 2023, https://www.thedailybeast.com/russia-says-injured-pregnant-woman-is-a-crisis-actor-shes-actually-a-pregnant-blogger.

6. Reuters, "Russia Accuses Ukraine of Trying to Frame It Over Mariupol Theatre Attack," March 17, 2023, https://www.reuters.com/article/ukraine-crisis-mariupol-theatre-russia-idINL2N2VK0SL.

7. Russian Embassy, UK, *Twitter*, March 7, 2022, https://x.com/RussianEmbassy/status/1500886096837849099?lang=en.

8. For one example, see UN Human Rights Council, "Report of the Independent International Commission of Inquiry on Ukraine," 2023, https://www.ohchr.org/sites/default/files/documents/hrbodies/hrcouncil/coiukraine/A_HRC_52_62_AUV_EN.pdf.

9. BBC Sounds, "Profile: Margarita Simonyan," March 17, 2018, https://www.bbc.co.uk/sounds/play/b09vx097.

10. Reuters, "Russia to Pay Damages for Beslan School Siege After European Court Ruling," September 19, 2017, https://www.reuters.com/article/us-russia-chechnya-beslan-rights

/russia-to-pay-damages-for-beslan-school-siege-after-european-court-ruling-ifax-reports
-idUSKCN1BU2MX.

11. Database of Free Russian Forum, "Simonyan Margarita," n.d., https://www.spisok-putina
.org/en/personas/simonyan-2; and US Department of State, "Faces of Kremlin Propaganda:
Margarita Simonyan," August 31, 2022, https://2021-2025.state.gov/disarming-disinformation
/faces-of-kremlin-propaganda-margarita-simonyan.

12. Interview with Luke Harding, June 2023.

13. Atlantic Council Digital Forensic Research Lab, "Question That: RT's Military Mission," January 8, 2018, https://medium.com/dfrlab/question-that-rts-military-mission
-4c4bd9f72c88.

14. Mona Elswah and Philip Howard, "'Anything that Causes Chaos': The Organizational
Behavior of Russia Today (RT)," *Journal of Communication* 70, no. 5 (2020): 623–45.

15. Gordon Ramsay and Sam Robertshaw, "Weaponising News: RT, Sputnik and Targeted
Disinformation," King's College London, 2019, https://www.kcl.ac.uk/policy-institute/assets
/weaponising-news.pdf.

16. Office of the Director of National Intelligence, USA, "Background to 'Assessing Russian
Activities and Intentions in Recent US Elections'," January 16, 2017, https://www.dni.gov
/files/documents/ICA_2017_01.pdf.

17. Office of the Director of National Intelligence, USA, "Background."

18. Martin Moore and Thomas Colley, "Two International Propaganda Models: Comparing
RT and CGTN's 2020 US Election Coverage," *Journalism Practice* 18, no. 5 (2022), 1306–28.

19. Julia Davis, "Kremlin Cronies Sent Reeling on Live TV Over U.S. Midterm Elections,"
November 9, 2022, https://www.thedailybeast.com/russian-state-media-sent-reeling-over-us
-midterm-election-results.

20. Reuters, "Russia's Prigozhin Admits Interfering in U.S. Elections," November 7, 2022,
https://www.reuters.com/world/us/russias-prigozhin-admits-interfering-us-elections
-2022-11-07/#:~:text=In%20comments%20posted%20by%20the,we%20know%20how
%20to%20do.%22.

21. Moore and Colley, "Two International Propaganda Models," 15.

22. Vera Tolz and Yuri Teper, "Broadcasting Agitainment: A New Media Strategy of Putin's
Third Presidency," *PostSoviet Affairs* 34, no. 4 (2018): 213–27.

23. Russia Media Monitor, "Russia's Top 10 Lies About Downed Malaysia Airliner," http://
www.russialies.com/russias-top-10-lies-about-downed-malaysia-airliner.

24. BBC, "UK Regulator Ofcom Backs BBC in Russian TV Case," September 21, 2015, https://
www.bbc.co.uk/news/entertainment-arts-34316047.

25. Jennifer Rankin, "Russian Media 'Spreading Covid-19 Disinformation'," *Guardian*, March 18,
2020, https://www.theguardian.com/world/2020/mar/18/russian-media-spreading-covid-19
-disinformation; and Sputnik, "Secret File Confirms Trump Claim: Obama, Hillary 'Founded
ISIS' to Oust Assad," August 14, 2016, https://sputnikglobe.com/20160813/trump-obama
-hillary-isis-syria-1044242978.html.

26. Christopher Paul et al., "The Russian 'Firehose of Falsehood' Propaganda Model," *RAND
Corporation*, 2016, https://www.rand.org/pubs/perspectives/PE198.html.

27. Ramsay and Robertshaw, "Weaponising News: RT, Sputnik and Targeted Disinformation."

28. Nick Holdsworth, "RT Boss Margarita Simonyan Eclipses Hillary Clinton on Forbes Power List," *The Times*, November 3, 2017, https://www.thetimes.com/world/article/rt-boss-margarita-simonyan-eclipses-hillary-clinton-on-forbes-power-list-2g6tpvo68.

29. Interview with Luke Harding, June 2023.

30. RT, "RT Editor-in-Chief Proclaimed 'Expert Troller'," September 17, 2024, https://www.rt.com/russia/604193-amanpour-cnn-simonyan-rubin.

31. Holdsworth, "RT Boss Margarita Simonyan."

32. Jade McGlynn, *Russia's War* (Polity Press, 2023).

33. Julia Davis, "Russian TV Host Cries About Losing His Italian Villa," *Yahoo*, February 27, 2022, https://www.yahoo.com/news/sanctioned-russian-tv-host-cries-033357258.html.

34. Russia Media Monitor, "Head of RT Wonders Why Russia Is So Disliked," July 15, 2023, *YouTube*, https://www.youtube.com/watch?v=rKkOkt4NDAQ.

35. Julia Davis, "Top Putin Lackey Urges Russians to Choose Violent Death Over War Defeat," *Daily Beast*, November 1, 2022, https://www.thedailybeast.com/margarita-simonyan-urges-russians-to-choose-death-over-defeat-in-ukraine-on-kremlin-state-tv.

36. McGlynn, *Russia's War.*

37. Paul Goode, "How Russian Television Normalizes the War," *Riddle*, July 14, 2023, https://ridl.io/how-russian-television-normalizes-the-war.

38. Andrew Buncombe, "What Are the Ukraine 'Biolabs' and Why Have They Become a Focus for Fox News and the US Right?," *Independent*, March 18, 2022, https://www.independent.co.uk/news/world/americas/us-politics/ukraine-biolabs-fox-tucker-carlson-tulsi-gabbard-b2039117.html.

39. McGlynn, *Russia's War.*

40. McGlynn, *Russia's War*, 115.

41. Interview with Paul Goode, May 2023.

42. Arkady Ostrovsky, *The Invention of Russia* (Viking, 2015), 63.

43. Interview with Paul Goode, May 2023.

44. Interview with Luke Harding, June 2023.

45. Emma Mayer, "Russia Anchorman Known as 'Putin's Voice' Wants Moscow to Take Stonehenge," *Newsweek*, May 30, 2022, https://www.newsweek.com/russia-anchorman-known-putins-voice-wants-moscow-take-stonehenge-1711482.

46. Holod Media, "Airborne Infection," *YouTube*, March 21, 2023, https://holod.media/en/2023/03/21/who-is-mr-solovyov/.

47. TV Rain, "Russia's Genocidal News Host," August 6, 2023, https://www.youtube.com/watch?v=sKgc9pLTDP8.

48. Tim McNulty, "Putin Humiliated as Propagandist Brands Ukraine War 'Terrible Crime' in Unearthed Footage," *Daily Express*, October 12, 2022, https://www.express.co.uk/news/world/1681453/Vladimir-Putin-Russia-latest-Vladimir-Solovyov-Ukraine-war-news-vn.

49. Alec Luhn, "Pro-Kremlin Journalists Win Medals for 'Objective' Coverage of Crimea," *Guardian*, May 5, 2014, https://www.theguardian.com/world/2014/may/05/vladimir-putin-pro-kremlin-journalists-medals-objective-crimea.

50. K Thor Jensen, "Russian Pundit Breaks Guinness World Record for Most TV Time in a Week," *Newsweek*, October 21, 2019, https://www.newsweek.com/russian-tv-host-guinness-world-record-1466703.

51. Ostrovsky, *The Invention of Russia*, 7–8.

52. Timothy Frye, *Weak Strongman: The Limits of Power in Putin's Russia* (Princeton University Press, 2021).

53. McGlynn, *Russia's War*.

54. Interview with James Rushton, May 2023.

55. Interview with Luke Harding, June 2023.

56. McGlynn, *Russia's War*.

57. Interview with Julia Davis, May 2023.

58. Brendan Cole, "Russian TV Says Ukraine No Longer Exists, Compares War to 'Deworming a Cat'," *Newsweek*, July 19, 2022, https://www.newsweek.com/russian-tv-ukraine-no-longer-exists-simonyan-russia-1-deworming-1726014#:~:text=Solovyev%20then%20went%20on%20to,%22exactly%2C%22%20to%20laughter.

59. Björn Alexander Düben, "'There Is No Ukraine': Fact-Checking the Kremlin's Version of Ukrainian History," *LSE Blogs*, 2020, https://blogs.lse.ac.uk/lseih/2020/07/01/there-is-no-ukraine-fact-checking-the-kremlins-version-of-ukrainian-history.

60. Julia Davis, "'Morality Shouldn't Get in the Way'—Russia's Genocidal State Media," *CEPA*, March 13, 2023, https://cepa.org/article/morality-shouldnt-get-in-the-way-russias-genocidal-state-media.

61. Russia Media Monitor, "Russian Propagandists Talk About Killing Millions of Ukrainians," *YouTube*, 2023, https://www.youtube.com/watch?v=I5yvjyJdDWo.

62. Ian Garner, *Z Generation: Into the Heart of Russia's Fascist Youth* (Hurst, 2023).

63. Peter Beaumont, "Video Appears to Show Russian Soldier Castrating Ukrainian Prisoner," *Guardian*, July 29, 2022, https://www.theguardian.com/world/2022/jul/29/video-appears-to-show-russian-soldier-castrating-ukrainian-prisoner; and UN Human Rights Council, "Report of the Independent International Commission of Inquiry on Ukraine."

64. Düben, "'There Is No Ukraine'."

65. Interview with Luke Harding, June 2023.

66. Kit Heren, "Russian TV Propagandist Claims British People Are Eating Squirrels Because of Food Shortages," *LBC News*, March 9, 2023, https://www.lbc.co.uk/news/russian-propagandist-britain-squirrels-olga-skabeeva.

67. Jeffrey Sonnonfeld and Steven Tian, "Tucker Carlson Is Only One Part of Putin's Disinformation War in the Western Media," *Time*, June 2, 2023, https://time.com/6276130/putins-disinfomation-war-western-media.

68. Luke Harding et al., "'Dumb and Lazy': The Flawed Films of Ukrainian 'Attacks' Made by Russia's 'Fake Factory'," *Guardian*, February 21, 2022, https://www.theguardian.com/world/2022/feb/21/dumb-and-lazy-the-flawed-films-of-ukrainian-attacks-made-by-russias-fake-factory.

69. Amnesty International, "Russia: 'Filtration' of Ukrainian Civilians a 'Shocking Violation' of People Forced to Flee War," September 8, 2022, https://www.amnesty.org/en/latest

/news/2022/09/russia-filtration-of-ukrainian-civilians-a-shocking-violation-of-people-forced-to-flee-war.

70. Khaleda Rahman, "Evacuation Route Offered to Fleeing Ukrainians Was Mined—Red Cross," *Newsweek*, March 7, 2022, https://www.newsweek.com/evacuation-route-offered-fleeing-ukrainians-mined-1685418.

71. Jade McGlynn and Ian Garner, "Russia's War Crime Denials Are Fuel for More Atrocities," *Foreign Policy*, April 23, 2022, https://foreignpolicy.com/2022/04/23/propaganda-russia-atrocity-bucha.

72. Alistair Coleman and Kayleen Devlin, "Ukraine Conflict: Russian Chemical Attack Claim Fact-Checked," *BBC*, May 15, 2022, https://www.bbc.co.uk/news/61439398.

73. Coleman and Devlin, "Ukraine Conflict."

74. Thomas Colley, "How Russia Attacks Ukrainian Civilians and Makes It Look Like Kyiv Is Doing It," *The I Newspaper*, June 26, 2023, https://inews.co.uk/news/world/russia-cynical-propaganda-war-attacks-civilians-opportunities-2432707?srsltid=AfmBOooFg2mfeGEy3UjOfBODXyaOZ5K1_Y95qGrqZl7TBi8HbdnAyZqv.

75. Reuters, "Russia's RT Registers as 'Foreign Agent' in USA—Editor," November 13, 2017, https://www.reuters.com/article/russia-usa-media-restrictions-rt-idUSL8N1NJ6IC.

76. Julia Davis, *Twitter*, April 13, 2022, https://x.com/JuliaDavisNews/status/1514339222118883334.

77. Jon Jackson, "Maps Show Where Russia Gained, Lost Territory Since Start of Ukraine War," *Newsweek*, July 31, 2023, https://www.newsweek.com/where-russia-gained-lost-territory-ukraine-war-maps-1812851.

78. "Russian State TV—'We Need More Censorship' Says Privileged Film Maker Tigran Keosayan," *YouTube*, June 8, 2023, https://www.youtube.com/watch?v=77pWusxtX4M.

79. Sergei Guriev and Daniel Treisman, *Spin Dictators: The Changing Face of Tyranny in the 21st Century* (Princeton University Press, 2022).

80. Frye, *Weak Strongman: The Limits of Power in Putin's Russia*, 135.

81. Nick Paton Walsh, "Putin Pulls Plug on Last Critical TV Channel," *Guardian*, June 23, 2018, https://www.theguardian.com/world/2003/jun/23/media.russia.

82. Frye, *Weak Strongman: The Limits of Power in Putin's Russia*.

83. Paul Mozur et al., "'They Are Watching': Inside Russia's Vast Surveillance State," *New York Times*, September 22, 2022, https://www.nytimes.com/interactive/2022/09/22/technology/russia-putin-surveillance-spying.html.

84. Reporters Without Borders, "Press Freedom Index 2021," https://rsf.org/en/index?year=2021.

85. Frye, *Weak Strongman: The Limits of Power in Putin's Russia*.

86. Luke Harding, *Invasion: Russia's Bloody War and Ukraine's Fight for Survival* (Guardian Faber, 2022).

87. Matt Murphy, "China's Protests: Blank Paper Becomes the Symbol of Rare Demonstrations," *BBC*, November 28, 2022, https://www.bbc.co.uk/news/world-asia-china-63778871.

88. Harding, *Invasion: Russia's Bloody War*.

89. OECD, "Disinformation and Russia's War of Aggression Against Ukraine," November 3, 2022, https://www.oecd.org/en/publications/disinformation-and-russia-s-war-of-aggression-against-ukraine_37186bde-en.html.

90. Andrew Roth, "Russia Bans Media Outlet that Published Vladimir Putin Scoops," *Guardian*, July 15, 2017, https://www.theguardian.com/world/2021/jul/15/russia-bans-media-outlet-that-published-vladimir-putin-scoops.

91. Reuters, "Russia Blocks BBC Website, Says It's Only Beginning of Its Response," March 16, 2022, https://www.reuters.com/world/russia-blocks-bbc-website-says-its-only-beginning-its-response-2022-03-16.

92. Kieran Devine, "Ukraine War: Russia Takes TV and Websites Offline as Part of Media Blackout in Occupied Territories," *Sky News*, June 28, 2022, https://news.sky.com/story/ukraine-war-russia-takes-tv-and-websites-offline-as-part-of-media-blackout-in-occupied-territories-12634539.

93. Andrew Roth, "Russia Uses Orwellian Propaganda News Vans in Mariupol," *Guardian*, May 26, 2022, https://www.theguardian.com/world/2022/may/26/russia-uses-orwellian-propaganda-news-vans-in-mariupol.

94. Devine, "Ukraine War: Russia Takes TV and Websites Offline."

95. David Lewis, "The Quiet Transformation of Occupied Ukraine," *Foreign Affairs*, January 18, 2024, https://www.foreignaffairs.com/ukraine/quiet-transformation-occupied-ukraine.

96. Human Rights Watch, "Death at the Station: Russian Cluster Munition Attack in Kramatorsk," 2022, https://www.hrw.org/video-photos/interactive/2023/02/21/death-at-the-station/russian-cluster-munition-attack-in-kramatorsk.

97. Tom Ball, "Russians Create Fake BBC News Video to Blame Ukraine for Bombing," *Times*, April 13, 2022, https://www.thetimes.com/world/russia-ukraine-war/article/russians-create-fake-bbc-news-video-to-blame-ukraine-for-bombing-vbkv96mfs.

98. Clemence Overeem, "Video Claiming 'Ukraine Responsible for Train Station Attack' Was Not Produced by BBC," *AFP*, April 25, 2022, https://factcheck.afp.com/doc.afp.com.328K3Y3.

99. Michael Sheldon. "Russia's Kramatorsk 'Facts' Versus the Evidence," *Bellingcat*, April 14, 2022, https://www.bellingcat.com/news/2022/04/14/russias-kramatorsk-facts-versus-the-evidence.

100. Human Rights Watch, "Death at the Station."

101. Statista, "Social Media in Russia—Statistics & Facts," March 24, 2023, https://www.statista.com/statistics/1024741/instagram-users-russia.

102. Piotr Sauer, "Russia Bans Facebook and Instagram Under 'Extremism' Law," *Guardian*, March 21, 2022, https://www.theguardian.com/world/2022/mar/21/russia-bans-facebook-and-instagram-under-extremism-law.

103. Associated Press, "Russia Convicts the Spokesperson for Facebook Owner Meta in a Swift Trial in Absentia," April 22, 2024, https://apnews.com/article/russia-ukraine-war-facebook-meta-andy-stone-8ebdc7bd118fa1150cab2abfdc032b59.

104. Sauer, "Russia Bans Facebook and Instagram."

105. McGlynn, *Russia's War*.

106. McGlynn, *Russia's War*, 143–44.

107. McGlynn, *Russia's War*, 94.

108. Aude Dejaifve and Arthur Bamas, "Fresh Round of Fake Videos Claim the Bucha Massacre Was Staged," *France 24*, April 6, 2022, https://observers.france24.com/en/europe/20220408-fresh-round-of-fake-videos-claim-the-bucha-massacre-was-staged.

109. For example see EUvsDisinfo, https://euvsdisinfo.eu. See also Ben Nimmo and Mike Torrey, "Taking Down Coordinated Inauthentic Behavior from Russia and China," *Meta*, September 2022, https://about.fb.com/wp-content/uploads/2022/10/CIB-Report_-China -Russia_Sept-2022-1-1.pdf.

110. Interview with Julia Davis, May 2023.

111. Vera Bergengruen, "Unmasking the Man Behind One of Russia's Most Popular Propaganda Channels," *Time*, March 15, 2023, https://time.com/6263308/war-on-fakes-man -behind-russian-propaganda.

112. Bergengruen, "Unmasking the Man Behind One of Russia's Most Popular Propaganda Channels."

113. Interview with James Rushton, May 2023.

114. Daniel Boffey, "'Often a Russian Mother Has a TV for a Brain': Ukraine YouTuber Films PoWs Calling Home," *Guardian*, April 5, 2022, https://www.theguardian.com/world /2022/apr/05/often-a-russian-mother-has-a-tv-for-a-brain-ukraine-youtuber-films-pows -calling-home.

115. Interview with Joanna Szostek, May 2023.

116. *McGlynn, Russia's War.*

117. Interview with Joanna Szostek, May 2023.

118. Interview with Joanna Szostek, May 2023.

119. Francis Scarr, "Inside Russia's Alternate Reality as TV News Anchors Claim 'Satanic Ukrainian Nazis' Are Shelling Civilians," *The I*, April 27, 2023, https://inews.co.uk/?ranMID =48016&ranEAID=je6NUbpObpQ&ranSiteID=je6NUbpObpQ-T65bV9depYw NrwNBna5lMw.

120. Interview with Joanna Szostek, May 2023.

121. Interview with Julia Davis, May 2023.

122. Nicholas O'Shaughnessy, "From Disinformation to Fake News: Forwards Into the Past," in Paul Baines et al., eds., *The SAGE Handbook of Propaganda* (SAGE, 2020), 56.

123. McGlynn, *Russia's War.*

124. Interview with Luke Harding, June 2023.

125. Maxime Popov, "Russia's Anti-War Lobby Goes Online," *Moscow Times*, February 26, 2022, https://www.themoscowtimes.com/2022/02/26/russias-anti-war-lobby-goes-online-a76616.

126. Wall Street Journal, "Prigozhin Is Dead: A Timeline of the Wagner Boss Since His Failed Mutiny," *YouTube*, August 24, 2023, https://www.youtube.com/watch?v=FqBoGooBULo.

127. Philip Churm, "Wagner Chief Says Ukraine Never Threatened to Attack Russia," *Euronews*, June 23, 2023, https://www.euronews.com/2023/06/23/wagner-chief-says-ukraine-never -threatened-to-attack-russia.

128. Goode, "How Russian Television Normalizes the War."

129. Russian Media Monitor, "Propagandists Are Displeased with Putin's Decision to Let Prigozhin Go," *YouTube*, July 2023, https://www.youtube.com/watch?v=u8tyn9Xr-68.

130. Andrew Osborn, "Pro-War Nationalist Putin Critic Girkin Charged with Inciting Extremism," *Reuters*, July 22, 2023, https://www.reuters.com/world/europe/russian-investigators -detain-pro-war-nationalist-putin-critic-igor-girkin-wife-2023-07-21.

131. ChrisO_wiki, *Twitter*, July 22, 2023, https://x.com/ChrisO_wiki/status/1682683244884500482.

132. Russian Media Monitor, "Russian Propagandists Deny There Was Mutiny," *YouTube*, July 2023, https://www.youtube.com/watch?v=MMgTpGz8aRw.

133. George Orwell, *1984* (Penguin, 1954), 7.

3. SELLING "DEMOCRACY": XI'S CHINA

1. Nathan Law, *Freedom: How We Lose It and How We Fight Back* (Penguin, 2021).

2. Amnesty International, "Hong Kong's National Security Law: 10 Things You Need to Know," July 17, 2020, https://www.amnesty.org/en/latest/news/2020/07/hong-kong-national-security-law-10-things-you-need-to-know.

3. Chris Lau, "Fugitive Hong Kong Ex-Lawmaker Nathan Law Blames West for Failing to Stand Up to China, Warns Hong Kong Now 'Police State'," *South China Morning Post*, December 10, 2021, https://www.scmp.com/news/hong-kong/politics/article/3159289/fugitive-hong-kong-ex-lawmaker-nathan-law-blames-west.

4. YouTube, "Nathan Law Speaking at the Summit for Democracy Day 2," December 10, 2021, https://www.youtube.com/watch?v=Q49Mt4vmXgs.

5. Urban Lehner, "China: The Overly Sensitive Superpower," *Asia Times*, September 21, 2021, https://asiatimes.com/2021/09/china-the-overly-sensitive-superpower.

6. Global Times, "Inviting Hong Kong Fugitive to 'Summit for Democracy' Proves US Desecration of Authentic Democracy," December 8, 2021, https://www.globaltimes.cn/page/202112/1241020.shtml.

7. Lau, "Fugitive Hong Kong Ex-Lawmaker Nathan Law Blames West."

8. Xinhua, "Full Text: Democracy That Works," December 14, 2021, https://www.chinadaily.com.cn/a/202112/04/WS61ab0795a310cdd39bc7957e.html.

9. Paul Tembe, "China's Whole-Process People's Democracy Revolutionizes Understandings on Democracy," *China Daily*, May 17, 2022, https://www.chinadaily.com.cn/a/202205/17/WS62834efba310fd2b29e5d392.html.

10. Global Times, "China's Democracy 'More Extensive, Genuine and Effective' than US Democracy: Official," December 4, 2021, https://www.globaltimes.cn/page/202112/1240628.shtml.

11. Thomas Colley and Martin Moore, "News as Geopolitics: China, CGTN and the 2020 US Presidential Election," *Journal of International Communication*, 2022, https://doi.org/10.1080/13216597.2022.2120522; and Martin Moore and Thomas Colley, "Two International Propaganda Models: Comparing RT and CGTN's 2020 US Election Coverage," *Journalism Practice* 18, no. 5 (2022): 1306–28.

12. Kai Strittmatter, *We Have Been Harmonised: Life in China's Surveillance State* (Old Street, 2019).

13. Economist Intelligence Unit, "Democracy Index 2021: The China Challenge," https://pages.eiu.com/rs/753-RIQ-438/images/eiu-democracy-index-2021.pdf.

14. Freedom House, "Freedom in the World 2022: China," https://freedomhouse.org/country/china/freedom-world/2022.

15. Constitution of the People's Republic of China, "Article 35," http://www.npc.gov.cn /zgrdw/englishnpc/Constitution/2007-11/15/content_1372964.htm#:~:text=Article%2035 %20Citizens%20of%20the,of%20procession%20and%20of%20demonstration.

16. Reporters Without Borders (RSF), "China," n.d., https://rsf.org/en/country/china.

17. United Nations, "OHCHR Assessment of Human Rights Concerns in the Xinjiang Uyghur Autonomous Region, People's Republic of China," August 31, 2022, https://www.ohchr .org/en/press-releases/2022/08/un-human-rights-office-issues-assessment-human-rights -concerns-xinjiang.

18. Freedom House, "Freedom in the World 2022: China."

19. Atlantic Council, "Chinese Discourse Power," December 2020, https://www.atlanticcouncil .org/in-depth-research-reports/report/chinese-discourse-power-ambitions-and-reality-in -the-digital-domain.

20. Sergei Guriev and Daniel Treisman, *Spin Dictators: The Changing Face of Tyranny in the 21st Century* (Princeton University Press, 2022); and Richard Wike et al., "Many Across the Globe Are Dissatisfied with How Democracy Is Working," *Pew Research Center*, April 29, 2019, https://www.pewresearch.org/global/2019/04/29/many-across-the-globe -are-dissatisfied-with-how-democracy-is-working.

21. Law, *Freedom: How We Lose It And How We Fight Back*, 9.

22. Law, *Freedom: How We Lose It And How We Fight Back*.

23. Louisa Lim and Julia Bergin, "Inside China's Audacious Global Propaganda Campaign," *Guardian*, December 7, 2018, https://www.theguardian.com/news/2018/dec/07/china-plan -for-global-media-dominance-propaganda-xi-jinping; Malin Oud and Katja Drinhausen, eds., "The Decoding China Dictionary," 2023, https://decodingchina.eu; and Reporters Without Borders (RSF), "China's Pursuit of a New World Media Order," 2019, https://rsf .org/en/rsf-report-chinas-pursuit-new-world-media-order.

24. Reporters Without Borders (RSF), "China's Pursuit of a New World Media Order."

25. Peter Humphrey, "Countering China's Forced Confessions," *The Diplomat*, November 23, 2019, https://thediplomat.com/2019/11/countering-chinas-forced-confessions.

26. Interview with Nathan Law, May 3, 2023.

27. "Reporters Without Borders Publishes the First Worldwide Press Freedom Index (October 2002)," https://rsf.org/en/reporters-without-borders-publishes-first-worldwide -press-freedom-index-october-2002.

28. Reporters Without Borders. "Index," 2023, https://rsf.org/en/index.

29. Colley and Moore, "News as Geopolitics."

30. Peter Singer and Emerson Brooking, *Likewar: The Weaponization of Social Media* (Hough-ton Mifflin Harcourt, 2018).

31. Leigh Hartman, "In China, You Can't Say These Words," *ShareAmerica*, June 3, 2020, https://share.america.gov/in-china-you-cant-say-these-words.

32. Helen Davidson and Lily Kuo, "Zoom Admits Cutting Off Activists' Accounts in Obe-dience to China," *Guardian*, June 12, 2020, https://www.theguardian.com/world/2020 /jun/12/zoom-admits-cutting-off-activists-accounts-in-obedience-to-china.

33. Cate Cadell, "China Launches Hotline for Netizens to Report 'Illegal' History Comments," *Reuters*, April 11, 2021, https://www.reuters.com/world/china/china-launches-hotline-netizens-report-illegal-history-comments-2021-04-11.
34. Reporters Without Borders (RSF), "The Great Leap Backwards of Journalism in China," 2021, https://rsf.org/en/unprecedented-rsf-investigation-great-leap-backwards-journalism-china.
35. Merriden Varrall, "Behind the News: Inside China's Global Television Network," *Lowy Institute*, 2020, https://www.lowyinstitute.org/publications/behind-news-inside-china-global-television-network#heading-1803.
36. Margaret Roberts, *Censored: Distraction and Diversion Inside China's Great Firewall* (Princeton University Press, 2018).
37. Roberts, *Censored: Distraction and Diversion.*
38. Roberts, *Censored: Distraction and Diversion.*
39. Colley and Moore, "News as Geopolitics."
40. Jacques Ellul, *Propaganda: The Formation of Men's Attitudes* (Vintage, 1973), 9.
41. Ellul, *Propaganda.*
42. Valentina Vellani et al., "The Illusory Truth Effect Leads to the Spread of Misinformation," *Cognition* 236 (2023): 105421.
43. Robyn Fivush, "Speaking Silence: The Social Construction of Silence in Autobiographical and Cultural Narratives," *Memory* 18, no. 2 (2010): 88–98.
44. Lim and Bergin, "Inside China's Audacious Global Propaganda Campaign."
45. Eleanor Albert, "China's Big Bet on Soft Power," *Council on Foreign Relations*, February 9, 2018, https://www.cfr.org/backgrounder/chinas-big-bet-soft-power.
46. Economist, "China Is Spending Billions to Make the World Love It," May 23, 2017, https://www.economist.com/china/2017/03/23/china-is-spending-billions-to-make-the-world-love-it; and Joshua Kurlantzick, *Beijing's Global Media Offensive: China's Uneven Campaign to Influence Asia and the World* (Oxford University Press, 2023), 426.
47. Alistair MacDonald, "Soft Power Superpowers," British Council, 2018, https://www.britishcouncil.org/sites/default/files/j119_thought_leadership_global_trends_in_soft_power_web.pdf.
48. Jim Waterson, "Hundreds of Jobs to Go as BBC Announces World Service Cutbacks," *Guardian*, September 29, 2022, https://www.theguardian.com/media/2022/sep/29/hundreds-of-jobs-to-go-as-bbc-announces-world-service-cutbacks.
49. Reporters Without Borders (RSF), "China's Pursuit of a New World Media Order."
50. Sarah Cook, "Beijing's Global Megaphone," *Freedom House*, 2020, https://freedomhouse.org/report/special-report/2020/beijings-global-megaphone.
51. CGTN, "Full Text: The Report on Human Rights Violations in the United States in 2022," April 21, 2023, https://news.cgtn.com/news/2023-03-28/Full-text-Report-on-human-rights-violations-in-U-S-in-2022-1ixlHB1qpfq/index.html.
52. The US was 30th on the Economist Intelligence Unit's Democracy Index in 2022. See "Democracy Index 2022," https://www.eiu.com/n/campaigns/democracy-index-2022.
53. CGTN, "A Look at China's Democracy: How Is It Unique and Distinctive?," March 24, 2023, https://news.cgtn.com/news/2023-03-24/A-look-at-China-s-democracy-How-is-it-unique-and-distinctive--1icxvUkIlmU/index.html.

54. Cao Siqi and Wan Hengyi, "Survey Shows Most Americans Believe US Not a Democracy, Reflects 'Discourse Woven by Elites Far Out of Touch with People's Feelings'," *Global Times*, June 1, 2022, https://www.globaltimes.cn/page/202206/1267104.shtml.

55. Aristotle, *Poetics* (Penguin, 1996).

56. Moore and Colley, "Two International Propaganda Models."

57. Moore and Colley, "Two International Propaganda Models."

58. Colley and Moore, "Two International Propaganda Models," 1314.

59. Moore and Colley, "Two International Propaganda Models."

60. Moore and Colley, "Two International Propaganda Models."

61. Moore and Colley, "Two International Propaganda Models."

62. Colley and Moore, "News as Geopolitics."

63. Colley and Moore, "News as Geopolitics."

64. Varrall, "Behind the News."

65. Moore and Colley, "Two International Propaganda Models."

66. Colley and Moore, "News as Geopolitics."

67. Ben Westcott and Steven Jiang, "Chinese Diplomat Promotes Conspiracy Theory that US Military Brought Coronavirus to Wuhan," *CNN*, March 13, 2020, https://edition.cnn.com/2020/03/13/asia/china-coronavirus-us-lijian-zhao-intl-hnk/index.html.

68. Economic Times, "China Scientists Claim Virus Born in India; West Experts Refute," November 30, 2020, https://economictimes.indiatimes.com/news/politics-and-nation/china-scientists-claim-virus-born-in-india-west-experts-refute/articleshow/79472030.cms; and Zhang Hui et al., "Italy Potentially Had COVID-19 Outbreak 'Earlier than Wuhan,' Study Shows," *Global Times*, December 10, 2020, https://www.globaltimes.cn/content/1209646.shtml.

69. Erhard Geissler and Robert Hunt Sprinkle, "Disinformation Squared: Was the HIV-from-Fort-Detrick Myth a Stasi Success?," *Politics and the Life Sciences* 32, no. 2 (2013): 2–99.

70. Fan Lingzhi, Huang Lanlan, and Zhang Hui, "Suspect No. 1: Why Fort Detrick Lab Should Be Investigated for Global COVID-19 Origins Tracing," *Global Times*, June 28, 2021, https://www.globaltimes.cn/page/202106/1227219.shtml.

71. China Daily, "US Animosity Toward Russia Root Cause of Ukraine Conflict: China Daily Editorial," February 24, 2022, https://www.chinadaily.com.cn/a/202302/24/WS63f8bf1aa-31057c47ebb0c5d.html.

72. CGTN, "Who Really Needs a War on Ukraine?," February 13, 2022, https://news.cgtn.com/news/2022-02-13/Who-really-needs-a-war-on-Ukraine--17CqJtCIAjS/index.html.

73. CGTN, "China Urges U.S. to Disclose More Details About Biolabs in Ukraine," March 8, 2022, https://news.cgtn.com/news/2022-03-08/China-urges-U-S-to-disclose-details-about-biolabs-in-Ukraine-18eA7VpwQRG/index.html.

74. Jennifer Conrad, "The War in Ukraine Is Keeping Chinese Social Media Censors Busy," *Wired*, March 4, 2023, https://www.wired.com/story/war-ukraine-chinese-social-media-censors-busy.

75. Tom Philips et al., "Beijing Rejects Tribunal's Ruling in South China Sea Case," *Guardian*, July 12, 2016, https://www.theguardian.com/world/2016/jul/12/philippines-wins-south-china-sea-case-against-china.

76. International Federation of Journalists (IFJ), "The China Network: Inside China's Global Media Mission in Asia, Africa and Latin America," 2022, https://www.ifj.org/media-centre/reports/detail/the-china-network-inside-chinas-global-media-mission-in-asia-africa-and-latin-america/category/publications; and Cliff Venzon, "Philippine News Agency Takes Down Xinhua's South China Sea Commentary," *Nikkei*, August 17, 2017, https://asia.nikkei.com/Politics/Philippine-News-Agency-takes-down-Xinhua-s-South-China-Sea-commentary2.

77. Lim and Bergin, "Inside China's Audacious Global Propaganda Campaign."

78. Kurlantzick, *Beijing's Global Media Offensive.*

79. Emily Feng, "China and the World: How Beijing Spreads the Message," *Financial Times*, July 12, 2018, https://www.ft.com/content/f5d00a86-3296-11e8-b5bf-23cb17fd1498.

80. Kurlantzick, *Beijing's Global Media Offensive.*

81. Emily Weinstein, "Covert Coverage: Xinhua as an Agent of Influence in the United States," *Project 2049 Institute*, March 7, 2018, https://project2049.net/2018/03/07/covert-coverage-xinhua-as-an-agent-of-influence-in-the-united-states.

82. China Media Project, "The Good Journalist," November 8, 2022, https://chinamediaproject.org/2022/11/08/the-good-journalist.

83. Dean Sterling Jones, "A British Newspaper Has Given Chinese Coronavirus Propaganda a Direct Line to the UK," *Buzzfeed*, April 8, 2020, https://www.buzzfeednews.com/article/deansterlingjones/coronavirus-british-newspaper-chinese-propaganda.

84. Paul Charon and Jean-Baptiste Jeangene Vilmer, "Chinese Influence Operations: A Machiavellian Moment," *IRSEM*, 2021, https://www.irsem.fr/report.html.

85. Kurlantzick, *Beijing's Global Media Offensive*, 195.

86. International Federation of Journalists, "The China Network."

87. Li Junru, "World Can Learn from China's Unique Model of Democracy," *Philippine News Agency*, October 15, 2022, https://www.pna.gov.ph/articles/1186273.

88. Independent Online (IOL), "Observing China's Whole-Process People's Democracy at Two Sessions," March 17, 2023, https://iol.co.za/news/partnered/2023-03-17-observing-chinas-whole-process-peoples-democracy-at-two-sessions.

89. Charon and Jeangene Vilmer, "Chinese Influence Operations," 185.

90. Kelsey Munro and Philip Wen, "Chinese Language Newspapers in Australia: Beijing Controls Messaging, Propaganda in Press," *Sydney Morning Herald*, July 8, 2016, https://www.smh.com.au/national/chinese-language-newspapers-in-australia-beijing-controls-messaging-propaganda-in-press-20160610-gpg0s3.html.

91. Koh Gui Qing and John Shiffman, "SPECIAL REPORT-Exposed: Beijing's Covert Global Radio Network," *Reuters*, November 2, 2015, https://www.reuters.com/article/china-radio-idUSL1N12U0ZZ20151102.

92. Sheng Zou, "Localisation Between Negotiating Forces: A Case Study of a Chinese Radio Station in the United States," *Westminster Papers in Communication and Culture* 13, no. 1 (2018), https://doi.org/10.16997/wpcc.273.

93. Raksha Kumar, "How China Uses the News Media as a Weapon in Its Propaganda War Against the West," *Reuters Institute*, November 2, 2021, https://reutersinstitute.politics.ox.ac.uk/news/how-china-uses-news-media-weapon-its-propaganda-war-against-west.

94. Azad Essa, "China Is Buying African Media's Silence," *Foreign Policy*, September 14, 2018, https://foreignpolicy.com/2018/09/14/china-is-buying-african-medias-silence.

95. Essa, "China Is Buying African Media's Silence."

96. StarSat, "What We're All About," n.d., https://starsat.co.za/about.

97. StarSat, "What We're All About."

98. Angela Lewis, "How a Pay TV Company Is Serving Up a Soft Power Win for China in Africa," *The Diplomat*, February 14, 2019, https://thediplomat.com/2019/02/how-a-pay -tv-company-is-serving-up-a-soft-power-win-for-china-in-africa.

99. Kenton Thibaut, "China's Discourse Power Operations in the Global South," *Atlantic Council*, 2022, https://www.atlanticcouncil.org/in-depth-research-reports/report/chinas-discourse -power-operations-in-the-global-south.

100. Lewis, "How a Pay TV Company Is Serving Up a Soft Power Win."

101. Richard McGregor, *The Party: The Secret World of China's Communist Rulers* (Allen Lane, 2010).

102. Economist, "Clicks and Control," March 23–29, 2024.

103. John Sudworth, "Xinjiang Police Files: Inside a Chinese Internment Camp," *BBC*, May 24, 2022, https://www.bbc.co.uk/news/resources/idt-8df450b3-5d6d-4ed8-bdcc-bd99137eadc3; Ted Regencia, "What You Should Know About China's Minority Uighurs," *Al Jazeera*, July 8, 2021, https://www.aljazeera.com/news/2021/7/8/uighurs-timeline#:~:text=In%20a%20report %20in%20June,of%20the%20country's%20Communist%20Party; United Nations, "OHCHR Assessment of Human Rights Concerns"; and World Uighur Congress, "Final Version of the Uyghur Tribunal Judgment," September 20, 2022, https://www.uyghurcongress.org/en /final-version-of-the-uyghur-tribunal-judgemnt-including-appendices.

104. Global Times, "US Hurts Own Interests by Politicizing Normal PV Trade with China: Analysts," December 6, 2022, https://www.globaltimes.cn/page/202212/1281259.shtml; and Global Times, "US Lie-of-the-Century About 'Genocide' in Xinjiang Fully Exposes Ill Intention to Politicize Olympics: Chinese FM," February 9, 2022, https://www.globaltimes .cn/page/202202/1251871.shtml.

105. Jeff Kao et al., "'We Are Very Free': How China Spreads Its Propaganda Version of Life in Xinjiang," *New York Times*, June 22, 2021, https://www.nytimes.com/interactive/2021/06/22 /technology/xinjiang-uighurs-china-propaganda.html.

106. Discover Xinjiang. *Twitter*, March 17, 2023, https://x.com/DXinjiang/status /1636532079814144000.

107. Charon and Jeangene Vilmer, "Chinese Influence Operations."

108. Vladimir Ilyich Lenin, "What Is to Be Done?," 1902, https://www.marxists.org/archive /lenin/works/1901/witbd/iii.htm.

109. Ben Nimmo et al., "Adversarial Threat Report: Second Quarter," *Meta*, August 2023, https://transparency.meta.com/en-gb/integrity-reports-q2-2023; and Donnie O'Sullivan et al., "China Is Using the World's Largest Known Online Disinformation Operation," *CNN*, November 13, 2023, https://edition.cnn.com/2023/11/13/us/china-online-disinformation -invs/index.html.

110. O'Sullivan et al., "China Is Using the World's Largest Known Online Disinformation Operation."

111. Elise Thomas, "Pro-CCP 'Spamouflage' Network Pivoting to Focus on US Presidential Election," *Institute for Strategic Dialogue*, February 15, 2024, https://www.isdglobal.org /digital_dispatches/pro-ccp-spamouflage-net-work-focuses-on-us-election.

112. Elise, "Pro-CCP 'Spamouflage' Network."

113. Moore and Colley, "Two International Propaganda Models."

114. Andrius Sylas, "Lithuania Says Throw Away Chinese Phones Due to Censorship Concerns," *Reuters*, September 21, 2021, https://www.reuters.com/business/media-telecom /lithuania-says-throw-away-chinese-phones-due-censorship-concerns-2021-09-21.

115. Sarah Cook, "China's Content Manipulation Reaches New Frontiers," *The Diplomat*, November 16, 2021, https://thediplomat.com/2021/11/chinas-content-manipulation-reaches -new-frontiers.

116. Charon and Jeangene Vilmer, "Chinese Influence Operations," 196.

117. Charon and Jeangene Vilmer, "Chinese Influence Operations"; Louise Matsakis, "How WeChat Censored the Coronavirus Pandemic," *Wired*, August 27, 2020, https://www .wired.com/story/wechat-chinese-internet-censorship-coronavirus; and Fergus Ryan et al., "TikTok and WeChat: Curating and Controlling Global Information Flows," *Australian Strategic Policy Institute*, no. 37, 2020, https://www.aspi.org.au/index.php/report /tiktok-wechat.

118. Interview with Nathan Law, May 3, 2023.

119. Ryan et al., "TikTok and WeChat."

120. Matsakis, "How WeChat Censored the Coronavirus Pandemic."

121. Alex Hern, "Revealed: How TikTok Censors Videos that Do Not Please Beijing," *Guardian*, September 26, 2019, https://www.theguardian.com/technology/2019/sep/25 /revealed-how-tiktok-censors-videos-that-do-not-please-beijing.

122. Ryan et al., "TikTok and WeChat."

123. Anna Gordon, "Here's All the Countries with TikTok Bans as Platform's Future in U.S. Hangs in Balance," *Time*, April 25, 2024, https://time.com/6971009/tiktok-banned -restrictions-worldwide-countries-united-states-law.

124. Gordon, "Here's All the Countries with TikTok Bans."

125. Economist, "China Is Spending Billions to Make the World Love It."

126. Abdirizak Guyo and Hong Yu, "China's News Media as Public Diplomacy in Africa: An Assessment of CCTV/CGTN Among Kenyan Audience," *Journal of Contemporary African Studies* 40, no. 3 (2022): 1–16.

127. Zhuoran Li and Gavin Xu, "Despite High Ambition, China's Media Influence Operation Is Far from Successful," *The Diplomat*, May 28, 2022, https://thediplomat.com/2022/05 /despite-high-ambition-chinas-media-influence-operation-is-far-from-successful.

128. Kurlantzick, *Beijing's Global Media Offensive*, 148.

129. Dani Madrid-Morales, "Who Set the Narrative? Assessing the Influence of Chinese Global Media on News Coverage of COVID-19 in 30 African Countries," *Global Media and China* 6, no. 2 (2021): 129–51.

130. Al Jazeera, "Taiwan's Push Against 'Red Media'," November 17, 2019, https://www .aljazeera.com/program/the-listening-post/2019/11/17/taiwans-push-against-red-media.

131. Fred Lewsey, "War in Ukraine Has Widened a Global Divide in Public Attitudes Toward US, China and Russia," *University of Cambridge*, 2022, https://www.cam.ac.uk/stories /worlddivided.

132. Wike et al., "Many Across the Globe Are Dissatisfied with How Democracy Is Working."

133. R. S. Foa et al., "Youth and Satisfaction with Democracy," *Centre for the Future of Democracy*, 2020, https://www.cam.ac.uk/stories/youthanddemocracy.

134. Daniel Mattingly et al., "Chinese State Media Persuades a Global Audience that the 'China Model' Is Superior: Evidence from a 19-Country Experiment," *OSF Preprints*, January 18, 2023, https://osf.io/5cafd.

135. Strittmatter, *We Have Been Harmonised.*

136. Reporters Without Borders (RSF), "China's Pursuit of a New World Media Order."

137. Marius Dragomir and Astrid Söderström, "The State of State Media," *CEU Democracy Institute*, 2021, https://cmds.ceu.edu/sites/cmcs.ceu.hu/files/attachment/article/2091 /thestateofstatemedia.pdf, 10.

138. Economist, "Why China's Economy Won't Be Fixed," August 24, 2023, https://www .economist.com/leaders/2023/08/24/why-chinas-economy-wont-be-fixed?ppcadID =&ppccampaignID=18156330227.

139. Law, *Freedom: How We Lose It and How We Fight Back*, 49.

4. A COUNTERFEIT PUBLIC SPHERE: ORBÁN'S HUNGARY

1. Origo, "Dollar Media: The Americans Have Already Poured Money Into the Hungarian Left-Wing Propaganda Press," December 15, 2022, https://www.origo.hu/itthon/2022/12 /dollarmedia-amerikai-segitseg-a-baloldali-sajtonak-is-3.

2. Origo, "Dollar Media: Brussels Pays Millions to Hungarian Left-Wing Propaganda Papers," December 17, 2022, https://www.origo.hu/itthon/2022/12/dollarmedia-kulfoldi -segitseg-a-baloldali-sajtonak-is-5.

3. Origo, "Amazing Data: George Soros Controls 253 News Sites with His People," December 28, 2022, https://www.origo.hu/nagyvilag/2022/12/soros-gyorgy-mediabefolyas; and Origo, "Dollar Media: Soros Maintains an Entire Organization to Produce Articles Attacking Hungary," December 29, 2022, https://www.origo.hu/itthon/2022/12/dollarmedia -sorospenzekbol-mukodik-a-hazankat-is-tamado-nemzetkozi-ujsagiro-szervezetet.

4. Origo, "Dollar Media: Brussels Pays"; and Origo, "Dollarmédia: Soros' Man Is Here, Who Directs the Anti-Hungarian Propaganda of the International Press," December 28, 2022, https://www.origo.hu/itthon/2022/12/soros-gyorgy-magyarorszag-elleni-lejarato-kampany -dollarmedia.

5. For example, see Magyar Nemzet, "Dollar Media: Soros Pays a Lot of Money to a Hungarian Propaganda Site to Serve His Interests," December 18, 2022, https://magyarnemzet.hu /belfold/2022/12/dollarmedia-soros-rengeteg-penzt-fizet-egy-magyar-propagandaoldalnak -hogy-az-o-erdekeit-szolgalja; and VAOL, "This Is How György Soros's Hungarian Dollar Media Was Built," December 19, 2022, https://www.vaol.hu/orszag-vilag/2022/12 /igy-epult-fel-soros-gyorgy-magyar-dollarmediaja.

6. Magyar Nemzet, "This Is How Soros's Dollar Media Networked Rural Hungary," April 26, 2023, https://magyarnemzet.hu/belfold/2023/04/igy-halozza-be-a-videk-magyarorszagat -soros-dollarmediaja.

7. András Szabó, "The Dollar Media and the Dollar Left Are on Ventilators," *Magyar Nemzet*, May 2, 2023, https://magyarnemzet.hu/velemeny/2023/05/lelegeztetogepen-a -dollarmedia-es-a-dollarbaloldal.

8. Tamás Fritz, "Who Is Behind Ursula von der Leyen?," *Magyar Nemzet*, March 9, 2022, https://magyarnemzet.hu/velemeny/2022/09/ki-all-ursula-von-der-leyen-mogott.

9. Origo, "America Spends a Huge Amount on the Pro-War Campaign in Hungary," April 20, 2023, https://www.origo.hu/itthon/2023/04/nyugati-palyan-amerikai-penzekbol-finanszirozzak -a-magyar-baloldalt.

10. Attila Barber, "The Evil Empire," *Magyar Nemzet*, February 16, 2023, https://magyarnemzet .hu/velemeny/2023/02/a-gonosz-birodalma.

11. Peter Plenta, "Conspiracy Theories as a Political Instrument: Utilization of Anti-Soros Narratives in Central Europe," *Contemporary Politics* 26, no. 5 (2020): 512–30; and Keno Verseck, "Hungary: Europe's Conspiracy Champion," *DW*, November 12, 2018, https:// www.dw.com/en/hungary-europes-champion-of-conspiracy-theories/a-46689822.

12. András Bozóki, *Rolling Transition and the Role of Intellectuals: The Case of Hungary* (Central European University Press, 2022), 69.

13. Bozóki, *Rolling Transition and the Role of Intellectuals.*

14. Jürgen Habermas, *The Structural Transformation of the Public Sphere* (Polity Press, 1992).

15. Jürgen Habermas et al., "The Public Sphere: An Encyclopedia Article," *New German Critique* 3 (1974): 49–55.

16. European Commission, "2020 Rule of Law Report Country: Chapter on the Rule of Law Situation in Hungary," September 30, 2020, https://eur-lex.europa.eu/legal-content/EN /TXT/PDF/?uri=CELEX:52020SC0316.

17. Shane Goldmacher, "Trump Endorses Viktor Orbán, Hungary's Far-Right Prime Minister," *New York Times*, January 3, 2022, https://www.nytimes.com/2022/01/03/us/politics /trump-endorses-viktor-orban-hungary.html.

18. Tucker Carlson, *Twitter*, August 3, 2021, https://x.com/TuckerCarlson/status /1422344832647712769.

19. Zoltán Kovács, "PM Viktor Orbán at CPAC Hungary: Hungary Is an Incubator for Shaping the Conservative Politics of the Future," *About Hungary*, May 4, 2023, https:// abouthungary.hu/blog/pm-viktor-orban-at-cpac-hungary-hungary-is-an-incubator-for -shaping-the-conservative-politics-of-the-future.

20. Marius Dragomir, "Media Capture in Europe," *Media Development Investment Fund*, 2019, http://www.mdif.org/wp-content/uploads/2023/10/MDIF-Report-Media-Capture-in -Europe.pdf.

21. Interview with Marius Dragomir, May 22, 2023.

22. "Act CLXXXV of 2010 on Media Services and on the Mass Media," chap. 2, section 4 and section 183, https://nmhh.hu/dokumentum/106487/act_clxxx_on_media_services_and_mass _media.pdf.

23. Krisztina Nagy, "It Turned Out That the Media Council Had Illegally Redrawn the Radio Market," *Tasz*, August 14, 2015, https://ataszjelenti.blog.hu/2015/08/14/pert_nyertunk _kiderult_hogy_a_mediatanacs_jogszerutlenul_rajzolta_at_a_radio_piacot.

24. Atlatszo, "Did You Know? The Government Does Not Campaign, but Informs for Social Purposes," August 9, 2016, https://vastagbor.atlatszo.hu/2016/08/09/tudta-a-kormany-nem -kampanyol-hanem-tarsadalmi-celbol-tajekoztat; and Mérték, "Party Service Media with Billions of Opaque Public Money," *Atlatszo*, November 2, 2021, https://mertek.atlatszo.hu /partszolgalati-media-atlathatatlan-kozpenz-milliardokbol.

25. Government of Hungary, "229/2018. (XII. 5.) Government Decree."

26. Reporters Without Borders (RSF), "Hungary," 2023, https://rsf.org/en/country/hungary.

27. Council of Europe, "Memorandum on Freedom of Expression and Media Freedom in Hungary," March 30, 2021, 13, https://rm.coe.int/memorandum-on-freedom-of-expression -and-media-freedom-in-hungary/1680a1e67e.

28. International Press Institute (IPI), "Mission Report: Media Freedom in Hungary Ahead of 2022 Election," March 21, 2022, https://ipi.media/wp-content/uploads/2022/03/HU _PressFreedomMission_Report_IPI_2022.pdf.

29. European Commission, "2020 Rule of Law Report Country: Chapter on the Rule of Law Situation in Hungary," https://eur-lex.europa.eu/legal-content/EN/TXT/PDF/?uri =CELEX:52020SC0316.

30. Mérték Media Monitor, "Four Shades of Censorship: State Intervention in the Central Eastern European Media Markets," 2021, https://mertek.eu/wp-content/uploads/2021/10 /Mertek-fuzetek_19.pdf.

31. Interview with András Koltay, June 21, 2023.

32. Isaiah Berlin, *Four Essays on Liberty* (Oxford University Press, 1969).

33. Judy Dempsey, "Hungary Waves Off Criticism Over Media Law," *New York Times*, December 15, 2010, https://www.nytimes.com/2010/12/26/world/europe/26hungary.html.

34. Mark Duke, "Balázs Bende, Who Regularly Bashes Soros on Public Television, Was Also Able to Study with a Soros Scholarship," *444*, April 6, 2020, https://444.hu/2020/04/06/a -kozteveben-rendszeresen-sorost-szapulo-bende-balazs-is-soros-osztondijjal-tanulhatott.

35. Mark Duke, "The Man Who Interprets the World for Public Television Viewers," *444*, April 5, 2020, https://444.hu/2020/04/05/az-ember-aki-ertelmezi-a-vilagot-a-kozteve-nezoinek.

36. Tamás Botos, "Impartial Public Media: In Next Year's Election, We Can Ensure that the Government Does Not Fall Into the Hands of Parties that Hate Everything that Is Hungarian," *444*, October 10, 2021, https://444.hu/2021/10/10/partatlan-kozmedia-a-jovo -evi-valasztason-biztosithatjuk-hogy-ne-keruljon-olyan-partok-kezebe-a-kormanyzas -akik-gyulolnek-mindent-ami-magyar.

37. Zoltán Haszan, "Public TV Presenter: The Entire West Is Delaying the End of the War by Supplying Weapons to Ukraine," *444*, March 5, 2022, https://444.hu/2022/03/05/a -kozteve-musorvezetoje-a-teljes-nyugat-a-haborut-veget-huzza-el-azzal-hogy-fegyvereket -szallit-ukrajnaba.

38. Mark Duke, "North Korean-Level Brain Death on Public Television," *444*, October 4, 2020, https://444.hu/2020/10/04/eszak-koreai-szintu-agyhalal-a-kozteven.

39. "Act CLXXXV," section 83(1)m.

40. Ákos Keller-Alánt, "Editorial Instruction at the Public Television: 'This Institution Does Not Support the Opposition Coalition'," *Szabad Europa*, November 12, 2020, https://www .szabadeuropa.hu/a/szerkesztoi-utasitas-a-koztevenel-ebben-az-intezmenyben-nem-az -ellenzeki-osszefogast-tamogatjak-mtva-fidesz/30940923.html.

41. Radio Free Europe, "RFE/RL Probe Finds Journalists at Hungarian State Broadcaster Instructed on News Coverage," November 12, 2020, https://www.rferl.org/a/leaked-audio -testimony-find-journalists-at-hungarian-state-broadcaster-instructed-on-news-coverage /30945077.html.

42. Keller-Alánt, "Editorial Instruction at the Public Television."

43. Mark Duke, "After the Leaked Audio Recordings, the Heads of the Public Media Claim that They Are Not Willing to Give in to Any Political Pressure," *444*, December 2, 2020, https://444.hu/2020/12/02/a-kozmedia-vezetoi-a-kiszivargott-hangfelvetelek-utan-azt -allitjak-semmilyen-politikai-nyomasgyakorlasnak-nem-hajlandok-engedni.

44. Zsuzsanna Wirth, "Leaked Documents Show How Orbán's Circle Dictates the News at Hungary's State News Agency—Part 1," *Direkt36*, March 4, 2022, https://www.direkt36.hu /en/kiszivargott-iratok-mutatjak-hogyan-diktalnak-orbanek-a-nemzeti-hirugynoksegnek; and Zsuzsanna Wirth, 'Please, Don't Report About this at All! Thanks!'—How the Hungarian State News Agency Censors Politically Unpleasant News—Part 2," *Direkt36*, March 7, 2022, https://www.direkt36.hu/en/ne-ird-meg-semmilyen-formaban-koszi-igy -hallgatja-el-a-kormanynak-kinos-hireket-az-allami-hirugynoksege.

45. Wirth, "Leaked Documents Show How Orbán's Circle Dictates the News"; and Wirth, "'Please, Don't Report About this at All!'"

46. Wirth, "Leaked Documents Show How Orbán's Circle Dictates the News."

47. "Act CLXXXV," section 82.

48. Farkas Csilla, "The Smell of Corpses and 'Bloody' Walls—Downsizing from the Perspective of a Fired MTV," *24*, December 1, 2011, https://24.hu/belfold/2011/12/01/hullaszag-es -veres-falak-leepites-egy-kirugott-mtv-s-szemszogebol.

49. Mandiner, "Zsolt Németh Became the New News Director of MTVA," April 3, 2013, https://mandiner.hu/belfold/2013/04/nemeth-zsolt-lett-az-mtva-uj-hirigazgatoja.

50. Mérték, "Public Life Content Before and After the New Media Law," *Mérték Media Analysis Workshop*, October 29, 2012, https://mertek.eu/2012/10/29/kozeleti-tartalom-az -uj-mediatorveny-elott-es-utan.

51. Democracy Reporting International, "Hungary's State-Owned TV Shows Bias in EU- Refugee Referendum," October 2, 2016, https://democracy-reporting.org/en/office/EU /news/hungarys-state-owned-tv-shows-bias-in-eu-refugee-referendum.

52. OSCE, "ODIHR Limited Election Observation Mission Final Report," June 27, 2018, 20, https://www.osce.org/files/f/documents/0/9/385959.pdf.

53. Mérték Media Monitor, "The Methods Are Old, the Cronies Are New: Soft Censorship in the Hungarian Media in 2015," *Mérték Booklets: Volume 9*, 2016, https://mertek .eu/wp-content/uploads/2017/01/softcensorship2015.pdf; and Mérték, "Funding for Public Service Media in Hungary—a Form of Unlawful State Aid?," *Mérték Médiaelemző Műhely*,

January 9, 2019, https://mertek.eu/en/2019/01/09/funding-for-public-service-media-in-hungary-a-form-of-unlawful-state-aid.

54. Kitti Fodi, "According to the Right-Wing Gábor Bencsik, M1's Political Bias Is Unsustainable," *444*, April 12, 2022, https://444.hu/2022/04/12/a-jobbos-bencsik-gabor-szerint-az-m1-politikai-elfogultsaga-tarthatatlan.

55. Hirado, "Bencsik Was Overtaken by Left-Wing Hysteria," April 12, 2022, https://hirado.hu/belfold/cikk/2022/04/12/bencsiket-utolerte-a-baloldali-hiszteria.

56. Jean-Philipp Baeck et al., "Press Freedom Under Attack in Hungary: Fighters on Orbán's Media Front," *Taz*, May 3, 2023, https://taz.de/Angegriffene-Pressefreiheit-in-Ungarn/!5928587.

57. About Hungary, "MTVA Head: Hungary's Public Media Is Balanced and Operates in Line with Professional Standards," February 19, 2023, https://abouthungary.hu/news-in-brief/mtva-head-hungarys-public-media-is-balanced-and-operates-in-line-with-professional-standards.

58. CMCS, "Public Service Media," n.d., http://medialaws.ceu.hu/public_service_media_more.html.

59. Attila Bátorfy et al., "Monitoring Media Pluralism in the Digital Era: Country Report—Hungary," *European University Institute*, 2022, https://cadmus.eui.eu/bitstream/handle/1814/74692/MPM2022-Hungary-EN.pdf.

60. József Spirk, "Bombardier Flew: Mészáros' Circle of Friends Traveled to Marbella to Watch a Practice Match," *24*, January 16, 2023, https://24.hu/belfold/2023/01/16/meszaros-lorinc-bombardier-barati-kor-marbellara-edzomeccs.

61. András Dezső, "God Also Played a Role in the Enrichment of Lőrinc Mészáros," *Index*, April 24, 2014, https://index.hu/belfold/2014/04/24/a_joisten_is_szerepet_jatszott_meszaros_lorinc_meggazdagodasaban.

62. Ákos Keller-Alánt et al., "Viktor Orbán's Favorite Mayor Goes on a Shopping Spree," *DW*, October 25, 2017, https://www.dw.com/en/in-hungary-viktor-orbans-favorite-mayor-goes-on-a-shopping-spree/a-41099347.

63. Attila Rovo, "The Silent Lord of Felcsút Makes Orbán's Dreams Come True," *Origo*, June 17, 2013, https://www.origo.hu/itthon/2013/06/portre-meszaros-lorinc-felcsuti-polgarmesterrol-a-puskas-akademia-elnokerol.

64. *Átlátszó*, "The Family Companies of Lőrinc Mészáros Have Been Enriched Predominantly from EU Funds in the Past Seven Years," January 15, 2018, https://atlatszo.hu/kozpenz/2018/01/15/tulnyomoreszt-unios-forrasokbol-gazdagodtak-meszaros-lorinc-csaladi-cegei-az-elmult-het-evben.

65. T. Mészáros, "Lőrinc Mészáros Could Be the Richest Man in the World by 2024," *Index*, August 4, 2017, https://index.hu/gazdasag/2017/08/04/meszaros_lorinc_2024-re_lesz_a_vilag_leggazdagabb_embere.

66. Átlátszó, "The Family Companies of Lőrinc Mészáros."

67. Átlátszó, "The Family Companies of Lőrinc Mészáros."

68. ESI (European Stability Initiative), "The Wizard, the Virus and a Pot of Gold—Viktor Orbán and the Future of European Solidarity," April 18, 2020, https://www.esiweb.org/publications/wizard-virus-and-pot-gold-viktor-orban-and-future-european-solidarity.

69. Dezső, "God Also Played a Role in the Enrichment of Lőrinc Mészáros."

70. Zoltán Kovács, "Meet Lajos Simicska: Fidesz's Enigmatic Oligarch," *The Budapest Beacon*, February 10, 2015, https://budapestbeacon.com/meet-lajos-simicska-fideszs-enigmatic-oligarch.

71. József Spirk, "Lajos Simicska: I Will Fire All Orbánists," *Index*, February 6, 2015, https://index.hu/belfold/2015/02/06/simicska_lajos_orban_egy_geci.

72. Tibor Lengyel, "Lajos Simicska: The Media War Is Not About Money," *Origo*, February 6, 2015, https://www.origo.hu/gazdasag/2015/02/simicska-lajos-szerint-a-mediahaboru-nem-a-penzrol-szol.

73. Attila Bátorfy, "Explore the Media Empire Friendly to the Government," *Átlátszó*, February 1, 2018, https://english.atlatszo.hu/2018/01/16/infographic-explore-the-media-empire-friendly-to-the-hungarian-government; and Attila Bátorfy, "Data Visualization: This Is How the Pro-Government Media Empire Owning 476 Outlets Was Formed," *Átlátszó*, November 30, 2018, https://english.atlatszo.hu/2018/11/30/data-visualization-this-is-how-the-pro-government-media-empire-owning-476-outlets-was-formed.

74. Interview with Attila Bátorfy, May 22, 2023.

75. Sándor Czinkóczi, "All County Newspapers Published the Same Central Orbán Interview the Day Before the Election," *444*, April 7, 2018, https://444.hu/2018/04/07/az-osszes-megyei-lap-ugyanazzal-a-kozponti-orban-interjuval-jelent-meg-a-valasztas-elotti-napon.

76. Interview with Attila Bátorfy, May 22, 2023.

77. Átlátszó, "Editor-in-Chief of *Átlátszó* to Media1: 'A Smear Campaign Has Been Launched Against Us Using the Methods of Putin's Russia'," January 13, 2023, https://english.atlatszo.hu/2023/01/13/editor-in-chief-of-atlatszo-to-media1-a-smear-campaign-has-been-launched-against-using-the-methods-of-putins-russia.

78. Tamás Pilhál, "They Got a Kick Out of the Papal Visit," *Magyar Nemzet*, May 4, 2023, https://magyarnemzet.hu/velemeny/2023/05/fraszt-kaptak-a-papalatogatastol.

79. Blanka Zöldi and András Pethő, "How Public Money Keeps Flowing to Orbán's Family Through Hungary's New Tycoon," *Direkt36*, May 13, 2019, https://www.direkt36.hu/en/igy-folyik-tovabb-a-kozpenz-meszaros-lorinctol-az-orban-csaladhoz.

80. Attila Borsodi, "They Are Preparing for a Fight with Facebook," *Magyar Nemzet*, November 19, 2021, https://magyarnemzet.hu/belfold/2021/11/harcra-keszulnek-a-facebookkal; and Tamás Fabián and Tamás Szilli, "Fidesz's Miracle Weapon that Will Change the Internet," *Telex*, February 7, 2023, https://telex.hu/video/2023/02/07/megafon-fidesz-valasztasi-kampany-facebook.

81. András Nagy Csomor, "'I'm Tired of the Ballib Steamroller, It's Time to Stop It!'—István Kovács, Founder of the Megafon Center for Mandiner," *Mandiner*, June 26, 2020, https://mandiner.hu/belfold/2020/06/unom-mar-a-ballib-gozhengert-itt-az-ideje-hogy-megallitsuk-kovacs-istvan-a-megafon-kozpont-alapitoja-a-mandinernek.

82. Ashley Johnson, "The Facts Behind Allegations of Political Bias on Social Media," *ITIF*, October 26, 2023, https://itif.org/publications/2023/10/26/the-facts-behind-allegations-of-political-bias-on-social-media; and Ryan Mac and Craig Silverman, "'Mark Changed the Rules': How Facebook Went Easy on Alex Jones and Other Right-Wing Figures," *Buzzfeed*, February 21, 2021, https://www.buzzfeednews.com/article/ryanmac/mark-zuckerberg-joel-kaplan-facebook-alex-jones.

83. Statista, "Number of Facebook Users in Hungary from September 2018 to March 2023," 2024, https://www.statista.com/statistics/1029770/facebook-users-hungary.

84. Magyar Nemzet, "More than Two Thousand People Have Already Registered on Megafon's Website," August 12, 2020, https://magyarnemzet.hu/belfold/2020/08/mar-tobb-mint-ketezren-regisztraltak-a-megafon-kepzesere.

85. Origo, "The Country's First Right-Wing Community Studio Is Under Construction," April 15, 2021, https://www.origo.hu/itthon/2021/04/epul-az-orszag-elso-jobboldali-kozossegi-studioja-interju-kovacs-istvannal.

86. Attila Kálmán, "Philip Rákay's Facebook Posts Were Pushed for Nearly HUF Five Million in a Single Month," 24, April 23, 2021, https://24.hu/kozelet/2021/04/23/megafon-kozpont-facebook-hirdetes-rakay-philip; and Marianna Kovács-Angel, "Megafon Központ Advertised a Single Post of a Pro-Government Facebook Page for HUF 1.6 Million," 24, April 7, 2021, https://24.hu/belfold/2021/04/07/a-kopasz-oszt-megafon-jakab-peter.

87. Zsolt Hanula, "We Have Reached Another Dream Limit: Megafon's Facebook Advertising Spending Has Exceeded Half a Billion Forints," January 3, 2022, https://telex.hu/belfold/2022/01/03/elertunk-egy-ujabb-alomhatart-atlepte-az-500-millio-forintot-a-megafon-facebookos-reklamkoltese.

88. Datawrapper, "Top Spending Political Advertisers on Facebook Since April 2019," 2022, https://datawrapper.dwcdn.net/41yrX/17/?fbclid=IwARowSIaPRPiKN4wo3P4TPbuaUVFFE-F2QOSmfOjQOwWcQjy8qqFQ-5dRoVY.

89. Interview with Attila Bátorfy, May 22, 2023.

90. János Molnár, "Megafon—Fighting the Dollar Media," Magyar Nemzet, December 12, 2022, https://magyarnemzet.hu/belfold/2022/12/megafon-harcban-a-dollarmediaval; and Barbara Vági, "We Want to Change the Internet," Origo, July 25, 2022, https://www.origo.hu/itthon/2022/07/sikeresek-a-jobboldali-velemenyvezerek-az-interneten-es-ez-a-baloldalt-nagyon-bosszantja-interju.

91. László Horváth, "A Quarter of a Billion Forints Flowed in from Private Individuals to the Pro-Government Megaphone Center," 24, January 6, 2021, https://24.hu/fn/gazdasag/2021/06/01/megafon-kozpont-kovacs-istvan-alapjogokert-kopont-tamogatas-maganszemely-rakay-philip-bayer-zsolt-rogan-antal.

92. Marianna Tóth-Biró and Kata Bálint, "They Are Hungry for Recognition from Public Money: This Is How the Billions Migrate to the Government's Favorite Experts," Telex, November 15, 2021, https://telex.hu/belfold/2021/11/25/kozpenz-milliardok-a-kormany-szakertoire-alapjogokert-kozpont-batthyany-lajos-alapitvany.

93. Balázs Bozzay, "Megafon Initiated Three Lawsuits Against Telex, But We Won All of Them at First Instance," Telex, February 8, 2022, https://telex.hu/belfold/2022/02/08/mindharom-per-megnyerte-telex-megafon-elso-fok.

94. Nikoletta Eket, "Hungarian, and Really Belonging to the Community—Hundub Started," Magyar Nemzet, December 27, 2020, https://magyarnemzet.hu/belfold/2020/12/magyar-es-tenyleg-a-kozossege-elindult-a-hundub; and József Spirk, "Public Debts and Liquidations Are Behind the Hungarian Facebook Rival," 24, December 31, 2020, https://tinyurl.com/3bypt3h3.

95. Krisztina Kincses, "István Kovács: Our Goals Go Beyond Electoral Victory," *Magyar Nemzet*, May 11, 2022, https://magyarnemzet.hu/belfold/2022/05/kovacs-istvan-a-mi-celjaink -tulmutatnak-a-valasztasi-gyozelmen.

96. Blikk, "The Rogáns Are Expecting a Baby!," *Blikk*, January 21, 2009, https://www.blikk.hu /aktualis/babat-varnak-roganek/nccqxkz; Fodor Bori, "Antal Rogán Got Engaged to His Young Love," *Cili*, January 21, 2009, https://www.blikk.hu/rogan-antal-eljegyezte-ifju -szerelmet-cilit/ql88rts; and Kordos Szabolcs, "Rogán Bandaged Cecília's Head," *Blikk*, January 21, 2009, https://www.blikk.hu/rogan-bekototte-cecilia-fejet/glp28cd.

97. Átlátszó, "Atlatszo.hu Unravels Intricate Web Behind Suspicious Budapest Real Estate Sellout," February 10, 2015, https://english.atlatszo.hu/2015/02/10/atlatszo-hu-unravels -intricate-web-behind-suspicious-budapest-real-estate-sellout.

98. Péter Erdélyi et al., "The Moneyman of Bashar al-Assad and a Suspect of a Serious International Crime Participated in Hungary's Golden Visa Program," *Direkt36*, March 28, 2018, https://www.direkt36.hu/en/sulyos-nemzetkozi-bunugy-gyanusitottja-es-a-sziriai -diktator-penzembere-is-magyar-papirokat-kapott-a-kotvenyprogramban.

99. Átlátszó, "Celebrity Politician Can't Put a Foot Wrong," September 8, 2016, https:// english.atlatszo.hu/2016/09/08/celebrity-politician-cant-put-a-foot-wrong.

100. Panyi Szabolcs et al., "We Present the Dark Side of Antal Rogán, Balázs Kertész Who Became a Phantom," *Index*, November 11, 2016, https://index.hu/belfold/2016/11/11/rogan _antal_titkos_talalkozoi_videon_kertesz_balazs_rogan-halozat.

101. Fred Siebert, Theodore Peterson, and Wilbur Schramm, *Four Theories of the Press* (University of Illinois Press, 1956).

102. Bátorfy et al., "Monitoring Media Pluralism."

103. Mérték Media Monitor, "Four Shades of Censorship."

104. Bátorfy et al., "Monitoring Media Pluralism."

105. Mérték Media Monitor, "The Methods Are Old."

106. Attila Bátorfy and Ágnes Urbán, "State Advertising as an Instrument of Transformation of the Media Market in Hungary," *East European Politics* 36, no. 1 (2020): 44–65.

107. Bátorfy et al., "Monitoring Media Pluralism."

108. Dániel Szőke, "How State Funds Help the Miracle Business of a Top Minister's Former Wife," *Direkt36*, July 22, 2022, https://www.direkt36.hu/en/rogan-hivatala-is -feltunik-korabbi-felesegenek-kiugroan-sikeres-uzlete-korul.

109. TWN, "Strange Reason: This Is Why You Shouldn't Pee While Showering, According to the Urologist," July 3, 2023, https://twn.hu/erdekes/2023/07/03/zuhanyzas-urologus -tik-tok-ok.

110. Mérték Media Monitor, "An Illiberal Model of Media Markets: Soft Censorship 2017," *Mérték Booklets: Volume 15*, July 2018, 38, https://mertek.eu/wp-content/uploads/2018/08 /MertekFuzetek15.pdf.

111. Gábor Kovács, "Antal Rogán 'Communicated' Twice as Much Money as He Legally Received," *HVG*, November 14, 2022, https://hvg.hu/gazdasag/20221114_Rogan_Antal _ketszer_annyi_penzt_kommunikalt_el_mint_terveztek?fbclid=IwAR1378f9EcqpF -6k9akJDAWntjJDyTwKCFd5cLlGRVknQyGzUYBvfXNPibM.

112. Dénes Csurgó, "From Now On, the Control of Public Funds Is Also Controlled by Rogán," *444*, September 14, 2022, https://444.hu/2022/09/14/mostantol-a-kozpenzek -ellenorzeset-is-rogan-ellenorzi; and Dénes Csurgó, "Rogán's Cabinet Empire Is Expanding Unstoppably," *444*, November 30, 2022, https://444.hu/2022/11/30/megallithatatlanul -bovul-rogan-kabinetbirodalma.

113. Balázs Gulyás, "The Government Gives 22 Billion to a Company Close to Fidesz for Media Monitoring," *Media1*, January 11, 2023, https://media1.hu/2023/01/11/22-milliardot -ad-mediafigyelesre-a-kormany-egy-fidesz-kozeli-cegnek.

114. Márton Nagy, "The Foundation Received a Grant of 133 Million, Where Rogán's Man Earned a Media Routine," *Átlátszó*, November 8, 2021, https://atlatszo.hu/kozpenz /2021/11/08/133-millios-tamogatast-kapott-az-alapitvany-ahol-rogan-embere-mediarutint -szerzett.

115. German Marshall Fund, "Russian Sites Sanctioned for Spreading Disinformation Ahead of War in Ukraine," March 2022, https://securingdemocracy.gmfus.org/incident /russian-sites-sanctioned-for-spreading-disinformation-ahead-of-war-in-ukraine.

116. Márton Nagy, "Minister's New Wife and Her Family Granted HUF 1.6 Billion Loan by a State Bank for Farmland Purchase," *Átlátszó*, February 4, 2021, https://english.atlatszo. hu/2021/02/04/ministers-new-wife-and-her-family-granted-huf-1-6-billion-loan-by-a -state-bank-for-farmland-purchase.

117. Krzysztof Dzięciołowski, "Is There a Chance for Non-Partisan Media in Poland?," Reuters Institute Fellowship Paper, University of Oxford, 2017, https://reutersinstitute .politics.ox.ac.uk/sites/default/files/2017-12/Is%20there%20a%20chance%20for%20non -partisan%20media%20in%20Poland%20-%20Krzysztof%20Dzieciolowsk%20Paper.pdf.

118. Maïa de la Baume, "Hungarian MEP Admits He Was at Lockdown 'Orgy'," *Politico*, December 1, 2020, https://www.politico.eu/article/police-arrests-20-people-including-eu-officials -at-lockdown-party-in-brussels; and Panyi Szabolcs, "Corruption Couldn't Shake Orbán's Credibility; A Sex Scandal Just Might," *Balkan Insight*, December 3, https://balkaninsight .com/2020/12/03/corruption-couldnt-shake-orbans-credibility-a-sex-scandal-just-might.

119. Károly Villányi, "Revenge from Brussels?," *Magyar Nemzet*, December 3, 2020, https:// magyarnemzet.hu/belfold/2020/12/bosszu-brusszelbol-2.

5. THE *GODI MEDIA*: MODI'S INDIA

1. Times of India, "'Tucker Carlson of India': John Oliver Takes Dig at Arnab Goswami," March 11, 2020, https://timesofindia.indiatimes.com/articleshow/74573376.cms.

2. Ananya Bhardwaj and Nayanima Basu, "'Bigger Than a Normal Strike' Against Pakistan, Arnab Goswami Said 3 Days Before Balakot," *The Print*, January 16, 2021, https://theprint .in/india/bigger-than-a-normal-strike-against-pakistan-arnab-goswami-said-3-days-before -balakot/586759.

3. The Hindu, "Ex-CEO of BARC Partho Dasgupta, Arrested in TRP Scam, Hospitalised," January 16, 2021, https://www.thehindu.com/news/cities/mumbai/ex-ceo-of-barc-partho -dasgupta-arrested-in-trp-scam-hospitalised/article33588641.ece.

4. The Wire, "TRP Scam: WhatsApp Messages Reveal Arnab Goswami's 'Collusion' with Former BARC Chief," January 16, 2021, https://theprint.in/india/bigger-than-a-normal -strike-against-pakistan-arnab-goswami-said-3-days-before-balakot/586759.

5. Republic TV, "The Debate with Arnab Goswami," February 26, 2022, https://www .youtube.com/watch?v=v64sgrsxPYE.

6. Salil Tripathi, "How the Fog of War Has Blinded Journalists to Their Roles," *The Caravan*, March 2, 2019, https://caravanmagazine.in/media/question-journalists-support -for-armed-forces.

7. Republic TV, "The Debate with Arnab Goswami," February 26, 2022.

8. Rahul Kanwal, cited in Tripathi, "How the Fog of War Has Blinded Journalists."

9. Rajdeep Sardesai, "Review: 2019: How Modi Won India," *Hindustan Times*, January 31, 2020.

10. Tim Groeling and Matthew Baum, "Crossing the Water's Edge: Elite Rhetoric, Media Coverage, and the Rally-Round-the-Flag Phenomenon," *The Journal of Politics* 70, no. 4 (2008): 1065–85.

11. Ravish Kumar, *The Free Voice: On Democracy, Culture and the Nation* (Speaking Tiger Books, 2019), 35.

12. Al Jazeera, "Expert Warns of Impending 'Genocide' of Muslims in India," January 16, 2022, https://www.aljazeera.com/news/2022/1/16/expert-warns-of-possible-genocide-against -muslims-in-india.

13. Indian Television, "Times Now dominates as No. 1 English News Channel During State Assembly Elections," December 15, 2023, https://indiantelevision.com/television /tv-channels/news-broadcasting/times-now-dominates-as-no.-1-english-news-channel -during-state-assembly-elections-231215.

14. Indian Television, "Times Now, Aaj Tak Retain Positions Even as Ratings Decline," January 6, 2024, https://www.indiantelevision.com/television/tv-channels/news-broadcasting /times-now-aaj-tak-retain-positions-even-as-ratings-decline-170106.

15. Krishn Kaushik, "The Tempest: Have Radhika and Pranny Roy Undermined NDTV?," *The Caravan*, December 1, 2015, https://caravanmagazine.in/reportage/the-tempest-prannoy -radhika-roy-ndtv.

16. Vanita Kohli-Khandekar, *The Indian Media Business: Pandemic and After* (SAGE, 2021), 113.

17. Rahul Bhatia, "Fast and Furious: The Turbulent Reign of Arnab Goswami," *The Caravan*, December 1, 2012, https://caravanmagazine.in/reportage/fast-and-furious.

18. MXMIndia, "What's Made Arnab the Face of News TV?," November 25, 2013, https:// www.mxmindia.com/uncategorized/whats-made-arnab-the-face-of-news-tv.

19. Times Now, "Mumbai Terror Attack—Part 3—Discussion on TIMES NOW," November 27, 2008," https://www.youtube.com/watch?v=vIF2LMMbd4Y.

20. Bhatia, "Fast and Furious."

21. Times Now, "The Newshour with Arnab Goswami on Times Now," August 1, 2014, https://www.youtube.com/watch?v=Mfm2Wk8X_PE.

22. Times of India, "Rahul Gandhi's First Interview: Full Text," January 28, 2014, https:// timesofindia.indiatimes.com/india/rahul-gandhis-first-interview-full-text/articleshow /29455665.cms.

23. Times Now, "Frankly Speaking with Narendra Modi: Full Interview," May 8, 2014, https://www.youtube.com/watch?v=JIjMGNwStto.

24. The Wire, "The 'Last Press Conference by an Indian PM in India' Was 10 Years Ago on This Day," January 3, 2024, https://thewire.in/government/last-press-conference-indian-prime-minister.

25. The Indian Express, "PM Modi's Interview with Arnab Goswami: Full Transcript," June 28, 2016, https://indianexpress.com/article/india/india-news-india/pm-modis-interview-with-arnab-goswami-full-transcript-2879832.

26. Manisha Pande, "'It's Not a Newsroom, It's a Durbar': Inside the Republic of Arnab Goswami," *News Laundry*, September 7, 2020, https://www.newslaundry.com/2020/09/07/its-not-a-newsroom-its-a-durbar-inside-the-republic-of-arnab-goswami.

27. Christophe Jaffrelot and Vihang Jumle, "A Study of 1,779 Republic TV Debates Reveals How the Channel Champions Narendra Modi," *The Caravan*, December 15, 2020, https://caravanmagazine.in/media/republic-debates-study-shows-channel-promotoes-modi-ndtv.

28. Interview of a former Times Now employee, June 28, 2022.

29. Interviews with three Indian journalists, June 10, 2022.

30. Kalyani Chadha and Michael Koliska, "Playing by a Different Set of Rules," *Journalism Practice* 10, no. 5 (2016): 617.

31. Chadha and Koliska, "Playing by a Different Set of Rules," 611.

32. Interviews with journalists, June 28, 2022.

33. For instance, see Republic World, "PM Modi Full Interview Before Elections 2022," February 9, 2022, https://www.youtube.com/watch?v=NoqR2Mw22Js.

34. Interviews with journalists, June 28, 2022.

35. Interviews with a journalist, June 10, 2022.

36. Interviews with journalists, June 28, 2022.

37. Interview with a journalist, June 10, 2022.

38. Times of India, "Govt's Pre-Election Ad Spends, Corporate Branding to Boost Print Media Revenues by 15 Percent in FY 24," July 11, 2023, https://timesofindia.indiatimes.com/india/govts-pre-election-ad-spends-corporate-branding-to-boost-print-media-revenues-by-15-in-fy24/articleshow/101664255.cms.

39. Times of India, "Govt's Pre-Election Ad Spends."

40. Adam Withnall, "How Modi Government Uses Ad Spending to 'Reward or Punish' Indian Media," *The Independent*, July 20, 2022, https://www.independent.co.uk/news/world/asia/india-modi-government-media-ad-spending-newspapers-press-freedom-a8990451.html.

41. Amit Shah, *Twitter*, November 4, 2020, https://x.com/AmitShah/status/1323863582027603970.

42. Gideon Rachman, *The Age of the Strongman: How the Cult of the Leader Threatens Democracy Around the World* (The Bodley Head, 2022).

43. Benjamin Parkin et al., "Is India's BJP the World's Most Ruthlessly Efficient Political Party?," *Financial Times*, April 17, 2024, https://www.ft.com/content/d5a1dfaa-ecfb-45c5-b60d-458f89228ea3.

44. Amrita Madhukalya, "50 Lakh WhatsApp Groups and Transmission Anywhere in 12 Minutes—What BJP Is Doing on Social Media for 2024," *Deccan Herald*, March 23, 2024, https://www.deccanherald.com/elections/india/political-theatre-bjp-on-social-media-2950186.

45. Manash Gohain, "BJP to Boost Social Media Drive Ahead of 2024 Lok Sabha Polls," *Times of India*, July 31, 2023, https://timesofindia.indiatimes.com/india/bjp-to-boost-social-media-drive-ahead-of-2024-lok-sabha-polls/articleshow/102257912.cms.

46. Economic Times, "YouTube Now Platform of Choice for 4 Out of 5 Indians Online, Shorts Usage Grows," September 27, 2023, https://economictimes.indiatimes.com/tech/technology/youtube-now-platform-of-choice-for-4-out-of-5-indians-online-shorts-usage-grows/articleshow/103990873.cms.

47. Laura Ceci, "Leading Countries Based on YouTube Audience Size as of January 2024," *Statista*, February 13, 2024, https://www.statista.com/statistics/280685/number-of-monthly-unique-youtube-users; Stacy Dixon, "Leading Countries Based on Instagram Audience Size as of January 2024," *Statista*, February 15, 2024, https://www.statista.com/statistics/578364/countries-with-most-instagram-users; and World Population Review, "WhatsApp Users by Country 2024," n.d., https://worldpopulationreview.com/country-rankings/whatsapp-users-by-country.

48. Rachman, *The Age of the Strongman.*

49. BBC, "Arnab Goswami: India's Most Loved and Loathed TV Anchor," November 22, 2020, https://www.bbc.co.uk/news/world-asia-india-54930379.

50. MXM Cast, "Arnab Goswami on Journalism, Republic TV and More," Podcast interview (26:45), September 25, 2020, https://apple.co/3JeQB2Q.

51. Interview with a former employee of Times Now, July 4, 2022.

52. Interview with a former employee of Times Now, July 4, 2022.

53. MXM Cast, "Arnab Goswami on Journalism."

54. Al Jazeera, "Brash and Bigoted: How Arnab Goswami Changed India's TV Debate," February 18, 2020, https://www.youtube.com/watch?v=GTyVp-sAXT4.

55. Arun George, "Exclusive: Arnab Goswami on His 'Republic,' The War on Big Media & Why He Has to Shout," *ScoopWhoop*, December 30, 2016, https://www.scoopwhoop.com/news/exclusive-arnab-goswami-on-his-republic-the-war-on-big-media-and-why-he-has-to-shout/.

56. Maya Tudor, "India's Nationalism in Historical Perspective: The Democratic Dangers of Ascendant Nativism," *Indian Politics and Policy* 1, no. 1 (2018): 1–24.

57. Arvind Sharma, "On the Difference Between Hinduism and Hindutva," *Education About Asia* 25, no. 1 (2020): 1–5.

58. Rachman, *The Age of the Strongman.*

59. Bela Bhatia, "The Naxalite Movement in Central Bihar," *Economic and Political Weekly* 40, no. 15 (2005): 1536–49.

60. Republic World, "Arnab Goswami's Open Letter Announcing Nationalist Collective to Fight Anti-India Forces," January 27, 2021, https://www.republicworld.com/india/arnab-goswamis-open-letter-announcing-nationalist-collective-to-fight-anti-india-forces.

61. Republic World, "Arnab Goswami's Open Letter."

62. Interview with the executive editor of News Laundry, June 24, 2022.

63. Cas Mudde, "The Populist Zeitgeist," *Government and Opposition* 39, no. 4 (2004): 541–63.

64. George, "Exclusive: Arnab Goswami on His 'Republic.'"

65. Republic World, "PM Modi Labels Congress Leader of 'Tukde-Tukde Gang' in Parliament Speech," February 7, 2022, https://www.youtube.com/watch?v=7PRokgd3iOw.

66. Republic World, "Arnab Goswami Speaks About Coining 'Tukde Tukde Gang,'" February 9, 2022, https://www.youtube.com/watch?v=aEpAuvqNawM.

67. See https://www.newslaundry.com/bloodlust-tv.

68. Harsh Mander, "Is India Lurching Into a Genocide?," *The Wire*, February 18, 2022, https://thewire.in/communalism/is-india-lurching-into-a-genocide.

69. Parth Sharma and Abhijit Anand, "Indian Media Coverage of Nizamuddin Markaz Event During COVID-19 Pandemic," *Asian Politics & Policy* 12, no. 4 (2020): 650–54.

70. ABP, "Tablighi Jamaat, the Human Bomb Which Can Explode Coronavirus Numbers," March 31, 2020, https://news.abplive.com/tv-show/master-stroke/tablighi-jamaat-the-human-bomb-which-can-explode-coronavirus-numbers-master-stroke-31032020-1186329.

71. Zee News, "DNA: Tablighi Jamaat Betrayed the Nation?," March 31, 2020, https://zeenews.india.com/video/india/dna-tablighi-jamaat-betrayed-the-nation-2273020.html.

72. Republic World, "Lockdown Negativity Gang Strikes Again," March 27, 2020, https://www.youtube.com/watch?v=HUc_udUBMPE.

73. Republic World, "The Debate with Arnab Goswami: PM Silences Vaccine Critics," March 1, 2021, https://www.youtube.com/watch?v=pcWTodxomSY.

74. Shekhar Gupta, "As Modi Govt Faces Up to Covid Disaster, BJP Learns a Tough Truth—The Virus Doesn't Vote," *The Print*, April 24, 2021, https://theprint.in/national-interest/as-modi-govt-faces-up-to-covid-disaster-bjp-learns-a-tough-truth-the-virus-doesnt-vote/644949.

75. Tanishka Sodhi, "Why Is Modi Getting Such Bad International Press?," *News Laundry*, May 11, 2021, https://www.newslaundry.com/2021/05/11/why-is-modi-getting-such-bad-international-press.

76. NDTV, "India in 'Endgame of Pandemic,' Says Health Minister," March 8, 2021, https://www.ndtv.com/india-news/coronavirus-india-in-endgame-of-pandemic-says-health-minister-2385882.

77. Krishna Das and Aftab Ahmed., "India's Modi Scorned Over Reckless Rallies, Religious Gathering Amid Virus Mayhem," *Reuters*, April 19, 2021, https://www.reuters.com/world/india/indias-modi-scorned-over-reckless-rallies-religious-gathering-amid-virus-mayhem-2021-04-19.

78. The Lancet, "India's COVID-19 Emergency," May 8, 2021, https://www.thelancet.com/journals/lancet/article/PIIS0140-6736(21)01052-7/fulltext.

79. Sodhi, "Why is Modi Getting Such Bad International Press?."

80. The Lancet, "India's COVID-19 Emergency."

81. Republic World, "COVID-19: Time for India to Unite, Not to Settle Political Scores," April 23, 2021, https://www.youtube.com/watch?v=b4FhTP9KJaU.

82. The Tribune, "Nationwide Strike Affects Normal Life in Kerala, Odisha, Other States; Over 25 Crore Workers Join Agitation: Trade Unions," November 26, 2020, https://www.tribuneindia.com/news/nation/trade-unions-go-on-strike-public-services-likely-to-be-hit-176123.

83. Gaurav Bhatnagar, "TV Channels Omit Coverage of Farmers Protest in Favour of Bollywood 'Drugs Mandli,'" *The Wire*, September 27, 2020, https://thewire.in/media/tv-channels-omit-coverage-of-farmers-protest-in-favour-of-bollywood-drugs-mandli.

84. Prabhjit Singh, "Farmers at Kundli Upset Over Media Misrepresentation, Accusations; Confront 'Godi Media,'" *The Caravan*, November 30, 2020, https://caravanmagazine.in/news/farmers-at-kundli-upset-over-media-misrepresentation-accusations-confront-godi-media.

85. Zee News, "DNA Exclusive: Farmers' Agitation Hijacked; Khalistani Terrorists Behind Violence During Protests?," November 28, 2020, https://zeenews.india.com/india/dna-exclusive-farmers-agitation-hijacked-khalistani-terrorists-behind-violence-during-protests-2327127.html.

86. Republic World, "Farmers' Protest: Haryana CM Manohar Lal Khattar Alleges Role of Khalistan in Agitation," November 28, 2020, https://www.youtube.com/watch?v=4Jv6TZGThGo.

87. For example, see Republic World, "Khalistani Group SFJ Offers $1 Million to Protesting Farmers at Delhi-Haryana Border," November 29, 2020, https://www.youtube.com/watch?v=So7bIHweStU.

88. Singh, "Farmers at Kundli Upset Over Media Misrepresentation."

89. Editors Guild of India, *Twitter*, December 4, 2020, https://x.com/IndEditorsGuild/status/1334804997230317571.

90. The Clarion India, "Irked by Misleading Reports, Farmers Boycott Pro-Govt TV News Channels," December 2, 2020, https://clarionindia.net/irked-by-misleading-reports-farmers-boycott-pro-govt-tv-news-channels.

91. Nidhi Suresh, "'Media Has Lost Our Trust': Why Protesting Farmers Are Angry with 'Godi Media,'" *News Laundry*, December 1, 2020, https://www.newslaundry.com/2020/12/01/media-has-lost-our-trust-why-are-protesting-farmers-angry-with-godi-media.

92. Rachman, *The Age of the Strongman.*

93. Sharma, "On the Difference Between Hinduism and Hindutva."

94. Times Now, "What Is Hinduphobia and Why Is It Important?," January 2022, https://www.youtube.com/watch?v=qgbgXWrjaN4&list=PLAQGzpyUo1aHWS5V4228Zmru3ws3NC4Uc&index=169.

95. Republic World, "Arnab Goswami on the Debate: Massive Outrage After Congress Leader Salman Khurshid Equates Hindutva to Terrorism," November 11, 2021, https://www.youtube.com/watch?v=8kCuL9xTdAo.

96. Onaiza Drabu, "Who Is the Muslim? Discursive Representations of the Muslims and Islam in Indian Prime-Time News," *Religions* 9, no. 9 (2018): 283.

97. Mariyam Alavi and Meher Pandey, "BJP Tops India's 'VIP' Hate Pandemic, NDTV Finds," *NDTV*, January 12, 2022, https://www.ndtv.com/india-news/bjp-tops-indias-vip-hate-pandemic-ndtv-finds-2703827.

98. Mander, "Is India Lurching Into a Genocide?."

99. Drabu, "Who Is the Muslim?."

100. Interview, June 24, 2022.

101. S. Meghnad and Deepanjana Pal, "Bloodlust TV: Aman Chopra Spitting Hate on Minorities with His 'Thook Jihad' Show," *News Laundry*, November 18, 2021, https://www.newslaundry.com/2021/11/18/bloodlust-tv-aman-chopra-spitting-hate-on-minorities-with-his-thook-jihad-show.

102. Alishan Jafri, "Thook Jihad? No, India Is Drowning in the Cesspool Our Reigning Spit Experts Have Created," *The Wire*, February 8, 2022.

103. Interview with Manisha Pande, June 24, 2022.

104. Amnesty International, "India: Persecution of Minorities and Shrinking Space for Dissent," November 2022, https://www.amnesty.org/en/wp-content/uploads/2022/04/ASA2054912022ENGLISH.pdf.

105. Human Rights Watch, "India: Dangerous Backsliding on Rights," January 13, 2022, https://www.hrw.org/news/2022/01/13/india-dangerous-backsliding-rights.

106. BBC, "Ayodhya Dispute: The Complex Legal History of India's Holy Site," November 9, 2019, https://www.bbc.co.uk/news/world-asia-india-50065277.

107. Editors Guild of India, "Recent Statements Issued," https://editorsguild.in/statements-issued.

108. Republic World, "Is Targeting One Religion Okay?," June 9, 2022, https://www.youtube.com/watch?v=T03ePlcoK10.

109. Soutik Biswas, "Why Journalists in India Are Under Attack," *BBC*, February 4, 2021, https://www.bbc.co.uk/news/world-asia-india-55906345.

110. Dakshina Murthy, "Covid-19: Indian Media Finally Muster Up Courage to Question Modi," *TRT World*, May 22, 2021, https://www.trtworld.com/opinion/covid-19-indian-media-finally-muster-up-courage-to-question-modi-46916.

111. Interview with Manisha Pande, June 24, 2022.

112. Sergei Guriev and Daniel Treisman, *Spin Dictators: The Changing Face of Tyranny in the 21st Century* (Princeton University Press, 2022).

113. Times of India, "'Tucker Carlson of India': John Oliver Takes Dig at Arnab Goswami."

114. New York Times, "Inside the Apocalyptic Worldview of 'Tucker Carlson Tonight,'" April 30, 2022, https://www.nytimes.com/interactive/2022/04/30/us/tucker-carlson-tonight.html.

115. New York Times, "Inside the Apocalyptic Worldview of 'Tucker Carlson Tonight.'"

116. Charlotte Alter, "Talking with Tucker Carlson, the Most Powerful Conservative in America," *Time*, July 15, 2021, https://time.com/6080432/tucker-carlson-profile.

117. Reuters, "Former UK Leader Johnson Takes New Role at GB News Broadcaster," October 27, 2023, https://www.reuters.com/world/uk/former-uk-leader-johnson-takes-new-role-gb-news-broadcaster-2023-10-27.

118. Kohli-Khandekar, *The Indian Media Business: Pandemic and After.*

119. Interview, June 28, 2022.

120. Rachman, *The Age of the Strongman.*

121. Nic Newman et al., "Reuters Institute Digital News Report, 2019," *University of Oxford*, 2019, https://www.digitalnewsreport.org/survey/2019/the-rise-of-populism-and-the-consequences-for-news-and-media-use.

122. Neha Sahgal et al., "Nationalism and Politics," Pew Research Center, June 29, 2021, https://pewrsr.ch/3cvcFtA.

123. Raju Gopalakrishnan, "Indian Journalists Say They Intimidated, Ostracized if They Criticize Modi and the BJP," *Reuters*, April 27, 2018, https://www.reuters.com/article/idUSKBN1HX1EK.

124. Chloe Cornish and Benjamin Parkin, "Asia's Richest Man Gautam Adani Reveals Global Media Ambitions," *Financial Times*, November 25, 2022, https://www.ft.com/content/d6c5ffa0-0b9b-436f-8c8b-ef417obedfe3.

125. Vidya Krishnan, "A Billionaire, a TV Network, and the Fight for a Free Press in India," *Nieman Reports*, July 24, 2023, https://niemanreports.org/india-ndtv-modi.

126. Advait Palepu and Chris Kay, "Billionaire Press Barons Are Squeezing Media Freedom in India," *Bloomberg*, February 26, 2024, https://www.bloomberg.com/news/features/2024-02-26/india-s-press-freedom-squeezed-as-billionaires-close-to-modi-take-over-newsrooms.

6. MASS DELUSION: BOLSONARO'S BRAZIL

1. Guy Debord, *Society of the Spectacle* (Rebel, 1992), 2.

2. @delucca, *Twitter*, January 8, 2023, https://x.com/delucca/status/1612219169063436288.

3. Jack Nicas, "What Drove a Mass Attack on Brazil's Capital? Mass Delusion," *New York Times*, January 9, 2023, https://www.nytimes.com/2023/01/09/world/americas/brazil-riots-bolsonaro-conspiracy-theories.html.

4. We Are Social, "Digital 2022 Global Overview Report," 2022, https://wearesocial.com/uk/blog/2022/01/digital-2022-another-year-of-bumper-growth-2.

5. Instituto Data Senado, "SenadoNoticias," December 12, 2019, https://www12.senado.leg.br/noticias/materias/2019/12/12/redes-sociais-influenciam-voto-de-45-da-populacao-indica-pesquisa-do-datasenado.

6. Fernanda Serboia, "The Rise of WhatsApp in Brazil Is About More Than Just Messaging," *Harvard Business Review*, April 15, 2016, https://hbr.org/2016/04/the-rise-of-whatsapp-in-brazil-is-about-more-than-just-messaging.

7. Barbara Simao et al., "2019 ICT Households," *CGI*, 2019, https://www.cetic.br/media/docs/publicacoes/2/20201123121817/tic_dom_2019_livro_eletronico.pdf#page=121.

8. Liriam Sponholz and Rogerio Christofoletti, "From Preachers to Comedians: Ideal Types of Hate Speakers in Brazil," *Global Media and Communication* 15, no. 1 (2019): 67–84.

9. Statista, "Leading Countries Based on YouTube Audience Size as of January 2023," https://www.statista.com/statistics/280685/number-of-monthly-unique-youtube-users; and We Are Social, "Instagram Users in Brazil in 2023," https://datareportal.com/reports/digital-2023-brazil.

10. We Are Social, "Digital 2022," 100.

11. Nic Newman et al., "Reuters Institute Digital News Report 2022, Brazil," *Reuters Institute*, 2023, https://reutersinstitute.politics.ox.ac.uk/digital-news-report/2022/brazil.

12. Economist, "Latin American Politicians Court Social-Media Stars, Often Ineptly," July 21, 2022, https://www.economist.com/the-americas/2022/07/21/latin-american-politicians-court-social-media-stars-often-ineptly; Folha de Sao Paulo, "Celebrities and TikTokers Are Young Voters in 2022," April 6, 2022, https://www1.folha.uol.com.br/podcasts/2022/04/celebridades-e-tiktokers-sao-cabos-eleitorais-dos-jovens-em-2022-ouca-podcast.shtml; and Statista, "The Influence of Influencers," June 5, 2022, https://www.omnesinfluencers.com/news/the-influence-of-influencers.

13. Alex Cuadros, *Brazillionaires: The Godfathers of Modern Brazil* (Profile, 2016).

14. Economist, "Latin American Politicians Court Social-Media Stars."

15. Lucas Patschiki, "Os litores da nossa burguesia: o Mídia sem Máscara em atuação partidária (2002–2011)," Dissertação Universidade Estadual do Oeste do Paraná, 2012, https://tede.unioeste.br/handle/tede/1789.

16. Benjamin Teitelbaum, *War for Eternity: The Return of Traditionalism and the Rise of the Populist Right* (Penguin, 2021), 136.

17. Gilberto Calil, "Olavo de Carvalho and the Rise of the Far Right," *Argumentum* 13, no. 2 (2021): 64–81, https://www.redalyc.org/journal/4755/475571195007/movil.

18. Natalia Cruz, "Neofascism and Brazilian Conspirationism: The Media Without a Mask and the 'Axis of Evil'," *Comparative History Magazine* 13, no. 2 (2019): 216–57.

19. Calil, "Olavo de Carvalho."

20. Terrence McCoy, "He's the Rush Limbaugh of Brazil. He Has Bolsonaro's Ear. And He Lives in Rural Virginia," *Washington Post*, July 14, 2019, https://www.washingtonpost.com/world/the_americas/hes-the-rush-limbaugh-of-brazil-he-has-bolsonaros-ear-and-he-lives-in-rural-virginia/2019/07/14/4f73dee2-8ac4-11e9-8f69-a2795fca3343_story.html.

21. Calil, "Olavo de Carvalho."

22. Antonio Gramsci, *Selections from the Prison Notebooks* (Lawrence and Wishart, 1971).

23. Calil, "Olavo de Carvalho."

24. Mitchell Abidor, "The Gramsci of the Brazilian Right," *Dissent Magazine*, 2020, https://www.dissentmagazine.org/article/the-gramsci-of-the-brazilian-right.

25. McCoy, "He's the Rush Limbaugh of Brazil."

26. Olavo de Carvalho, in Patschiki, "Os litores da nossa burguesia," note 307.

27. McCoy, "He's the Rush Limbaugh of Brazil."

28. YouTube, "Deputado Flávio Bolsonaro entrega medalha Tiradentes a Olavo de Carvalho," July 13, 2012, https://youtu.be/CboJGA8oiLo.

29. YouTube, "O começo do 'Gabinete do Ódio': A primeira conversa entre Olavo de Carvalho com a família Bolsonaro," February 13, 2014, https://www.youtube.com/watch?v=ZMpoOJ-NAzg.

30. Mauro Porto and João Brant, "Social Media and the 2013 Protests in Brazil: The Contradictory Nature of Political Mobilization in the Digital Era," in Lina Dencik and Oliver Leistert, eds., *Critical Perspectives on Social Media and Protest* (Rowman & Littlefield, 2015), 181–202.

31. Stuart Davis, "MídiaNINJA and the Rise of Citizen Journalism in Brazil," in Eric Gordon and Paul Mihailides, eds., *Civic Media: Technology, Design, Practice* (MIT Press, 2016), 527–32.

32. Armando Boito and Alfredo Saad-Filho, "State, State Institutions, and Political Power in Brazil," *Latin American Perspectives* 43, no. 2 (2016): 190–206.

33. Porto and Brant, "Social Media and the 2013 Protests in Brazil."

34. Stuart Davis and Joe Straubhaar, "Producing Antipetismo: Media Activism and the Rise of the Radical, Nationalist Right in Contemporary Brazil," *International Communication Gazette*, 82, no. 1 (2020): 82–100.

35. Richard Romancini, "From 'Gay Kit' to 'Indoctrination Monitor': The Conservative Reaction in Brazil," *Contracampo—Brazilian Journal of Communication* 37, no. 2 (2018): 85–106.

36. Pragmatismo, "Filho de Bolsonaro pode sofrer condenação por comentário homofóbico," June 13, 2012, https://www.pragmatismopolitico.com.br/2012/06/filho-de-bolsonaro-pode-sofrer-condenacao-por-comentario-homofobico.html.

37. FamiliaBolsonaro, "Jair Bolsonaro: 'Sou preconceituoso, com muito orgulho'," July 4, 2011, https://web.archive.org/web/20110719042108/http:/familiabolsonaro.blogspot.com.

38. Ranier Bragon, "Bolsonaro defendeu esterilização de pobres para combater miséria e crime," *Folha de Sao Paulo*, June 11, 2018, https://www1.folha.uol.com.br/poder/2018/06/bolsonaro-defendeu-esterilizacao-de-pobres-para-combater-miseria-e-crime.shtml.

39. FamiliaBolsonaro, "Filmes Do Kit-Gay Rendem Mais De R$ 1,5 Milhão Para Ong LGBT," May 23, 2011, https://familiabolsonaro.blogspot.com/2011/05/filmes-do-kit-gay-rendem-mais-de-r-15.html; and Folha de Sao Paulo, "Preta Gil discutindo valores é algo humorístico, diz filho de deputado," March 29, 2011, https://www1.folha.uol.com.br/ilustrada/2011/03/895376-preta-gil-discutindo-valores-e-algo-humoristico-diz-filho-de-deputado.shtml.

40. Daniel Pereira and Ricardo Chapola, "Sniper do Planalto: como Carlos Bolsonaro atua nos bastidores da campanha," *Veja*, May 13, 2022, https://veja.abril.com.br/politica/sniper-do-planalto-como-carlos-bolsonaro-atua-nos-bastidores-da-campanha.

41. Carlos Bolsonaro, *Twitter*, October 18, 2018, https://x.com/CarlosBolsonaro/status/1052911803406147585.

42. Pereira and Chapola, "Sniper do Planalto."

43. Familia Bolsonaro, "Mais Votado No RJ Para a Camara e Terceiro Do Brasil, Bolsonaro Mira a Presidencia em 2018," October 8, 2014, https://familiabolsonaro.blogspot.com/2014/10/mais-votado-no-rj-para-camara-e.html.

44. Rose Santini et al., "When Machine Behavior Targets Future Voters: The Use of Social Bots to Test Narratives for Political Campaigns in Brazil," *International Journal of Communication* 15 (2021): 1220–43.

45. Santini et al., "When Machine Behavior Targets Future Voters."

46. Santini et al., "When Machine Behavior Targets Future Voters."

47. Rubens Valente, "WhatsApp Groups Simulate Military Organization and Share Support for Bolsonaro," *Folha de Sao Paulo*, October 26, 2018, https://www1.folha.uol.com.br/poder/2018/10/grupos-de-whatsapp-simulam-organizacao-militar-e-compartilham-apoio-a-bolsonaro.shtml.

48. See "Curso Online de Filosofia: Olavo De Carvalho," https://sl.seminariodefilosofia.org/assinatura-cof.

49. David Nemer, "The Human Infrastructure of Fake News in Brazil," *Items: Insights from the Social Sciences 6*, 2021, https://items.ssrc.org/extremism-online/the-human-infrastructure -of-fake-news-in-brazil.

50. Rafael Evangelista and Fernanda Bruno., "WhatsApp and Political Instability in Brazil: Targeted Messages and Political Radicalisation," *Internet Policy Review* 8, no. 4 (2019): 1–23.

51. Patricia Campos Mello, "Empresários bancam campanha contra o PT pelo WhatsApp," *Folha de Sao Paulo*, October 18, 2018, https://www1.folha.uol.com.br/poder/2018/10 /empresarios-bancam-campanha-contra-o-pt-pelo-whatsapp.shtml.

52. Alice Cravo, "Dono da SmartFit pedia em grupo de empresários dinheiro para impul-sionar mensagens contra o Legislativo," *O Globo*, May 27, 2020, https://oglobo.globo.com /politica/dono-da-smartfit-pedia-em-grupo-de-empresarios-dinheiro-para-impulsionar -mensagens-contra-legislativo-1-24449359.

53. Mello, "Empresários"; and Fernanda Mena, "Estudo aponta para automação no envio de mensagens e orquestração entre grupos de WhatsApp pró-Bolsonaro," *Folha de Sao Paulo*, October 26, 2018, https://www1.folha.uol.com.br/poder/2018/10/estudo-aponta-para -automacao-no-envio-de-mensagens-e-orquestracao-entre-grupos-de-whatsapp-pro -bolsonaro.shtml.

54. Claire Wardle et al., "An Evaluation of the Impact of a Collaborative Journalism Project on Brazilian Journalists and Audiences," *Comprova/First Draft*, 2019, https://firstdraftnews .org/wp-content/uploads/2019/06/Comprova-Full-Report-Final.pdf?x21167.

55. Mello, "Empresários."

56. Patricia Pasquini, "90 percent dos eleitores de Bolsonaro acreditaram em fake news, diz estudo," *Folha de Sao Paulo*, November 2, 2018, https://www1.folha.uol.com.br/poder/2018 /11/90-dos-eleitores-de-bolsonaro-acreditaram-em-fake-news-diz-estudo.shtml.

57. Mello, "Empresários."

58. Folha de Sao Paulo, "Carlos me pôs na Presidência e deveria ser ministro, diz Bolsonaro sobre filho," April 8, 2019, https://www1.folha.uol.com.br/poder/2019/04/carlos-me-pos -na-presidencia-e-deveria-ser-ministro-diz-bolsonaro-sobre-filho.shtml.

59. Talita Fernandes and Gabriela Sa Pessoa, "Bolsonaro escolhe Bebianno como ministro da Secretaria-Geral," *Folha de Sao Paulo*, November 21, 2018, https://www1.folha.uol.com.br /poder/2018/11/bolsonaro-escolhe-bebianno-como-ministro-da-secretaria-geral.shtml.

60. Manuel Castells, "A Network Theory of Power," *International Journal of Communication* 5, no. 15 (2011): 773–87, https://ijoc.org/index.php/ijoc/article/view/1136.

61. STF 4828 Inquiry Into Anti-Democratic Acts, 2021.

62. Talita Fernandes, "Bolsonaro diz que tendência é indicação de filho para Secom mor-rer," *Folha de Sao Paulo*, November 22, 2018, https://www1.folha.uol.com.br/poder/2018/11 /bolsonaro-diz-que-tendencia-e-que-indicacao-de-filho-para-secom-morra.shtml.

63. Nemer, "The Human Infrastructure of Fake News in Brazil."

64. Roula Khalaf et al., "The Rise of 'o3': Bolsonaro's Third Son Is Crucial Link to Trump's Inner Circle," *Financial Times*, July 31, 2022, https://www.ft.com/content /4f150c07-41d7-4021-a911-a70ecacacb08.

65. Igor Mello, "PF aponta como o 'gabinete do ódio' se expandiu além do Palácio do Plan-alto," *UOL*, June 13, 2021, https://noticias.uol.com.br/politica/ultimas-noticias/2021/06/13/gabinete-do-odio.htm.

66. Ana Costa, "Who Is Filipe Martins, the Eyes and Ears of Olavo de Carvalho in Plan-alto?," *O Globo*, March 28, 2019, https://oglobo.globo.com/epoca/quem-filipe-martins-os-olhos-ouvidos-de-olavo-de-carvalho-no-planalto-23556449.

67. Costa, "Who Is Filipe Martins."

68. For a longer report on the *Gabinete de Odio*, see Patricia Campos Mello, *A máquina do ódio: notas de uma repórter sobre fake news e violência digital* (Companhia das Letras, 2020).

69. Talita Fernandes, "Após vencer com uso das redes, Bolsonaro estuda comunicação profissional," *Folha de Sao Paulo*, November 19, 2018, https://www1.folha.uol.com.br/poder/2018/11/apos-vencer-com-uso-das-redes-bolsonaro-estuda-comunicacao-profissional.shtml.

70. Folha de Sao Paulo, "Novo chanceler, Ernesto Araújo foi indicado por Olavo de Carvalho," November 14, 2018, https://www1.folha.uol.com.br/mundo/2018/11/novo-chanceler-ernesto-araujo-foi-indicado-por-olavo-de-carvalho.shtml.

71. Patricia Campos Mello, "Chefe de departamento do Itamaraty usa blog para fazer cam-panha para Bolsonaro," *Folha de Sao Paulo*, October 1, 2018, https://www1.folha.uol.com.br/mundo/2018/10/chefe-de-departamento-do-itamaraty-usa-blog-para-fazer-campanha-para-bolsonaro.shtml.

72. Brian Winter, "Jair Bolsonaro's Guru," *Americas Quarterly*, December 17, 2018, https://www.americasquarterly.org/article/jair-bolsonaros-guru.

73. Nathaniel Gleicher, "Removing Coordinated Inauthentic Behavior," *Meta*, July 8, 2020, https://about.fb.com/news/2020/07/removing-political-coordinated-inauthentic-behavior.

74. STF 4781, Airton Vieira Report, from testimony of Congressman Heitor Rodrigo Pereira Freire, February 5, 2020.

75. Talita Fernandes, "Bolsonaro escolhe 'discípulo' de Olavo de Carvalho como assessor inter-nacional," *Folha de Sao Paulo*, January 3, 2019, https://www1.folha.uol.com.br/mundo/2019/01/bolsonaro-escolhe-discipulo-de-olavo-de-carvalho-como-assessor-internacional.shtml.

76. Por Amanda Ribeiro and Luiz Fernando Menezes, "Jornal da Cidade Online usa perfis apócrifos para atacar políticos e magistrados," *Jornal da Cidade*, July 4, 2019, https://www.aosfatos.org/noticias/jornal-da-cidade-online-usa-perfis-apocrifos-para-atacar-politicos-e-magistrados.

77. Patricia Campos Mello, "Site campeão de compartilhamentos no WhatsApp e no Telegram lidera comunicação bolsonarista," *Folha de Sao Paulo*, August 16, 2021, https://www1.folha.uol.com.br/poder/2021/08/site-campeao-de-compartilhamentos-no-whatsapp-e-no-telegram-lidera-comunicacao-bolsonarista.shtml; and Ethel Rudnitzki et al., "Desinfor-mação eleitoral alcança 30 milhões impulsionada por Telegram, WhatsApp e anúncios do Google," September 19, 2022, https://www.aosfatos.org/noticias/desinformacao-eleitoral-alcanca-30-milhoes-impulsionada-por-telegram-whatsapp-e-anuncios-do-google.

78. Victor Bursztyn and Larry Birnbaum, "Thousands of Small, Constant Rallies: A Large-Scale Analysis of Partisan WhatsApp Groups," *ASONAM* 19 (2019): 484–88, https://doi.org/10.1145/3341161.3342905.

79. Thais Lazzeri, "Denialist Film About the Environment in Brazil Is One of the Top 10 Most-Posted Videos on Telegram," *InfoAmazonia*, January 26, 2022, https://infoamazonia .org/en/2022/01/26/telegram-extrema-direita-fake-news-meio-ambiente.

80. Marcelo Rocha, "Moraes, do STF, concede prisão domiciliar ao blogueiro bolsonarista Oswaldo Eustáquio," January 26, 2021, https://www1.folha.uol.com.br/poder/2021/01/moraes -do-stf-concede-prisao-domiciliar-ao-blogueiro-bolsonarista-oswaldo-eustaquio.shtml.

81. João Barbosa, "From the New Right to Bolsonarism: Uses of the Brazilian Military Dictatorship by the YouTube Channel Folha Política" (master's thesis, Federal University of Goiás, Goiânia, 2022), https://repositorio.bc.ufg.br/tede/items/da0703a7-12bf-4130-a758-2f7343aa0e1e.

82. Olavo de Carvalho, "Bernardo Küster—No quintal do Olavão," *YouTube*, 2019, https:// www.youtube.com/watch?v=V_gdMyzMN3w.

83. Center for Countering Digital Hate, "The Disinformation Dozen: Why Platforms Must Act on Twelve Leading Online Anti-Vaxxers," 2022, https://counterhate.com/wp-content /uploads/2022/05/210324-The-Disinformation-Dozen.pdf.

84. STF 4781, Airton Vieira Report. From testimony of Congresswoman Joice Hasselmann, December 17, 2019. See also Poder 360, "List of Followers Became Evidence in STF Investigation," August 29, 2022, https://www.poder360.com.br/justica/lista-de-seguidores -virou-prova-em-inquerito-do-stf.

85. Joice Hasselmann, "É CRIME!," Evidence submitted to CPMI Fake News Inquiry, 2019, 10.

86. STF 4781, Airton Vieira Report.

87. Paula Ramón, "The Fake-News Kingpin of Brazil," *Columbia Journalism Review*, April 13, 2022, https://www.cjr.org/analysis/brazil-bolsonaro-lula-allan-dos-santos.php.

88. STF 4781, Airton Vieira Report.

89. Fabio Zanini, "Google Says That Bolsonarist Allan dos Santos Acts Disloyally, Toxic and Romanticizes Violence," *Folha de Sao Paulo*, August 20, 2021, https://www1.folha.uol.com .br/colunas/painel/2021/08/google-diz-que-bolsonarista-allan-dos-santos-age-de-modo -desleal-toxico-e-romantiza-violencia.shtml.

90. Alice Maciel and Ana Beatriz Anjos, "Acusado de financiar fake news, Fakhoury deu din-heiro a ONG dos Weintraub e Força Brasil," *El Pais*, September 30, 2021, https://brasil .elpais.com/brasil/2021-09-30/acusado-de-financiar-fake-news-fakhoury-deu-dinheiro -a-ong-dos-weintraub-e-forca-brasil.html.

91. See "Critica Nacional," 2020, archived at https://web.archive.org/web/20200426154748 /https://criticanacional.com.br/; and Jose Fucs, "Rede bolsonarista 'jacobina' promove lin-chamento virtual até de aliados," *Estadao de Sao Paulo*, March 16, 2019, https://www.estadao .com.br/politica/rede-bolsonarista-jacobina-promove-linchamento-virtual-ate-de-aliados.

92. Mello, "Empresários."

93. Igor Mello and Juliana Dal Piva, "Líder do 'gabinete do ódio' repassou vídeos para canal bolsonarista," *UOL*, July 6, 2021, https://noticias.uol.com.br/politica/ultimas-noticias/2021 /06/07/lider-gabinete-odio-pf.htm.

94. O Globo, "Hate Office Servers Fed Bolsonarist Website That Profited Up to \$R100,000 Per Month," April 12, 2020, https://oglobo.globo.com/politica/servidores-de-gabinete-do -odio-alimentavam-sites-bolsonaristas-que-lucravam-ate-100-mil-por-mes-24781083.

95. Por Breno Pires and Rafael Moraes Moura, "Alvorada 'é local de apoiadores,' diz youtuber bolsonarista que faturou R$ 1,76 milhão," *Estadao de Sao Paulo*, April 12, 2020, https://www.estadao.com.br/politica/alvorada-e-local-de-apoiadores-diz-youtuber-bolsonarista-que-faturou-r-1-76-milhao.

96. Reynaldo Turollo Jr., "Channels Targeted by the TSE Earned R$10 Million on YouTube in Two Years," *Veja*, September 20, 2021, https://veja.abril.com.br/politica/canais-na-mira-do-tse-faturaram-r-10-milhoes-no-youtube-em-dois-anos.

97. Painel, "Canal bolsonarista alvo do TSE e STF recebeu cerca de R$ 200 mil só em publicidade antes de ser excluído do YouTube," *Folha de Sao Paulo*, August 22, 2021, https://www1.folha.uol.com.br/colunas/painel/2021/08/canal-bolsonarista-alvo-do-tse-e-stf-recebeu-cerca-de-r-200-mil-so-em-publicidade-antes-de-ser-excluido-do-youtube.shtml.

98. Luiza Bandeira, "Well-Known Disinfo Spreader on YouTube Reappears Ahead of Brazilian Local Elections," *DFR Lab*, October 20, 2020, https://medium.com/dfrlab/well-known-disinfo-spreader-on-youtube-reappears-ahead-of-brazilian-local-elections-cc495dff79f8.

99. Patricia Campos Mello, "Verba publicitária de Bolsonaro irrigou sites de jogos de azar e de fake news na reforma da Previdência," May 9, 2020, https://www1.folha.uol.com.br/poder/2020/05/verba-publicitaria-de-bolsonaro-irrigou-sites-de-jogos-de-azar-e-de-fake-news-na-reforma-da-previdencia.shtml.

100. Paula Soprana and Patricia Campos Mello, "Movimento contra fake news chega ao Brasil e cobra 30 empresas por anúncios em site suspeito," May 22, 2020, https://www1.folha.uol.com.br/mercado/2020/05/movimento-que-cobra-empresas-por-anuncios-em-sites-de-fake-news-chega-ao-brasil.shtml.

101. Painel, "Após reclamação de Carlos Bolsonaro, Banco do Brasil volta atrás e mantém publicidade em site," *Folha de Sao Paulo*, May 21, 2020, https://www1.folha.uol.com.br/colunas/painel/2020/05/apos-reclamacao-de-carlos-bolsonaro-banco-do-brasil-volta-atras-e-mantem-publicidade-em-site.shtml.

102. "Inquerito Policial: 2021.0052061 (INQ_STF n° 4874-DF)," n.d., https://static.poder360.com.br/2022/02/peca_257_Inq_4874-40-45.pdf.

103. Congress Nacional, "CPMI—Fake News," n.d., http://legis.senado.leg.br/sdleg-getter/documento/download/00cd6400-c47c-4c60-ab45-1ed4f930840a.

104. UOL, "Polícia Investiga Cabeça De Porco Enviada De 'Presente' A Deputada Eleita," December 5, 2018, https://www.congressoemfoco.com.br/noticia/32945/policia-investiga-cabeca-de-porco-enviada-de-presente-a-deputada-eleita; and Joice Hasselmann, *Twitter*, November 30, 2018, https://x.com/joicehasselmann/status/1068554791633203201.

105. Hasselmann, "É CRIME!."

106. Folha de Sao Paulo, "Carlos Bolsonaro fez 'macumba psicológica' na cabeça do presidente, diz Bebianno," February 19, 2019, https://www1.folha.uol.com.br/poder/2019/02/carlos-bolsonaro-fez-macumba-psicologica-na-cabeca-do-presidente-diz-bebianno.shtml.

107. Luiza Bandeira, "How Bolsonaro's disinfo machine targeted Brazil's pro-quarantine health minister," *DFR Lab*, April 21, 2020, https://tinyurl.com/yhxynwbb.

108. Monica Bergamo, "Doria recebe ameaça de morte e faz boletim de ocorrência," *Folha de Sao Paulo*, March 26, 2020, https://www1.folha.uol.com.br/colunas/monicabergamo/2020/03/doria-recebe-ameaca-de-morte-e-fara-boletim-de-ocorrencia.shtml.

109. Patricia Campos Mello, "2021 Reuters Memorial Lecture: How to Rescue Journalism in an Age of Lies," University of Oxford, June 8, 2021, https://reutersinstitute.politics.ox.ac.uk/news/full-text-patricia-campos-mellos-2021-reuters-memorial-lecture-how-rescue-journalism-age-lies.

110. David Nemer, "Eduardo E Flávio Bolsonaro São Os Criadores De Grupos De Whatsapp De Mentiras Contra Jornalista Da Folha," *The Intercept*, February 14, 2020, https://www.intercept.com.br/2020/02/14/eduardo-flavio-bolsonaro-criadores-whatsapp-mentiras-jornalista.

111. STF 4781, Airton Vieira Report. From testimony of Congressman Alexandre Frota, December 17, 2019.

112. I. Kalil and R. M. Santini, "Coronavírus, Pandemia, Infodemia e Política," *FESPSP*, 2020, https://sxpolitics.org/ptbr/wp-content/uploads/sites/2/2020/04/Coronavirus-e-infodemia.pdf.

113. Kalil and Santini, "Coronavirus."

114. Carolina. Linhares, "Na Paulista, apoiadores de Bolsonaro atacam Congresso e STF e chamam coronavírus de 'mentira'," *Folha de Sao Paulo*, March 15, 2020, https://www1.folha.uol.com.br/poder/2020/03/na-paulista-apoiadores-de-bolsonaro-atacam-congresso-e-stf-e-chamam-coronavirus-de-mentira.shtml.

115. Ricardo Coletta and Renato Onofre, "Não queremos negociar nada, diz Bolsonaro em ato pró-intervenção militar diante do QG do Exército," *Folha de Sao Paulo*, April 19, 2020, https://www1.folha.uol.com.br/poder/2020/04/nao-queremos-negociar-nada-diz-bolsonaro-em-carreata-anti-isolamento-em-brasilia.shtml.

116. Folha de Sao Paulo, "Veja possíveis crimes cometidos por Bolsonaro em ato pró-golpe; leia discurso comentado," April 20, 2020, https://www1.folha.uol.com.br/poder/2020/04/veja-possiveis-crimes-cometidos-por-bolsonaro-em-ato-pro-golpe-leia-discurso-comentado.shtml.

117. STF 4828 Inquiry, n.d., https://portal.stf.jus.br/processos/detalhe.asp?incidente=5895367.

118. Elon Musk. *X*, August 30, 2024, https://x.com/elonmusk/status/1829308905177956551; and Elon Musk. *X*, August 30, 2024, https://x.com/elonmusk/status/1829625536777277754.

119. Constança Rezende and Renato Machado, "Eduardo Bolsonaro ofereceu ajuda para blogueiro investigado pelo STF deixar o país, apontam mensagens," *Folha de Sao Paulo*, October 1, 2021, https://www1.folha.uol.com.br/poder/2021/10/eduardo-bolsonaro-ofereceu-ajuda-para-blogueiro-investigado-pelo-stf-deixar-o-pais-apontam-mensagens.shtml.

120. Julie Ricard and Juliano Medeiros, "Using Misinformation as a Political Weapon: COVID-19 and Bolsonaro in Brazil," *Harvard Kennedy School Misinformation Review*, April 17, 2020, https://doi.org/10.37016/mr-2020-013.

121. Felipe Soares et al., "Research Note: Bolsonaro's Firehose: How Covid-19 Disinformation on WhatsApp Was Used to Fight a Government Political Crisis in Brazil," *Harvard Kennedy School Misinformation Review*, January 29, 2021, https://doi.org/10.37016/mr-2020-54.

122. Paulo Fonseca et al., "Demarcating Patriotic Science on Digital Platforms: Covid-19, Chloroquine and the Institutionalisation of Ignorance in Brazil," *Science as Culture* 31, no. 4 (2022): 530–54.

123. Sandro Cabral et al., "The Disastrous Effects of Leaders in Denial: Evidence from the COVID-19 Crisis in Brazil," *SSRN*, 2021, https://ssrn.com/abstract=3836147.

124. WHO, "COVID-19. Data Up to 29 March 2023," https://data.who.int/dashboards/covid19/cases.

125. Johns Hopkins Coronavirus Resource Center, "Mortality Analyses," 2023, https://coronavirus.jhu.edu/data/mortality.

126. Jan Rocha, "Bolsonaro's Genocide of the Yanomami," *Latin America Bureau*, January 27, 2023, https://lab.org.uk/bolsonaros-genocide-of-the-yanomami.

127. Oswaldo Braga de Souza, "What You Need to Know to Understand the Crisis in the Yanomami Indigenous Land," *Instituto Socioambiental*, January 31, 2023, https://www.socioambiental.org/en/socio-environmental-news/What-you-need-to-know-to-understand-the-crisis-in-the-Yanomami-indigenous-land.

128. Sanya Mansoor, "Why Lula Accused Bolsonaro of 'Genocide' Against Brazil's Yanomami People," *Time*, January 23, 2023, https://time.com/6249369/lula-accuses-bolsonaro-genocide-yanomami.

129. Conectas, "Yanomami Tragedy: The Warnings That the Bolsonaro Government Didn't Want to Hear," January 30, 2023, https://www.conectas.org/en/noticias/yanomami-tragedy-the-warnings-that-the-bolsonaro-government-didnt-want-to-hear.

130. Folha Politica, "Bolsonaro marcha ao lado de General Heleno e de ministro da Defesa e presencia ceri," *YouTube*, August 18, 2019, https://www.youtube.com/watch?v=m2e8pOIpI3c&feature=youtu.be.

131. Leandro Melito et al., "Amazônia inventada: 70 milhões de visualizações no Youtube, cliques e dinheiro em vídeos que desinformam sobre a floresta e os povos indígenas," *InfoAmazonia*, April 14, 2022, https://infoamazonia.org/2022/04/14/amazonia-inventada-70-milhoes-de-visualizacoes-no-youtube-cliques-e-dinheiro-em-videos-que-desinformam-sobre-a-floresta-e-os-povos-indigenas.

132. Lupa, "Pare e reflita: quantas mensagens suspeitas sobre desmatamento você já recebeu?," October 11, 2022, https://lupa.uol.com.br/institucional/2022/10/11/pare-e-reflita-desmatamento.

133. Bruno Nomura et al., "Com mentiras recicladas, Bolsonaro usa Jovem Pan para atacar urnas e se defender de acusações de corrupção," *Lupa*, September 6, 2022, https://lupa.uol.com.br/jornalismo/2022/09/06/jovem-pan-entrevista-bolsonaro; and Bruno Nomura et al., "Em reunião com embaixadores, Bolsonaro insiste em mentiras para atacar sistema eleitoral," *Lupa*, July 18, 2022, https://lupa.uol.com.br/jornalismo/2022/07/18/bolsonaro-embaixadores-sistema-eleitoral.

134. For example, see Italo Rômany, "Lula's Video Is Manipulated to Make It Appear That the Former President Was 'Drunk'," *Lupa*, September 3, 2021. See also Marcelo Alves et al., "Disinformation and 2022 Elections in Brazil: Lessons Learned from a South-to-South Context," *INCT*, 2023, https://inctdsi.uff.br/wp-content/uploads/sites/699/2023/11/Disinformation-and-2022-Elections-in-Brazil.pdf.

135. Alves et al., "Disinformation and 2022 Elections in Brazil."

136. Paula Costa, "Ombudsman: Não há chance de luz quando se questiona a existência do túnel," *Lupa*, October 14, 2022, https://lupa.uol.com.br/jornalismo/2022/10/14/ombudsman-paula-cesarino-costa-existencia-do-tunel.

137. Thaisa Galvao, "Deputada Carla Zambelli saca arma e entra em bar do Jardins, em São Paulo," *YouTube*, October 29, 2022, https://www.youtube.com/watch?v=R1RqBpoPCdo.

138. Gabriel Amora, "Atlas Poll: Only 56.4 Percent of Brazilians Believe in Lula's Victory," *Focus*, January 10, 2023, https://focuspoder.com.br/pesquisa-atlas-56-4-dos-brasileiros-acreditam -que-lula-venceu-as-eleicoes-enquanto-39-7-apontam-que-nao.

139. Arthur Stabile, "Com 214 casos em 2022, violência política cresceu 335 percent no Brasil em três anos," *O Globo*, July 13, 2022, https://g1.globo.com/politica/eleicoes/2022/noticia /2022/07/13/com-214-casos-em-2022-violencia-politica-cresceu-335percent-no-brasil-em -tres-anos.ghtml.

140. Liz Nobrega, "Brasileiros apoiam combate à desinformação, mas não confiam nas instituições que o propõem," *Desinformante*, August 3, 2022, https://desinformante.com.br/brasileiros -apoiam-combate-a-desinformacao-mas-nao-confiam-nas-instituicoes-que-o-propoem.

141. Estadao de Sao Paulo, "Brasil é o sétimo mais polarizado entre 28 países analisados, diz pesquisa," January 26, 2023, https://www.estadao.com.br/politica/pesquisa-edelman-trust -barometer-2023-polarizacao-brasil.

7. THE GOSPEL TRUTH: AMLO's MEXICO

1. Jorge Muñoz and Pablo Aguirre, "Morning Conferences: From Dialogue to the Sacrificial Rite and the Formation of Scapegoats," *Journal of Foreign Languages and Cultures* 5, no. 2 (2021): 74–89.

2. Luis Estrada, *El imperio de los otros datos: Tres años de falsedades y engaños desde palacio*, 2022; *Financial Times*, "AMLO's Media Naming and Shaming Shows a Flexible Approach to Facts," July 6, 2021, https://www.ft.com/content/80338157-156c-401c-8797-1a735e83c80a; and Spin TCP, "Sigue el análisis de SPIN-TCP, sobre las conferencias de prensa matu-tinas del presidente Andrés Manuel López Obrador," 2019, http://www.spintcp.com /conferenciapresidente.

3. Mañanera, June 30, 2021, https://lopezobrador.org.mx/2021/06/30/version-estenografica -de-la-conferencia-de-prensa-matutina-del-presidente-andres-manuel-lopez-obrador-563.

4. *Financial Times*, "AMLO's Media Naming and Shaming."

5. Mañanera, June 30, 2021.

6. Reuters, "Mexico, the Deadliest Country for Journalists in 2022: Watchdog," December 14, 2022, https://www.reuters.com/world/americas/mexico-deadliest-country-journalists-2022 -watchdog-2022-12-14/.

7. Mañanera, June 30, 2021.

8. Associated Press, "Press Groups Slam Mexican Leader's 'Lie of the Week' Contest," July 3, 2021, https://uk.news.yahoo.com/press-groups-slam-mexican-leaders-003755623.html.

9. George Grayson, *Mexican Messiah: Andrés Manuel López Obrador* (Pennsylvania State University Press, 2007).

10. Grayson, *Mexican Messiah*.

11. Cas Mudde and Cristóbal Kaltwasser, *Populism: A Very Short Introduction* (Oxford University Press, 2017).

12. Grayson, *Mexican Messiah*.

13. Michael Sproule, "Authorship and Origins of the Seven Propaganda Devices: A Research Note," *Rhetoric and Public Affairs* 4, no. 1 (2001): 135–43.

14. Reuters, "Mexico's Presidential Jet Sold to Tajikistan," April 12, 2023, https://www.reuters.com/world/americas/mexicos-presidential-jet-sold-tajikistan-latest-twist-political-saga-2023-04-21/#:~:text=MEXICO%20CITY%2C%20April%2020%20(Reuters,the%20excesses%20of%20his%20predecessors.

15. Grayson, *Mexican Messiah*.

16. Paolo Demuru, "Conspiracy Theories, Messianic Populism and Everyday Social Media Use in Contemporary Brazil: A Glocal Semiotic Perspective," *Glocalism: Journal of Culture, Politics and Innovation* 3 (2020), https://doi.org/10.12893/gjcpi.2020.3.12.

17. William Berg, "The Rhetoric of Narcissism: Trump's Tweets on Writing," *Rhetoric and Public Affairs* 25, no. 2 (2022): 91–117; Business Standard, "Sycophancy Bug Bites BJP Leaders, Hail Modi as 'God's Gift' and 'Messiah'," March 21, 2016, https://www.business-standard.com/article/current-affairs/sycophancy-bug-bites-bjp-leaders-hail-modi-as-god-s-gift-and-messiah-116032100145_1.html; and Ben Winter, "Messiah Complex: How Brazil Made Bolsonaro," *Foreign Affairs* 99, no. 5 (2020), https://www.foreignaffairs.com/articles/brazil/2020-08-11/jair-bolsonaro-messiah-complex.

18. Business Standard, "Sycophancy Bug Bites BJP Leaders."

19. David Smith, "'I Am Your Retribution': Trump Rules Supreme at CPAC as He Relaunches Bid for White House," *Guardian*, March 5, 2021, https://www.theguardian.com/us-news/2023/mar/05/i-am-your-retribution-trump-rules-supreme-at-cpac-as-he-relaunches-bid-for-white-house.

20. Gregor Fitzl et al., eds., *Populism and the Crisis of Democracy*. Vol. 1, *Concepts and Theory* (Routledge, 2019).

21. Grayson, *Mexican Messiah*, 173 and 167.

22. Kathleen Bruhn, "'To Hell with Your Corrupt Institutions': AMLO and Populism in Mexico," in Cas Mudde and Cristóbal Kaltwasser, eds., *Populism in Europe and the Americas: Threat or Corrective for Democracy?* (Cambridge University Press, 2012), 88–112.

23. Felipe Higaredo, "AMLO's Social Communication Strategies: Are They Enhancing the Deliberative Quality of the Mexican Public Sphere?," July 2019, https://doi.org/10.13140/RG.2.2.17925.88808.

24. Higaredo, "AMLO's Social Communication Strategies."

25. Mark Stevenson, "Mexican President Mounts Campaign Against Social Media Bans," Associated Press, January 15, 2021, https://apnews.com/article/donald-trump-marcelo-ebrard-mexico-media-social-media-a5303f532810447575ccf2af6692a2d4.

26. Andrea Diaz and Jessica Campisi, "Mexico Goes to the Polls This Weekend," *CNN*, July 2, 2018, https://edition.cnn.com/2018/06/27/americas/mexico-political-deaths-election-season-trnd/index.html.

27. The first three "transformations," according to AMLO, were the Mexican War of Independence (1810–1821), the Reform War (1858–1861), and the Mexican Revolution (1910–1917).
28. Jan Albert Hootsen, "López Obrador's Anti-Press Rhetoric Leaves Mexico's Journalists Feeling Exposed," *Committee to Protect Journalists*, May 6, 2019, https://cpj.org/2019/05/mexico-president-lopez-obrador-press-rhetoric-threatened/.
29. Cyntia Diaz and Nacha Cattan, "Twitter Mobs Bash Those Who Dare Challenge AMLO in Mexico Press," *Bloomberg*, April 12, 2019, https://www.bloomberg.com/news/articles/2019-04-12/twitter-mobs-bash-those-who-dare-challenge-amlo-in-mexico-press.
30. Tom Philips, "Mexico media say president's attacks on journalists are 'invitation to violence'," *Guardian*, December 21, 2022, https://www.theguardian.com/world/2022/dec/21/mexico-journalist-safety-andres-manuel-lopez-obrador-amlo#:~:text=Some%20believe%20such%20verbal%20attacks,during%20his%20predecessor's%20entire%20administration.
31. Elena López-Dóriga, "The Skyrocketing Number of Journalists Murdered in Mexico: AMLO's Polemic Against Reporters," *Universidad de Navarra*, May 26, 2022, https://www.unav.edu/en/web/global-affairs/the-skyrocketing-number-of-journalists-murdered-in-mexico#:~:text=Article%2019%2C%20a%20civil%20organisation,in%20their%20first%20three%20years.
32. Phillips, "Mexico Media."
33. Mañanera, June 30, 2021.
34. Mañanera, May 4, 2022, https://www.youtube.com/watch?v=20Xp4eLEm14.
35. Mañanera, November 3, 2021, https://www.youtube.com/watch?v=HJVwXENSyZg; and World Justice Project Rule of Law Index 2021, https://worldjusticeproject.org/sites/default/files/documents/WJP-INDEX-2021.pdf.
36. Mañanera, November 3, 2021.
37. Mañanera, May 4, 2022.
38. Mañanera, June 30, 2021; and "Noticias falsas contra AMLO trass u visita a EUA," *Capital 21 TV*, July 20, 2022, https://www.facebook.com/Capital21/videos/5395077257181678.
39. Mañanera, August 2, 2023, https://www.youtube.com/watch?v=hzDitgpXHgk.
40. Mañanera, April 26, 2023, https://www.youtube.com/watch?v=zgP7_62lKhs.
41. Mañanera, June 30, 2021; and Mañanera, November 3, 2021.
42. Mañanera, May 18, 2022, https://www.youtube.com/watch?v=EIWAkjgIoyw.
43. Joel Simon, "Defending Vanguard Journalists," in Anya Schiffrin, ed., *Media Capture: How Money, Digital Platforms, and Governments Control the News* (Columbia University Press, 2021), 277–90.
44. Muñoz, and Aguirre, "Morning Conferences."
45. Kevin Celestino, "Las 'mañaneras' de AMLO y los abusos de la comunicacion presidencial," *Centro de Estudios Espinosa Yglesias*, 2022, https://ceey.org.mx/las-mananeras-de-amlo-y-los-abusos-de-la-comunicacion-presidencial.
46. Ioan Grillo, "Mexico, the Coronavirus and the Hugging President," *New York Times*, March 23, 2020, https://www.nytimes.com/2020/03/23/opinion/mexico-coronavirus-amlo.html.
47. Grillo, "Mexico, the Coronavirus and the Hugging President."

48. Estrada, *El imperio rio de los otros datos*; and Spin TCP, "Sigue el análisis de SPIN-TCP."

49. Muñoz and Aguirre, "Morning Conferences."

50. Muñoz and Aguirre, "Morning Conferences"; and Estrada, "El imperio *rio de los otros datos*."

51. Muñoz and Aguirre, "Morning Conferences."

52. Muñoz and Aguirre, "Morning Conferences," 75.

53. Celestino, "Las 'mañaneras'."

54. @lopezobrador, X, January 31, 2024, https://twitter.com/lopezobrador; and @carlosloret, X, January 31, 2024, https://twitter.com/carlosloret?lang=en.

55. Mexico News Daily, "AMLO on Offensive After Story Reveals Son's Million-Dollar Home in US," February 1, 2022, https://mexiconewsdaily.com/news/amlos-sons -million-dollar-us-home/?lp_txn_id=297361.

56. César López Linares, "Mexico's President Reveals Journalist's Income," *LatAm Journalism Review*, February 15, 2022, https://latamjournalismreview.org/articles/mexicos-president -reveals-journalists-income-and-the-public-reacts-in-unprecedented-ways-on-social -media.

57. Mexico News Daily, "AMLO on Offensive."

58. Linares, "Mexico's President Reveals Journalist's Income."

59. Linares, "Mexico's President Reveals Journalist's Income."

60. "Carlos Loret de Mola's father denounces robbery; 'AMLO' message is left nailed with a knife," *ContentEngine Noticias Financieras* November 2, 2023, https://go.gale.com/ps/i .do?id=GALE%7CA771687363&sid=sitemap&v=2.1&it=r&p=IFME&sw=w&userGroup Name=anon%7Edf482d56&aty=open-web-entry.

61. Steve Devitt, "Porfirian Influence on Mexican Journalism: An Enduring Legacy of Economic Control," University of Montana, 1987, https://scholarworks.umt.edu/cgi /viewcontent.cgi?article=6120&context=etd.

62. United Nations, "Universal Declaration of Human Rights," n.d., https://www.un.org/en /about-us/universal-declaration-of-human-rights#:~:text=Article%2019,media%20and %20regardless%20of%20frontiers.

63. Article 19, "Mexico: AMLO Attacks ARTICLE 19 on World Press Freedom Day," May 4, 2023, https://www.article19.org/resources/mexico-amlo-attacks-article-19-on-world-press -freedom-day.

64. Mexico News Daily, "Article 19: Nearly 3,000 Attacks on Mexican Press Since 2018," September 20, 2023, https://mexiconewsdaily.com/news/article-19-nearly-3000-attacks -on-mexican-press-since-2018.

65. Article 19, "Mexico: AMLO Attacks ARTICLE 19"; and Associated Press. "Mexico President Complains US Is Funding Opposition," May 3, 2023, https://apnews.com/article /mexico-united-states-funding-organizations-098797034e179df1f42bedb9a8e7b682.

66. Grayson, *Mexican Messiah*, 6, 5.

67. El Pais, "Journalist Jorge Ramos Confronts López Obrador in La Mañanera," January 30, 2024, https://elpais.com/mexico/2024-01-30/el-periodista-jorge-ramos-confronta-a -lopez-obrador-en-la-mananera.html.

68. William Finnegan, "The Man Who Wouldn't Sit Down," *New Yorker*, September 28, 2015, https://www.newyorker.com/magazine/2015/10/05/the-man-who-wouldnt-sit-down.

69. Katie Reilly, "Here Are All the Times Donald Trump Insulted Mexico," *Time*, August 31, 2016, https://time.com/4473972/donald-trump-mexico-meeting-insult.

70. Meg James, "Journalist Jorge Ramos Detained and Released in Venezuela," *Los Angeles Times*, February 25, 2019, https://www.latimes.com/business/hollywood/la-fi-ct-jorge-ramos-univision-captive-venezuela-20190225-story.html.

71. Mañanera, April 15, 2019, https://www.youtube.com/watch?v=t5MXe7wqQro.

72. France 24, "For Media Covering Mexico's AMLO, Access Comes with Attacks," June 18, 2019, https://www.france24.com/en/20190618-media-covering-mexicos-amlo-access-comes-with-attacks.

73. Esther Mosqueda, "Authorities Must Protect the Director of Reform for Attacks Against Him," *Article 19*, April 25, 2019, https://articulo19.org/autoridades-deben-proteger-a-director-de-reforma-por-agresiones-en-su-contra.

74. Diaz and Cattan, "Twitter Mobs Bash Those Who Dare Challenge AMLO."

75. International Journalism Festival, "Rana Ayyub Receives Online Rape and Death Threats," January 28, 2022, https://www.journalismfestival.com/news/rana-ayyub-receives-online-rape-and-death-threats-third-mexican-journalist-killed-this-year-and-how-big-beef-is-fueling-the-amazons-destruction.

76. Diaz and Cattan, "Twitter Mobs Bash Those Who Dare Challenge AMLO."

77. Phillips, "Mexico Media."

78. Eduardo Dina, "AMLO se solidariza con Ciro Gómez Leyva tras ataque; antes dijo que por escucharlo podía salir un tumor," *El Universal*, December 16, 2022, https://www.eluniversal.com.mx/nacion/amlo-se-solidariza-con-ciro-gomez-leyva-tras-ataque-antes-dijo-que-por-escucharlo-podia-salir-un-tumor.

79. Dina, "AMLO se solidariza con Ciro Gómez Leyva tras ataque."

80. Natalie Kitroeff, "Gunmen Tried to Kill a Famous TV Anchor. Mexico's Leader Suggested It Was Staged," *New York Times*, December 21, 2022, https://www.nytimes.com/2022/12/21/world/americas/mexico-journalist-attack-ciro-gomez-leyva.html.

81. Article 19, "Mexico: AMLO Attacks ARTICLE 19"; and Phillips, "Mexico Media."

82. Jug Suraiya, "Messiah Modi," *Times of India*, September 24, 2013, https://timesofindia.indiatimes.com/blogs/jugglebandhi/messiah-modi.

83. Samantha Bradshaw et al., "Industrialized Disinformation: 2020 Global Inventory of Organized Social Media Manipulation," University of Oxford, 2020, https://demtech.oii.ox.ac.uk/research/posts/industrialized-disinformation; and Samuel Woolley and Philip Howard, *Computational Propaganda: Political Parties, Politicians and Political Manipulation on Social Media* (Oxford University Press, 2019).

84. Swati Chaturvedi, *I Am a Troll: Inside the Secret World of the BJP's Digital Army* (Juggernaut Books, 2016).

85. Lucina Melesio, "Mexico Tightens Its Belt, and the Press Feels the Squeeze," *Al Jazeera*, August 9, 2019, https://www.aljazeera.com/economy/2019/8/9/mexico-tightens-its-belt-and-the-press-feels-the-squeeze.

86. Signa Lab ITESO, "Democracy, Freedom of Expression and the Digital Sphere," February 28, 2019, https://signalab.iteso.mx/informes/informe_redamlove.html.

87. Melesio, "Mexico Tightens Its Belt."

88. Alberto Najar, "How Much Power Do the Peñabots, the Tweeters Who Combat Criticism in Mexico, Have?," *BBC News*, March 17, 2015, https://www.bbc.com/mundo /noticias/2015/03/150317_mexico_internet_poder_penabot_an; and J. M. Porup, "How Mexican Twitter Bots Shut Down Dissent," *Vice*, August 24, 2015, https://www.vice .com/en/article/how-mexican-twitter-bots-shut-down-dissent.

89. Economist, "Narendra Modi Is the World's Most Popular Leader," July 15, 2023, https:// www.economist.com/asia/2023/06/15/narendra-modi-is-the-worlds-most-popular-leader.

90. Taberez Neyazi and Ralph Shroeder, "Was the 2019 Indian Election Won by Digital Media?," *The Communication Review* 24, no. 2 (2021): 87–106.

91. Prasun Sonwalkar, "How London Techies Helped Modi Create Campaign Buzz," *Hindustan Times*, May 25, 2014, https://www.hindustantimes.com/india/how-london-techies -helped-modi-create-campaign-buzz/story-qyIwywmPnsRg3YohLtRBgL.html.

92. See https://www.narendramodi.in/mann-ki-baat.

93. Narendra Modi, "Mann Ki Baat: A Decade of Dialogue, Diversity, and Driving Social Change," February 15, 2024, https://www.narendramodi.in/mann-ki-baat-a-decade-of -dialogue-diversity-and-driving-social-change-579475.

94. Economic Times, "Mann Ki Baat Transformed Country's Mindset, Initiated Mass Movements on Social Causes: Report," May 1, 2023, https://economictimes.indiatimes.com /news/politics-and-nation/mann-ki-baat-transformed-countrys-mindset-initiated-mass -movements-on-social-causes-report/articleshow/99915907.cms?from=mdr.

95. NDTV, "Through Mann Ki Baat, Mass Movements Came Into Being: PM in Episode 100," April 30, 2023, https://www.ndtv.com/india-news/pm-modis-100th-mann-ki -baat-address-today-to-go-global-live-10-points-3991795.

96. Swati Chaturvedi, "Mute Modi: Why Is the PM Terrified of Holding Even a Single Press Conference?," *The Wire*, January 4, 2018, https://thewire.in/politics/narendra-modi -press-conference.

97. Hans-Hartwig Blomeier and Luis Téllez, "Journalists Under Pressure," *Konrad Adernauer Stiftung*, September 28, 2021, https://www.kas.de/en/web/auslandsinformationen/artikel /detail/-/content/journalists-under-pressure.

98. X, "Permanent Suspension of @realDonaldTrump," January 8, 2021, https://blog.x.com /en_us/topics/company/2020/suspension.

99. Klaus Kamps, *Commander-in-Tweet: Donald Trump and the Deformed Presidency* (Springer, 2020).

100. Gideon Rachman, *The Age of the Strongman: How the Cult of the Leader Threatens Democracy Around the World* (The Bodley Head, 2022), 170.

101. Mark Stevenson, "Mexican President Mounts Campaign Against Social Media Bans," Associated Press, January 15, 2021, https://apnews.com/article/donald-trump-marcelo-ebrard -mexico-media-social-media-a5303f532810447575ccf2af6692a2d4.

102. Stevenson, "Mexican President Mounts Campaign Against Social Media Bans."

103. Mexico News Daily, "Facebookóatl? AMLO Moves to Create Social Media Network for Mexicans," January 14, 2021, https://mexiconewsdaily.com/news/amlo-moves-to-create -social-media-network.

104. Jacob Jarvis, "Fact Check: TRUTH Social Users Must Agree Not to 'Disparage' the Site," *Newsweek*, October 21, 2021, https://www.newsweek.com/fact-check-truth-social -users-terms-donald-trump-1641183.

105. Patrick Gerard et al., "Truth Social Dataset," *ICWSM 2023*, https://ojs.aaai.org/index.php /ICWSM/article/view/22211/21990.

106. Derek Hawkins et al., "How Trump Has Become Angrier and More Isolated on Truth Social," *Washington Post*, April 22, 2024.

107. The Independent, "Trump Shares Bizarre 'God Made Trump' Campaign Video," January 15, 2024, https://www.youtube.com/watch?v=lIYQfyA_1Hc.

108. Gerard et al., "Truth Social Dataset."

109. Jarvis, "Fact Check."

110. David Rosen, "Truth Social's Censorship, Terms of Service Defy Free Speech Promises," *Public Citizen*, September 2022, https://www.citizen.org/news/truth-socials-censorship -terms-of-service-defy-free-speech-promises.

111. Darragh Roche, "Donald Trump's TRUTH Social Prohibits 'Excessive Use of Capital Letters'," *Newsweek*, October 21, 2021, https://www.newsweek.com/donald-trump-truth -social-prohibits-excessive-capital-letters-social-media-1641107.

112. Kai Strittmatter, *We Have Been Harmonised: Life in China's Surveillance State* (Old Street, 2019).

113. Philip Dunwoody et al., "The Fascist Authoritarian Model of Illiberal Democracy," *Frontiers in Political Science* 4 (2022), https://www.frontiersin.org/journals/political-science /articles/10.3389/fpos.2022.907681/full.

114. Hannah Arendt, *Between Past and Future* (Viking, 1961), 257.

115. Associated Press, "Trump's Social Media Company Gains in Its First Day of Trading on Nasdaq," March 26, 2024, https://apnews.com/article/trump-media-truth-social-nasdaq -stock-106d7c423174ca1d7cc3cc9a3f3897a0; and Reuters, "Trump's Truth Social Reports $31.6m Net Loss Since Launch to Mid-2023," November 22, 2023, https://www.reuters.com /technology/trumps-truth-social-reports-net-loss-since-launch-mid-2023-2023-11-22.

116. Reporters Without Borders, "Index," 2023, https://rsf.org/en/index.

117. GB News, "GB News Stars Urge Viewers to Support The People's Channel," https://www .gbnews.com/news/gb-news-membership-stars-urge-viewers-to-support-the-peoples-channel.

118. Ofcom, "Ofcom Finds GB News in Breach of Broadcasting Rules for a Second Time," May 9, 2023, https://www.ofcom.org.uk/tv-radio-and-on-demand/broadcast-standards /ofcom-finds-gb-news-in-breach-of-broadcasting-rules-for-a-second-time.

119. Conrad Duncan, "Andrew Neil Says He Quit GB News Because He Didn't Want to Work for 'British Fox'," September 17, 2021, https://www.independent.co.uk/news/media /andrew-neil-gb-news-question-time-b1921793.html; and GB News, "Chancellor Jeremy Hunt Looks Ahead to His Spring Budget in a GB News EXCLUSIVE Interview," March 11, 2023, https://www.youtube.com/watch?v=CFLkzoney3Q.

120. GB News, "Chancellor Jeremy Hunt Looks Ahead."

121. Reporters Without Borders, "Index."

122. GB News, "Chancellor Jeremy Hunt Looks Ahead."

123. Sky News, "GB News Breached Impartiality Rules After Chancellor Interviewed by Tory MPs, Ofcom Finds," September 18, 2023, https://news.sky.com/story/gb-news-breached -impartiality-rules-after-chancellor-interviewed-by-tory-mps-ofcom-finds-12964234 #:~:text=GB%20News%20breached%20impartiality%20rules%20after%20Chancellor %20Jeremy%20Hunt%20was,Philip%20Davies%2C%20Ofcom%20has%20found.

124. Lewis Goodall, "GB News Isn't a News Channel—It's Tory TV," *The New Statesman*, November 8, 2023, https://www.newstatesman.com/comment/2023/11/gb-news-tory-tv; and William Mata, "How Many Tory MPs Have Joined GB News? Boris Johnson Set to Host Own Show," *The Standard*, October 27, 2023, https://www.standard.co.uk/news/uk /gb-news-tory-mps-how-many-boris-johnson-b1116498.html.

125. Jim Waterman, "No Rule to Stop Tory MP Interviewing Minister on GB News, Says Ofcom Boss," *Guardian*, September 28, 2023, https://www.theguardian.com/media/2023 /sep/28/no-rule-to-stop-tory-mp-interviewing-minister-on-gb-news-says-ofcom-boss.

126. Guardian, "Braverman Criticised for Shutting Out Guardian and BBC from Rwanda Trip," March 18, 2023, https://www.theguardian.com/politics/2023/mar/18/braverman -criticised-for-shutting-out-guardian-and-bbc-from-rwanda-trip.

127. Rowena Mason and Andrew Sparrow, "Political Journalists Boycott No 10 Briefing After Reporter Ban," *Guardian*, February 3, 2020, https://www.theguardian.com/politics /2020/feb/03/political-journalists-boycott-no-10-briefing-after-reporter-ban; and Charlotte Tobitt, "Guardian, FT and Mirror Journalists 'Excluded' from Home Secretary's Rwanda Trip," *Press Gazette*, April 25, 2022, https://pressgazette.co.uk/news/guardian-ft -mirror-journalists-rwanda-priti-patel.

128. Conrad Duncan, "Boris Johnson Hides in Fridge on Live TV While Dodging Interview on Eve of Election," *The Independent*, December 11, 2019, https://www.independent .co.uk/news/uk/politics/boris-johnson-hides-fridge-general-election-piers-morgan-good -morning-britain-live-tv-a9241631.html; and Jessica Ní Mhainín, "The UK and Media Freedom: An Urgent Need to Lead by Example," *The Foreign Policy Centre*, December 9, 2020, https://fpc.org.uk/the-uk-and-media-freedom-an-urgent-need-to-lead-by-example.

129. David Smith, "Camera Shy v Media Hog," *The Observer*, February 18, 2024, https://www .theguardian.com/us-news/2024/feb/18/biden-trump-media-coverage-journalism.

130. Andy Gregory, "Ofcom Investigating Whether David Lammy's LBC Show Broke Broadcasting Rules," *Independent*, April 9, 2024, https://www.independent.co.uk/news/uk /politics/david-lammy-lbc-ofcom-rules-labour-b2525058.html.

131. George Orwell, *Animal Farm* (New American Library, 1946), 120.

132. Viri Rios, "The Real Reasons for AMLO's Popularity," *Americas Quarterly*, December 13, 2023, https://americasquarterly.org/article/the-real-reasons-for-amlos-popularity.

133. Luis Rubio, *Unmasked: Lopez Obrador and the End of Make-Believe* (Wilson Center, 2019), B.

134. Rios, "The Real Reasons for AMLO's Popularity."

135. Ní Mhainín, "The UK and Media Freedom."

8. THE TRUTH-SEEKERS: VERIFYING GOVERNMENT NARRATIVES

1. Interview with Alex Murray, November 8, 2023.
2. James Tweedie, "Russia and China Lead Multipolar Development as US Pours Fuel on Israeli Fire," *Sputnik*, October 18, 2023, https://sputnikglobe.com/20231018/russia-and-china-lead-multipolar-development-as-us-pours-fuel-on-israeli-fire-1114295992.html.
3. Hannah Arendt, *Between Past and Future* (Viking, 1961), 229.
4. Dan Gillmor, *We the Media: Grassroots Journalism By the People, For the People* (O'Reilly Media, 2006).
5. UK House of Commons, "Report of the Official Account of the Bombings in London on 7th July 2005," *HC 1087*, May 11, 2006, https://assets.publishing.service.gov.uk/media/5a7c7bc84of0b626628ac62e/1087.pdf.
6. Interview with Alex Murray, November 8, 2023.
7. Jasper Jackson, "BBC Sets Up Team to Debunk Fake News," *Guardian*, January 12, 2017, https://www.theguardian.com/media/2017/jan/12/bbc-sets-up-team-to-debunk-fake-news.
8. Interview with Matthew Eltringham, January 5, 2024.
9. Lucas Graves et al., "Understanding Innovations in Journalistic Practice: A Field Experiment Examining Motivations for Fact-Checking," *Journal of Communication* 66, no. 1 (2016): 102–38.
10. "FactCheck.org: Celebrating 15 Years of Holding Politicians Accountable," *University of Pennsylvania Almanac* 65, no. 24 (2019), https://almanac.upenn.edu/articles/factcheck.org-celebrating-15-years-of-holding-politicians-accountable.
11. Duke Reporters' Lab, "Duke Lab Gives Fact-Checkers, Researchers New Tools to Thwart Misinformation," December 15, 2023, https://reporterslab.org/category/fact-checking.
12. Lucas Graves, "Boundaries Not Drawn: Mapping the Institutional Roots of the Global Fact-Checking Movement," *Journalism Studies* 19, no. 5 (2018): 613–31.
13. Mark Stencel et al., "Misinformation Spreads, But Fact-Checking Has Leveled Off," *Duke Reporters' Lab*, June 21, 2023, https://reporterslab.org/tag/international-fact-checking-network.
14. Poynter, "About the International Fact-Checking Network," https://www.poynter.org/ifcn/about-ifcn/.
15. IFCN, "Verified Signatories of the IFCN Code of Principles," February 2024, https://ifcncodeofprinciples.poynter.org/signatories.
16. Valérie Bélair-Gagnon et al., "Knowledge Work in Platform Fact-Checking Partnerships," *International Journal of Communication* 17 (2023): 1169–89.
17. Michelle Amazeen, "Journalistic Interventions: The Structural Factors Affecting the Global Emergence of Fact-Checking," *Journalism* 21, no. 1 (2020): 95–111.
18. Lucas Graves, *Deciding What's True* (Columbia University Press, 2016).
19. Tom McCarthy, "Zuckerberg Says Facebook Won't Be 'Arbiters of Truth' After Trump Threat," *Guardian*, May 28, 2020, https://www.theguardian.com/technology/2020/may/28/zuckerberg-facebook-police-online-speech-trump.
20. Eliot Higgins, *We Are Bellingcat* (Bloomsbury, 2021).

21. Nina Müller and Jenny Wiik, "From Gatekeeper to Gate-Opener: Open-Source Spaces in Investigative Journalism," *Journalism Practice* 17, no. 2 (2023): 197.

22. Paul Mena, "Principles and Boundaries of Fact-Checking: Journalists' Perceptions," *Journalism Practice* 13, no. 6 (2019): 657–72.

23. Mena, "Principles and Boundaries of Fact-Checking", 664.

24. Müller and Wiik, "From Gatekeeper to Gate-Opener", 202.

25. Timothy Cook, *Governing with the News: The News Media as a Political Institution* (University of Chicago Press, 2005), 70–71.

26. Müller and Wiik, "From Gatekeeper to Gate-Opener."

27. Johanna Wild, "These Are the Tools Open Source Researchers Say They Need," *Bellingcat*, August 12, 2022, https://www.bellingcat.com/resources/2022/08/12/these-are-the-tools-open -source-researchers-say-they-need.

28. Bélair-Gagnon et al., "Knowledge Work in Platform Fact-Checking Partnerships."

29. Rachel Leingang, "Meta's factchecking partners brace for layoffs", *Guardian*, January 8, 2025, https://www.theguardian.com/technology/2025/jan/08/meta-layoffs-factchecking -partners.

30. Dean Jones, "The Co-Founder of Snopes Wrote Dozens of Plagiarized Articles for the Fact-Checking Site," *Buzzfeed*, August 13, 2021, https://www.buzzfeednews.com/article /deansterlingjones/snopes-cofounder-plagiarism-mikkelson.

31. Pooja Chaudhuri, "Images of 2015 Pak Heatwave Viral as Casualties of the Balakot Airstrike by IAF," *Alt News*, March 7, 2019, https://www.altnews.in/images-of-2015-pak-heatwave -viral-as-casualties-of-the-balakot-airstrike-by-iaf.

32. Pooja Chaudhuri, "Old, Unrelated Video Shared as Muslims Licking Utensils to Spread Coronavirus Infection," *Alt News*, March 30, 2020, https://www.altnews.in/old-unrelated -video-shared-as-muslims-licking-utensils-to-spread-coronavirus-infection; Jignesh Patel and Ayushi Tiwari, "Truth About 'Sting' Claiming Shaheen Bagh Women Were Paid Rs 500: Alt News-News Laundry Joint Investigation," *Alt News*, February 4, 2020, https:// www.altnews.in/truth-about-sting-claiming-shaheen-bagh-women-were-paid-rs-500 -alt-news-newslaundry-joint-investigation; and Pooja Chaudhuri, "Jamia Violence: Media Misreport Wallet as 'Stone' in Student's Hand," *Alt News*, February 18, 2020, https://www .altnews.in/jamia-violence-media-misreport-wallet-as-stone-in-students-hand.

33. Arfa Sherwani, "Mohammed Zubair Is Being Targeted for the Work Alt News Does: Pratik Sinha," *The Wire*, September 8, 2020, https://thewire.in/media/alt-news -pratik-sinha-zubair-fir.

34. Prateek Goyal, "Now, a New Hate Campaign Against Zubair with Wild Claims About His Time in Jail," *News Laundry*, November 22, 2023, https://www.newslaundry.com /2023/11/22/now-a-new-hate-campaign-against-zubair-with-wild-claims-about-his-time -in-jail.

35. "Case 3:23-cv-00571." In the United States District Court for the Western District of Louisiana Monroe Division, May 2, 2023, paragraph 1, America First Legal, https://media .aflegal.org/wp-content/uploads/2023/05/09040857/Doc-1-Complaint.pdf?_ga=2.180847458 .4702543.1708693918-529472059.1708693917.

36. "Case 3:23-cv-00571," paragraph 147.
37. Yochai Benkler et al., "Mail-In Voter Fraud: Anatomy of a Disinformation Campaign," *Research Publication No. 2020–6* (2020), https://ssrn.com/abstract=3703701; and Yochai Benkler et al., *Network Propaganda: Manipulation, Disinformation and Radicalization in American Politics* (Oxford University Press, 2018).
38. America First Legal, "The Mission," n.d., https://aflegal.org/about.
39. Renee DiResta, "My Encounter with the Fantasy-Industrial Complex," *The Atlantic*, June 15, 2024, https://www.theatlantic.com/ideas/archive/2024/06/cia-renee-censorship-conspiracy -twitter/678688.
40. Naomi Nix, Cat Zakrzewski, and Joseph Menn, "Misinformation Research Is Buckling Under GOP Legal Attacks," *Washington Post*, September 25, 2023, https://www .washingtonpost.com/technology/2023/09/23/online-misinformation-jim-jordan.
41. Eliot Higgins, "Written Evidence from Eliot Higgins, Founder and CEO of Bellingcat (GMF0038)," *UK Parliament*, July 2019, https://committees.parliament.uk/writtenevidence /104168/html/#_ftn1.
42. Eric van der Beek, "Is Bellingcat Being Played by the CIA?," *Sputnik*, January 26, 2021, https://sputnikglobe.com/20210126/is-bellingcat-played-by-the-cia-1081883373.html.
43. Higgins, *We Are Bellingcat*, 186.
44. Press Information Bureau, "PIB Fact Check Unit," n.d., Government of India, https://pib .gov.in/aboutfactchecke.aspx?reg=3&lang=1.
45. Times of India, "Internet Firms to Lose Safe Harbour on Not Removing Content Flagged by Govt Notified Fact Checker," April 6, 2023, https://timesofindia.indiatimes.com/india /internet-firms-to-lose-safe-harbour-on-not-removing-content-flagged-by-govt-notified -fact-checker/articleshow/99305319.cms.
46. Editors Guild of India, "Press Statement," April 7, 2023, https://x.com/IndEditorsGuild /status/1644212343692222466.
47. Economic Times, "Karnataka Floats Expression of Interest for Fact Checking Unit," October 5, 2023, https://m.economictimes.com/tech/tech-bytes/karnataka-floats-expression -of-interest-for-fact-checking-unit/articleshow/104181815.cms.
48. Lasse Schuldt, "Official Truths in a War on Fake News: Governmental Fact-Checking in Malaysia, Singapore, and Thailand," *Journal of Current Southeast Asian Affairs* 40, no. 2 (2021): 340–71.
49. Elias Meseret, "A Global Rise in Government-Led Fact-Checking Initiatives Cause Concern, Worries of Misuse," *Poynter*, February 8, 2024, https://www.poynter.org/ifcn/2024 /government-fact-checking-initiatives-worldwide.
50. Schuldt, "Official Truths in a War on Fake News."
51. Amber Sinha, "Sanity Prevails as Bombay High Court Strikes Down India Government's Fact Check Unit," *Tech Policy Press*, September 26, 2024, https://www.techpolicy.press /sanity-prevails-as-bombay-high-court-strikes-down-india-governments-fact-check-unit.
52. Herman Wasserman, ed., "Meeting the Challenges of Information Disorder in the Global South," *IRDC*, 2022, 224, https://idl-bnc-idrc.dspacedirect.org/items/5aad1667-cf56-44bf -b85f-8695cb5f11dd.

53. Steven Myers and Nico Grant, "Combating Disinformation Wanes at Social Media Giants," *New York Times*, February 14, 2023, https://www.nytimes.com/2023/02/14 /technology/disinformation-moderation-social-media.html; and Erin Woo, "Musk's X Cuts Half of Election Integrity Team After Promising to Expand It," *The Information*, September 27, 2023, https://www.theinformation.com/articles/musks-x-cuts-half-of -election-integrity-team-after-promising-to-expand-it.

54. Joel Kaplan, "More Speech and Fewer Mistakes," *Meta*, January 7, 2025, https://about .fb.com/news/2025/01/meta-more-speech-fewer-mistakes; and David Gilbert, "Meta's Fact-Checking Partners Say They Were 'Blindsided' by Decision to Axe Them," *Wired*, January 7, 2025, https://www.wired.com/story/metas-fact-checking-partners-blindsided.

55. Hannah Murphy et al., "Elon Musk Moves to Address Content Issues as He Takes Control of Twitter," *Financial Times*, October 29, 2022, https://www.ft.com/content /8ccae1fb-2727-4c60-be28-91a5bad05a33.

56. Lucas Graves et al., "From Public Reason to Public Health: Professional Implications of the 'Debunking Turn' in the Global Fact-Checking Field," *Digital Journalism* (2023), https://doi.org/10.1080/21670811.2023.2218454.

57. Otávio Vinhas and Marco Bastos, "When Fact-Checking Is Not WEIRD: Negotiating Consensus Outside Western, Educated, Industrialized, Rich, and Democratic Countries," *International Journal of Press/Politics*, 2024, https://doi.org/10.1177/19401612231221801.

58. Lucas Graves and Federico Cherubini, "The Rise of Fact-Checking Sites in Europe," *Reuters Institute*, 2016, https://reutersinstitute.politics.ox.ac.uk/our-research/rise-fact -checking-sites-europe.

59. Jay Jennings and Natalie Stroud, "Asymmetric Adjustment: Partisanship and Correcting Misinformation on Facebook," *New Media & Society* 25, no. 7 (2023): 1501–21.

60. Drew Westen, *The Political Brain: The Role of Emotion in Deciding the Fate of the Nation* (Public Affairs, 2007).

61. Monmouth Poll Reports, "Partisan Identity Determines Which Specific Rights People Feel Are at Risk," June 20, 2023, https://www.monmouth.edu/polling-institute/reports /monmouthpoll_US_062023.

62. Tiffany Hsu and Stuart Thompson, "Fact Checkers Take Stock of Their Efforts: 'It's Not Getting Better'," *New York Times*, September 29, 2023, https://www.nytimes.com /2023/09/29/business/media/fact-checkers-misinformation.html.

63. Jennings and Stroud, "Asymmetric Adjustment."

64. Bill Adair and Rebecca Ianucci, "Heroes or Hacks: The Partisan Divide Over Fact-Checking," *Duke Reporters' Lab*, June 7, 2017, https://reporterslab.org/2017/06/07/heroes -hacks-partisan-divide-fact-checking.

65. Jason Walker and Jeffrey Gottfried, "Republicans Far More Likely Than Democrats to Say Fact-Checkers Tend to Favor One Side," *Pew Research Center*, June 27, 2019, https://www .pewresearch.org/short-reads/2019/06/27/republicans-far-more-likely-than-democrats-to -say-fact-checkers-tend-to-favor-one-side.

66. Mike Howell, "Fact Check: Fact-Checkers Falsely Claim They Are Fact-Checkers," *The Heritage Foundation*, January 7, 2022, https://www.heritage.org/progressivism/commentary /fact-check-fact-checkers-falsely-claim-they-are-fact-checkers.

67. Jacob Siegel, "Invasion of the Fact-Checkers," *Tablet*, March 22, 2022, https://www
.tabletmag.com/sections/news/articles/invasion-fact-checkers.

68. House Judiciary Committee, "The Weaponization of 'Disinformation' Pseudo-Experts
and Bureaucrats: How the Federal Government Partnered with Universities to Censor
Americans' Political Speech," November 6, 2023, https://judiciary.house.gov/sites/evo
-subsites/republicans-judiciary.house.gov/files/evo-media-document/EIP_Jira-Ticket
-Staff-Report-11-7-23-Clean.pdf.

69. Angela Fu, "It's Easy to Find Misinformation on Social Media. It's Even Easier on X,"
Poynter, September 19, 2024, https://www.poynter.org/fact-checking/2024/how-elon-musk
-twitter-takeover-accelerated-misinformation; and Elon Musk (@elonmusk). *X.com*, June
14, 2023, https://x.com/elonmusk/status/1669017475659251713.

70. Daniel Funke, "These Fact-Checkers Were Attacked Online After Partnering with
Facebook," *Poynter*, September 10, 2018, https://www.poynter.org/fact-checking/2018/these
-fact-checkers-were-attacked-online-after-partnering-with-facebook.

71. Seth Smalley, "Brazil's Fact-Checkers Concerned with Their Impact Ahead of Oct. 30
Runoff," *Poynter*, October 13, 2022, https://www.poynter.org/fact-checking/2022/brazils
-fact-checkers-concerned-with-their-impact-ahead-of-oct-30-runoff.

72. Manuel Mogato, "Philippines Complains Facebook Fact-Checkers Are Biased," *Reuters*,
April 16, 2018, https://www.reuters.com/article/us-philippines-facebook/philippines
-complains-facebook-fact-checkers-are-biased-idUSKBN1HN1EN.

73. Stencel et al., "Misinformation Spreads, But Fact-Checking Has Leveled Off."

74. European Broadcasting Union, "Public Service Media," 2024, https://www.ebu.ch/home.

75. John Reith in Asa Briggs, *The History of Broadcasting in the United Kingdom*, vol. 1 (Oxford
University Press, 1995), 215.

76. Edward Malnick, "Margaret Thatcher Conducted Covert War Against BBC," *Tele-graph*, December 30, 2014, https://www.telegraph.co.uk/news/politics/margaret-thatcher
/11313380/Margaret-Thatcher-conducted-covert-war-against-BBC.html; and Jim Pickard et
al., "Tony Blair Tried to Change BBC Tone on Iraq on Eve of 2003 Invasion," *Financial Times*,
December 29, 2023, https://www.ft.com/content/c8cbbb7d-ec12-4abd-8d74-769129e2a173.

77. Charlotte Higgins, *This New Noise: the Extraordinary Birth and Troubled Life of the BBC*
(Faber and Faber, 2015).

78. Jean Seaton, *Pinkoes and Traitors: The BBC and the Nation, 1974–1987* (Profile, 2015), 3.

79. Kofi Annan, "Implications of the BBC World Service Cuts," Written Evidence,
February 10, 2011, https://publications.parliament.uk/pa/cm201011/cmselect/cmfaff/writev
/849/ws25.htm.

80. H. M. Government, "Broadcasting: Copy of Royal Charter for the Continuance of
the British Broadcasting Corporation," December 2016, https://downloads.bbc.co.uk
/bbctrust/assets/files/pdf/about/how_we_govern/2016/charter.pdf.

81. Matthew Hill et al., "'Their Goal Is to Destroy Everyone': Uighur Camp Detainees
Allege Systematic Rape," *BBC*, February 2, 2021, https://www.bbc.co.uk/news/world
-asia-china-55794071.

82. Joe Tidy, "Evil Corp: 'My Hunt for the World's Most Wanted Hackers'," *BBC*, November
17, 2021, https://www.bbc.co.uk/news/technology-59297187.

83. BBC, "Reporting Iran Inside BBC Persian 2023," *YouTube*, March 19, 2023, https://www
.youtube.com/watch?v=3c_i8c3i0Dw.

84. BBC, "India: The Modi Question," 2023, https://www.bbc.co.uk/programmes/podkb144.

85. Sarah Rainsford, "Sarah Rainsford: My Last Despatch Before Russian Expulsion," *BBC*,
August 31, 2021, https://www.bbc.co.uk/news/world-europe-58395121.

86. BBC, "'A Club to the Head': What It's Like to Be a Foreign Agent in Russia," December
27, 2021, https://www.bbc.com/russian/media-59790853.

87. First Voice, "Even in Running, John Sudworth Sees China Through 'Underworld
Filter'," *CGTN*, April 1, 2021, https://news.cgtn.com/news/2021-04-01/Even-in-running
-John-Sudworth-sees-China-through-underworld-filter--Z6A57dpwqc/index.html.

88. BBC, "BBC China Correspondent John Sudworth Moves to Taiwan After Threats,"
March 31, 2021, https://www.bbc.co.uk/news/world-asia-china-56586655.

89. Reuters, "Moscow Says BBC Being Used to Undermine Political Situation in Russia," March 3, 2022, https://www.reuters.com/world/europe/russia-says-bbc-being-used
-undermine-internal-political-situation-2022-03-03.

90. Lijian Zhao, *Twitter*, June 22, 2019, https://archive.vn/iuDNe.

91. William Langley, "Chinese State Media Denies BBC Reports of Forced Labour in
Xinjiang Cotton Fields," *South China Morning Post*, December 29, 2020, https://www
.scmp.com/news/china/diplomacy/article/3115595/chinese-state-media-denies-bbc
-reports-forced-labour-xinjiang.

92. First Voice, "BBC Acts as a Propaganda Weapon by Spreading Lies on Xinjiang," *CGTN*,
February 3, 2021, https://news.cgtn.com/news/2021-02-03/BBC-acts-as-a-propaganda
-weapon-by-spreading-lies-on-Xinjiang-XzZSBZngiI/index.html.

93. Jacob Wallis et al., "Trigger Warning. The CCP's Coordinated Information Effort to Discredit the BBC," *Australian Strategic Policy Institute*, 2021, https://www.aspi.org.au/report
/trigger-warning.

94. Spokesperson, "Remarks by Spokesperson of the Embassy on BBC's Inaccurate Coverage
About Xinjiang," Embassy of the People's Republic of China in New Zealand, May 31,
2022, http://nz.china-embassy.gov.cn/eng/fyrbt/sgfyr/202303/t20230309_11038369.htm.

95. Insikt Group, "China Propaganda Network Targets BBC Media, UK in Influence
Campaign," August 18, 2021, https://www.recordedfuture.com/research/china-propaganda
-targets-bbc-uk; and Wallis et al., "Trigger Warning."

96. Wallis et al., "Trigger Warning."

97. Sidhant Sibal, *X*, January 21, 2023, https://x.com/sidhant/status/1616760933883449345.

98. First Voice, "BBC World News Is ousted! Why?," *CGTN*, February 12, 2021, https://news
.cgtn.com/news/2021-02-12/BBC-World-News-is-ousted-Why—XNQK8CFfxK/index.html.

99. Good Morning Britain, "Lucy Frazer Addressed BBC Review as Ofcom Is Given Powers to
Investigate Bias," *ITV*, January 22, 2024, https://www.youtube.com/watch?v=McOalKxr2ac.

100. Pippa Crerar, "Downing Street Denies Having Anti-BBC Agenda After Bias Accusations,"
Guardian, January 22, 2024, https://www.theguardian.com/media/2024/jan/22/downing
-street-denies-having-anti-bbc-agenda-after-bias-accusations.

101. Georgina Cutler, "BBC Facing New Clampdown as Broadcaster Blasted by Audiences Over Claims of Bias," *GB News*, January 22, 2024, https://www.gbnews.com/news/bbc-bias-ofcom-new-rules-lucy-frazer.

102. Jake Kanter, "Op-Ed: The UK Government Spent a Day Bashing the 'Bias' BBC, But Its Claims Were Misleading," *Deadline*, January 23, 2024, https://deadline.com/2024/01/bbc-bias-claims-unevidenced-lucy-frazer-1235801799.

103. BBC, "Global News Services," https://www.bbc.com/aboutthebbc/whatwedo/worldservice; and "Written Evidence Submitted by BBC World Service (TFP0035)," June 2021, https://committees.parliament.uk/writtenevidence/36976/pdf.

104. Patrick Barwise and Peter York, *The War Against the BBC* (Penguin, 2020).

105. Toby Helm, "Jeremy Hunt: Why I Don't Mind 'Scum' and Other 4-Letter Words," *Guardian*, December 11, 2010, https://www.theguardian.com/politics/2010/dec/11/jeremy-hunt-interview-james-naughtie.

106. Jane Martinson, "BBC Today Show Debate 'Very, Very Anti-Tory,' Says Culture Minister," *Guardian*, April 29, 2015, https://www.theguardian.com/media/2015/apr/29/bbc-today-show-debate-very-anti-tory-says-culture-minister-sajid-javid.

107. Anita Singh, "BBC Output Must Reflect Entire Nation, Culture Secretary Says as He Pledges to Tackle Bias," *Telegraph*, March 5, 2020, https://www.telegraph.co.uk/politics/2020/03/05/bbc-output-must-reflect-entire-nation-culture-secretary-says.

108. Press Gazette, "Culture Sec Nadine Dorries Says BBC May Not Exist in 10 Years and Slams Impartiality 'Problem'," October 4, 2021, https://pressgazette.co.uk/news/nadine-dorries-bbc-10-years-impartiality.

109. Tiana Corbin and Toby Codd, "Jacob Rees-Mogg Says BBC Licence Fee 'Needs to Go' After Gary Lineker Row," *Somerset Live*, March 14, 2023, https://www.somersetlive.co.uk/news/somerset-news/jacob-rees-mogg-says-bbc-8248380.

110. David Maddox, "BBC Branded 'a Safe Haven for Perverts' with Tory MPs Demanding Licence Fee Is Scrapped," *Express*, July 10, 2023, https://www.express.co.uk/news/politics/1789369/lee-anderson-bbc-perverts-licence-fee-scrapped-tory-mps.

111. Ofcom, "News Consumption in the UK: Supporting Data," July 20, 2023, 32, https://www.ofcom.org.uk/siteassets/resources/documents/research-and-data/tv-radio-and-on-demand-research/tv-research/news/news-consumption-2023/news-consumption-in-the-uk-2023-supporting-data?v=329964.

112. BBC, "Tim Davie's Introductory Speech as BBC Director-General," September 3, 2020, https://www.bbc.co.uk/mediacentre/speeches/2020/tim-davie-intro-speech.

113. Jay Rosen, "The View from Nowhere: Questions and Answers," *PressThink*, November 10, 2010, https://pressthink.org/2010/11/the-view-from-nowhere-questions-and-answers.

114. Interview with Richard Sambrook, August 1, 2023.

115. Press Gazette, "Boris Johnson Condemns 'Statist, Corporatist, Defeatist, Anti-Business' and 'Biased to Left' BBC News," May 14, 2012, https://pressgazette.co.uk/news/boris-johnson-condemns-statist-corporatist-defeatist-anti-business-and-biased-to-left-bbc-news.

116. Boris Johnson, "The 2013 Margaret Thatcher Lecture—Boris Johnson," *Centre for Policy Studies*, November 27, 2013, https://cps.org.uk/events/post/2013/the-2013-margaret -thatcher-lecture-boris-johnson.

117. Christopher Hope, "Conservatives Make Formal Complaint to BBC About 'Biased' Leaders' Election Debate," *Telegraph*, June 1, 2017, https://www.telegraph.co.uk/news/2017 /06/01/conservatives-make-formal-complaint-bbc-biased-leaders-election.

118. Rowena Mason and Jim Waterson, "Boris Johnson 'Looking at' Abolishing TV Licence Fee for BBC," *Guardian*, December 9, 2019, https://www.theguardian.com/politics/2019 /dec/09/boris-johnson-looking-at-abolishing-tv-licence-fee-for-bbc.

119. Interview with Fran Unsworth, July 31, 2023.

120. Culture, Media and Sport Committee, "Fourth Report: BBC Licence Fee Settlement and Annual Report," *UK Parliament*, May 2011, https://publications.parliament.uk/pa /cm201012/cmselect/cmcumeds/454/45405.htm#a1.

121. Nadine Dorries, *Twitter*, January 16, 2022, https://x.com/NadineDorries/status/1482622722 228240387?s=20.

122. BBC, "BBC Value for Audiences," February 2021, https://downloads.bbc.co.uk/aboutthebbc /reports/reports/value-for-audiences-2021.pdf.

123. Alistair Gray, "BBC World Service to Cut 400 Jobs in Funding Squeeze," *Financial Times*, September 29, 2022, https://www.ft.com/content/12be030f-b4da-401b-adb4-2c5588a8bcb2; and Yasmin Rufo, "BBC World Service to cut 130 jobs in savings plan," BBC, January 29, 2025, https://www.bbc.co.uk/news/articles/cpqlivvdn580.

124. Interview with Richard Sambrook, August 1, 2023.

125. Lucy Fisher and Daniel Thomas, "BBC World Service Secures Budget Bump in Government Funding," *Financial Times*, October 31, 2024, https://www.ft.com/content/e5495b79 -29e7-41f1-80a3-654bb419fc61.

126. The State of Israel Official Twitter Account, *X*, October 19, 2023, https://x.com/Israel /status/1714913106340557236.

127. Interview with Alex Murray, November 8, 2023.

128. Interview with Lindsay McCoy, November 2, 2023.

129. Andrew Messenger, "Liz Truss Urges Conservatives to 'Defund State Media' as She Rails Against Left at Australian CPAC Event," *Guardian*, October 5, 2024, https://www .theguardian.com/politics/2024/oct/05/liz-truss-bbc-abc-state-media-left-australian-cpac -event-brisbane.

130. Israel Defense Forces, *X*, October 17, 2023, https://x.com/IDF/status/1714403025136017784.

131. Israel Defense Forces, *X*, October 19, 2023, https://x.com/i/broadcasts/1BRJjPbkaRQKw.

132. Michael Biesecker, "New AP Analysis of Last Month's Deadly Gaza Hospital Explosion Rules Out Widely Cited Video," Associated Press, November 22, 2023, https://apnews. com/article/israel-palestinians-hamas-war-hospital-rocket-gaza-e0fa550faa4678f024797- b72132452e3.

133. Julian Borger and Emma Graham-Harrison, "Biden Backs Israel's Stance on Deadly Blast at Gaza Hospital," *Guardian*, October 18, 2023, https://www.theguardian.com/world/2023

/oct/18/joe-biden-israel-news-gaza-al-ahli-baptist-hospital-explosion-jordan-summit
-cancelled-protests.

134. Aric Toler et al., "A Close Look at Some Key Evidence in the Gaza Hospital Blast,"
New York Times, October 24, 2023, https://www.nytimes.com/2023/10/24/world/middleeast
/gaza-hospital-israel-hamas-video.html. See also Forensic Architecture, "Israeli Disinformation: Al-Ahli Hospital," February 15, 2024, https://forensic-architecture.org/investigation
/israeli-disinformation-al-ahli-hospital.

135. Al Jazeera, "Video Investigation: What Hit al-Ahli Hospital in Gaza?," October 19, 2023,
https://www.aljazeera.com/news/2023/10/19/what-hit-ahli-hospital-in-gaza.

9. BACK TO REALITY

1. Greg Jaffe and Jose Real, "Life Amid the Ruins of QAnon: 'I Wanted My Family Back',"
Washington Post, February 23, 2021, https://www.washingtonpost.com/nation/interactive
/2021/conspiracy-theories-qanon-family-members/?tid=ss_tw.

2. Yochai Benkler et al., "Mail-In Voter Fraud: Anatomy of a Disinformation Campaign,"
Research Publication No. 2020–6 (2020), https://ssrn.com/abstract=3703701.

3. "Dominion Voting Systems vs Fox News Network, Case No. N21C-03-257 EMD,
Consolidated Public Version," February 16, 2023, 25, https://courts.delaware.gov/Opinions
/Download.aspx?id=345820.

4. Ben Kamisar, "Almost a Third of Americans Still Believe the 2020 Election Result
Was Fraudulent," *NBC*, June 20, 2023, https://www.nbcnews.com/meet-the-press
/meetthepressblog/almost-third-americans-still-believe-2020-election-result-was-fraudule
-rcna90145.

5. Benjamin Netanyahu, *X*, November 6, 2024, https://x.com/netanyahu/status
/1854070348926328965.

6. For example, see Andrea Tate, "My Husband and His Family Voted for Trump—So I'm
Canceling Thanksgiving and Christmas," *Huffington Post*, November 21, 2024.

7. Lorenzo Tondo and Mark Rice-Oxley, " 'They Don't Believe It's Real': How War Has
Split Ukrainian-Russian Families," *Guardian*, March 18, 2022, https://www.theguardian
.com/world/2022/mar/18/ukraine-russia-families-divided-over-war.

8. Shannon Tiezzi, "What Do Chinese People Think Is Happening in Xinjiang?," *The
Diplomat*, May 29, 2021, https://thediplomat.com/2021/05/what-do-chinese-people-think
-is-happening-in-xinjiang.

9. ICU Nurse, "It's Bizarre to See a Covid Patient Deny Covid Exists While Gasping for
Breath," *Guardian*, October 17, 2021, https://www.theguardian.com/commentisfree/2021
/oct/18/its-bizarre-to-see-a-covid-patient-deny-covid-exists-while-gasping-for-breath.

10. Evan Dyer, "Mexico's Choice: Amulets or Science to Fight COVID-19," *CBC News*,
March 29, 2020, https://www.cbc.ca/news/politics/mexico-s-choice-amulets-or-science-to
-fight-covid-19-1.5513973; and Chiara Giordano, "Coronavirus: Bolsonaro Claims Media

'Tricking' Brazilians Over Severity of Pandemic," *Independent*, March 24, 2020, https:// www.independent.co.uk/news/world/americas/coronavirus-brazil-bolsonaro-death-toll -cases-covid-19-latest-a9420911.html.

11. Morgan Marietta and David Barker, *One Nation, Two Realities* (Oxford University Press, 2019), xi.

12. Marietta and Barker, *One Nation, Two Realities*, 9.

13. Rush Limbaugh, in *The Constitution of Knowledge: A Defense of Truth*, by Jonathan Rauch (Brookings Institution, 2021), 174.

14. Emanuel Adler and Alena Drieschova, "The Epistemological Challenge of Truth Subversion to the Liberal International Order," *International Organization* 75, no. 2 (2021): 362.

15. Adler and Drieschova, "The Epistemological Challenge," 361.

16. Francis Fukuyama, "The End of History?," *The National Interest*, no. 16 (1989): 3–18.

17. Ruchir Sharma, "Indian Democracy with East Asian Characteristics," *Financial Times*, April 8, 2024, https://www.ft.com/content/509b30c4-8033-4984-afce-eed847b903a0.

18. David Goldman, "What Just Happened? It Was the Economy, Stupid," *CNN*, November 6, 2024, https://edition.cnn.com/2024/11/06/economy/economy-trump-reelection/index.html.

19. World Health Organization, "The COVID-19 Infodemic," https://www.who.int/health -topics/infodemic/the-covid-19-infodemic#tab=tab_1.

20. Marc Andrejevic, *Infoglut: How Too Much Information Is Changing the Way We Think and Know* (Routledge, 2013).

21. Martin Moore, "Fake Accounts on Social Media, Epistemic Uncertainty and the Need for an Independent Auditing of Accounts," *Internet Policy Review* 12, no. 1 (2023), https://doi .org/10.14763/2023.1.1680.

22. Rasmus Nielsen, "Forget Technology—Politicians Pose the Gravest Misinformation Threat," *Financial Times*, January 2, 2024, https://www.ft.com/content/5da52770-b474-4547 -8d1b-9c46a3c3bac9.

23. Kate Farhall et al., "Political Elites' Use of Fake News Discourse Across Communications Platforms," *International Journal of Communication* 13 (2019): 4353–75.

24. Mark Galeotti, *The Weaponization of Everything: A Field Guide to the New Way of War* (Yale University Press, 2022).

25. Karl von Clausewitz, *On War* (Oxford University Press, 2007), 30.

26. Philip Taylor, *Munitions of the Mind* (Manchester University Press, 1990).

27. Yashraj Sharma, "Twitter Accused of Censorship in India as It Blocks Modi Critics," *Guardian*, April 5, 2023, https://www.theguardian.com/world/2023/apr/05/twitter-accused-of-censorship -in-india-as-it-blocks-modi-critics-elon-musk.

28. Jerome Bruner, "The Narrative Construction of Reality," *Critical Inquiry* 18, no. 1 (1991): 9.

29. See, for example, Kendall Haven, *Story Proof: The Science Behind the Startling Power of Story* (Libraries Unlimited, 2007).

30. Thomas Colley, *Always at War: British Public Narratives of War* (University of Michigan Press, 2019).

31. Colley, *Always at War*.

32. Stephen Colbert, in *The Constitution of Knowledge: A Defense of Truth*, Jonathan Rauch (Brookings Institution, 2021), 260.
33. Bruner, "The Narrative Construction of Reality," 9.
34. J. D. Vance, *X*, September 10, 2024, https://x.com/JDVance/status/1833505359513661762?ref _src=twsrc%5Etfw%7Ctwcamp%5Etweetembed%7Ctwterm%5E1833505359513661762 %7Ctwgr%5Eadc112c3eeaead7e5ef9c61f0a26d882310f4958%7Ctwcon%5Es1_&ref_url =https%3A%2F%2Fnews.sky.com%2Fstory%2Fhow-trumps-claims-of-immigrants -eating-pets-started-and-spiralled-online-13213476.
35. Zeeshan Aleem, "JD Vance Is Openly Defending the Idea of Making Things Up," *MSNBC*, September 17, 2024, https://www.msnbc.com/opinion/msnbc-opinion/jd-vance -make-up-pet-eating-story-haitian-rcna171326.
36. Peter Oborne, *The Assault on Truth* (Simon & Schuster, 2021), 132.
37. Melanie Green and Timothy Brock, "The Role of Transportation in the Persuasiveness of Public Narratives," *Journal of Personality and Social Psychology* 79, no. 5 (2000): 701–21.
38. Thomas Colley, "Strategic Narratives and War Propaganda," in *The Sage Handbook of Propaganda*, ed. Paul Baines et al. 38–54 (SAGE, 2020); and Michael Slater and Donna Rouner, "Entertainment-Education and Elaboration Likelihood: Understanding the Processing of Narrative Persuasion," *Communication Theory* 12, no. 2 (2002): 173–91.
39. Tim Reid, "Trump Predicts the End of U.S. Democracy if He Loses 2024 Election," *Reuters*, March 17, 2024, https://www.reuters.com/world/us/trump-predicts-end-us -democracy-if-he-loses-2024-election-2024-03-17.
40. Philip Smith, *Why War: The Cultural Logic of Iraq, The Gulf War, and Suez* (University of Chicago Press, 2005).
41. Jonathan Rauch, *The Constitution of Knowledge: A Defense of Truth* (Brookings Institution, 2021).
42. Rauch, *The Constitution of Knowledge*, 100.
43. Rauch, *The Constitution of Knowledge*, 7.
44. Rauch, *The Constitution of Knowledge*.
45. Rauch, *The Constitution of Knowledge*, 182.
46. Rauch, *The Constitution of Knowledge*.
47. Jade McGlynn, *Russia's War* (Polity Press, 2023).
48. Hannah Arendt, *Between Past and Future* (Viking, 1961), 13.

SELECTED BIBLIOGRAPHY

Adair, Bill, and Rebecca Ianucci. "Heroes or Hacks: The Partisan Divide Over Fact-Checking." *Duke Reporters' Lab*, June 7, 2017. https://reporterslab.org/2017/06/07/heroes-hacks-partisan-divide-fact-checking.

Adler, Emanuel, and Alena Drieschova. "The Epistemological Challenge of Truth Subversion to the Liberal International Order." *International Organization* 75, no. 2 (2021): 359–86.

Albert, Eleanor. "China's Big Bet on Soft Power." *Council on Foreign Relations*, February 9, 2018. https://www.cfr.org/backgrounder/chinas-big-bet-soft-power.

Alves, Marcelo, et al. "Disinformation and 2022 Elections in Brazil: Lessons Learned from a South-to-South Context." *INCT* (2023). https://inctdsi.uff.br/wp-content/uploads/sites/699/2023/11/Disinformation-and-2022-Elections-in-Brazil.pdf.

Amazeen, Michelle. "Journalistic Interventions: The Structural Factors Affecting the Global Emergence of Fact-Checking." *Journalism* 21, no. 1 (2020): 95–111.

Amerisov, Alexander. "A Chronology of Soviet Media Coverage." *Bulletin of the Atomic Scientists*, 42, no. 7 (1986): 38–39.

Andrejevic, Marc. *Infoglut: How Too Much Information Is Changing the Way We Think and Know.* Routledge, 2013.

Arendt, Hannah. *Between Past and Future.* Viking, 1961.

Aristotle. *Poetics.* Penguin, 1996.

Atlantic Council. "Chinese Discourse Power." December 2020. https://www.atlanticcouncil.org/in-depth-research-reports/report/chinese-discourse-power-ambitions-and-reality-in-the-digital-domain.

Barbosa, João. "From the New Right to Bolsonarism: Uses of the Brazilian Military Dictatorship by the YouTube Channel Folha Política." MA diss., Federal University of Goiás. Goiânia, 2022. https://repositorio.bc.ufg.br/tede/items/da0703a7-12bf-4130-a758-2f7343aa0e1e.

Barwise, Patrick, and Peter York. *The War Against the BBC*. Penguin, 2020.

Bátorfy, Attila, and Ágnes Urbán. "State Advertising as an Instrument of Transformation of the Media Market in Hungary." *East European Politics* 36, no. 1 (2020): 44–65.

Bátorfy, Attila, et al. "Monitoring Media Pluralism in the Digital Era: Country Report—Hungary." *European University Institute*, 2022. https://cadmus.eui.eu/bitstream/handle/1814/74692/MPM2022-Hungary-EN.pdf.

Baudrillard, Jean. *The Gulf War Did Not Take Place*. Trans. Paul Patton. Indiana University Press, 1995.

Bélair-Gagnon, Valérie, et al. "Knowledge Work in Platform Fact-Checking Partnerships." *International Journal of Communication* 17 (2023): 1169–89.

Benkler, Yochai, Robert Faris, and Hal Roberts. "Mail-In Voter Fraud: Anatomy of a Disinformation Campaign." *Research Publication No. 2020–6* (2020). https://ssrn.com/abstract=3703701.

——. *Network Propaganda: Manipulation, Disinformation and Radicalization in American Politics*. Oxford University Press, 2018.

Berg, William. "The Rhetoric of Narcissism: Trump's Tweets on Writing." *Rhetoric and Public Affairs* 25, no. 2 (2022): 91–117.

Berlin, Isaiah. *Four Essays on Liberty*. Oxford University Press, 1969.

Bernays, Edward. *Propaganda*. Ig, 2005. First published in 1928.

Bhatia, Bela. "The Naxalite Movement in Central Bihar." *Economic and Political Weekly* 40, no. 15 (2005): 1536–49.

Blomeier, Hans-Hartwig, and Luis Téllez. "Journalists Under Pressure." *Konrad Adernauer Stiftung*, September 28, 2021. https://www.kas.de/en/web/auslandsinformationen/artikel/detail/-/content/journalists-under-pressure.

Boito, Armando, and Alfredo Saad-Filho. "State, State Institutions, and Political Power in Brazil." *Latin American Perspectives* 43, no. 2 (2016): 190–206.

Bozóki, András. *Rolling Transition and the Role of Intellectuals: The Case of Hungary*. Central European University Press, 2022.

Bradshaw, Samantha, et al. "Industrialized Disinformation: 2020 Global Inventory of Organized Social Media Manipulation." University of Oxford, 2020. https://demtech.oii.ox.ac.uk/research/posts/industrialized-disinformation.

Brady, Anne-Marie. *Marketing Dictatorship: Propaganda and Thought Work in Contemporary China*. Rowman and Littlefield, 2008.

Briggs, Asa. *The History of Broadcasting in the United Kingdom*, vol. 1. Oxford University Press, 1995.

Bruhn, Kathleen. "'To Hell with Your Corrupt Institutions': AMLO and Populism in Mexico." In *Populism in Europe and the Americas: Threat or Corrective for Democracy?*, ed. Cas Mudde and Cristóbal Kaltwasser, 88–112. Cambridge University Press, 2012.

Bruner, Jerome. "The Narrative Construction of Reality." *Critical Inquiry* 18, no. 1 (1991): 1–21.

Bursztyn, Victor, and Larry Birnbaum. "Thousands of Small, Constant Rallies: A Large-Scale Analysis of Partisan WhatsApp Groups." *ASONAM* 19 (2019): 484–88. https://doi.org /10.1145/3341161.3342905.

Cabral, Sandro, et al. "The Disastrous Effects of Leaders in Denial: Evidence from the COVID-19 Crisis in Brazil." *SSRN*, 2021. https://ssrn.com/abstract=3836147.

Calil, Gilberto. "Olavo de Carvalho and the Rise of the Far Right." *Argumentum* 13, no. 2 (2021): 64–81. https://www.redalyc.org/journal/4755/475571195007/movil/.

Campos Mello, Patricia. *A máquina do ódio: notas de uma repórter sobre fake news e violência digital.* Companhia das Letras, 2020.

Castells, Manuel. *Communication Power.* Oxford University Press, 2013.

——. "A Network Theory of Power." *International Journal of Communication* 5, no. 15 (2011): 773–87.

Chadha, Kalyani, and Michael Koliska. "Playing by a Different Set of Rules." *Journalism Practice* 10, no. 5 (2016): 608–25.

Charon, Paul, and Jean-Baptiste Jeangene Vilmer. "Chinese Influence Operations: A Machiavellian Moment," *IRSEM*, 2021. https://www.irsem.fr/report.html.

Chaturvedi, Swati. *I Am a Troll: Inside the Secret World of the BJP's Digital Army.* Juggernaut Books, 2016.

China Media Project. "The Good Journalist." November 8, 2022. https://chinamediaproject .org/2022/11/08/the-good-journalist.

Colley, Thomas. *Always at War: British Public Narratives of War.* University of Michigan Press, 2019.

Colley, Thomas. "How Russia Attacks Ukrainian Civilians and Makes It Look Like Kyiv Is Doing It," *The I Newspaper,* June 26, 2023. https://inews.co.uk/?ranMID=48016&ranEAID =je6NUbpObpQ&ranSiteID=je6NUbpObpQ-giGYpLRxt2Ky2UdRfqidug.

Colley, Thomas. "Strategic Narratives and War Propaganda." In *The Sage Handbook of Propaganda,* ed. Paul Baines et al., 38–54. SAGE, 2020.

Colley, Thomas, and Martin Moore. "News as Geopolitics: China, CGTN and the 2020 US Presidential Election." *Journal of International Communication,* 2022. https://doi.org/10 .1080/13216597.2022.2120522.

Colley, Thomas, and Carolijn van Noort. *Strategic Narratives, Ontological Security and Global Policy: Responses to China's Belt and Road Initiative.* Palgrave MacMillan, 2022.

Cook, Sarah. "Beijing's Global Megaphone." *Freedom House,* 2020. https://freedomhouse.org /report/special-report/2020/beijings-global-megaphone.

——. "China's Content Manipulation Reaches New Frontiers." *The Diplomat,* November 16, 2021. https://thediplomat.com/2021/11/chinas-content-manipulation-reaches-new-frontiers.

Cook, Timothy. *Governing with the News: The News Media as a Political Institution.* University of Chicago Press, 2005.

Cruz, Natalia. "Neofascism and Brazilian Conspirationism: The Media Without a Mask and the 'Axis of Evil'." *Comparative History Magazine* 13, no. 2 (2019): 216–57.

Cuadros, Alex. *Brazillionaires: The Godfathers of Modern Brazil.* Profile, 2016.

da Empoli, Giuliano. *The Wizard of the Kremlin*. Pushkin Press, 2023.

Davis, Stuart. "MídiaNINJA and the Rise of Citizen Journalism in Brazil." In *Civic Media: Technology, Design, Practice*, ed. Eric Gordon and Paul Mihailides, 527–32. MIT Press, 2016.

Davis, Stuart, and Joe Straubhaar. "Producing Antipetismo: Media Activism and the Rise of the Radical, Nationalist Right in Contemporary Brazil." *International Communication Gazette*, 82, no. 1 (2020): 82–100.

Debord, Guy. *Society of the Spectacle*. Rebel, 1992.

Demuru, Paolo. "Conspiracy Theories, Messianic Populism and Everyday Social Media Use in Contemporary Brazil: A Glocal Semiotic Perspective." *Glocalism: Journal of Culture, Politics and Innovation* 3 (2020). https://doi.org/10.12893/gjcpi.2020.3.12.

Devitt, Steve. "Porfirian Influence on Mexican Journalism: An Enduring Legacy of Economic Control." *University of Montana*, 1987. https://scholarworks.umt.edu/cgi/viewcontent.cgi?article=6120&context=etd.

Drabu, Onaiza. "Who Is the Muslim? Discursive Representations of the Muslims and Islam in Indian Prime-Time News." *Religions* 9, no. 9 (2018): 1–22.

Dragomir, Marius. "Media Capture in Europe." *Media Development Investment Fund*, 2019. https://www.mdif.org/news/mdif-publishes-report-on-media-capture-in-europe.

Dragomir, Marius, and Astrid Söderström. "The State of State Media." *CEU Democracy Institute*, 2021. https://cmds.ceu.edu/sites/cmcs.ceu.hu/files/attachment/article/2091/thestateofstatemedia.pdf.

Dunwoody, Philip, et al. "The Fascist Authoritarian Model of Illiberal Democracy." *Frontiers in Political Science* 4 (2022). https://doi.org/10.3389/fpos.2022.907681.

Dzięciołowski, Krzysztof. "Is There a Chance for Non-Partisan Media in Poland?" *Reuters Institute Fellowship Paper*. University of Oxford, 2017. https://reutersinstitute.politics.ox.ac.uk/sites/default/files/2017-12/Is%20there%20a%20chance%20for%20non-partisan%20media%20in%20Poland%20-%20Krzysztof%20Dzieciolowsk%20Paper.pdf.

Ellul, Jacques. *Propaganda: The Formation of Men's Attitudes*. Vintage, 1973.

Elswah, Mona, and Philip Howard. "'Anything that Causes Chaos': The Organizational Behavior of Russia Today (RT)," *Journal of Communication* 70, no. 5 (2020): 623–45.

Essa, Azad. "China Is Buying African Media's Silence." *Foreign Policy*, September 14, 2018. https://foreignpolicy.com/2018/09/14/china-is-buying-african-medias-silence.

Estrada, Luis. *El imperio de los otros datos: Tres años de falsedades y engaños desde palacio.* 2022.

European Broadcasting Union. "Public Service Media," 2024. https://www.ebu.ch/home.

European Commission. "2020 Rule of Law Report Country: Chapter on the Rule of Law Situation in Hungary." September 30, 2020. https://eur-lex.europa.eu/legal-content/EN/TXT/PDF/?uri=CELEX:52020SC0316.

Evangelista, Rafael, and Fernanda Bruno. "WhatsApp and Political Instability in Brazil: Targeted Messages and Political Radicalisation." *Internet Policy Review* 8, no. 4 (2019): 1–23.

Farhall, Kate, et al. "Political Elites' Use of Fake News Discourse Across Communications Platforms." *International Journal of Communication* 13 (2019): 4353–75.

Fitzl, Gregor, et al., eds. *Populism and the Crisis of Democracy*. Vol. 1, *Concepts and Theory*. Routledge, 2019.

Fivush, Robyn. "Speaking Silence: The Social Construction of Silence in Autobiographical and Cultural Narratives." *Memory* 18, no. 2 (2010): 88–98.

Foa, R. S., et al. "Youth and Satisfaction with Democracy." *Centre for the Future of Democracy*, 2020. https://www.cam.ac.uk/stories/youthanddemocracy.

Fonseca, Paulo, et al. "Demarcating Patriotic Science on Digital Platforms: Covid-19, Chloroquine and the Institutionalisation of Ignorance in Brazil." *Science as Culture* 31, no. 4 (2022): 530–54.

Frye, Timothy. *Weak Strongman: The Limits of Power in Putin's Russia*. Princeton University Press, 2021.

Fukuyama, Francis. "The End of History?." *The National Interest*, no. 16 (1989): 3–18.

Galeotti, Mark. *The Weaponization of Everything: A Field Guide to the New Way of War*. Yale University Press, 2022.

Gans, Herbert. *Deciding What's News*. Constable, 1980.

Garner, Ian. *Z Generation: Into the Heart of Russia's Fascist Youth*. Hurst, 2023.

Geissler, Erhard, and Robert Hunt Sprinkle. "Disinformation Squared: Was the HIV-from-Fort-Detrick Myth a Stasi Success?" *Politics and the Life Sciences* 32, no. 2 (2013): 2–99.

Gerard, Patrick, et al. "Truth Social Dataset." *ICWSM*, 2023. https://ojs.aaai.org/index.php /ICWSM/article/view/22211/21990.

Gillmor, Dan. *We the Media: Grassroots Journalism By the People, For the People*. O'Reilly Media, 2006.

Gleicher, Nathaniel. "Removing Coordinated Inauthentic Behavior." *Meta*, July 8, 2020. https:// about.fb.com/news/2020/07/removing-political-coordinated-inauthentic-behavior.

Goode, Paul. "How Russian Television Normalizes the War." *Riddle*, July 14, 2023. https://ridl.io /how-russian-television-normalizes-the-war.

Gramsci, Antonio. *Selections from the Prison Notebooks*. Lawrence and Wishart, 1971.

Graves, Lucas. "Boundaries Not Drawn: Mapping the Institutional Roots of the Global Fact-Checking Movement." *Journalism Studies* 19, no. 5 (2018): 613–31.

——. *Deciding What's True*. Columbia University Press, 2016.

Graves, Lucas, and Federico Cherubini. "The Rise of Fact-Checking Sites in Europe." *Reuters Institute*, 2016. https://reutersinstitute.politics.ox.ac.uk/our-research/rise-fact-checking-sites -europe.

Graves, Lucas, et al. "From Public Reason to Public Health: Professional Implications of the 'Debunking Turn' in the Global Fact-Checking Field." *Digital Journalism* (2023). https://doi .org/10.1080/21670811.2023.2218454.

Graves, Lucas, et al. "Understanding Innovations in Journalistic Practice: A Field Experiment Examining Motivations for Fact-Checking." *Journal of Communication* 66, no. 1 (2016): 102–38.

Grayson, George. *Mexican Messiah: Andrés Manuel López Obrador*. Pennsylvania State University Press, 2007.

Green, Melanie, and Timothy Brock. "The Role of Transportation in the Persuasiveness of Public Narratives." *Journal of Personality and Social Psychology* 79, no. 5 (2000): 701–21.

Groeling, Tim, and Matthew Baum. "Crossing the Water's Edge: Elite Rhetoric, Media Coverage, and the Rally-Round-the-Flag Phenomenon." *The Journal of Politics* 70, no. 4 (2008): 1065–85.

Guriev, Sergei, and Daniel Treisman. *Spin Dictators: The Changing Face of Tyranny in the 21st Century*. Princeton University Press, 2022.

Guyo, Abdirizak, and Hong Yu. "China's News Media as Public Diplomacy in Africa: An Assessment of CCTV/CGTN Among Kenyan Audience." *Journal of Contemporary African Studies* 40, no. 3 (2022): 1–16.

Habermas, Jürgen. *The Structural Transformation of the Public Sphere*. Polity Press, 1992.

Habermas, Jürgen, et al. "The Public Sphere: An Encyclopedia Article." *New German Critique* 3 (1974): 49–55.

Hagström, Linus, and Karl Gustafsson. "Narrative Power: How Storytelling Shapes East Asian International Politics." *Cambridge Review of International Affairs* 32, no. 4 (2019): 387–406.

Harding, Luke. *Invasion: Russia's Bloody War and Ukraine's Fight for Survival*. Guardian Faber, 2022.

Haven, Kendall. *Story Proof: The Science Behind the Startling Power of Story*. Libraries Unlimited, 2007.

Higaredo, Felipe. "AMLO's Social Communication Strategies: Are They Enhancing the Deliberative Quality of the Mexican Public Sphere?." July 2019. https://doi.org/10.13140 /RG.2.2.17925.88808.

Higgins, Charlotte. *This New Noise: the Extraordinary Birth and Troubled Life of the BBC*. Faber and Faber, 2015.

Higgins, Eliot. *We Are Bellingcat*. Bloomsbury, 2021.

——. "Written Evidence from Eliot Higgins, Founder and CEO of Bellingcat (GMF0038)," *UK Parliament*, July 2019. https://committees.parliament.uk/writtenevidence/104168/html /#_ftn1.

Hothschild, Jennifer, and Katherine Einstein. "Do Facts Matter? Information and Misinformation in American Politics." *Political Science Quarterly* 130, no. 4 (2015): 585–624.

Humphrey, Peter. "Countering China's Forced Confessions." *The Diplomat*, November 23, 2019. https://thediplomat.com/2019/11/countering-chinas-forced-confessions.

Hung, Tzu-Chieh, and Tzu-Wei Hung. "How China's Cognitive Warfare Works: A Frontline Perspective of Taiwan's Anti-Disinformation Wars." *Journal of Global Security Studies* 7, no. 4 (2022). https://doi.org/10.1093/jogss/ogac016.

International Federation of Journalists (IFJ). "The China Network: Inside China's Global Media Mission in Asia, Africa and Latin America," 2022. https://www.ifj.org/media-centre/reports /detail/the-china-network-inside-chinas-global-media-mission-in-asia-africa-and-latin -america/category/publications.

International Press Institute (IPI). "Mission Report: Media Freedom in Hungary Ahead of 2022 Election." March 21, 2022. https://ipi.media/wp-content/uploads/2022/03/HU _PressFreedomMission_Report_IPI_2022.pdf.

Jennings, Jay, and Natalie Stroud. "Asymmetric Adjustment: Partisanship and Correcting Misinformation on Facebook." *New Media & Society* 25, no. 7 (2023): 1501–21.

Johnson, Ashley. "The Facts Behind Allegations of Political Bias on Social Media." *ITIF*, October 26, 2023. https://itif.org/publications/2023/10/26/the-facts-behind-allegations-of -political-bias-on-social-media.

Kalil, Isabela, and R. Marie Santini. "Coronavírus, Pandemia, Infodemia e Política." *FESPSP*, 2020. https://www.netlab.eco.br/en/post/coronavirus-pandemic-infodemic-and-politics.

Kamps, Klaus. *Commander-in-Tweet: Donald Trump and the Deformed Presidency*. Springer, 2020.

Karolewski, Ireneusz, et al. "Carl Schmitt and Democratic Backsliding." *Contemporary Political Theory* 22 (2023): 406–37.

Kohli-Khandekar, Vanita. *The Indian Media Business: Pandemic and After*. SAGE, 2021.

Kumar, Ravish. *The Free Voice: On Democracy, Culture and the Nation*. Speaking Tiger, 2019.

Kurlantzick, Joshua. *Beijing's Global Media Offensive: China's Uneven Campaign to Influence Asia and the World*. Oxford University Press, 2023.

Law, Nathan. *Freedom: How We Lose It and How We Fight Back*. Penguin, 2021.

Lenin, Vladimir Ilyich. "What Is to Be Done?," 1902. https://www.marxists.org/archive/lenin/works/1901/witbd/iii.htm.

Lewis, Angela. "How a Pay TV Company Is Serving Up a Soft Power Win for China in Africa." *The Diplomat*, February 14, 2019. https://thediplomat.com/2019/02/how-a-pay-tv-company-is-serving-up-a-soft-power-win-for-china-in-africa.

Lewis, David. "The Quiet Transformation of Occupied Ukraine." *Foreign Affairs*. https://www.foreignaffairs.com/ukraine/quiet-transformation-occupied-ukraine.

Lewsey, Fred. "War in Ukraine Has Widened a Global Divide in Public Attitudes Toward US, China and Russia." *University of Cambridge*, 2022. https://www.cam.ac.uk/stories/worlddivided.

Li, Zhuoran, and Gavin Xu. "Despite High Ambition, China's Media Influence Operation Is Far From Successful." *The Diplomat*, May 28, 2022. https://thediplomat.com/2022/05/despite-high-ambition-chinas-media-influence-operation-is-far-from-successful.

Linares, César López. "Mexico's President Reveals Journalist's Income." *LatAm Journalism Review*, February 15, 2022. https://latamjournalismreview.org/articles/mexicos-president-reveals-journalists-income-and-the-public-reacts-in-unprecedented-ways-on-social-media.

Lippmann, Walter. *Liberty and the News*. Dover, 2010.

López-Dóriga, Elena. "The Skyrocketing Number of Journalists Murdered in Mexico: AMLO's Polemic Against Reporters." *Universidad de Navarra*, May 26, 2022. https://www.unav.edu/en/web/global-affairs/the-skyrocketing-number-of-journalists-murdered-in-mexico#:~:text=Article%2019%2C%20a%20civil%20organisation,in%20their%20first%20three%20years.

MacDonald, Alistair. "Soft Power Superpowers." *British Council*, 2018. https://www.britishcouncil.org/sites/default/files/j119_thought_leadership_global_trends_in_soft_power_web.pdf.

Madrid-Morales, Dani. "Who Set the Narrative? Assessing the Influence of Chinese Global Media on News Coverage of COVID-19 in 30 African Countries." *Global Media and China* 6, no. 2 (2021): 129–51.

Marietta, Morgan, and David Barker. *One Nation, Two Realities*. Oxford University Press, 2019.

Markham, James. *Voices of the Red Giants: Communications in Russia and China*. University of Iowa Press, 1967.

Mattingly, Daniel, et al. "Chinese State Media Persuades a Global Audience That the 'China Model' is Superior: Evidence from a 19-Country Experiment." *OSF Preprints*, January 18, 2023. https://osf.io/5cafd/download.

McGlynn, Jade. *Russia's War*. Polity Press, 2023.

McGlynn, Jade, and Ian Garner. "Russia's War Crime Denials Are Fuel for More Atrocities." *Foreign Policy*, April 23, 2022. https://foreignpolicy.com/2022/04/23/propaganda-russia-atrocity -bucha.

McGregor, Richard. *The Party: The Secret World of China's Communist Rulers*. Allen Lane, 2010.

Mello, Patricia Campos. "2021 Reuters Memorial Lecture: How to Rescue Journalism in an Age of Lies." *University of Oxford*, June 8, 2021. https://reutersinstitute.politics.ox.ac.uk/news/full -text-patricia-campos-mellos-2021-reuters-memorial-lecture-how-rescue-journalism-age-lies.

Mena, Paul. "Principles and Boundaries of Fact-Checking: Journalists' Perceptions." *Journalism Practice* 13, no. 6 (2019): 657–72.

Moore, Martin. "Fake Accounts on Social Media, Epistemic Uncertainty and the Need for an Independent Auditing of Accounts." *Internet Policy Review* 12, no. 1 (2023). https://doi .org/10.14763/2023.1.1680.

Moore, Martin, and Thomas Colley. "Two International Propaganda Models: Comparing RT and CGTN's 2020 US Election Coverage." *Journalism Practice* 18, no. 5 (2022): 1306–28.

Mudde, Cas. "The Populist Zeitgeist." *Government and Opposition* 39, no. 4 (2004): 541–63.

Mudde, Cas, and Cristóbal Kaltwasser. *Populism: A Very Short Introduction*. Oxford University Press, 2017.

Müller, Nina, and Jenny Wiik. "From Gatekeeper to Gate-Opener: Open-Source Spaces in Investigative Journalism." *Journalism Practice* 17, no. 2 (2023): 189–208.

Mungiu-Pippidi, Alina. "How Media and Politics Shape Each Other in the New Europe." *Romanian Journal of Political Science* 8, no. 1 (2008): 69–78.

Muñoz, Jorge, and Pablo Aguirre. "Morning Conferences: From Dialogue to the Sacrificial Rite and the Formation of Scapegoats." *Journal of Foreign Languages and Cultures* 5, no. 2 (2021): 74–89.

Nemer, David. "'The Human Infrastructure of Fake News in Brazil." *Items: Insights from the Social Sciences* 6, (2021). https://items.ssrc.org/extremism-online/the-human-infrastructure -of-fake-news-in-brazil.

Newman, Nic, et al. "Reuters Institute Digital News Report 2019." University of Oxford, 2019. https://www.digitalnewsreport.org/survey/2019/the-rise-of-populism-and-the-consequences -for-news-and-media-use.

——. "Reuters Institute Digital News Report 2022, Brazil." University of Oxford, 2023. https:// reutersinstitute.politics.ox.ac.uk/digital-news-report/2022/brazil.

Neyazi, Taberez, and Ralph Shroeder. "Was the 2019 Indian Election Won by Digital Media?." *The Communication Review* 24, no. 2 (2021): 87–106.

Nimmo, Ben, et al. "Adversarial Threat Report: Second Quarter." *Meta*, August 2023. https:// transparency.meta.com/en-gb/integrity-reports-q2-2023.

Nimmo, Ben, and Mike Torrey. "Taking Down Coordinated Inauthentic Behavior from Russia and China." *Meta*, September 2022. https://about.fb.com/wp-content/uploads/2022/10 /CIB-Report_-China-Russia_Sept-2022-1-1.pdf.

O'Shaughnessy, Nicholas. "From Disinformation to Fake News: Forwards Into the Past." In *The SAGE Handbook of Propaganda*, ed. Paul Baines et al. SAGE, 2020.

Obama, Barack. *Dreams from My Father: A Story of Race and Inheritance*. Three Rivers, 2004.

Oborne, Peter. *The Assault on Truth*. Simon & Schuster, 2021.

OECD. "Disinformation and Russia's War of Aggression Against Ukraine." November 3, 2022. https://www.oecd.org/en/publications/disinformation-and-russia-s-war-of-aggression-against-ukraine_37186bde-en.html.

Office of the Director of National Intelligence, USA. "Background to 'Assessing Russian Activities and Intentions in Recent US Elections'." January 16, 2017. https://www.dni.gov/files/documents/ICA_2017_01.pdf.

Orwell, George. *Animal Farm*. New American Library, 1946.

——. *1984*. Penguin, 1954.

——. *Notes on Nationalism*. London, 1945. https://orwell.ru/library/essays/nationalism/english/e_nat#google_vignette.

OSCE. "ODIHR Limited Election Observation Mission Final Report." June 27, 2018. https://www.osce.org/files/f/documents/0/9/385959.pdf.

Ostrovsky, Arkady. *The Invention of Russia*. Viking, 2015.

Oud, Malin, and Katja Drinhausen, eds. "The Decoding China Dictionary," 2023. https://decodingchina.eu.

Patschiki, Lucas. "Os litores da nossa burguesia: o Mídia sem Máscara em atuação partidária (2002–2011)." *Dissertação Universidade Estadual do Oeste do Paraná*, 2012. https://tede.unioeste.br/handle/tede/1789.

Paul, Christopher, et al. "The Russian 'Firehose of Falsehood' Propaganda Model." *RAND Corporation*, 2016. https://www.rand.org/pubs/perspectives/PE198.html.

Plenta, Peter. "Conspiracy Theories as a Political Instrument: Utilization of Anti-Soros Narratives in Central Europe." *Contemporary Politics* 26, no. 5 (2020): 512–30.

Popper, Karl. *The Logic of Scientific Discovery*. Routledge, 2002.

Porto, Mauro, and João Brant. "Social Media and the 2013 Protests in Brazil: The Contradictory Nature of Political Mobilization in the Digital Era." In *Critical Perspectives on Social Media and Protest*, ed. Lina Dencik and Oliver Leistert, 181–202. Rowman & Littlefield, 2015.

Rachman, Gideon. *The Age of the Strongman: How the Cult of the Leader Threatens Democracy Around the World*. The Bodley Head, 2022.

Ramón, Paula. "The Fake-News Kingpin of Brazil." *Columbia Journalism Review*, April 13, 2022. https://www.cjr.org/analysis/brazil-bolsonaro-lula-allan-dos-santos.php.

Ramsay, Gordon, and Sam Robertshaw. "Weaponising News: RT, Sputnik and Targeted Disinformation." *King's College London*, 2019. https://www.kcl.ac.uk/policy-institute/assets/weaponising-news.pdf.

Rauch, Jonathan. *The Constitution of Knowledge: A Defense of Truth*. Brookings Institution, 2021.

Reporters Without Borders (RSF). "China's Pursuit of a New World Media Order," 2019. https://rsf.org/en/rsf-report-chinas-pursuit-new-world-media-order.

——. "The Great Leap Backwards of Journalism in China," 2021. https://rsf.org/en/unprecedented-rsf-investigation-great-leap-backwards-journalism-china.

——. "Hungary," 2023. https://rsf.org/en/country/hungary.

Ricard, Julie, and Juliano Medeiros. "Using Misinformation as a Political Weapon: COVID-19 and Bolsonaro in Brazil." *Harvard Kennedy School Misinformation Review*, April 17, 2020. https://doi.org/10.37016/mr-2020-013.

Rios, Viri. "The Real Reasons for AMLO's Popularity." *Americas Quarterly*, December 13, 2023. https://americasquarterly.org/article/the-real-reasons-for-amlos-popularity.

Roberts, Margaret. *Censored: Distraction and Diversion Inside China's Great Firewall*. Princeton University Press, 2018.

Robinson, Piers. "The CNN Effect: Can the News Media Drive Foreign Policy?." *Review of International Studies* 25, no. 2 (1999): 301–9.

Romancini, Richard. "From 'Gay Kit' to 'Indoctrination Monitor': The Conservative Reaction in Brazil." *Contracampo—Brazilian Journal of Communication* 37, no. 2 (2018): 85–106.

Rosen, Jay. "The View from Nowhere: Questions and Answers." *PressThink*, November 10, 2010. https://pressthink.org/2010/11/the-view-from-nowhere-questions-and-answers.

Rubio, Luis. *Unmasked: Lopez Obrador and the End of Make-Believe*. Wilson Center, 2019.

Ryan, Fergus, et al. "TikTok and WeChat: Curating and Controlling Global Information Flows." *Australian Strategic Policy Institute*. Report no. 37, 2020. https://www.aspi.org.au/report/tiktok-wechat.

Sahgal, Neha, et al. "Nationalism and Politics." *Pew Research Center*, June 29, 2021. https://www.pewresearch.org/religion/2021/06/29/nationalism-and-politics.

Santini, Rose, et al. "When Machine Behavior Targets Future Voters: The Use of Social Bots to Test Narratives for Political Campaigns in Brazil." *International Journal of Communication* 15 (2021): 1220–43.

Schiffrin, Anya, ed. *Media Capture: How Money, Digital Platforms and Governments Control the News*. Columbia University Press, 2021.

Schmitt, Carl. *The Concept of the Political*. University of Chicago Press, 1986.

Schudson, Michael. "The Politics of Narrative Form: The Emergence of News Conventions in Print and Television." *Daedalus* 111, no. 4 (1982): 97–112.

Schuldt, Lasse. "Official Truths in a War on Fake News: Governmental Fact-Checking in Malaysia, Singapore, and Thailand." *Journal of Current Southeast Asian Affairs* 40, no. 2 (2021): 340–71.

Seaton, Jean. *Pinkoes and Traitors: The BBC and the Nation, 1974–1987*. Profile, 2015.

Sharma, Arvind. "On the Difference Between Hinduism and Hindutva." *Education About Asia* 25, no. 1 (2020): 1–5.

Sharma, Parth, and Abhijit Anand. "Indian Media Coverage of Nizamuddin Markaz Event During COVID-19 Pandemic." *Asian Politics & Policy* 12, no. 4 (2020): 650–54.

Siebert, Fred, Theodore Peterson, and Wilbur Schramm. *Four Theories of the Press*. University of Illinois Press, 1956.

Signa Lab ITESO. "Democracy, Freedom of Expression and the Digital Sphere." February 28, 2019. https://signalab.iteso.mx/informes/informe_redamlove.html.

Singer, Peter, and Emerson Brooking. *Likewar: The Weaponization of Social Media*. Houghton Mifflin Harcourt, 2018.

Slater, Michael, and Donna Rouner. "Entertainment-Education and Elaboration Likelihood: Understanding the Processing of Narrative Persuasion." *Communication Theory* 12, no. 2 (2002): 173–91.

Smith, Philip. *Why War: The Cultural Logic of Iraq, The Gulf War, and Suez*. University of Chicago Press, 2005.

Soares, Felipe, et al. "Research Note: Bolsonaro's Firehose: How Covid-19 Disinformation on WhatsApp Was Used to Fight a Government Political Crisis in Brazil." *Harvard Kennedy School Misinformation Review*, January 29, 2021. https://doi.org/10.37016/mr-2020-54.

Solzhenitsyn, Alexandr. "Nobel Lecture." 1970. https://www.nobelprize.org/prizes/literature /1970/solzhenitsyn/lecture.

Spin TCP. "Sigue el análisis de SPIN-TCP, sobre las conferencias de prensa matutinas del presidente Andrés Manuel López Obrador." 2019. https://conferenciapresidente.spintcp.com.

Sponholz, Liriam, and Rogerio Christofoletti. "From Preachers to Comedians: Ideal Types of Hate Speakers in Brazil." *Global Media and Communication* 15, no. 1 (2019): 67–84.

Sproule, Michael. "Authorship and Origins of the Seven Propaganda Devices: A Research Note." *Rhetoric and Public Affairs* 4, no. 1 (2001): 135–43.

Stencel, Mark, et al. "Misinformation Spreads, But Fact-Checking Has Leveled Off." *Duke Reporters' Lab*, June 21, 2023. https://reporterslab.org/tag/international-fact-checking-network.

Strittmatter, Kai. *We Have Been Harmonised: Life in China's Surveillance State*. Old Street, 2019.

Subotić, Jelena. "Narrative, Ontological Security, and Foreign Policy Change." *Foreign Policy Analysis* 12, no. 4 (2015): 610–27.

Taylor, Philip. *Munitions of the Mind*. Manchester University Press, 1990.

Teitelbaum, Benjamin. *War for Eternity: The Return of Traditionalism and the Rise of the Populist Right*. Penguin, 2021.

The Lancet. "India's COVID-19 Emergency." May 8, 2021. https://www.thelancet.com/journals /lancet/article/PIIS0140-6736(21)01052-7/fulltext.

Thibaut, Kenton. "China's Discourse Power Operations in the Global South." *Atlantic Council*, 2022. https://www.atlanticcouncil.org/in-depth-research-reports/report/chinas-discourse -power-operations-in-the-global-south.

Thomas, Elise. "Pro-CCP 'Spamouflage' Network Pivoting to Focus on US Presidential Election." *Institute for Strategic Dialogue*, February 15, 2024. https://www.isdglobal.org /digital_dispatches/pro-ccp-spamouflage-net-work-focuses-on-us-election.

Thussu, Daya, et al. *China's Media Go Global*. Routledge, 2018.

Tieri, Silvia, and Amit Ranjan. "Covid-19, Communalism, and Islamophobia: India Facing the Disease." *Social Identities* 29, no. 1 (2023): 62–78.

Tiezzi, Shannon. "What Do Chinese People Think Is Happening in Xinjiang?." *The Diplomat*, May 29, 2021. https://thediplomat.com/2021/05/what-do-chinese-people-think-is-happening -in-xinjiang.

Tolz, Vera, and Yuri Teper. "Broadcasting Agitainment: A New Media Strategy of Putin's Third Presidency." *PostSoviet Affairs* 34, no. 4 (2018): 213–27.

Trump, Donald. *The Art of the Deal*. Ballantine, 1987.

Tudor, Maya. "India's Nationalism in Historical Perspective: The Democratic Dangers of Ascendant Nativism." *Indian Politics and Policy* 1, no. 1 (2018): 1–24.

UK House of Commons. "Report of the Official Account of the Bombings in London on 7th July 2005." *HC 1087*, May 11, 2006. https://assets.publishing.service.gov.uk/media/5a7c7bc840fob6 26628ac62e/1087.pdf.

United Nations. "OHCHR Assessment of Human Rights Concerns in the Xinjiang Uyghur Autonomous Region, People's Republic of China." August 31, 2022. https://

www.ohchr.org/en/press-releases/2022/08/un-human-rights-office-issues-assessment
-human-rights-concerns-xinjiang.

——. "Universal Declaration of Human Rights." n.d. https://www.un.org/en/about-us/universal
-declaration-of-human-rights#:~:text=Article%2019,media%20and%20regardless%20of
%20frontiers.

United Nations Human Rights Council. "Report of the Independent International Commission of Inquiry on Ukraine." 2023. https://www.ohchr.org/en/press-releases/2023/03
/war-crimes-indiscriminate-attacks-infrastructure-systematic-and-widespread.

Varrall, Merriden. "Behind the News: Inside China's Global Television Network." *Lowy Institute*,
2020. https://www.lowyinstitute.org/publications/behind-news-inside-china-global-television
-network#heading-1803.

Vellani, Valentina, et al. "The Illusory Truth Effect Leads to the Spread of Misinformation."
Cognition 236 (2023): 105421.

Vinhas, Otávio, and Marco Bastos. "When Fact-Checking Is Not WEIRD: Negotiating
Consensus Outside Western, Educated, Industrialized, Rich, and Democratic Countries."
International Journal of Press/Politics, 2024. https://doi.org/10.1177/19401612231221801.

von Clausewitz, Karl. *On War*. Oxford University Press, 2007.

Wallis, Jacob, et al. "Trigger Warning. The CCP's Coordinated Information Effort to Discredit the BBC." *Australian Strategic Policy Institute*, 2021. https://www.aspi.org.au/report
/trigger-warning.

Wardle, Claire, et al. "An Evaluation of the Impact of a Collaborative Journalism Project on
Brazilian Journalists and Audiences." *Comprova/First Draft*, 2019. https://firstdraftnews.org
/wp-content/uploads/2019/06/Comprova-Full-Report-Final.pdf?x21167.

Wasserman, Herman, ed. "Meeting the Challenges of Information Disorder in the Global
South." *IRDC*, 2022. https://idl-bnc-idrc.dspacedirect.org/items/5aad1667-cf56-44bf-b85f
-8695cb5f11dd.

Westen, Drew. *The Political Brain: The Role of Emotion in Deciding the Fate of the Nation*. Public
Affairs, 2007.

Wiener, Philip, ed. *Charles S. Peirce: Selected Writings*. Dover, 1966.

Winter, Ben. "Messiah Complex: How Brazil Made Bolsonaro." *Foreign Affairs* 99, no. 5 (2020).
https://www.foreignaffairs.com/articles/brazil/2020-08-11/jair-bolsonaro-messiah-complex.

Woolley, Samuel, and Philip Howard. *Computational Propaganda: Political Parties, Politicians and
Political Manipulation on Social Media*. Oxford University Press, 2019.

World Uighur Congress. "Final Version of the Uyghur Tribunal Judgment." September 20,
2022. https://www.uyghurcongress.org/en/final-version-of-the-uyghur-tribunal-judgemnt
-including-appendices.

INDEX

Adani, Gautam, 146
advertising in news, 10, 40, 71, 97, 101, 109–112,
    209, 220, 223, 242; in Brazil, 168–169, 172,
    180; changes in digital age, 71, 144–145;
    government spending on, 10, 119; in
    Hungary, 91–2, 98–99, 109–112, 114; in
    India, 119, 126, 144–145
agenda-setting, 89, 97, 236–238; and
    Brazilian news, 153, 160–161; and Chinese
    international state news, 57, 63–64, 82–84;
    and Indian news, 124–125, 128, 133, 144; and
    Mexican news, 183–185, 188, 190, 193; and
    Russian news, 33–34
algorithms, 80, 255
Al Jazeera, 4, 72, 76, 147, 242, 244–245
Alt News, 224–225
alternative reality. *See* parallel realities
Amazon region, 13, 150, 159, 175; and
    Yanomami deaths, 177–178
AMLO. *See* Andrés Manuel López Obrador
Amnesty International, 20, 139

Andrés Manuel López Obrador: approach to
    news, 7, 11, 182–213, 249, 251; background,
    185–190; comparison with Donald Trump,
    185–186, 204; comparison with Narendra
    Modi, 201; criticism of journalists,
    189–200; disinformation, use of, 192,
    197–199, 248; *mañaneras*, use of, 182–185,
    187–200, 249, 251; as messianic populist,
    186–188, 193–196, 203, 260, 263; popularity
    of, 201, 211–212; social media usage of, 188,
    204. *See also* mañaneras
Andropov, Yuri, 2–3
antipetismo, 155–156, 159, 163
Arab Spring, 215, 219–220
Araujo, Ernesto, 162
Arnaud, Tercio, 161, 165, 169
Artificial Intelligence, 46, 78, 256
Associated Press, 20, 71–72, 220
Australia, 72, 74, 80, 101, 199
authoritarianism: approach to news, 7, 12,
    18, 88–89, 104, 203, 207, 213, 253–4,

GPSR Authorized Representative: Easy Access System Europe, Mustamäe tee 50, 10621 Tallinn, Estonia, gpsr.requests@easproject.com